A CULTURAL HISTORY OF FURNITURE

VOLUME 5

A Cultural History of Furniture
General Editor: Christina M. Anderson

Volume 1
A Cultural History of Furniture in Antiquity
Edited by Dimitra Andrianou

Volume 2
A Cultural History of Furniture in the Middle Ages and Renaissance
Edited by Erin J. Campbell and Stephanie R. Miller

Volume 3
A Cultural History of Furniture in the Age of Exploration
Edited by Christina M. Anderson and Elizabeth A. Carroll

Volume 4
A Cultural History of Furniture in the Age of Enlightenment
Edited by Sylvain Cordier, Christina M. Anderson, and Laura Houliston

Volume 5
A Cultural History of Furniture in the Age of Empire and Industry
Edited by Catherine L. Futter and Christina M. Anderson

Volume 6
A Cultural History of Furniture in the Modern Age
Edited by Claire I.R. O'Mahony

A CULTURAL HISTORY OF FURNITURE

IN THE AGE OF EMPIRE AND INDUSTRY

Edited by Catherine L. Futter and Christina M. Anderson

BLOOMSBURY ACADEMIC
LONDON • NEW YORK • OXFORD • NEW DELHI • SYDNEY

BLOOMSBURY ACADEMIC
Bloomsbury Publishing Plc
50 Bedford Square, London, WC1B 3DP, UK
1385 Broadway, New York, NY 10018, USA
29 Earlsfort Terrace, Dublin 2, Ireland

BLOOMSBURY, BLOOMSBURY ACADEMIC and the Diana logo are
trademarks of Bloomsbury Publishing Plc

First published in Great Britain 2022

Series design: Raven Design.
Cover image: Illustrated plate of "The Great Exhibition" (1854). Prominent objects
on display included wood carving by machinery and Leslie's patent gas fittings.
(© SSPL/Getty Images)

A catalogue record for this book is available from the British Library.

A catalog record for this book is available from the Library of Congress.

ISBN: Pack: 978-1-4725-7789-4
HB: 978-1-4725-7787-0

Series: The Cultural Histories Series

Typeset by Integra Software Services Pvt. Ltd.
Printed and bound in Great Britain

To find out more about our authors and books visit www.bloomsbury.com
and sign up for our newsletters.

CONTENTS

LIST OF ILLUSTRATIONS

PLATES

FIGURES

CONTRIBUTORS

Megan Aldrich is an independent scholar who lectures, writes, and teaches aspects of architectural and design history, including interiors and furniture, and consults in the heritage sector. Recent publications include *Antiquaries and Archaists* (2009); *Art and Authenticity* (2012); *Thomas Rickman and the Victorians* (2019); and articles in the journals of *Garden History* (2016), and *Furniture History* (2018). She is a Fellow of the Society of Antiquaries.

Christina M. Anderson worked in the furniture department of Sotheby's London before founding her own art research consultancy. She has a degree in history from Yale University, a postgraduate certificate in architectural heritage from the Catholic University of Leuven, and a doctorate in art history from the University of Oxford. A former Fulbright scholar, Belgian American Educational Foundation fellow, and British Academy Postdoctoral Fellow, she currently holds a senior research fellowship at University College London.

Sylvain Cordier is Paul Mellon Curator and Head of the Department of European Art at the Virginia Museum of Fine Arts in Richmond, Virginia. Prior to this, he was Curator of Early Decorative Arts at the Montreal Museum of Fine Arts. He completed his Ph.D. in Art History at the Paris Sorbonne University. He has published widely on the history of taste for furniture and the relation between decorative arts and the discourse of power in early nineteenth-century France.

Emma Ferry teaches at Hereford College of Arts, UK. She has published several book chapters and articles from her Ph.D. on Macmillan's 'Art at Home' series (1876–83). Her research interests relate to Victorian interior design and decoration.

Catherine L. Futter is Senior Curator of Decorative Arts at the Brooklyn Museum. Previously, she was at the Nelson-Atkins Museum of Art as the Director, Curatorial Affairs and the Helen Jane and R. Hugh "Pat" Uhlmann Curator of Architecture, Design and Decorative Arts. Catherine earned her doctorate from Yale University, where her focus was on American decorative arts. She has curated a number of permanent collection installations of European and American art and numerous exhibitions, including the international loan exhibition and award-winning catalogue *Inventing the Modern World: Decorative Arts at the World's Fairs, 1851–1939*.

Caroline McCaffrey-Howarth is Curator of 17th and 18th Century Ceramics & Glass and Lecturer in History of Design at the Victoria and Albert Museum. She is an art and design historian specializing in the visual and material culture of Britain and France (*c.* 1550–1900), with a particular focus on the histories of collecting, designing, and displaying decorative arts. She received her Ph.D. in Art History from the University of Leeds in 2019, which is the subject of her forthcoming book, provisionally entitled *Sèvres-mania: The Craft of Ceramics Connoisseurship*.

Camille Mestdagh is a lecturer in the history of the decorative arts and their markets (IESA, ICART, Paris). She completed her Ph.D. on the Beurdeley dynasty, dealers in antiques and furniture makers in 19th century Paris (winner of the INHA/CTHS Prize – forthcoming). Her first research on furniture workshops was published as a book *L'Ameublement d'art français (1850–1900)*. More recently, she has focused on the development of decorative arts and their commerce, in relation to the development of museum collections and specialised historiography. She has participated in recent publications, notably *Art Markets, Agents and Collectors: Collecting Strategies in Europe and the United States* (2021) and *Questions de style. L'historicisme dans les arts décoratifs français au XIXe siècle* (2020).

David Oakey is a specialist researcher in architectural history and the decorative arts, who has held positions in the museum and commercial art sectors and is currently Curator of a private collection.

Amy G. Richter is Associate Professor of History at Clark University. Her work focuses on nineteenth- and twentieth-century American cultural history, with an emphasis on women's and urban history. She is the author of *Home on the Rails: Women, the Railroad, and the Rise of Public Domesticity* (2005) and *At Home in Nineteenth-Century America: A Documentary History* (2015).

SERIES PREFACE

A Cultural History of Furniture is a six-volume series examining the changing cultural framework within which furniture was designed, produced, and used, as well as the cultural construction of furniture itself, from antiquity through to the present day in the Western tradition. All the volumes follow the same structure: an editorial overview of the historical context of the period under consideration is followed by chapters written by specialists that each correspond to one of the following themes: design and motifs; makers, making, and materials; types and uses; the domestic setting; the public setting; exhibition and display; furniture and architecture; visual representations; and verbal representations. The configuration of the series means that readers can use the material synchronically or diachronically: an individual volume provides a thorough grounding in the furniture of a particular period while following one distinct theme across all volumes presents the reader with the evolution of a specific aspect of furniture over time. The six volumes divide the history of furniture in this way:

Volume 1: A Cultural History of Furniture in Antiquity (From the beginnings to CE)
Volume 2: A Cultural History of Furniture in the Middle Ages and Renaissance (500–1500)
Volume 3: A Cultural History of Furniture in the Age of Exploration (1500–1700)
Volume 4: A Cultural History of Furniture in the Age of Enlightenment (1700–1800)
Volume 5: A Cultural History of Furniture in the Age of Empire and Industry (1800–1900)
Volume 6: A Cultural History of Furniture in the Modern Age (1900–twenty-first century)

Christina M. Anderson
General Editor

Introduction

CATHERINE L. FUTTER AND CHRISTINA M. ANDERSON

> *On entering the building, for the first time, the eye is completely dazzled by the rich variety of hues which burst upon it on every side; and it is not until this partial bewilderment has subsided, that we are in a condition to appreciate as it deserves its real magnificence and the harmonious beauty of effect produced by the artistical arrangement of the glowing and varied hues which blaze along its grand and simple lines.*
>
> —"History of the Great Exhibition" (1851: 25)

Those that visited London's Hyde Park in the spring of 1851 for the Great Exhibition of the Industry of All Nations encountered a new experience—for the first-time visitors from all walks of life could see and experience the architectural marvel of the Crystal Palace (Plate 1). The traditions and aspirations, the accomplishments and adaptations, and the handicraft and machinery of many nations filled the glass and iron structure. Not only was there a Medieval Court with the latest Gothic Revival designs, there were enormous machines of war and industry (Plate 2). There were many underlying motivations of the fair—to inspire improvements in design of the industrial or decorative arts; to proclaim nationalistic superiority in industry and colonialism; and to educate a consumer class. This fair, as well as the dozens of international expositions held around the world for the rest of the century and into the next century, firmly established the role that these events had as a forum for displaying technological advancements and defining fashionable taste. There were over fifty expositions that can be defined as international in the period 1851–99, held in the large metropolises of London, Paris, and Chicago as well as colonial outposts such as Calcutta, Melbourne, and Kingston. The fairs educated numerous generations of artists, manufacturers, and consumers, and influenced the establishment of cultural and artistic institutions. They were the impetus for the foundation of institutions such as what is now known as the Victoria and Albert Museum in London, the Museum of Applied Arts–Contemporary Art (MAK) in Vienna, and the Carnegie Museum of Art in Pittsburgh. In their day, the fairs were the topic of hundreds of books, from jury reports and critical analyses to travel guides and personal recollections in diaries and postcards. Images circulated through wood engravings, metal engravings, new chromolithographic images, and in the new technology of photography.

During the nineteenth century, a variety of terms were used to refer to these impressive and magnificent events, including universal exhibition, international exhibition, and exposition universelle; yet, at their heart, they were the most important vehicles for debuting objects and products to an international audience on a large scale. Countries from all over the globe participated in the fairs, presenting marvels such as the sewing machine and the telephone as well as architectural wonders such as the Eiffel Tower (Paris, 1889) and the Ferris Wheel (Chicago, 1893). In the category of furniture, innovative materials and technological marvels such as bentwood, tubular steel, and papier-mâché were exhibited. Makers employed Irish bog peat or native hard stones in their designs to proclaim national natural resources, while manufacturers revived historical styles to advertise their long and impressive histories. Colonial displays also included raw materials as well as finished goods to indicate potential economic development. At times, Indigenous peoples were brought to the fairs, often unwillingly, to illustrate the types of labor employed to work the materials needed for the manufacture of the displayed goods. These sent a message of numerous inexpensive laborers in the service of colonial enterprises and endorsed the racial hierarchies already present at the fair in countless exhibits.

Many fairs were broad in scope, displaying decorative arts alongside paintings, sculpture, machines, and agricultural products. They functioned as showcases and marketplaces for design. The exhibitions democratized design in an entirely new way. Decorative arts, particularly objects crafted in metal, glass, clay, textile, and wood, were the physical manifestations of the progressive, economic, and technological ideals embodied in the exhibitions. Unfortunately, the stages or backdrops for these displays were ephemeral, yet many of the objects displayed at them, especially outstanding examples of furniture, have survived. Many of these models are now found in museums of decorative arts or in royal collections around the world. They were appreciated at the time and preserved as masterpieces of design and craftsmanship. These innovative designs represented the pinnacle of the scientific and artistic achievements of their time. In their forms, styles, methods, and materials, they signaled a better and brighter future.

If we only look at the furniture displayed at the fairs during the nineteenth century, we can see a variety of themes and trends. The designs and manufactured products not only illustrate inventive or revived fabrication techniques, but also embody cross-cultural and cross-national influences, and reflect the significant nationalistic objectives and folkloric customs that drove the competition inherent in these events. Although one thinks of modernism as being a twentieth-century concept, the constant push and pull between historicism and modernism and innovation during the second half of the nineteenth century generated some of the most exciting and inventive developments in decorative arts, especially furniture. This volume addresses many of the same themes as those explored at the international exhibitions: that furniture can be studied and understood in its social, political, economic, stylistic, and representational contexts; and that designers, fabricators, patrons, and consumers played an important role in the discovery, dissemination, innovation, and understanding of the craftsmanship and manufacture of cabinetmaking. Finally, the exhibition and display through these momentous events as well as the establishment of museums and other display spaces encouraged designers, manufacturers, consumers, and students of all ages. The ways in which furniture and other decorative arts were displayed and written about influenced and was reacted against in the ensuing centuries.

One of the most important documents of the 1851 Great Exhibition was the *Reports by the Juries on the Subjects in the Thirty Classes into Which the Exhibition was Divided* (1852). Included in this large volume was a "Supplementary Report on Design" by the eminent English designer and critic Richard Redgrave (1804–88). In this lengthy essay, Redgrave discusses design as displayed at the 1851 Great Exhibition. As a member of the Royal Academy and a friend of Henry Cole (1808–82), the primary organizer of this international event, Redgrave must have known the motivations for the Great Exhibition: to encourage an educated consumer class and to stimulate British designers and manufacturers not only to compete with but also surpass French design. The exhibition organizers were cognizant that although British manufacturing was thought to be on a par with or even exceeding French production in many fields, French design was considered far superior. Redgrave had also worked with Cole on one of his earliest endeavors to improve and transform British design: Summerly's Art Manufacturers founded in 1847. Summerly, the pseudonym of Cole, hoped to unite art and industry by employing artists to design for manufacturers. The most famous product of this venture was a glass flower vase, known as *Well Spring*, enamel decorated with water plants designed by Redgrave and manufactured by A.J.F. Christy, Stangate Glass Works of Lambeth. Although progressive, the Art Manufacturers was not successful and only a handful of decorative objects were designed and produced; no examples of furniture were among those that did go into fabrication. This enterprise, however, can be seen as a precursor of the role of the industrial designer. The mid- and late nineteenth century saw the introduction of designers such as

Christopher Dresser (1834–1904) and, later, Philip Webb (1831–1915), among others, who worked with a variety of manufacturers to produce "well-designed" goods, including wooden and even cast iron furniture.

Although the "Supplementary Report on Design" concerns itself with all kinds of manufacturing or goods shown at the 1851 exhibition, Redgrave's observations can be applied to the issues surrounding nineteenth-century furniture. At the exhibition, British furniture could be found in a number of locations: in Class 26 and in areas for metalwork and other material-driven categories. Visitors found furniture produced by other nations and even British colonies in separate sections.

Redgrave's essay can orient us to many of the issues of the day that concerned the decorative arts. He begins with a distinction between design and ornament: design pertaining to the construction "for both use and beauty," while "ornament is merely the decoration of a thing constructed" (*Reports by the Juries on the Subjects in the Thirty Classes into Which the Exhibition was Divided* 1852: 1589). His overall impression of the fair is that the majority of the displays at the exhibition showed that "utility and construction are made secondary to decoration" (1589). This is a criticism regarding nineteenth-century design, particularly in furniture, perpetuated throughout the century. Inlaid, marquetry, carved, turned, and painted ornament covered every surface, with no focus on the construction. For Redgrave, the

> display of gilding ... for brilliancy and sparkle in metal and ormolu work, showy and glittering beyond anything attainable in the simpler forms of Renaissance or classical antiquity. From these qualities it has long maintained its hold on the public taste; and in its florid and gorgeous tinsel still prevails in three-fourths of the works in the Great Exhibition, notwithstanding the gross contempt of constructive principles.
>
> (*Reports by the Juries on the Subjects in the Thirty Classes into Which the Exhibition was Divided* 1852: 1591)

For the nineteenth-century critic, the application of ornament derived from one material, such as stone, applied to another, such as wood or metal, created "senseless anomalies of all kinds" (1591). Redgrave observed that there are only two types of "ornamentists": those he calls the "traditional," who "superstitiously reverence the remains of past ages and are wedded in practice to existing styles." For the others, Redgrave claims they "despise the past" and freely adapt ornament from nature and are looking only for novelty (1591). These designers copy or imitate nature in a variety of materials: "enormous wreaths of flowers, fish, games, fruits, &c., imitated *à merveille*, dangle round sideboards, beds, and picture-frames" (1592). What Redgrave proposes is that the designer shed all forms of imitation in search of defined and sound principles upon which he can create "to attain through fitness and truth." It was not until soon after 1851 that designers, such as William Morris and others in Britain and the United States, stripped designs down to their bones, eliminating what was seen as unnecessary or lacking any function. Construction elements such as tenons became ornaments, rather than profuse carving. The designers that did follow Redgrave and others' condemnation of profuse decoration produced works that sought to restore the function of the object—especially in a less elaborate or flamboyant version of the Gothic style, often called Reform Gothic.

Redgrave addresses another issue that was to torment the nineteenth century: the dichotomy between handcrafted and machine-made works and the place of the designer, artisan, and manufacturer. Although machines allowed more people, mainly the middle class, to acquire and furnish their homes, they also dehumanized the labor force. In addition, mass production led to "all products" being "rigidly the same, whence arises a sickening monotony, a tiresome sameness, unknown in the works of nature and peculiar to these artificial works of man: the varying mind has no share in their production, and man himself becomes only the servant of the machine" (1594). By the middle of the century, and with increasingly loud voices, critics expounded on the lack of humanity, and lack of "piety" and "love" that the artisan who labored in the factories felt as they produced vast quantities of inferior goods. Not only were the laborers degraded by the act of creation, but the consumer did not respect these cheap products. In 1851, Redgrave proposed that designers be more valued and paid better for their contributions; that the manufacturer not alter the design and that the consumer be more educated in good taste and appreciate skillful workmanship (1595). In his essay, Redgrave points out that some of the French, German, Bavarian, and Italian manufactures not only designed the products but executed them as well—with excellent results. In furniture, Redgrave highlights the work of the French manufacturer Michel-Joseph-Napoléon Liénard (1810–70), who was awarded the Council Medal (the highest medal at the fair) for a clock case decorated with a carved boar hunt. In fact, the French furniture manufacturers Liénard, Henri-Auguste Fourdinois (1830–1907), and Ferdinand Barbedienne (1810–92) won the highest awards at the fair.

During the nineteenth century, designers and cabinetmakers became increasingly well known amongst manufacturers and the general public due to a rise in the number of trade publications, ladies' journals, articles on exhibitions, advertising and other means of promotion, and international expositions. In addition to designers, the work of critics also promoted "good design" and "improved taste." One of the most important of these was the author Charles Locke Eastlake (1836–1906), who although not a designer himself, published an extremely influential doctrine, *Hints on Household Taste* (1868), on interiors that promoted "Eastlake" furniture to English-speaking audiences on both sides of the Atlantic (Figure 0.1). This is just one example of the influence that books

XII.

Dining-room Sideboard,

executed from a Design by Charles L. Eastlake.

FIGURE 0.1 Dining room sideboard in Charles L. Eastlake's *Hints on Household Taste in Furniture, Upholstery, and Other Details* (1869). Image courtesy of University of California Libraries/Internet Archive.

on interiors had on middle-class audiences with wealth to spend on domestic furnishings and interior decoration.

Government-sponsored schools of design were established around the world during the nineteenth century. Redgrave decries that although there are schools teaching ornamental art in some of the large manufacturing towns in England, there is not one such national school focused on design. He also praises the royal and imperial government-sponsored manufacturing of France, Germany, Italy, and Belgium for their support of good quality and well-designed products. The schools hired the "best painters, sculptors, and designers as well as men of the most scientific acquirements in botany, mineralogy, and chemistry" to teach. In addition, these schools and workshops, as they were state-sponsored, could experiment and innovate (1596). Private manufacturers benefited from the skilled workmen trained by the schools, who brought the latest tools, materials, technologies, and processes to industry.

The nineteenth century was a period of intense interest in typologies of all objects, including furniture. In his discourse, Redgrave systematically addresses the displays at the fair. Beginning with architecture, he continues with domestic furniture, followed by domestic utensils and finally garment fabrics. In the section on architecture, Redgrave continues to praise the French in their use of ornament. He discusses the use of new materials such as gutta-percha, putty, carton pierre, etc., which he sees as having the potential for "often doing greater injury, from the tasteless, misplaced, and false decoration arising from their use, than good, by ministering to decorative purposes" (1602). He declares that because they are cheaper to use, these materials are used immoderately. They carry with them "the sense of untruth," which corrupts the consumer who increasingly grows accustomed to these falsehoods. Redgrave also criticizes the inappropriate scale and the overabundance of ornament used in the decorative arts. In the use of iron as a material in design, Redgrave much prefers wrought iron over cast. He appreciates the "varied beauty," the "greater durability, its tenacity," as it is wrought by hand rather than "cast from a mold (thereby leaving the fancy and the feeling of the workman untrammeled)" (1615). He does, however, praise the workmanship of the Coalbrookdale Company, in this case with designs by Charles Crookes. The same firm was to go on to greater recognition with garden and hall seating furniture designed by Christopher Dresser (1834–1904) in the following decades. Redgrave, however, heaps disdain on the cast iron seating at the fair that imitated tree branches and foliage.

With this, Redgrave turns to "Domestic and other Furniture." Here, he sees all the same complaints that so perturbed him earlier: the "ornamental" that "prevails to the exclusion of the useful." Furniture that should be comfortable and "fitted for convenience, rest and repose" are considered "objects of art" (1616). He praises the quality of past or historical English workmanship: drawers moved easily; wood was seasoned appropriately; and furniture was handed from father to son due to its craftsmanship. Now, he feels that these basic and solid tenets have been replaced by an obsession with "decoration and display" (1616). He fears that the English manufacturers in their race to meet foreign competition have abandoned the advantages and strengths of their workmanship to apply the most ornament to these large cabinet pieces. He advocates that the designers and manufacturers return to the basics: that the first consideration of the designer should be "*perfect adaptation to intended use*"; that every piece of furniture has a "specific purpose." Walking through the fair he saw ample indication that there are "a multitude of objects offending against this rule." He saw examples both by British and foreign manufacturers, citing a pianoforte "surrounded by bristling bushrushes, which must always be catching in the dresses of those who approach it" and "chairs so heavy that they must be fixtures instead of moveables" (1617). Manufacturers should think about convenience and accommodation "in the least amount of space" so that furniture can be suitable to the location for which it is intended. Redgrave favors solid designs, criticizes the rococo style for its flimsiness and instability, and declares that "simplicity is the safest guide to beauty" (1617). "Ornament should arise out of construction," not the inverse. He praises the craftsman of New Zealand, the Swiss shepherd, and the Indian woodworker, who construct their forms and then simply and with "refined taste" decorate them. He also commends the French manufacturers, returning to one of the opinions of the Great Exhibition, that French manufacturers and designers were superior to the British in their suitable use of ornament, integrating flowers and fruits more successfully into their designs (1618).

Redgrave also addresses the use of materials. One of his, and later designer reformers, pieces of advice is to use appropriate materials. He feels that one substance should not imitate another, that the material should be used properly, that color should be homogenous, and that the finishes should be applied judiciously. Again, he finds that the French succeed more frequently, especially when employing the Renaissance style. He does not like, however, the French rococo style works with multihued veneers and inset porcelain panels. He strongly rejects the use of nature in furniture, and in one of the most evocative and descriptive passages, he declares that:

> there seems no fitness, for instance, in surrounding the frame of a pier-glass with dead birds, game, shell-fish, nets, &c., although they may be excellent specimens of carving; nor is it clear why eagles should support a sideboard, or dogs form the arms of an elbow-chair; nor again, why swans should make their nests under a table, at the risk of having their necks broken by every one seated at it.
>
> (1620)

Redgrave does find at least one piece of cabinetry to praise, the enormous walnut sideboard by Fourdinois, which does not seem to have survived (Figure 0.2). He exclaims that it "is an apt illustration of ornament, having a just and characteristic significance ... of rare excellence and merit in design, and of skillful and artistic execution as to carving, and although of highly decorative character, is fitted for

FIGURE 0.2 Alexandre-Georges Fourdinois (maker). Carved walnut sideboard, 1851. Photograph courtesy of Artokoloro/Alamy Stock Photo.

the purpose for which it is intended" (*Reports by the Juries on the Subjects in the Thirty Classes into Which the Exhibition was Divided* 1852: 1620–1). Six nearly life-size dogs supported the display surface of the sideboard, which in turn buttressed a console that bore four carved female figures from four areas of the world, each holding their agricultural attributes. The whole was surmounted with the figure of Plenty. Carving of fruits and vegetables covered almost every surface. Yet, Redgrave approves of the ornament that communicates the sideboard's function. He also commends the scale and the craftsmanship, the use of a fifteenth-century Renaissance form and a thirteenth-century style of carving. He lists the best works exhibited at the fair that convey styles from the past, including a wardrobe by T.F. Wirth of Stuttgart and a console table and glass by Angiolo Barbetti (1805–73) of Siena (V&A, O59304). He praises the cabinet by Auguste-Emile Ringuet-Leprince (1801–86) and Michel-Joseph-Napoléon Liénard (sold at Sotheby's February 24, 2016, sale L16317, lot 110) (Plate 3), for having "high merit"; a picture frame by Liénard; a boxwood cradle designed by W. Harry Rogers (1825–73) and carved by his father William Gibbs Rogers (1792–1875) (Royal Collection, RCIN 1516) (Plate 4); and a sideboard by a student of the School of Design in Sheffield. Redgrave also approved of the oak cabinet bookcase displayed in the Medieval Court designed by Augustus Welby Northmore Pugin (1812–52) and manufactured by J.G. Crace (V&A, 25:1 to 3–1852) (Plate 5) as well as other works in this style that were exhibited in the Court. He singles out their sound construction and the "very judicious manner in which ornament is made subservient to it." He also extols the use of metalwork on the bookcase, which complements the constructive treatment of the wood (1622). For Redgrave, the works in the Medieval Court "deserve commendation for their illustration of truth, and as showing what one man, by earnest and well-directed attention, can achieve in the reformation of taste, and in the training and forming of other minds to assist in his truthful labors. Their unity of character, moreover, is not the least among their many excellences" (1623). These sentiments were to echo into the twentieth century, with their emphasis on the honesty of construction, the appropriate use of materials and ornament, and the commendation of workmanship and the single craftsman. From William Morris (1834–96), who is said to have refused to enter the 1851 Great Exhibition, and Arts and Crafts movement designers and artisans, these principles were to govern their products and marketing.

Redgrave continues his reflections with a discussion of the materials used in furniture at the fair. He approves of the use of inlays of metals, mother-of-pearl, and tortoiseshell, as long as they are employed sparingly. He notes some of the Boulle work displayed in the French Court; a wood mosaic table with geometric patterns by Marcelin of Paris; and a *pietra dura* table by Benedetto Boschetti (fl. *c.* 1820–79), a similar table by Luigi Moglia is in the collection of Osborne House (RCIN 41310). The revival of techniques was another characteristic of the period, as designers and manufacturers not only looked to the styles of the past but also processes. Materials such as hard stones, Boulle work of tortoiseshell and brass, inlaid ivory into ebony, and gilded metalwork recalled the past through luxurious materials and complex techniques. Another work exhibited by the Austrian cabinetmaker Carl Leistler (1805–57) of Vienna made a tremendous impression, not only on Redgrave. Designed by Bernardo di Bernardis (1807–68) and carved by Anton Dominik Fernkorn (1813–78), this Gothic Revival bookcase was purchased by Austrian Emperor Franz Josef (1830–1916) as a gift for Queen Victoria (1819–1901) (Figure 0.3). Franz Josef filled the bookcase with books and albums of watercolors to augment the cabinet. Originally, Prince Albert (1819–61) used the bookcase at Buckingham Palace, but later it was moved to Holyroodhouse. In 1923, King George V gave the bookcase to the University of Edinburgh, and in 1967 it entered the collection of the V&A (W.12–1967). The patronage of royalty and aristocracy at these events not only drew attention to their importance, but also works of furniture entered these august collections.

FIGURE 0.3 Carl Leistler & Sons (maker), Bookcase in neo-Gothic style, carved oak, *c*. 1851. Photograph courtesy of Artokoloro/Alamy Stock Photo.

It is no surprise that papier-mâché furniture repulsed Redgrave. He did not despise the technique so much as the ornament. He saw that the lightness, strength, and ease of manufacture could be a positive in furniture production, but the finishes of mother-of-pearl and gilding led him to declare that papier-mâché work "is the most gaudily decorated of all manufactures, and seems quite beyond the pale of any just principles of ornament" (1624). He continues that "it is a mass of barborous splendor that offends the eye and quarrels with every other kind of manufacture with which it comes into contact." Redgrave suggests that the British manufacturers look to "the simple lacquered work of India" as a source for the decoration on papier-mâché due to the sensitivity of the application of gold and color, which is "a lesson of richness without gaudiness."

Redgrave does not devote all of his criticism to the British exhibitors; he upbraids the Austrians for their deficiency in addressing function in their furniture. He points out that one of the Austrian beds evokes a coffin rather than a place of repose. For him, the Belgians use inappropriate materials: the carving in wood imitates stonework.

At the end of his essay, Redgrave returns to the education of the worker, especially in the superiority of French training in craftsmanship. He emphasizes skillful carving on pieces by Ringuet-LePrince, Fourdinois, and Liénard—works by these makers entered the collection of the South Kensington Museum and they are still appreciated today. Redgrave's praise is faint when he mentions English carving by Holland and Son and Johann Martin Levien (1811–71). Again, he calls for improvements in education in the form of technical skills as well as printed materials to teach workers, and one supposes, the public, in the finer points of furniture manufacture and consumption.

The jury reports for the international exhibitions always ended with list of medal winners, with lists of makers, their nationalities and their prize-winning works denoted for all to see. These publications acted as memories of the great events, promotional materials for the exhibitors, and sources for designers, manufacturers, students, and later, historians. Today, scholars and students can mine these editions for information on a wide range of topics.

As the international exhibitions were one of the great inventions of the nineteenth century, they can act as the starting point for much of our investigation of this transformational period in design history.

SETTING THE STAGE FOR DEVELOPMENTS IN THE FURNITURE INDUSTRY

Although the previous century triggered many of the developments that we see as central to the nineteenth century, it was during this revolutionary period that so many radical changes, discussions, and innovations came to maturity. The nineteenth century saw seismic shifts in society, industry, science, communication, internationalism, globalism, and nationalism. It was a time when more people moved to cities, from small and large estates, small towns, and villages. Industry replaced agriculture as the main form of employment as well as basis of the economy—especially in Europe and the new United States, but this was also a global shift. Throughout the century, huge numbers of people were displaced or sought new opportunities during and following revolutions and wars, both civil and foreign. Governments formed and reformed from monarchies to republics and back again. These developments often affected international trade, and countries such as France, Britain, and the United States went through periods of protectionism and free trade. Economies were volatile with changes in governments, wars, droughts, strikes, and the like.

New institutions in the urban environment gradually replaced the rural economy and traditions. Although the middle class had been steadily increasing in numbers since the sixteenth century, it was during the nineteenth century that the divisions between the classes became even more differentiated. Yet, there were also more opportunities from the middle to the end of the century for upward social mobility as industrialists became some of the wealthiest individuals, outstripping the fortunes of the large, often aristocratic, landowners.

The century also saw a sweeping technological revolution. The major source of light, for example, would change from candles to kerosene lamps and then to electric light bulbs. Transportation evolved from walking and horse power to steam-powered locomotives, to electric trolley cars, to gasoline-powered automobiles. Many were born into a society in which the vast majority of people were involved in agriculture, yet, they were to experience an industrial revolution that radically changed the ways millions of people worked and where they lived. In the United States, millions of people migrated from rural America to the nation's rapidly growing cities. Europe too saw an enormous influx of new residents to urban areas as industrial cities boomed and housing needs had to be met. Tenements and crowded terrace houses sprang up to house workers. From birth until death, from farm to city, from industrial country to undeveloped territory, the world underwent profound, extreme, and fundamental changes during the nineteenth century.

INDUSTRY AND LABOR

Although the previous century saw the start of the Industrial Revolution, with time-saving machines transforming menial tasks, from sorting or combing cotton to the initial uses of the steam engine, it was the nineteenth century that saw tremendous developments in technology and the organization of industry. In the early years of the century, Napoleon transformed France with a series of modernizing economic acts: he abolished the system of guilds, monopolies, and trade restrictions and introduced the metric system for uniformity and standardization. He did block all trade with Britain, which had the effect of spurring British industrialization and innovation (as well as smuggling). Most of the industry within France during the Napoleonic Wars developed to fabricate munitions and other products for battle. Following the wars, there was some attention to developing industry in France, but most of these attempts were small in comparison to Britain's efforts. While Britain built its successful global textile industry, the French manufactured on a much smaller scale. One of the industries of the post-Napoleonic Wars that pertained to the furniture industry was brass and gilt-metal work used to adorn furniture. American industries were just beginning and would not begin to surpass European manufacturing until after the Civil War ended in 1865.

Various revolutions, including the revolutions of 1848 that occurred throughout Europe, led to mass exodus and movement of people throughout the continent, although the majority left for the seemingly more peaceful United States. The new country was seen as a land of economic opportunity and one with greater personal freedom from political and religious persecution. Between 1870 and 1900 nearly twelve million immigrants, mainly from Germany, Ireland, and England arrived in the United States. Other immigrants came from Asia and arrived along the west coast cities of the United States. Although many of these new immigrants stayed in the port cities and ended up working in urban industries, others settled in less populated and more rural centers. The majority of these immigrants brought with them their traditions and preferences from their countries of origin. German and French immigrants brought with them their manufacturing techniques as well as the styles fashionable in their homelands and they were consumers who welcomed both new styles as well as the ones with which they were most familiar. The mix of people throughout the world was increasingly global.[1]

In addition, immigrants were not the only changes to European and American economies. Women, especially young, single women, increasingly played a more important role in the economy, not only as factory workers but also as consumers. These women now had more disposable income and, if they could afford it, leisure time in which to spend their earnings. They became a significant focus of marketing efforts of various domestic industries, such as household goods, throughout the second half of the nineteenth century.[2] For Africans, especially those that worked as slave labor on plantations, there was little economic power until the end of the century. African slaves made up much of the labor force on cotton plantations that not only produced cotton for clothing but for upholstering furniture. Many of the factories that turned the cotton into cloth refused to employ freed Blacks, so they worked in unskilled labor or in small workshops. Even after Reconstruction in the 1870s, African Americans still did not have the same rights and economic freedoms as those of white workers and business owners. Chinese and Mexican workers were limited in their economic abilities too, serving mainly as unskilled laborers for new industries such as coal mining, railroad building, and steel manufacturing.

As machines increasingly took over some manual labor jobs, often children replaced adults in industrial work that did not require adult strength. Children served as both skilled and unskilled labor. Throughout the century, 20 percent of boys and 10 percent of girls under the age of fifteen held full-time jobs, were paid very minimal wages, working sixty to eight hours per week. The majority of these children did not receive an education, creating greater disparity between laborers and white-collar workers. Although social reformers decried the use of children in industrial jobs, it was not until the middle of the century in Britain and even later in the United States, that effective child labor laws were enacted to protect the young and ensure that adults were the major wage earners for families. In his speech of 1864 to the International Working Men's Association, Karl Marx (1818–83) cited the 1863 "Report of the Children's Employment Commission" that "the unhealthy child is an unhealthy parent in his turn" (Marx 1864). Charles Dickens (1812–70) was well known for his vehement criticism of child labor, stemming from his own experiences as a boy working in a blacking factory. From 1837 to 1839, his realistic and highly critical novel *Oliver Twist* was serialized in *Bentley's Miscellany*. Dickens highlighted the hard life Twist endured following his birth in a workhouse, apprenticeship to an undertaker, and his participation later in a gang of young London pickpockets. Dickens's message to readers was clear: take action against child labor.

The nineteenth century also saw the rise of trade unions and organized labor. The first one in the United States, the Mechanics' Union of Trade Associations in Philadelphia, was formed in 1827. This group began as an alliance of different craft unions within a single city. By 1852, the International Typographical Union brought local unions of the same trade from across the United States and Canada (hence the designation international) together. During this period, trade union membership was limited to skilled, rather than industrial, workers. In the 1830s, workingmen's political parties started, advocating equal rights and a series of reforms. Two of these groups were the National Labor Union, which began in 1866, and the Knights of Labor, which was its most influential in the mid-1880s. Initially, the Knights of Labor welcomed all forms of membership, regardless of gender, race, or skilled or unskilled laborer. Contemporary reform movements were not always in concert with the trade unions: the reformers sought cooperative commonwealth rather than higher wages for all levels of production, not just for workers toiling for daily wages. The reformers also did not endorse the trade union's reliance on strikes and boycotts. While the reformers dealt with the future well-being of the worker, trade unions were more concerned with immediate issues. Yet, by 1886, these two constituents joined to form the American Federation of Labor (AFL), which focused on the short-term needs of workers and not on long-term labor reform. The AFL advocated for an eight-hour workday in 1891, insisting that the shortened workday would improve workers' minds. The AFL also negotiated for wage increases and enhanced workplace safety. Yet, by 1895, the AFL was for whites and men only. It was also a time when workers, whether in unions or not, organized strikes, including a general strike in 1842 across Britain, affecting a number of industries, and in Philadelphia in 1835, St. Louis in 1877, the Great Railroad Strike of 1877 across the United States, and the 1892 New Orleans general strike.

Over the hundred-year span, there were a great number of economic changes around the world, through physical and commercial expansion into foreign markets, industrialization, but also revolutions, wars, and economic collapses that saw recessions and depressions. Early in the century, with the basis of most economies in agriculture, the scarcity of arable land restricted growth. In the United States, however, especially after the Louisiana Purchase in 1804, new areas of the country opened up to development—mainly to agriculture. Regions of the United States, partly due to land and climate conditions, divided into areas of farming and ranching in the west, cotton plantations in the south, and industry in the northeast. Ports, whether along the Atlantic, Pacific, or Gulf of Mexico coasts or along the major rivers such as the Mississippi, Missouri, and Ohio served as the distribution centers for raw materials and finished goods. Within Europe, there were also designated centers of industry adjacent to sources of water to use in manufacturing or to bring in raw materials or disperse finished products. European nations after the defeat of Napoleon worked to restore their economies and reassert political power.

INDUSTRIAL INVENTIONS

All sectors of industry witnessed tremendous changes in technologies over the century, many of them affecting the furniture industry. With the invention of the Jacquard loom in Lyon, France, in 1800, the production of textiles for upholstery was altered, enabling furniture manufacturers to work with industrially produced fabrics in an endless number of standardized and easily reproducible patterns. In 1830, Barthélemy Thimonnier (1793–1857) patented the sewing machine, replicating and yet standardizing hand stitching, although it was not until the patent of the American inventor Elias Howe (1819–67) in 1845, and Isaac Singer (1811–75) in 1851, that the lockstitch machine was universally employed. The Howe sewing machine won a gold medal at the 1867 Paris Universelle Exposition and the same year Howe was awarded the Légion d'honneur by Napoleon III for his invention. In the 1844, in Lancashire, England, the chemist John Mercer (1791–1866) developed a process, now called mercerized cotton, whereby cotton threads are treated with sodium hydroxide, to strengthen the fibers and give them a lustrous appearance. Although invented earlier in the century, mercerization, which produced stronger textiles that could be more easily dyed, did not become popular until the 1890s. Artificial fibers such as rayon were also developed, some successfully, such as Swiss chemist Georges Audemars's rayon in 1855 and a later development of the same material by Hilaire, Count de Chardonnet (1839–1924) in 1884. Tables and seating furniture were more easily moved around within interiors after vulcanized rubber was patented in 1839, as the casters on the legs of the furniture pieces were outfitted with small rubber wheels.

The dissemination of imagery of furniture by various visual means evolved throughout the century from woodcuts, engravings, and etchings to lithographs, chromolithographs, and finally, to photography. These processes stimulated the promotion of furniture in the popular press, journals, exhibition catalogs, and books. In addition, the adoption of wood pulp paper in the 1840s and the simultaneous mechanization of paper production radically changed the amount of paper that could be easily fabricated, thereby decreasing the cost of paper and increasing the availability to broader audiences. What was once limited by cost and time now was a booming market and marketplace for the presentation and advertising of all consumer goods.

Images of furniture, interiors, and architecture also changed during the century. Lithography, and subsequently chromolithography, replaced traditional means of illustration or image reproduction: woodcuts, engravings, and etchings. Although the Bavarian Alois Senefelder (1771–1834) invented lithography in 1796, it was during the middle of the nineteenth century that it became a preferred medium for printing images. By the 1850s, photolithography, whereby photographic images were reproduced through the lithographic process, had been introduced and was used more broadly. Another development in printed images came from the 1837 patent for chromolithography, or the introduction of color into the printed images, by Godefroy Engelmann (1788–1839) of Mulhouse, France. This printing technique, although it still used labor-intensive multiple stone blocks to achieve different colors within an image, replaced time-consuming hand coloring during the 1850s. The architect and designer Owen Jones's (1809–74) *Plans, Elevations, Sections and Details of the Alhambra*, published in twelve parts from 1836 to 1845, is considered the first significant work to employ chromolithography. With these new technologies, printing runs could be larger and the distribution, through developments in transportation, meant that more people at various levels of society saw more images. What was previously the exclusive purview of the wealthy was now accessible to a greater number of consumers. At least visually, more consumers had access to the range of goods, from expensive to cheap, that were in the marketplace.

The introduction of photography also revolutionized the distribution of imagery of furniture. Capturing still images through the first Calotype photograph by William Henry Fox Talbot (1800–77) in about 1835 and the daguerreotype by Louis Daguerre (1787–1851) and Joseph Nicéphore Niépce (1765–1833) in 1839, realistically conveyed how furniture looked. The earliest photographic portraits often included seating furniture, as the sitters were required to remain still while an image was captured through a long exposure. These images have also served as documents of the fashions and tastes of the period, locations, and social aspirations of their subjects. Originally promoting the use of glass plates, the American entrepreneur George Eastman (1854–1932) introduced paper-strip, or roll, photographic film in 1885. This and his subsequent launch of the trademark Kodak camera, in 1888, allowed for faster, less cumbersome, and far more numerous (up to one hundred exposures on a roll) recordings of images by cameras. By the end of the century, many journals were able to reproduce photographic images in articles and advertising. The sepia-toned image became the standard for most consumers in which to evaluate goods.

Images were also disseminated through catalogs; in 1872, the first mail-order catalog was published by the American entrepreneur Aaron Montgomery Ward (1843–1913), based in Chicago. These free catalogs, filled with images of consumer goods, allowed customers, often in remote areas of the United States, access to goods from around the country and later the world, ordered from the comfort of their homes. The new railroads not only helped to distribute the catalogs but also to deliver the wares expeditiously.

TRANSPORTATION

Transportation also underwent radical changes during this period, with the invention of the steam engine at the beginning of the century and the internal combustion engine at the end of the century. These developments affected the furniture industry by fundamentally and drastically altering the access of consumers and the workforce to furniture as well as affecting the distribution of finished products. Although the viability of steamboats in Britain and the United States had been established in the 1780s, it was in the nineteenth century that steamboats and, later, steamships became common modes of transportation for materials, finished goods, and passengers. Engineered by William Symington (1764–1831), the *Charlotte Dundas*, propelled by steam-powered paddle wheels, carried passengers and hauled barges up the Forth and Clyde Canal in Scotland in its inaugural voyage of 1803. The same year, the American engineer and inventor Robert Fulton (1765–1815), who was present at the *Charlotte Dundas* trials, collaborated with another Scottish engineer, Henry Bell (1767–1830), to sail up the River Seine in France in his steamboat. Fulton was to develop his own steamship in the United States, establishing the North River Steamboat to bring passengers and goods up and down the Hudson River from New York City to Albany beginning in 1807. Engineers and entrepreneurs worked to prepare vessels to cross the oceans as the technology could help move people and goods with more accuracy than ships with sails, reliant on prevailing winds. The first seagoing steamship was launched in 1813; and in 1822, the first iron steamship, the *Aaron Manby*, crossed the English Channel, carrying passengers and freight. In 1827, although it was not able to make the entire journey under steam-power, the Dutch ship *Curaçao* made a voyage between Rotterdam and Surinam. The first regularly scheduled transatlantic crossings began in 1833 with the British side-wheel paddle steamer *SS Great Western* built by the noted engineer Isambard Kingdom Brunel (1806–59) in 1838. The introduction of the smaller, fully submerged, screw-propeller method of propulsion, in Britain in 1839 and the United States in 1844, replaced paddle wheels. Ships could now enter shallower waters, and the submersion of the propeller meant that there was less damage to the mechanism. The development of trade routes accessible through steam-powered vessels was essential to sourcing of raw materials and distribution of finished goods. The Liverpool engineer and merchant Alfred Holt (1829–1911) launched the screw-propelled *Agamemnon* in 1865 with a trip from London to China, with a stop to take on more coal in Mauritius. With the opening of the Suez Canal in 1869, the journey from Britain to Asia was substantially shortened, allowing for more trade between distant lands. Passengers too were able to make voyages far quicker and more economically with new ocean liners, with accommodations for a variety of classes. In 1870, the White Star Line's RMS *Oceanic* introduced first-class cabins, with amenities such as electricity and running water, and with large portholes. From 1880 into the next century, ocean liners increased in size to accommodate the needs of the increase in migration to the United States and Australia.

Ships were not the only means of transportation impacted by technological advancements during the century. The Stockton and Darlington Railway in Durham, England, introduced the first commercially viable steam locomotive in 1825, although passengers continued to be carried in horse-drawn coaches until carriages hauled by steam locomotives were introduced in 1833. The Liverpool and Manchester Railway opened in 1830, making exclusive use of steam power for passenger and goods trains. The steam engine was not the only development in transportation during this period, as, in 1837, the Scottish chemist Robert Davidson (1804–94) introduced the first electric locomotive, powered by galvanic cells (batteries). By 1879, Werner von Siemens (1816–92) demonstrated an electric railway in Berlin and the world's first electric tramline, also built by Siemens, the Gross-Lichterfelde Tramway, opened near Berlin in 1881. Electric tramways, including one introduced in 1883 in Brighton, England, that remains operational today, sprang up in cities such as Vienna and Richmond, Virginia, and linked cities such as Baltimore and New York. By the end of the century, most street railways were electrified. The London Underground, the world's oldest underground railway, opened in 1863, and began operating electric services for the City and South London Railway in 1890. The diesel engine was invented in 1895, although it was not put into commercial use until 1912. Goods could now travel greater distances, more reliably than by horse and carriage to diversify the marketplace.

People were able to communicate over greater distances as the century progressed. The first telegraph using static electricity was built in 1816, although it was Samuel F.B. Morse's electrical telegraph of 1837 and his subsequent invention of a machine that recorded messages on paper tape that proved successful. By 1851, there were over 32,000 kilometers of telegraph lines crossing the United States. In 1858, a cable was laid across the Atlantic, linking Ireland and Newfoundland, and by 1866, there was a cable connecting Bombay (now Mumbai) to Saudi Arabia; by 1872, telegraph cables linked Bombay to London. Continents, nations, and businesses now enjoyed improved communication for trade.

In 1800, the electric battery was introduced; it would transform society and allow for developments in a number of industries. By 1804, gas lighting had been patented, and towns, cities, homes, and businesses would soon be lit with a stable and reliable light. This was to be supplanted by the introduction of the electrical lightbulb in 1879 by the English physicist, chemist, and inventor Sir Joseph Wilson Swan (1828–1914). Swan was responsible for developing and supplying the first incandescent lights used to illuminate homes and public buildings, including the Savoy Theatre, London, in 1881. Almost simultaneously during the 1880s, two American entrepreneurs Thomas Alva Edison (1847–1931) and George Westinghouse (1846–1914) competed to electrify the United States with incandescent light bulbs and a safe, stable, and constant flow of electricity.

Steam-power, coal, and later, diesel engines, all affected the manufacture of furniture during this period. The technologies that specifically altered the production of furniture can be explored in greater depth in Christina M. Anderson's chapter in this volume.

CROSS-CULTURALISM, IMPERIALISM, AND COLONIALISM

Increased methods of communication and transportation seemingly had a positive effect on goods, including furniture. European and American designers and manufacturers became more familiar with examples of raw materials and goods from far away and designers in India and Asia catered to the markets in London, Paris, Vienna, New York, Chicago, and San Francisco. Printed materials circulated with images that transported audiences to India, Japan, and China and educated readers in differing ways of life. Goods from these global markets flooded the shops and transformed the interiors of middle- and upper-class residences. In turn, Asian manufacturers, and their customers, became more aware of European and American styles and models. The nineteenth century saw the first true global marketplace, where goods from all nations moved with greater ease and were accessible to more people than ever before. There was, however, a more nuanced and negative perspective to this global marketplace.

Although European nations sought to influence and control lands around the world, especially in Asia and Africa, before the nineteenth century, it was this period that saw the greatest expression and demonstration of political and economic dominance of European nations over peoples in Africa, Asia, and South America. This was expressed in imperial and colonial enterprises that shaped the world, mainly in very negative ways promoting ideas of uncivilized, illiterate, and uncultured peoples and fomenting intolerance. What differentiates imperialism and colonialism has been the subject of much discussion among historians. For the purposes of this chapter, the definitions of imperialism and colonialism established by the historian and critic Edward W. Said (1935–2003) will serve as parameters for these terms. For Said, imperialism is "the practice, the theory, and the attitudes of a dominating metropolitan center ruling a distant territory. Colonialism, which is almost always a consequence of imperialism, is the implantation of settlements on distant territory" (Said 1993: 8). Most of the European nations sought to enlarge their economic supremacy in the acquisition of raw materials, labor, and markets for manufactured goods. There were some economic successes for the European nations: the Indian states were profitable for the British and King Leopold II of Belgium, although the most brutal of the imperialist rulers, found the Belgian Congo lucrative as a private enterprise. Natural resources, from timber to cotton to rubber, were made available through imperialism. The world's fairs were the most visible evidence of imperialism and colonialism as the displays were organized according to each imperial nation's holdings. The London 1851 Great Exhibition of the Works of Industry of All Nations reinforced the reality and perception of Britain as the greatest empire in the world with large displays of goods from the Indian subcontinent. Subsequent fairs supported the claims of the host nation as supreme in their imperial and colonial holdings. Although these expositions highlighted industrial production, they also displayed peoples from the colonies in living dioramas or working villages. Although often promoted as educational, in fact these displays hardened racial stereotyping and led to increased intolerance for non-Europeans.

The rise of nationalism, seen through the prism of imperialist and colonial holdings, international competitions, and the xenophobia that accompanied it, was one of the key characteristics of the nineteenth century. Early in the century, Napoleon's conquest of German and Italian states aroused patriotism with the vanquished, creating intense enmity between France and the rest of Europe. By dissolving the Holy Roman Empire in 1806 and organizing the Confederation of the Rhine, Napoleon generated a feeling of German unity. It was not until the efforts of Otto von Bismark (1815–98) that Germany achieved unification in 1871. Nationalism was the impetus for the unification of the Italian city-states into the Kingdom of Italy in 1861. In the 1820s, Greece revolutionaries staged a series of conflicts with the Ottoman Empire, finally achieving independence in 1832. In South and Central America, former colonies of Spain became self-ruled by the middle of the century. In addition to military conflicts, such as the Franco-Prussian War in 1870 or the Boer War in South Africa in 1880, nationalism played a role in economic confrontations that took place less violently at the international expositions. Designers and manufacturers too supported nationalism through the incorporation of traditional motifs or techniques into their products. During the second half of the century, designers drew on folk and vernacular styles to promote nationalistic sentiments. The architecture and furnishings of national pavilions at the international expositions disseminated patriotic symbols and styles. As nationalistic sentiments intensified there was more evidence of patriotic motifs incorporated into designs for decorative arts, such American eagles or German bears, carved in wooden seating furniture.

EDUCATION

The nineteenth century was a period of intense classification. Although the eighteenth-century Swedish botanist Carl Linnaeus (1707–78) revolutionized and advanced modern taxonomies, standardizing a binomial naming system for animal and plant species through class, order, genus, and species, it was during the nineteenth century that categorization and classification became universal. From the taxonomies of the natural world to the classes of the manufactured world, nineteenth-century scientists divided and categorized the world around them. Each part had its place. This carried over to the designation of art, craft, design, and the educational systems for these interconnected categories.

Education, and especially art design education, became an increasingly important topic in the national and international competition, with those countries with nationally sponsored art education the envy of those that did not have such systems. One of the most successful programs in art and design education was in France. Founded in the seventeenth century, the French schools of art had been training artists and designers in many of the major cities. In 1766, Jean-Jacques Bachelier (1724–1806) founded the École royale gratuite de dessin (Royal Free School of Art) with a program to train designers to improve the quality of manufactured goods. The curriculum combined art, design, technique, fabrication, and an apprenticeship, and in 1877 the school became the National School of Decorative Arts (École nationale des arts décoratifs). In Britain, the House of Commons established the first schools of art and design in 1835, one for young men and another for women. The schools, however, were deemed a failure—as shown from the criticism of British design at the 1851 Great Exhibition. The year after the Great Exhibition, the government appointed Henry Cole, one of the organizers of the fair, to be the first General Superintendent of the Department of Practical Art, to improve standards of art and design education in Britain with reference to their applicability to industry. In this capacity, Cole was instrumental in the development of the Museum of Ornamental Art in Marlborough House, later to become the South Kensington Museum and, still later, the Victoria and Albert Museum. Cole was the museum's first director of the museum from 1857 to 1873. A full study of this development in the exhibition and access to view furniture and other decorative arts and the role of art education is examined in Chapter 6 in this volume on exhibition and display.

In 1854, another English art school was founded by the Reverend Robert Gregory: the City and Guilds of London Art School, called the Lambeth School of Art. Its first program was night classes, but with the support of Cole, the school prospered and it became a leader for instruction in applied art and design for working artisans, many of whom were employed by local manufacturing firms. The school was so successful that it expanded to new premises in 1860.

CONCLUSION

The chapters that follow elaborate on many of the social, economic, technological, and political themes through the lens of furniture and its use, fabrication, and symbolic role in the cultural life of the nineteenth century. Without improved transportation and communication, the materials used to construct or produce furniture would not have been possible and the distribution limited to regional areas. New shipping employing steamships and railroads resulted in the availability of finished goods in shops, expositions, and other wholesale and retail outlets. The growth of the middle class supplied consumers able to buy works fabricated by great industry and without the industrialists who made their fortunes through the work of unskilled and skilled laborers, the finest works would not have been commissioned for their luxurious interiors. Improved transportation and communication had tremendous impact on the distribution of imagery through advertising, journals, catalogs, and newspapers leading to consumers being more knowledgeable and more aspirational in their desire for the latest and most fashionable goods. The invention of lithography, chromolithography, and later, photography more accurately transmitted images to the public, designers, and manufacturers. The adoption of wood pulp paper as the primary material for printed documents, lowered costs, which also spurred the tremendous growth in the number of published pamphlets, brochures, magazines, and books available to a greater variety of the public. Changes in styles, from neoclassical to Art Nouveau, were recorded, disseminated, and appreciated through these technological advancements. With a burgeoning middle class, more entrepreneurs in the industrial economy, society became more fluid. The so-called robber barons of the United States, who had made their fortunes in railroads and other industries, rather than in agriculture, had more disposable income for changing fashions and luxurious homes. In addition, local, national, and colonial governments invested in new civic buildings, which needed to be furnished with works that communicated history and power. All of these revolutionary activities are investigated in greater detail in this volume.

CHAPTER ONE

Design and Motifs

MEGAN ALDRICH

We must not make use of tradition for its own sake; through scholarly research we must penetrate its spiritual and material qualities in order to arrive at an apprehension of the essential nature of tradition and an understanding of its forms. Only then will we be able to decide what part of tradition merely belongs to the past … and what part contains eternal truth, is valid for all future generations, and therefore must be accepted and retained by us. This would be true eclecticism.

—Karl Gottlieb Wilhelm Bötticher, 1846

The words above are taken from the transcription of an 1846 speech made by Karl Gottlieb Wilhelm Bötticher (1806–89), an influential professor of classical architecture at the University of Berlin; he later became head of the sculpture department of what eventually became the Pergamon Museum in Berlin. In this speech, he was celebrating the birthday of the late Prussian neoclassical architect and furniture designer Karl Schinkel (1781–1841) (Herrmann 1992). Architecture and furniture design were closely linked during the nineteenth century, and Bötticher voiced an almost universal concern—that is, what stylistic and ornamental choices designers should make when carrying out work in the industrial age, with its wealth of new materials, new types of interiors, and new patrons.

THE CONTEXT FOR FURNITURE DESIGN IN THE NINETEENTH CENTURY

Nineteenth-century design is known for the complex layering of visual and stylistic references, and the study and reuse of historical styles is one of its defining characteristics. This referencing of the past in nineteenth-century design was rarely done capriciously. In fact, designers, writers, and critics often cited and promoted the revival of these historical styles for their nationalistic, patriotic, imperial, and religious connotations and denotations. The inclusion of a style or a particular motif could recall times of nationalistic superiority and inspire or motivate political movements or regimes. This layering was also an outgrowth of the tremendous social, economic, technological, and political transformations taking place during this period. Designers were focused on the incorporation of the most innovative materials and technologies to express these revival styles. Often the most conservative of styles would be expressed through the most modern materials or technologies—Gothic Revival in cast iron or Rococo Revival in laminated wood—historicizing styles fabricated through substances and technologies that were quintessentially "modern."

Although the long-established classical language of design familiar to Bötticher was never entirely superseded during the nineteenth century, nonetheless from 1800 to 1900 a series of styles ranging from the Gothic to Art Nouveau unfolded and coexisted alongside classicism and drew mainly upon earlier art historical periods. This stylistic succession included, but was not confined to, neo-medievalism or the "Gothic Revival," which encompassed a range of different styles referencing the Middle Ages; the "Old French" style, which embraced French design from the seventeenth and eighteenth centuries up to the period of the French Revolution; the more specialized Renaissance Revival and the neoclassical revival, both of which examined past styles of classicism; and the referencing of non-European styles seen in design phenomena such as Egyptian Revival, as well as Japonism and Orientalism, the latter encompassing a wave of interest in design inspired by travel to Egypt and the Middle East. Toward the end of the century, "reforming" styles such as Aestheticism and the Arts and Crafts movement attempted to move away from strict historical revivalism. In continental Europe, the dialectic between classicism and neo-medievalism remained the dominant stylistic force in design until the 1860s, while in the English-speaking world, perhaps due to the impact of factory production and industrialization as well as a more developed market economy with a thirst for innovation, a rapid succession of stylistic experimentations took place with decorative art in general, and with regard to the design of furniture and interiors, in particular.

The principal expression of "style" was found in the ornament and decorative motifs employed in a design. Traceried patterns with pointed arches signified the Gothic, and all of its associations, while C-scrolls and shells signaled the rococo style and its eighteenth-century references. In furniture design, forms changed to reflect different styles but ultimately remained within a narrow range of possibilities, given the practical demands of furniture. Any form of seat furniture, for example, had to be strong enough to support and conform to the proportions of the human frame. Although new materials such as iron began to be used for furniture on an experimental basis before the middle of the century, most manufacturers and the buying public preferred traditional materials—mainly woods—for the furniture they acquired for domestic use.

Leading architects and designers of the nineteenth century in Europe were concerned with the appropriate referencing of past art historical styles and with the adaptation of this rich, inherited language of forms and ornament for use with new, industrial materials such as cast iron, and with new processes of manufacture. For example, the viscous nature of metals when heated during production facilitated the use of naturalistic ornament, especially leafy forms, which became a tremendously popular type of motif during the century in interior elements, such as architectural brackets and light fittings. Therefore, innovations in technology helped to drive the styles and ornamental vocabularies used in the production of goods during the nineteenth century.

However, in addition to this technological progress and innovation, the nineteenth century was also an era of near-constant political upheaval, much of it stemming from France, the dominant political force in Europe during the early years of the century. Events such as the Napoleonic Wars, the Congress of Vienna of 1815, the rise and eventual overthrow of the Second Empire under Napoleon III, and the Franco-Prussian War all had an impact on design and encouraged designers to look back to established, historical periods such as the eighteenth century, which became viewed as a "golden age" of civilization. Karl Bötticher, whose ideas influenced the great French architectural and design theorist Eugène-Emmanuel Viollet-le-Duc (1814–79), made a call for "true eclecticism" (Hübsch 1992), which he felt would be a positive development as it would allow nineteenth-century designers to take the best of historical design and reapply it to design problems of the modern era. Viollet-le-Duc, for example, embraced the use of cast iron in his widely read *Entretiens sur l'architecture* (Lectures on Architecture, 1863–72), arguably one of the most prominent publications on design of the nineteenth century. Although he restored a number of important medieval buildings and was known as the leading Gothic Revival architect and designer in France, Viollet-le-Duc mixed up his Gothic forms with other more exotic elements such as domes and mosaic ornament derived from Byzantine culture. In his work we find the "eclecticism" of which Bötticher spoke. The sinuous forms and leafy ornament Viollet-le-Duc developed in his eclectic furniture designs of the 1860s helped to lay the foundations for the development of the Art Nouveau style at the end of the century—several of his followers became leading Art Nouveau designers.

SOURCES FOR ORNAMENT AND DESIGN

Since the eighteenth century pattern books had become essential tools for the furniture maker's workshop, and this tradition of published designs continued into the nineteenth century. Some earlier publications such as Daniel Marot's rich, late baroque designs, which were issued in Amsterdam at the beginning of the eighteenth century, or Thomas Chippendale's famous pattern book of designs from the 1750s and early 1760s, were republished and served as a resource for revivalism in design. Another interesting aspect of nineteenth-century publishing saw the development of books that specialized in ornament, some of which were comprehensive or even encyclopaedic in scope.

Although no one country, culture, or location dominated the literature on ornament and design of the nineteenth century, French designers continued to lead the way from the eighteenth into the nineteenth century. Because of the years of turmoil extending from the French Revolution of 1789, through the Terror of the 1790s, into the Napoleonic Wars, which ended in 1815, many ambitious young Frenchmen traveled to other cities, including London, which profited by such skilled immigration. The leading *marchand-mercier* Dominique Daguerre (active 1772–96) maintained a presence in Paris during the Revolutionary period but found fruitful employment at the Francophile court of George IV in Britain, feeding the taste for fashionable French neoclassical furnishings. Napoleon's court designers, Charles Percier and Pierre François Léonard Fontaine's influential pattern book, the *Recueil de decoration* of 1801 and 1812 (see below), featured not only classical ornament but actual examples of furniture executed by leading furniture makers according to their designs. Theirs was an exercise aimed at the French elite of the early nineteenth century, but their designs were disseminated to a more middle-class audience both within and outside of France via design periodicals, a relatively new type of literature akin to the design and decorating magazines still with us today. This phenomenon will be discussed further in the section on neoclassical design, below.

The architectural draughtsman Augustus Charles Pugin (1769–1832) settled in London to study at the Royal Academy while the fierce aftermath of the French Revolution was in full swing in Paris. He published close studies of ornament, especially foliate, or leafy, ornament, taken from motifs of Gothic architecture, which set a new standard in terms of their detailed observation, making them ready for use as patterns to be followed by craftsmen and carvers. The plates from Pugin's publication were used as a direct source in his own furniture designs of the 1820s, and in the early furniture designs by his more famous son, Augustus Welby Northmore Pugin (1812–52), a dominant figure in the Gothic Revival of the nineteenth century who published his own highly important "manifestos" of design, which will be discussed in the section on the Gothic, below.

By the time of the 1851 Exhibition in London, British design publications began to assume the leading role in the study of design and ornament. Ralph Nicholson Wornum (1812–77) was one of the first writers in Britain to attempt a comprehensive survey of ornament and styles, beginning with antiquity. In 1856, when Keeper of the National Gallery in London, Wornum published an influential book: *Analysis of Ornament. The Characteristics of Styles: An Introduction to the Study of the History of Ornamental Art*, which went through several editions. Wornum's *Analysis* was based on a series of lectures he gave to students at the Government Schools of Design in London, which were intended to prepare young people for careers as professional designers. In chapter five, Wornum set out "The Styles," as he saw them, beginning with the Egyptians, proceeding through Greece, Rome, and Byzantium to the European Middle Ages, and ending with three "modern" styles: the Renaissance, the Cinquecento, and "Louis Quatorze." Each style was divided into subheadings and accompanied by illustrations of architectural and ornamental details; each chapter begins with a meaty list of "Illustrated Literature" for further reading. As will be discussed in this chapter, subsequent writers on nineteenth-century design have adopted different terminology to that used by Wornum, which is now seen as somewhat eccentric. However, broadly speaking he captured the principal revived styles up to about 1870, which are still recognized by design historians today. His was very much a study of the established, European styles.

Wornum's great contemporary in terms of the study of design and motifs, generally, was Owen Jones (1809–74), the talented son of a Welsh antiquary whom nowadays would probably be described as a "product designer," a term that implies both three-dimensional and graphic design. In 1856, the year in which Wornum's *Analysis* was published, Jones produced an important book in glowing chromolithography. *The Grammar of Ornament* set new standards of color printing and at the same time moved directly into the study of non-European ornament and design outside of the classical tradition. Jones had published *Plans, Elevations, Sections, and Details of the Alhambra* in instalments between 1836 and 1845 in the new method of color printing, chromolithography, based upon his firsthand knowledge of the more important building of Moorish Spain. Jones displayed a strong interest in the motifs and design of the Arab world and went on to decorate the Crystal Palace, which housed the 1851 Exhibition in London, in stenciled designs in primary colors. It was a step in the direction of abstract design, but he was not without contemporaries, as some of the later designs by A.W.N. Pugin of the 1840s displayed the same interest in flat, unrelieved pattern. These were used not only in interior decoration but also to paint the surfaces of furniture, a fashionable technique in some of the more extreme Gothic and exotic designs of the later nineteenth century, such as that produced by William Burges and William Morris, which will be discussed toward the end of this chapter.

A different, perhaps more "scientific," approach was taken by the German writer, Franz Sales Meyer (1849–1927), a professor of design at the Grand Ducal School of Applied Art in Karlsruhe. His comprehensive *Handbook of Ornament* was published in Karlsruhe in 1888; it subsequently went through several more editions before 1900. It provides an extremely clear, rational approach to the often complex study of ornamental design. In his introduction, Meyer tells us that the style of an object should be determined by its intended use and by the material it is to be made out of, and that style may be varied without being arbitrary. In a sense, Meyer is suggesting a concept that was to be embraced by the modernists of the early twentieth century—that is, that form should follow function. This is different from the eclecticism promoted by Bötticher earlier in the century, for Meyer's concern was not so much to create a new style by studying the underlying principles of design of the past, a concern shared by designers such as A.W.N. Pugin and Viollet-le-Duc. Instead, Meyer gave copious illustrations of patterns, decorative details, and forms that might be adapted by the modern designer. Unlike the majority of nineteenth-century design books, Meyer's *Handbook* includes a chapter dedicated to furniture that succinctly discusses the development of historical forms, shapes, and types by means of identified examples of seat, table, and carcase furniture, as well as a brief discussion of frames. His is one of the first publications to study the history of shapes in furniture design, as opposed to the examination of ornamental features, making it an important milestone in the historiography of furniture.

Such design literature was complemented later in the century by interior decorating manuals, which were intended to guide a middle-class clientèle in selecting furnishings and creating stylish interiors. Such activities came to be seen as an important means of signaling one's tastes and position in society, as well as one's social aspirations. Such publications provide useful insight into the nineteenth-century phenomenon of revivalism and the eclecticism of design, which exerted a powerful impact on the look of furniture during this period. The international best seller of this genre was *Hints on Household Taste* of 1868 by Charles Locke Eastlake (1836–1906), who gave his name to an entire style of decorating in the United States. Such decorating manuals, which always include furniture within their broader context of the interior, are characteristic of the second half of the nineteenth century and will be discussed in the section on Aestheticism later in this chapter, as will the phenomenon of Orientalism and late chinoiserie. By about 1800, the British East India Company was the largest corporation in the world, bringing great wealth into Britain and creating an enormous demand for exotic goods, including imported furniture. Partly because of this globalized trade, and because of the influx of talented designers from other cities who worked alongside native designers, such as Alexandre-Eugène

Prignot working with the London firm of Jackson and Graham (see Victoria and Albert Museum [hereafter V&A], 7247:1 to 13-1860), furniture design in Britain assumed a leading position in terms of setting the styles of design in the nineteenth century, and its impact was felt internationally throughout its colonial empire, and beyond.

NEOCLASSICISM IN THE NINETEENTH CENTURY

For centuries in Europe, the fashionable arrangement of interiors and the creation of the most refined and expensive furnishings rested with designers who worked for princes and courts. An alternative model developed in the trading nations—particularly in Portugal, the Netherlands, Belgium, and Great Britain, where wealthy merchants with new fortunes provided a strong, alternative kind of patronage for luxury goods and furnishings. At the outset of the nineteenth century, European governments were still predominantly located in courts and monarchies, although these had been shaken to their foundations by the French Revolution of 1789 with the execution of the king and queen, followed by the rise of the self-styled emperor of the French, Napoleon Bonaparte (1769–1821), who crowned himself at Fontainebleau in 1804. Until his final defeat in 1815 at the Battle of Waterloo, Napoleon created and controlled his own distinctive court style of bold classicism, which self-consciously referenced motifs from imperial Rome and the emperors of the classical period of antiquity. His politically inspired brand of imperial classicism outlasted his own reign and was copied and adopted from Russia to Greece to the new American federal republic.

The century's first highly influential guide to furniture and interiors, the *Recueil de Décorations Intérieures*, was published in 1801, and enlarged and republished in 1812. The authors were Charles Percier (1764–1838) and Pierre François Léonard Fontaine (1762–1853), the court designers to the emperor Napoleon. Their *Recueil* showcased the bold style of classicism they created, which broke new ground in terms of block-like forms of seats and cabinets, compact, circular tables, and a high degree of contrast between dark woods and lavish gilt-bronze mounts. In a departure from design publications of the eighteenth century, the *Recueil* even depicted actual examples of furniture executed for prominent figures at the imperial court, accompanied by a simple explanatory text. Many of these designs were made into furniture by Jacob Frères of Paris in mahogany with gilt-brass mounts. It is probably not an overstatement to claim that Percier and Fontaine transformed the look of neoclassical furniture from the linear forms and delicate ornament of classical design during the second half of the eighteenth century to archaeologically based forms, often derived from ancient Roman models, and simplified but powerful ornament highlighted in gilding against a ground of dark or figured woods such as mahogany, thuja, and amboyna—woods that rarely appeared in the tradition of French furniture making until the period of the Revolution. These dark woods, provided a contrasting background for high-quality, low-relief gilt-bronze mounts in bold silhouettes of classical forms such as stars, masks of deities, or classical architectural motifs. Decorative motifs included imperial eagles, griffins, and lion monopodia taken from ancient sources, often sculptural ones. The firm of Pierre-Philippe Thomire (1751–1843) of Paris supplied much of the most exquisite metalwork, including candelabra and clocks as well as the characteristic mounts on what has come to be known as French Empire furniture.

This powerful new style was captured in one of the most famous portraits of Napoleon by the French neoclassical painter Jacques-Louis David, now in the National Gallery in Washington, DC (Plate 6). In this image, which was in fact commissioned not by a member of Napoleon's court but by an admiring British aristocrat, the emperor stands at his desk with his hand resting on an ivory globe used as a decorative finial on the armrest of the simple but boldly modeled rectangular mahogany chair. The firm of Georges Jacob (1739–1814), which predated the French Revolution but prospered well into the nineteenth century, made much of the Napoleonic court furniture and supplied studio furniture to the painter David (Ledoux-Lebard 1965). The Jacob firm created many pieces of furniture which were closely based on the designs of Percier and Fontaine and popularized in the widely disseminated designs published by Pierre Antoine Leboux de la Mésangère (1761–1831), which were enthusiastically received in the new American republic. De la Mésangère, a Catholic priest, had lost his teaching position at the time of the French Revolution, so he took over the editorship of a fashion magazine, the *Journal des Dames et des Modes*, which contained an influential and widely disseminated supplement on the design of furniture and works of art, the *Collection de Meubles et Objets de Goût*, published during the period 1802–35. De la Mésangère went on to publish several more books on design, costume, and fashion, an unexpected if successful career for an unemployed man of the church.

European courts from Brussels to Munich to Athens followed the stylistic lead of France and its imperial style of design during the first third of the nineteenth century. The emperor of the French was particularly fascinated by the Republic of Venice, and during the brief moment of French rule, which was much resented by Venetians, local designers were commissioned to create new, neoclassical-style interiors and furniture. The talented decorative artist and designer Giuseppe Borsato (1771–1849), who designed exquisite neoclassical interiors for the Napoleonic wing of what is now the Museo Correr in Saint Mark's Square, also designed Empire-style walnut furniture of uncomplicated forms decorated with prominent winged sphinxes for the rooms by Andrea

Palladio on the site of the Accademia Museum in Venice, the subject of a major refurbishment in 2015. Napoleonic influence extended to the New World, for Napoleon's younger brother, Jerome, had married an American heiress from Baltimore, and there was a moment of French Empire style in the new republic. This was led by Charles-Honoré Lannuier (1779–1819), a cabinetmaker born and trained in France who emigrated in 1803 to New York due to the political and economic upheaval in France, where he established a very successful career. During his relatively short life, Lannuier produced a distinctive version of the French Empire style with prominent gilt sphinxes on mahogany console tables for smart New York houses during the Federal period (Kenny, Bretter, and Leben 1998). Lannuier's furniture and French Empire designs were highly sought after in the New Republic, alongside the designs by De la Mésangère. Other designers in the early American republic such as the Scottish-born cabinetmaker Duncan Phyfe (1770–1854) created versions of this European classical furniture, while in Austria and Germany cabinetmakers simplified French forms and used local, native timbers to create plain furniture, known as "Biedermeier."

In the English-speaking world, this paradigm shift in classical design away from the more two-dimensional and refined neoclassicism of the eighteenth century can be tracked via the first and last publications of Thomas Sheraton (1751–1806). Sheraton, a drawing-master from the north of England, published two widely influential books: *The Cabinet Maker's and Upholsterer's Drawing Book*, published in series from 1791 to 1793, 2nd edition in 1794 and revised edition 1802, and *The Cabinet-Maker, Upholsterer and General Artist's Encyclopedia* of 1806. The *Drawing Book* was very much a product of the eighteenth-century classical tradition that Robert Adam, the great neoclassical architect and furniture designer of the eighteenth century, would have recognized. The *Encyclopedia* heralded the new century and the influence of Percier and Fontaine combined with that of Thomas Hope (see below). The drawing master Richard Brown (active 1804–45), whose own publications followed the lead of those by Sheraton for the next generation, captured the change in neoclassical furniture design thus:

> [There is a] new character, bold in the outline, rich and chaste in the ornaments, and durable from the rejection of little parts. This style, although in too many instances resembling the Greek tombs, has evidently arisen in a great measure from Mr. Hope's mythological work on Household Furniture, Mr. Smith's excellent book of Unique Design, and Percier's splendid French work on Interior Decoration.
>
> (Brown 1822)

Brown was referring to the squared-off, block-like profiles particularly of furniture in classical styles, which Sheraton was picking up from the designs of all three men referred to above: Percier, Hope, and Smith. Plate 45 of Sheraton's *Encyclopedia*, a design for a sofa (Figure 1.1), displays a solid silhouette. The design also features three-dimensional masks, which decorate the arched sofa ends, reflecting a new interest in incorporating archaeological references even in the design of a sofa for a fashionable drawing room. For example, either side of the sofa back has been ornamented with acroteria, the spade-shaped projections noted by early travelers to Greece along the rooflines of later Greek temples and shrines. The work done by archaeologist-designers such as Robert Adam and James Stuart in the eighteenth century was still being studied in the nineteenth, and the fourth volume of Stuart's highly important study of Greek ornament and architecture, *The Antiquities of Athens*, did not appear until 1814, after his death. Napoleon's military expedition into Egypt in 1799 and the resulting publication of Egyptian antiquities by Baron Denon caused a sensation in Europe and sparked the earliest examples of Egyptian styles. Likewise, antiquaries were becoming archaeologists in the nineteenth century and were turning their attention toward medieval architecture as well. Scholarly references and erudite, antiquarian enquiry had become fashionable.

Sheraton's later publication clearly displays the influence of the Amsterdam-born collector and scholarly designer Thomas Hope (1769–1831), who settled

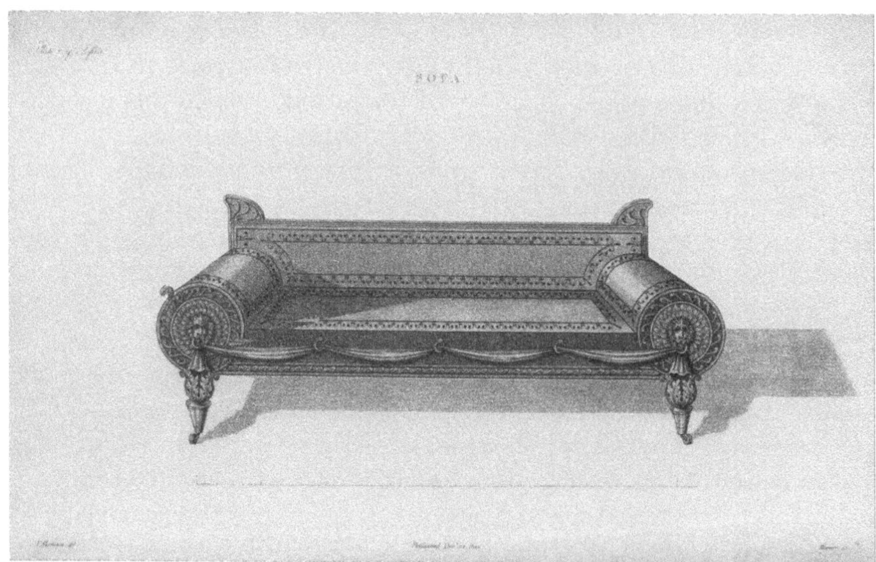

FIGURE 1.1 Thomas Sheraton, *The Cabinet-Maker, Upholsterer and General Artist's Encyclopaedia* (1806). Harris Brisbane Dick Fund, 1932/Metropolitan Museum of Art. Photograph courtesy of the Metropolitan Museum of Art.

in London in 1799 and began remodeling an eighteenth-century townhouse on Duchess Street that had been designed by Robert Adam. Once Hope's interiors had taken shape, and his archaeological collections of Egyptian, Greek, and Roman sculptures were installed, he allowed access to his house through ticketed open houses. Hope's collection, on its own, was remarkable for its variety, quality, and refinement, indicating a sophisticated eye. Hope's selection of a variety of ancient sculptures was also reflected in the designs for his furniture. His interest in ancient Egyptian design, both in his collection and his furniture designs, was displayed in pylon shapes and sphinx-like ornament. Not all visitors were entranced with Hope's new vision of classicism, as evidenced by the eyewitness account of the German traveler Prince Pückler-Muskau, who made two extended trips to Britain in 1814 and 1826:

> Mr Hope, who is rather remarkable for his reserve ... appeared to me no ordinary man. He is very rich, and his house full of treasures of art, and of luxuries which I shall describe hereafter. His furniture theory, which is fashioned on the antique, I cannot praise in practice: – the chairs are ungovernable; other trophy-like structures look ridiculous, and the sophas have such sharp salient points in all directions, that an incautious sitter might hurt himself seriously.
>
> (Butler 1957)

Hope eventually published a guide to understanding his own distinctive interiors and furniture in 1807 (Watkin and Hewat-Jaboor 2008). His *Household Furniture and Interior Decoration* was the second guide of major importance to nineteenth-century classical design after Percier and Fontaine's *Recueil*. In contrast to the Napoleonic court designers, who stayed close to Roman Imperial sources ultimately for political reasons and the celebration of empire, Hope was raised amongst a family of renowned art collectors and he was widely traveled, having taken a lengthy Grand Tour in his youth. In addition to Italy, Hope traveled through the Balkans on his way to Greece, and then on to Egypt, sketching and studying all the while. His contribution to the history of nineteenth-century classicism was to incorporate what were then perceived as more exotic motifs from pre-classical Greece, including the Archaic period, and from Egypt. Such use of bold new forms of classicism in his furniture, as in his famous "Egyptian room," which was furnished with gilt and ebonized daybeds decorated with scarab beetles and fake hieroglyphics, sparked a fashion for more diverse forms of antique referencing, including Egyptian forms and motifs.

The more commercially minded British pattern books that publicized Hope's style in furniture and interiors included Sheraton's *Encyclopedia* and the influential design magazine the *Repository of the Arts*, published by the German émigré Rudolph Ackermann (1764–1834), who also ran a successful shop in London. Designs were also published by the prolific but somewhat mysterious George Smith (dates unknown), whose works began to appear in 1806 and continued until 1826–8 with his last book, the *Cabinet-Maker's and Upholsterer's Guide, Drawing Book and Repository*, the title neatly referencing the well-known published design compilations of Sheraton and Ackermann. Smith, who made the seemingly false claim to have been upholder to the Prince of Wales, was far more commercially minded than Thomas Hope, who strove for archaeological purity (Collard 1985). Smith's designs for furniture, interiors, and upholstery included the full range of styles current in Britain during the period of the Regency (1811–20), and the subsequent reign of George IV (1820–30). As an alternative stylistic tradition to classicism, Gothic (a term often used quite loosely to embrace a range of neo-medieval revivalisms) was undoubtedly the most significant; Gothic Revival design will be discussed shortly. However, Smith's published designs also included Louis XIV, discussed below, and chinoiserie, the European phenomenon of adopting Chinese and other East Asian decorative motifs, which was spectacularly showcased in the Royal Pavilion at Brighton.

The neoclassical style, in its more geometric and more archaeologically accurate interpretation as well as the more delicate versions from the late eighteenth century, was also popular throughout Germany and Austria as well as Scandinavia. German and Austrian Biedermeier was named for the pseudonym of a German poet, Adolph Kussmaul (1822–1902), who wrote about the comfortable, non-political *petit-bourgeois*. Like French Empire furniture, Biedermeier designs display the characteristic bold outlines of this period and were often based on ancient Greek and Roman models. They diverge from the French models in their use of strong contrasting wood tones, black against pale, and unconventional forms such as spherical sewing tables or large lyre-shaped secretary bookcases. Upholstery, too, was dramatic and brilliantly colored.

The Chinese-style interiors and furnishings at Brighton were being developed between 1802 and about 1822 for the Prince Regent, later George IV, by a design team led by John Crace (1754–1819) and his son Frederick (1779–1859). After the Royal Pavilion, however, it was nearly half a century before Asian-inspired designs once again became highly visible, most notably in Aesthetic design and Japonism, discussed later in this chapter. In the meantime, the long shadow of the French Revolution was still felt across Europe, bringing with it a reexamination of what was perceived as a lost golden age of European design—the furniture, interiors, and decorative art produced for the "Louis" kings of France: Louis XIV, XV, and XVI.

THE "OLD FRENCH" STYLE AND THE ROCOCO REVIVAL

The cultural conservatism sparked by the Congress of Vienna in 1815, where there was an attempt to reestablish the European order as it was before the advent of Napoleon, encouraged a nostalgic look backward to the glories of the French *ancien régime* on both sides of the Channel. The phenomenon took some time to establish itself in Continental Europe, where Napoleonic classicism remained surprisingly tenacious long after the defeat of the emperor at Waterloo. In fact, it was British patrons and collectors, led by King George IV and his circle, who were often the most enthusiastic admirers of what came to be known as the "Old French Style," as it was first called by a leading practitioner in London, John Gregory Crace (1809–89), the son of Frederick Crace who had worked at the Royal Pavilion in Brighton.

Terminology has always been an issue with regard to capturing this interesting stylistic phenomenon, and contemporary stylistic descriptors lacked precision. Writers in the nineteenth century were fond of the term "Louis Quatorze"—that is, after the court style of the Sun King at Versailles in the seventeenth century—to describe designs that were, in fact, not very baroque at all, aside from the occasional borrowing of specific motifs. It was rather French eighteenth-century design before the Revolution that provided the inspiration for this style. Most modern writers of the twentieth century have tended to use the term "Rococo Revival" as a replacement for "Old French Style," although, in fact, the Rococo Revival included aspects of design from the baroque period under Louis XIV; an even greater number of elements from the neoclassical period under Louis XVI; and rococo designs and motifs from the period of Louis XV and his famous mistress Madame du Pompadour. Less reverent, perhaps, was the term "tous les louis" (literally "all the Louis"), which conveyed the jumble of *ancien régime* references in these complex designs.

One of the first writers on ornament and design to discuss the French style in any detail was Ralph Nicholson Wornum. In his *Analysis of Ornament*, however, Wornum was distinctly lukewarm about its virtues: "Had the knowledge of styles been a little more disseminated in the present day, we should not have found the Louis XV, and the rococo, as the prevailing English tastes of the Great Exhibition of 1851." In other words, Wornum is suggesting it might have been ignorance of the alternatives that resulted in so many manufacturers exhibiting objects which came to be associated with the Rococo Revival in its broader sense at the Great Exhibition in London. The term "Rococo Revival" suggests a more commercial version of J.G. Crace's refined, aristocratic "Old French Style," a term he used in commissions for country houses such as the redecorating and furnishing of the Lower Library at Chatsworth of 1840–4 (Aldrich 1990). Crace's furniture in maple and amaranth for the Chatsworth Lower Library, however, revived baroque forms of furniture rather than rococo ones. For example, the suite of library furniture he created for the 6th Duke of Devonshire, Chatworth's owner, featured x-frame stools and armchairs, looking both to French and Netherlandish seventeenth-century precedents. An equivalent to Crace's "Old French" could be found in the work of some Paris makers who created historicist work, such as Pierre Bellangé, court cabinetmaker to Charles X, the younger brother of Louis XVI, the French king who was guillotined during the Revolution. Bellangé sometimes combined porcelain plaques on rococo-style furniture with lavish gilt mounts and rosewood veneers. Rosewood was used in high-end baroque and nineteenth-century furniture but was less common in eighteenth-century French pieces, while the incorporation of porcelain plaques was a feature very much associated with French neoclassical furniture. In the work of both J.G. Crace and Pierre Bellangé, therefore, we see the layered referencing of different stylistic periods in the creation of a new, hybrid style. That style represented, perhaps, the more conservative end of furniture and interior design, one which was compatible with existing historic buildings and that looked back to the golden age of European design.

The decade of the 1840s was undoubtedly the period in which the older French styles flourished, and Wornum's comment on the plethora of rococo-style objects at the Great Exhibition of 1851 in London reflects this. Manufacturers focused on production and techniques, demonstrating the accomplishments of their factories and workshops; but where rococo objects were poorly designed or functioned simply as a vehicle to show off carving, gilding, and ornament, the results could be unappealing. Plate 7, on the other hand, illustrates a beautifully made example of this genre, which won a medal at the Paris Exposition of 1855, held four years after the Great Exhibition in London. This enormous cabinet was designed by a Frenchman named Alexandre-Eugène Prignot, who was working for the London firm of Jackson and Graham, in whose workshops the cabinet was made (V&A, 7247:1 to 13-1860). The firm had a reputation for high-quality workmanship and was well known at the large, international exhibitions of the nineteenth century. The scale is too vast for this piece to have been intended for domestic use. It combines the shape of an eighteenth-century rectangular commode of breakfront design with an enormous mirror incorporating candleholders, a type of object not produced in this form during the eighteenth century. Moreover, its rich ornamentation and variety of materials, combined with its eccentric form, confirm that it was a piece designed to be noticed and to provoke comment at a large exhibition.

Technical innovations are evident in the cabinet's manufacture, and to some extent led its design and influenced its form, producing a work that suggested an eighteenth-century piece of French furniture but certainly could only have been produced in the nineteenth century. The lower portion of the cabinet has expensive, machine-cut marquetry of tropical woods decorated by lavish electroplated gilt mounts, a new industrial technique superseding the traditional mercury gilding, and porcelain plaques painted in the eighteenth-century neoclassical style, surmounted by a mirror the size of which would have been technically impossible to produce during the eighteenth century (Meyer 2006). The combination of technical innovation, lavish decoration, and large silhouettes is typical of many exhibition pieces. The Jackson and Graham cabinet demonstrates a combination of French baroque, rococo, and neoclassical motifs, forms, and techniques, which is typical of this stylistic phenomenon. Overall, although it is more neoclassical, or Louis XVI, in character than anything else, this cabinet would still be broadly classified as an object of the "Rococo Revival."

A variation on the French-inspired Rococo Revival came via pattern books from past periods of design. In 1822, Thomas Chippendale the Younger (1749–1822) died after a lengthy and successful career. He was the long-lived son of the great Thomas Chippendale the Elder (1718–79), who published the famous eighteenth-century pattern book, the *Gentleman and Cabinet Makers' Director*. In the Chippendale studio, which had been founded in the early 1750s in London, were collections of designs for furniture by leading figures of the English rococo such as Matthias Lock, Thomas Johnson, and Thomas Chippendale the Elder. These designs became available at Chippendale the Younger's death and were reissued beginning in 1834 by the London publisher John Weale. They were immediately picked up and used by furniture designers, principally in the English-speaking world. The complex and often fantastical designs of Thomas Johnson, in particular, which incorporated elements of chinoiserie, seem to have captivated a nineteenth-century audience with its insatiable taste for novelty. Many objects, particularly mirrors, were produced as near copies of these re-released, eighteenth-century designs. For owners of genuine eighteenth-century objects who wanted to enlarge their suites of furniture, items made in the eighteenth-century English styles were very useful. One example in the neoclassical style can be found in the Red Drawing Room of Syon House, near London, when in the late 1820s the furniture maker Robert Hughes created a suite of seat furniture after earlier objects designed by Robert Adam. Adam had created the interiors of Syon when he remodeled the house in the 1760s and early 1770s; in the nineteenth century, owing to changes in fashion for entertaining, more seat furniture was needed. It was therefore often a pragmatic decision that led country house owners to commission new furniture to harmonize with existing historic interiors and collections.

Elsewhere in Europe, revived rococo styles took hold more slowly and complicated the "duopoly" of styles—that is, classical and Gothic—remarked upon by writers on design. In Vienna, which had a strong court culture during the eighteenth century, it is not surprising to see the older classical style based upon the French Empire model give way to the curved forms and scrolls of the rococo during the 1830s and 1840s. Vienna, after all, had been the location of the pan-European congress of 1815, whose aim was to restore political order in Europe after the defeat of the emperor Napoleon. It is interesting to observe that these conservative rococo forms—that is, the court style of the autocratic French kings—should have inspired the first truly mass-produced furniture in Europe. The German furniture maker Michael Thonet (1796–1871) began experimenting with laminated wood in about 1830; the technique was already known and laminated furniture had been produced in Belgium since the late eighteenth century, but Thonet embraced and promoted this technology to its full potential. In Germany, he exhibited chairs of sinuous form produced via this technique in the 1840s, by which time he had moved to Vienna, where he collaborated with the leading commercial furniture manufacturer, Carl Leistler. In Vienna, Thonet acquired a powerful patron, the Prince Lichtenstein, and between 1836 and 1847 he began to work at the Palais Lichtenstein (now known as the Lichtenstein City Palace). Thonet helped to create some of the most sumptuous neo-rococo interiors in Europe, exemplified by the palace's ballroom, which evokes a lost age of white and gilt splendor, the gilded rococo scrolls, shells, and foliage taking the form of encrusted ornament running around the room and somewhat obscuring its structure. The same approach was taken with neo-rococo furniture design, whereby the ornament often seemed to overtake the frame of the chair, cabinet, or table.

However, it was his inexpensive, lightweight, industrially produced bentwood furniture for which Thonet gained greatest fame. From the scrolls of Viennese revived rococo designs came groundbreaking mass-produced furniture that has never really gone out of fashion since it was first designed and made. Early bentwood chairs by the Thonet firm were made in Vienna in the 1850s and shown at the International Exhibition in London in 1862. The backs of the chairs retain the outlined form of the mainstream Rococo Revival chairs fashionable at the time, including the so-called balloon back chairs of Victorian drawing rooms. These rounded forms dominated pattern books intended for use by commercial cabinetmakers, such as *The Cabinet-Maker's Assistant* (1853), and can also be seen in the highly encrusted, naturalistic ornament and extreme bentwood designs manufactured by the American firm of John Henry Belter, who was active in New York from 1845 to 1865. It is indicative of the complexity and paradoxical qualities of nineteenth-century furniture design that bentwood furniture inspired by the Rococo Revival, the most conservative and opulent of nineteenth-century design movements, was collected by the great twentieth-century modernist Le Corbusier, whose radical tubular steel furniture it inspired.

GOTHIC AND NEO-MEDIEVALISM

In 1863 John Burley Waring published *Masterpieces of Industrial Art*, a review of the London International Exhibition of 1862. In it, he expressed opinions that an audience of today might find contrary to conventional wisdom, for he considered the neoclassical period of the later eighteenth century to have been a "dark age" of design. He continued that, during the past half a century—that is, the period 1812–62—"we have every reason to be satisfied with our progress," for in 1812, "we were fed with the simple food of ancient Greece ... a poor reflex of the pseudo-Greek style of the French Empire, as practiced by the architects Percier and Fontaine ... From that period the desire for works of a more ornamental nature was rapidly developed." Waring credited the Gothic Revival architect, designer, and theorist A.W.N. Pugin with promoting the reintroduction of ornament into the design of furniture, interior design, and architecture.

The younger Pugin was the son of Auguste Charles Pugin, a French architectural draughtsman and designer who had emigrated to London in the chaotic aftermath of the French Revolution, and Catherine Welby Pugin, an Englishwoman who made considerable contributions in her own right to her husband's architectural and design publications (Hill 2007). A.W.N. Pugin, their only child, was brought up in a bilingual household in London where architecture and design reigned supreme; he had an enormous impact on furniture design of the nineteenth century by introducing the lavish kinds of Gothic leaf ornament published in his father's books while all the time insisting upon the primacy of form over ornament, with a strong nod toward functionality.

The phenomenon of antiquarianism—that is, the study of the physical remains of the past—is linked to the history of the Gothic Revival. Neither began in the nineteenth century. As with the Rococo Revival, the Gothic Revival represented a complex stylistic mix in which various forms of medieval referencing were found, and the meanings and associations of these medieval references changed over time. In addition to the occasional use of Romanesque motifs and tracery from various periods of Gothic design (once they were understood), aspects of what we would term today the Northern Renaissance also formed part of this stylistic phenomenon. In particular, design during the Tudor period and the reign of Elizabeth I was enthusiastically invoked as a kind of lost golden age of the British Isles, much as the eighteenth century and "Louis Quatorze" period was seen as the high point of historical French design. Antiquarian publications such as Henry Shaw's *Specimens of Ancient Furniture* of 1836, which featured

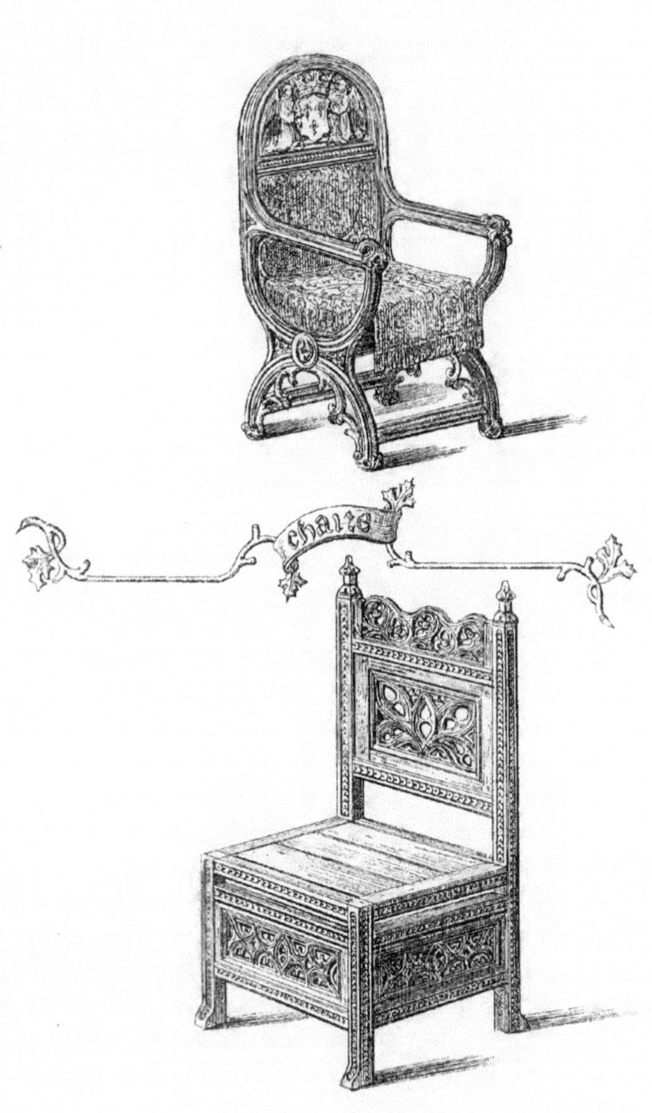

Figure 1.2 Design for two chairs from A.W. Pugin, *Gothic Furniture in the Style of the Fifteenth Century*, 1835. Image courtesy of Open Library/Internet Archive.

furniture and interiors from the fifteenth to seventeenth centuries, were influential on Gothic Revival designers, and Pugin's father, Augustus Charles, was a major contributor through his extensive topographical publications. Beginning with the *Microcosm of London* (1808–10), which was published by Rudolph Ackermann in his *Repository of the Arts*, Pugin the Elder extensively published illustrations of architectural monuments in England and in his native France, with a concentration on medieval structures. He was assisted by his young son, A.W.N. Pugin, as well as by apprentices in his architectural draughting office in London (Ferrey 1978).

Beginning in 1821 with *Specimens of Gothic Architecture*, A.C. Pugin began to break new ground with the highly detailed, accurately drawn ornaments, panels of Gothic tracery, and architectural details, which appeared in his publications. These were beautifully rendered in lithographs that, through shading, demonstrated the contours and three-dimensionality of the sources, which were identified. Therefore, craftsmen, designers, and architects engaged in creating medieval-style buildings and furnishings could have ready access to real medieval models as inspiration for their own designs. At the same moment in France, the dedicated antiquary Thomas Willemin was at work in Paris recording the antiquities and collections that had suffered during the recent decades of political turmoil.

In England, other antiquarian authors who worked directly from medieval sources such as illuminated manuscripts were A.W.N. Pugin and Henry Shaw. Shaw gave detailed depictions of "ancient furniture" found in illuminated manuscripts, late Gothic and Renaissance panel paintings, and occasionally surviving objects. His sources include a mixture of objects from the sixteenth and seventeenth centuries, including some baroque furniture. The younger Pugin also relied on Renaissance and baroque illustrated sources when designing Gothic furniture, as there was a lack of genuine medieval examples available to use as models. For example, Figure 1.2 illustrates two designs for medieval-style seat furniture from A.W.N. Pugin's *Gothic Furniture in the Style of the Fifteenth Century*, one of his early publications of 1835. Here Pugin was borrowing directly from antiquarian prints. The upper design is an x-frame chair, an ancient furniture type, but the placement of the x on the side of the chair frame indicates it is a type made popular in the seventeenth century. Pugin owned furniture designs published in the 1640s by Crispin de Passe the Younger of Utrecht (Wainwright 1994: 131–2). De Passe had published designs for x-frame chairs and stools, including the model for this design, to which Pugin simply added angels displaying a shield on the back of the chair, and some Gothic leaf ornaments, called crockets, and cusping, or points within tracery, on the base. Two years later Pugin used this design as the basis for carved oak chairs he supplied to Scarisbrick Hall in Lancashire, one of his important early country house commissions. Pugin focused on the later Gothic period for his furniture designs because there were more objects and pictorial representations available to him, but he supplemented medieval sources with seventeenth-century designs and extant furniture. This mixing of medieval and later sources is typical of Gothic Revival designs for furniture in the nineteenth century.

It could be argued that A.W.N. Pugin's most significant contribution to the history of nineteenth-century design was his writing of two bold manifestos: *Contrasts: or, A Parallel between the Noble Edifices of the Fourteenth and Fifteenth Centuries, and Corresponding Buildings of the Present Day; shewing the Present Decay of Taste* of 1836, with a second edition in 1841; and *The True Principles of Pointed or Christian Architecture* of 1841. Pugin, a convert to Catholicism, had already linked morality and the health of society to good design in *Contrasts*, a work that was highly critical of the Protestant Reformation; *The True Principles* is of greater relevance to the design of furniture and interiors. The text was based on a series of lectures he had given as Professor of Ecclesiastical Antiquities at St Mary's College, Oscott, near Birmingham. Not only were there illustrated examples—both good and bad—of furniture and wallpaper design, textiles and fringes, metalwork, paving tiles, and more, but Pugin's "two great rules for design," which have reverberated throughout the nineteenth and twentieth centuries, were set out thus on the opening page:

> The two great rules for design are these: 1st, that there should be no features about a building which are not necessary for convenience, construction, or propriety; 2nd, that all ornament should consist of enrichment of the essential construction of the building. The neglect of these two rules is the cause of all the bad architecture of the present time ... the smallest detail should *have a meaning or serve a purpose;* and even the construction itself *should vary with the material employed,* and the designs should be adapted to the material in which they are executed.
>
> (Pugin 1841)

The remarks above were equally applied to furniture design and had some far-reaching consequences by the end of the century. It was the art critic and Oxford lecturer John Ruskin (1819–1900) who took Pugin's principles unacknowledged and applied them to the criticism of design, linking ornament to form, and form with function. Later design movements such as the Arts and Crafts Exhibition Society in England, and the Bauhaus in Germany, developed these same ideas with radically different results. However, in *The True Principles*, Pugin went on to explain that, "Strange as it may appear at first sight, it is in *pointed architecture alone that these great principles have been carried out*" (Pugin 1841: 1). He then proceeded to demonstrate how Gothic design, with its modularity and stylized ornament based on nature, was used in the medieval period to enrich structural elements and perform a function. For example, Pugin praised the elongated strap hinges found on Gothic chests for combining beauty with utility. Not only did medieval hinges reveal the structure that they supported, they added beauty to the structure—that is, "enrichment of the essential construction," in Pugin's own words, encapsulating his "second great rule of design".

Pugin's Gothic designs were inspired by the rich, traceried ornament he observed on fifteenth-century Continental Gothic carving, particularly choir stalls and wall paneling. An accomplished sailor, Pugin made multiple trips to Belgium and France in his sailing boat. In the wake of Napoleon's reign, the Belgian monasteries were being stripped of their treasures, and high-quality medieval material was available on the market (Tracy 2001). Pugin bought as much medieval carving and decorative art as he could carry home. His genius, however, was to observe and employ this rich Gothic vocabulary in his own designs, while keeping the use of ornament under tight control. He contained ornament within carefully proportioned, geometrical panels, and it was typically executed in low relief so as not to interrupt the overall form. In other words, although Pugin's Gothic furniture can appear highly ornamented to a modern viewer, he practiced what he preached in terms of insisting that ornament enrich but not obscure structure.

The application of these design principles can be seen by examining a large stained oak and brass armoire cabinet designed by Pugin and made by J.G. Crace, with whom he had formed a Gothic house decorating partnership in 1844 (Aldrich 1990). The cabinet occupied a prominent position in the Medieval Court of the Great Exhibition. It is illustrated in the *Art Journal Illustrated Catalogue* of the 1851 exhibition, and in *Dickinson's Comprehensive Pictures* of the Great Exhibition; today the cabinet is in the Victoria and Albert Museum in London (25, 1 to 3-1852). Pugin and Crace's Gothic cabinet maintains its simple rectangular silhouette despite being decorated with recessed panels of carved, low-relief tracery in the Gothic style of the fifteenth century. Contrasting brass metalwork includes pronounced strap hinges of the variety praised in *The True Principles* some ten years earlier. In this elaborate example, which was intentionally designed for an important international exhibition, ornament remains clearly subsidiary to the overall structure.

Another large Gothic cabinet shown at the 1851 exhibition in London creates a strong point of contrast to Pugin's cabinet. Made of light oak, it is a richly carved and very architectural bookcase cabinet designed by Bernardo di Bernadis (1807–68), carved by Anton Dominik Fernkorn (1813–78), and made by the firm of Carl Leistler in Vienna (Figure 0.3). Leistler was also collaborating with Michael Thonet in the revived rococo interiors for the Lichtenstein Palace at the same time his firm was producing this massive, Gothic "cathedral in wood" with two domed revolving glazed bookcases. Like Pugin's armoire, this piece is also in the collection of the Victoria and Albert Museum (W.12-1967). However, the Leistler bookcase cabinet is far more three-dimensional.

Crocketted pinnacles, flying buttresses, and other Gothic architectural features such as tracery, the system of flat, interlocking pointed arches typical of Gothic design, cover the upper stages of the cabinet and somewhat obscure its overall form. Moreover, this piece of furniture looks like a scale model of a fictitious cathedral, unlike the flat, rectangular form that dominates Pugin's cabinet. The Leistler cabinet was also made to impress at an international exhibition. In a comparison between the two, Pugin's work appears markedly restrained.

DIVERGENCE FROM THE GOTHIC TRADITION

One style of design and ornament that inserted itself into the midst of the lengthy Gothic Revival was the Renaissance style, a complex stylistic phenomenon that incorporated late Gothic, Renaissance, classical, and Middle Eastern influences. One of its purest expressions can be seen in the courtyard of the former South Kensington Museum, now known as the Victoria and Albert Museum in London. Founded one year after the Great Exhibition of 1851 in London, the museum was initially known as the Museum of Manufactures and expressed the mid-nineteenth-century concern for finding appropriate models of design combined with the use of new technology to inform the manufacture of furnishings and luxury goods. The courtyard survives with its decorative scheme relatively intact—during the late 1850s and 1860s the supervising architect was an army engineer, Captain Francis Fowke, who worked for the influential director of the museum, Henry Cole (1808–82). The courtyard's brick arcades have been decorated with stone and terra-cotta sculpture and mosaics directly inspired by the architecture and monuments of Renaissance Italy. The association of the Renaissance with learning and artistic culture was very much in evidence during this period. One example is the West Library created for the financier J.P. Morgan, now part of a complex known as the Morgan Library and Museum (main building 1902–7) in New York. The interior designer and artist Harry Siddons Mowbray (1858–1928) used painting and plasterwork inspired by the Renaissance artist Raphael for the design of the ceiling. The Renaissance style was promoted as a fashionable style for the discerning traveler to the Italian cities of Rome, Venice, and especially Florence, an association reinforced by the activity of dealers such as the great Stefano Bardini (1836–1922) in Florence, who not only stocked genuine antiquities, paintings, and furniture, which he restored, but also his own creations using Renaissance and older fragments within new objects, which he sold from a beautifully decorated, restored "palazzo" in Florence created out of a deconsecrated church and convent. Such activity served to promote the Renaissance as the fashionable style during the third quarter of the nineteenth century, especially to the Anglo-American community who frequented his showroom.

The Renaissance Revival was, perhaps, more in evidence in the United States than in Europe as a style of domestic architecture, as in the famous Newport,

Rhode Island, "cottage," The Breakers, designed by Richard Morris Hunt (1827–95) in 1870 as an Italianate summer palace on the New England seacoast for a fabulously wealthy patron, Cornelius Vanderbilt. During the 1860s the Herter Brothers of New York (active 1864–1906) developed some very fine examples of revived Renaissance furniture of intricately carved walnut with motifs borrowed from Italian Renaissance designs such as arabesques, griffins, and intricately entwined foliate scrolls. Later on, as was the case with many designers who used Renaissance motifs, the Herter's style took on influences from further afield, mixing Asian motifs to create an American version of the Aesthetic movement (see below).

During the 1840s and 1850s, excitement rose over the "discovery" of Islamic interiors and decorative motifs, which were often seen as linked to European Gothic design. The Alhambra in Granada had been made popular by the book *Tales of the Alhambra* (1832; revised edition 1851) by the American writer Washington Irving, who actually lived for a time at the site. Even before Irving's residency at the Alhambra, the traveler and architectural draughtsman Owen Jones (1809–74) had traveled through Egypt, Turkey, and southern Spain during the 1830s. His groundbreaking publication, *Plans, Details and Sections of the Alhambra* of 1836–45, gave designers the models they needed, and Jones's publication was lavishly illustrated in color. The book was particularly influential in the field of tiles and ceramics, as well as colored, or polychromatic, architectural decoration, which Pugin had already established as a fundamental feature of Gothic interiors.

While designers such as J.G. Crace and Edward Welby Pugin (1834–75), the eldest son of A.W.N. Pugin, continued to produce Gothic designs and furniture that developed the ideas of A.W.N. Pugin, other designers began to develop the Gothic style in a different direction. William Burges (1827–81) was an architect and designer who had been articled to the antiquarian architect Edward Blore (1787–1879) in 1844; Burges was directly inspired by the designs and writings of A.W.N. Pugin, as was his entire generation of Gothic Revival designers. During the 1850s Burges won several important design competitions, including that for Lille Cathedral in France, and he began to develop his ideas around the simpler medieval design of the thirteenth century, deliberately looking back further in time than the elaborate, fifteenth-century Gothic favored by Pugin. Burges combined simple forms with archaic design, and his Gothic furniture was considered shockingly crude by many visitors to the London Architectural Exhibition of 1859 and the Medieval Court of the 1862 London International Exhibition. Burges used simple, repetitive painted patterns and "cartoon strip" narratives on crude wooden boxes and cabinets, inspired by French medieval furniture published by antiquaries in France. His later Gothic designs were on occasion referred to as "muscular Gothic" for the boldness and simplicity of the forms he used (Crook 1981).

Burges was not alone in this new, deliberately primitive aesthetic, for a group of young designers led by William Morris (1834–96) and Edward Burne-Jones (1833–98), with their friend the architect Philip Webb (1831–1915), were designing very similar objects with medievalizing, painted decoration on simple, boxlike forms of crude construction. The St George Cabinet of 1861–2 (Plate 8) takes the form of a primitive, rectangular chest made of mahogany, pine, and oak on a stand with curved braces resembling the "cruck" construction of medieval timbered barns with characteristic split, v-shaped beams (V&A, 341:1 to 8–1906). Philip Webb, who trained in the office of the Oxford architect G.E. Street (1824–81), designed the form of the St George Cabinet, a pattern that was repeated on many occasions during the history of production of furniture by the firm of William Morris. The cabinet is of interest because it survives as the sole example of furniture painted by William Morris himself, in the style developed by his good friend Edward Burne-Jones. Morris went on to lead the famous decorating and design firm that bore his name, and became a brilliant designer of textiles, wallpapers, and patterns. The St George Cabinet was shown alongside the similarly distinctive furniture of William Burges in the Medieval Court of the 1862 Exhibition, demonstrating that change was afoot in the realm of the Gothic Revival.

ASIAN AND NON-WESTERN STYLISTIC INFLUENCES

At the 1862 Exhibition in London, William Burges was struck by objects that were exhibited in the Japanese Court, which he called "the real medieval court of the exhibition" (Jervis 1984); simple animal forms observed from Japanese carved *netsuke* began to appear in his designs mixed with his thirteenth-century Gothic motifs. Nor was he alone in this, for the furniture designs of Philip Webb also began to exhibit traces of Japanese influence in the referencing of the *mon*, or Japanese armorial badge, along with the simulation of embossed leather designs most evident in a series of canopied sideboards of ebonized mahogany with colorful panels of decoration, beginning in the 1860s. The form goes back to the Gothic-style sideboard revived by Pugin, but Webb developed the form into something more abstract in shape, and more richly ornamented in a kind of hybrid freestyle, which moves between a memory of the European Gothic tradition and Japonist design. One such example dating to *c.* 1880 is in the collection of the Musée d'Orsay in Paris; it has bold designs of swirling, stylized leaves in the decorative panels, and Japanese *mon* designs on the drawers in the center of the piece (Musée d'Orsay, OAO 449).

Burges and Webb were not the only Gothic Revivalists to observe and begin to incorporate elements of Japanese and other non-Western styles of design. While Burges began experimenting with Islamic design, culminating in the remarkable Arab Room at Cardiff Castle, Wales, of 1881, another Gothic Revival architect was moving into a purer vision of Japanese design. Edward William Godwin (1833–86) was trained in Bristol and had some success with early commissions in Ireland which were essentially abstractions of Gothic design. In 1862 he decorated his own house in Bristol with Japanese prints, Persian rugs (Islamic carpets had been recommended by both Pugin and Morris), and antique furniture. This bohemian mixed style was shortly to be recommended in Charles Eastlake's influential decorating guide, *Hints on Household Taste in Furniture, Upholstery and Other Details* (1868), which had a strong impact on taste in the United States. Eastlake, who wrote the first history of the Gothic Revival, advocated the mixing of antique with modern furnishings, as well as combining European with imported designs to create a tastefully decorated domestic interior. His audience was the well-educated, progressive middle class who also shopped at William Morris's premises on Oxford Street. In the United States, "Eastlake" came to be a term associated with the Gothic style, but Eastlake himself was far more eclectic in his design recommendations, and today he is associated with that eclectic phenomenon known as the Aesthetic movement, a middle-class phenomenon of design that combined elements of eighteenth-century seat furniture and English Regency mirrors with peacock feathers, sunflowers, and Chinese and Japanese pots and decorative elements. Those who aspired to the Aesthetic, or Eastlake, look could shop for Asian decorative art at Farmer and Rogers' emporium in London, where an ambitious young man named Arthur Lasenby Liberty worked until 1875, when he founded his own shop, which still bears his name. Liberty's sold the *accoutrements* of the Aesthetic interior, with Japanese items, Middle Eastern carpets, and the textiles produced by the William Morris firm.

Godwin established his avant-garde credentials with his own important style book of 1877: *Art Furniture, with Hints and Suggestions on Art Furniture and Decorations*. The title page (see Figure 9.5 in Chapter 9) was unashamedly Japonist in design, featuring bell-shaped openings, paper lanterns, and other rather obvious references to what was understood of Japanese design; his partner, the famous Shakespearean actress Ellen Terry, is the figure portrayed in a kimono on the title page. Godwin's furniture in the "Anglo–Japanese" style, as part of the broader Aesthetic movement, was probably more copied than any other style of Victorian furniture, possibly because his designs were fashionable amongst the intelligentsia and were relatively easy to reproduce commercially. In common with Philip Webb, he used ebonized wood, typically mahogany, to create linear black shapes in space constructed of contrasting horizontals and verticals, and solids and voids. So abstract are the designs of his famous series of sideboards (produced *c*. 1865–80 by the manufacturer William Watt) that they seem to anticipate the radical modernism of the early twentieth century (for example, see V&A, CIRC.38:1 to 5–1953). However, Godwin's black forms were intended to be seen against the rich colors and complex patterns of Aesthetic movement wallpapers and textiles, and to be loaded with the bold, colorful ceramics being produced during this period of design.

Another designer whose furniture designs share a kinship with those of Godwin is Dr Christopher Dresser (1834–1904). Dresser's "art furniture" was executed in narrow, turned black elements decorated with simple geometrical incising picked out in gilding (for example, V&A, W.35–1992). Combining a variety of sources of inspiration, Dresser was perhaps best known for his ceramics and radically simple metalwork designs, and he was perhaps the first important European designer to travel to Japan.

In France there was equal fascination with all things Japanese, but furniture design tended to feature more literal borrowing of Asian motifs. The abstraction of Godwin and other British designers such as the eclectic William Eden Nesfield (1835–88) was not echoed in Paris, where the firm of Georges-Alphonse-Bonifacio Monbro (1807–84) specialized in producing expensive, beautifully crafted ebony furniture reviving the baroque style of André Charles Boulle at the court of Louis XIV (for example, Musèe d'Orsay, OAO 497). In addition, the firm produced pieces that displayed panels of black and gold lacquer and Chinese-style paintings and carvings (for example, Musèe d'Orsay, OAO 497). Originally founded in 1801 in Paris by Monbro's father, there was also a Monbro shop in London during the 1860s to 1880s. The deluxe nature of these designs was removed from the more bohemian, middle-class character of the Aesthetic movement in England, which did not attempt to cater to the demands of high-end clients, who continued to shop in Paris. However, the literal referencing of Asian design in the phenomenon of *Japonism* in France, which can be seen as distinct from the more hybrid form of Japonism practiced in Britain and America, did exert a powerful influence on the formation of the most distinctive of later nineteenth-century styles in Continental Europe: the new style, or Art Nouveau.

The name Art Nouveau was taken from the influential Parisian shop founded in 1895 by the German émigré Siegfried Bing (1838–1905). In addition to textiles and wallpapers by the Morris firm, Bing sold the work of Belgian, French, and German designers who were creating furniture with a sinuous curved outline recalling aspects of the Rococo Revival. The rococo style had once again come to the fore in France during the third quarter of the nineteenth century with the Second Empire under Napoleon III, when historicist design was still very much in evidence. In contrast, Art Nouveau designers used abstract linear forms as a basis for their furniture designs. These included the pioneering Belgian designer Victor Horta (1861–1947); the Frenchman Emile Gallé (1846–1904), who combined inspiration from nature, from the rococo tradition of his native Lorraine, and most importantly Japanese design; the French designer Paul Follot (1877–1941), who moved into Art Deco design in the twentieth century; and the Paris designer Hector Guimard (1867–1942), best known for the remarkable twisting, naturalistic designs for the Paris Metro. Looking back to the strong Continental tradition of rococo design, Art Nouveau designers mixed curvilinear form with aspects of Japonist pictorial design. In some designers' work like that of Guimard, a Gothic lineage was also evident via the elongated designs of the 1860s and 1870s of Viollet-le-Duc (Figure 1.3).

FIGURE 1.3 Eugène-Emmanuel Viollet-le–Duc, plate from *Entretiens sur l'architecture* showing the use of cast iron columns in an imaginary auditorium, 1872. Photograph courtesy of the Picture Art Collection/Alamy Stock Photo.

Viollet-le-Duc, in his lectures on architecture, argued that designers should create a new style for their own age, and a number of Art Nouveau architects and furniture designers, for instance, Guimard and the Swiss designer Eugène Grasset (1845–1917), were directly influenced by him. Likewise, the German variation on Art Nouveau, known as "Jugendstil," led by Bavarian furniture designers such as Hermann Obrist (1862–1927) and Richard Riemerschmid (1868–1957), featured the sinuous profiles and whiplash curves of French and Belgian Art Nouveau, but with a more abstract character. Riemerschmid, in particular, demonstrated a debt to Viollet-le-Duc through his chairs for the House of a Music Lover, exhibited at the Paris 1900 Exposition, which featured the long diagonal strut favored by Viollet-le-Duc in his own chair designs for the Château of Pierrefonds in the 1860s.

By 1900 Art Nouveau design had already attracted some severe critics. The northern Protestant nations in Scandinavia, many parts of Germany, the Netherlands, and especially Britain and its colonies never really favored the style; in America, elements of ornament in the work of architects such as Louis Sullivan of Chicago (1856–1924) are sometimes associated with the style, but it was not embraced with enthusiasm. Instead, an alternative design tradition arose out of the later Gothic Revival and the writings and influential designs of William Morris. This tradition of simplified, "reformed" Gothic design of the 1860s and 1870s was mixed with nostalgia for the more rustic aspects of traditional, vernacular design. It became known as the Arts and Crafts movement. The Exhibition Society of the same name was founded in the office of the architect Richard Norman Shaw (1831–1912); the first Arts and Crafts Exhibition was held in 1888 at the New Gallery in Regent Street, London. The exhibitions continued well into the twentieth century. Arts and Crafts was not really a style, but rather an attitude toward design. The whitewashed country cottage and simple, joined oak furniture with strap hinges derived from Pugin suggest one kind of Arts and Crafts tradition, as seen in the ash and beech ladderback chair, a traditional form interpreted by Ernest Gimson (1864–1919) in 1888, the year of the first Arts and Crafts Society exhibition (Plate 9).

Gimson's career is representative of many aspects of the Arts and Crafts movement, including its concern for rapidly disappearing traditional crafts. The son of an industrialist, he studied architecture and furniture design and was greatly inspired by a meeting with William Morris in 1884. The chair in Plate 9 was the product of his apprenticeship to a traditional country chair maker. However, despite the deceptively rustic appearance of the chair, Gimson created an object of metropolitan sophistication with graduated back slats and beautifully elongated and tapered upright supports (Greensted 1991). This seeming paradox of Arts and Crafts design, with its sophisticated rusticity and updated archaic forms, was inherited directly from the Gothic Revival tradition of the first half of the nineteenth century. Just as Art Nouveau drew upon elements of historicism mixed with exotic influences, so too did the Arts and Crafts movement represent a development from, and not a complete break with, furniture design earlier in the nineteenth century.

CONCLUSION

Throughout the nineteenth century there was continual experimentation with motifs, styles, materials, technology, and forms to express the new industrial era. Britain had retained its monarchy under Queen Victoria's long reign (1837–1901), but not without periods of unrest and uncertainty, as was the case with all the surviving monarchies across Europe. Although court styles tended to be more conservative, looking back to traditional designs and methods of furniture production, there ran in parallel a rich seam of industrially driven design catering for a more middle-class market, which was showcased at a series of international exhibitions and in specialist shops. It is therefore unsurprising that, perhaps more than any other era, the nineteenth century saw an astonishing variety of styles of design take hold in European furniture. New materials and ways of furnishing interior spaces drove innovation, and a plethora of design literature bombarded professionals and amateurs alike. The second half of the nineteenth century, in particular, saw a strong interest in design from other, non-European cultures; however, the dominant design centers for nearly the whole of the nineteenth century remained Paris and London, the two cities that had also dominated furniture design of the eighteenth century. Thus, in the face of so much rapid change, there was continuity as well. The great majority of European and American furniture designers looked to these two great cities for models and inspiration. However, the outbreak of the First World War in 1914 radically changed this design landscape forever.

CHAPTER TWO

Makers, Making, and Materials

CHRISTINA M. ANDERSON

It can be difficult to see furniture making across the nineteenth century as part of a continuum with each decade building on the developments of the previous one. Instead, it can seem that furniture production stubbornly held on to the past until mid-century, then lurched ahead into questionable territory. Indeed, furniture historians have traditionally seen 1840 as a benchmark, a date by which the neoclassicism of the preceding era had essentially given way to the Gothic Revival and by when large, comprehensive firms that could provide a full service—from drapery to dining room tables and from installation to maintenance and cleaning—largely replaced smaller workshops working in traditional ways. This is evidenced, for example, by the *Dictionary of English Furniture Makers*, published by the Furniture History Society in 1986, that covers the years 1660 to 1840 and follows the lead taken by Howard Colvin's *A Biographical Dictionary of British Architects, 1600–1840* (1978). What is also implied by both publications' abrupt finish of coverage in 1840 is that a new period of what was thought of as questionable taste begins at this point. The nineteenth century often embarrasses those who favor earlier periods when the furniture studied tends to have been made for elite clients. In the middle of the nineteenth century, on the other hand, a growing percentage of the furniture was produced for the burgeoning middle classes whose taste, by comparison, is often viewed as untrustworthy. This is borne out by an exhibition organized by the Rijksmuseum in 1995 titled *The Age of Ugliness*, the catalog for which states that

> That was how in the twentieth century the Dutch often referred to this period in their history—or at least, those Dutch people who prided themselves on their good taste. It was generally held that the nineteenth century lacked a style of its own.
>
> (Schoemaker and Judikje 1995: 1)

What these critics fail to appreciate, however, is that the "age of ugliness" was actually a time of great experimentation, innovation, and creativity, which can best be seen not so much in terms of style as in the way furniture was made, the materials that were used, and the people who were producing it. This chapter will examine the roles of migration, the increasing use of machines and patents, the production of artistic furniture and reproductions, and the use of novel materials to illuminate both the originality and uniqueness of developments in nineteenth-century furniture making.

MAKERS

At the beginning of the nineteenth century, furniture was still being made in workshops much as it had been in the 1700s. These workplaces could be quite grand and well established, such as that of the Jacob family in Paris, which received imperial commissions and, as discussed elsewhere in this volume, realized the designs of Percier and Fontaine. Political, economic, and social upheaval, as well as opportunity, however, changed this, encouraging a distinct trend for greater mobility among designers and makers. Perhaps nowhere is this more evident than in the United States, where makers from Europe were often responsible for establishing taste.

Immigrant cabinetmakers, particularly those from the British and Channel Isles, had already made their mark in the seventeenth and eighteenth centuries in North America's New England, some of these, or their descendants, continued to operate into the nineteenth century. John Seymour (1738–1818) and his family, for example, left Axminster, Devon, in 1784 and settled first in Falmouth (later Portland), Maine, moving to Boston in 1793 (Mussey 2002: 1, 26). Working in a refined neoclassical (i.e., Sheratonesque) style, Thomas (1771–1848), whose talents really came into their own at the start of the nineteenth century, employed other immigrant cabinetmakers. Although success did not come easily, he was able to capitalize on the fact that Boston was undergoing expansion at this time—socially, economically, and intellectually. Not only was there an increasingly wealthy part of the population who were building new houses and interested in high-quality furniture, but also the exotic woods utilized by the Seymours, such as mahogany and rosewood, were available through Boston's global reach as a port city (28–78).

Undoubtedly, though, the most famous early nineteenth-century cabinetmaker active in the United States was Duncan Phyfe (1770–1854), a Scotsman (born Duncan Fife) who emigrated with his family in 1784. The Phyfes settled first in Albany, relocating to New York City in 1791. It is often lamented that despite Phyfe's reputation for high-quality craftsmanship and widespread influence on taste in interiors, particularly in New York where he founded his business, so few pieces that can be securely attributed to him survive (Ketchum with the Museum of American Folk Art 1995: 259–61). For most of his career, and that of his sons who entered the family business, the firm was based in Partition, later Fulton, Street in Manhattan. They successfully adapted to all the successive neoclassical styles, but faltered when other, historicist styles started to dominate from around 1840.[1] Phyfe's name, nonetheless, continues to be well known. Another immigrant furniture maker in the United States, the German Ernest Hagen (1830–1913), was among the first to spur renewed interest in the Scotsman through documenting his career and creating pieces in the Phyfe style (Metropolitan Museum of Art, 61.254).[2] For furniture historians, perhaps Phyfe's most significant commission, due to the large number of pieces ordered and the documentation concerning it that is still extant, was for William Bayard's home on State Street, on the tip of Manhattan. This is certainly the earliest known of Phyfe's commissions for which pieces are still extant, an armchair from this commission held by the Winterthur Museum, Delaware (1957.0720.001; Figure 8.2). Phyfe supplied Bayard with pieces at the cutting edge of taste in a new version of the neoclassical style, which was just becoming available in New York, and at which Phyfe excelled and with which he is enduringly associated (Kenny et al. 2011: 3–64, 115–18, 158–65).

The makers described here were bringing highly developed skills to the United States (although Phyfe is supposed to have apprenticed in New York) as well as firsthand knowledge of the sophisticated ways in which styles were being interpreted in Europe. Almost contemporaneous with Phyfe was the Frenchman Charles-Honoré Lannuier (1779–1819), who also worked in New York City. His Empire-style furniture illustrates his unique blending of a pure French *goût antique* with English-style elements from the New York-Phyfe school of furniture design (Kenny, Bretter, and Leben 1998: 75–9). Trained as an *ébéniste* (cabinetmaker) by his brother, Nicolas-Louis-Cyrille Lannuier, and an uncle, Jean-Baptiste Cochois, Lannuier migrated to the United States in 1803. Although the exact reasons for his departure from France are unknown, no doubt the introduction of conscription in his home country, the better economic opportunities available in New York, and the presence of his older brother Auguste there all played a part in his decision (3, 31–2). His work, like that of Phyfe, benefited from the availability of exotic woods, especially mahogany from Santo Domingo in the Caribbean, and a stable, growing economy (154–8). Lannuier, however, also incorporated expensive features such as mirrors, marble, and ormolu, unlike Phyfe who relied on fine carving and some gilding for decoration. Following French custom, and again in contrast to Phyfe, Lannuier also regularly labeled or stamped his furniture, so that a sizeable body of extant pieces is known. Among these is a pair of card tables purchased in 1817 by William Bayard, who as mentioned above patronized Phyfe as well, now in the Metropolitan Museum of Art (Plate 10) (Kenny, Bretter, and Leben 1998: 110, 117, 210).

Later political troubles in Europe also encouraged other cabinetmakers to emigrate to the United States. Gustave Herter (1830–92), for example, left Germany for New York City in 1848. He was one of a number of emigrants affected by the wave of European revolutions that year which left many in search of stability after suffering famine and economic and political upheaval in their home countries. Trained as an architect, Gustave first worked for the New York business Tiffany, Young & Ellis, then entered a short-lived partnership with the French emigré Auguste Pottier, which was followed by collaboration with the established furniture maker Erastus Bulkley (1798–1872) in 1852. For New York's 1853 Exhibition of the Industry of All Nations, Herter designed a monumental Gothic Revival bookcase, made by Bulkely with detailed carving by the German-American sculptor Ernst Plassmann (1823–77). This colossal bookcase demonstrated not only that American makers could compete with their European counterparts in style and craftsmanship but also that abundant American materials such as oak were appropriate for use in the most sophisticated furniture. Gustave went on to establish his own business in 1858, which, like those discussed elsewhere in this chapter, strove to be comprehensive in offering both furniture making and decorating services. In 1859 his brother Christian (1839–83) followed him to New York and together they formed Herter Brothers in 1865. Gustave's early furniture embodies a robust historicist approach, mainly in the Renaissance revival style, while later in the century a preoccupation with ebonized "art" furniture is apparent in the firm's output. Christian eventually took Herter Brothers over in 1870, by which time the company was engaged in business with many of the leading industrialists in the United States, from New York to Chicago to San Francisco. One of the firm's most important commissions involved supplying the furnishings for all the private and public interiors of the William H. Vanderbilt mansion on New York's Fifth Avenue. These reflected a variety of styles—from Renaissance to Japanesque—and utilized the finest materials including exotic inlaid timbers in complex marquetry panels and carved and gilded woods (Howe, Cooney Frelinghuysen, and Hoover Voorsanger 1994: 13–14; Plate 18).

Others crossing national boundaries include the German-born John Henry Belter (1804–63) who set up a furniture manufactory in New York and was associated with the Rococo Revival. Belter stands out as a notable nineteenth-century maker not only for his immigrant status but also for his use of patents to register and protect his devising of a new construction method. He developed a type of plywood that consisted of layers of different kinds of less-valuable wood sandwiched between outer layers of rosewood. The resultant panels could be shaped through steam and carved. In many ways, his laminated rosewood furniture shares similarities with the bent, veneered wood utilized by Austrian Biedermeier manufacturers, particularly in their chairs. It also parallels the techniques employed by Michael Thonet (1796–1871) in Austria early in his career, which led to his solid bentwood furniture, discussed elsewhere in this volume (Vincent 1967: 97–8). Clare Vincent describes how Belter made a table now in the Museum of the City of New York: "If we look closely at the pierced, hand-carved aprons ... we see that they were constructed by gluing a number of layers of wood together, bending them to the desired shape, and applying smaller pieces of wood to them to be carved in high relief wherever necessary" (92 and plate 25). Two of Belter's patents apply to his chairs in which he "replaced the typical rail and stile construction of the preceding centuries with a one-piece back of laminated wood or plywood which had been bent, pierced, carved and upholstered" (93 and plate 26B). An earlier patent covers a kind of jigsaw that Belter developed that allowed him to create the complicated, irregular, and lacy designs for which he is best known (95–7) (Plate 11).

Craftspeople were also migrating between European countries. The movement of skilled artisans was not new, both the French royal *ébéniste* Jean-Henri Riesener (1734–1806) and his master Jean-François Oeben (1721–63), for example, had been born in Germany but had made their careers in eighteenth-century France. In nineteenth-century Europe, however, just as with the United States, individuals were fleeing political upheavals on the Continent. According to Elizabeth Aslin, for example, "Around 1848 numbers of French designers and artisans came to England and from then on there were French, Italians and Germans working in the [English] cabinet trades for some years, though their influence on design was negligible after the mid-sixties" (1962: 38). The London firm Jackson and Graham, for instance, hired a number of French cabinetmakers at mid-century in addition to the designer they relied on for some of their showiest pieces, Alexandre-Eugène Prignot (b.1822). Prignot had trained with the great French cabinetmaker Henri-Auguste Fourdinois (1830–1907) (Figure 9.4) and designed for Jackson and Graham a magnificent sideboard that looked back to eighteenth-century French styles. It won a gold medal at the 1855 Paris exhibition (V&A, 7247:1 to 13–1860; Plate 7).

Other notable immigrant designers, makers, and dealers across nineteenth-century Europe include Jean-Adam and Philippe Dexheimer who established premises in London in mid-century; Jean-Henri-Chrétien and

Jean-Henri-Christophe Wassmus who were born in Hanover but set up shop together in 1810 in Paris (although it was really the elder brother's son Henri-Léonard who supplied the energy behind the firm); and the German Joseph-Emmanuel Zwiener (*c.* 1848–95) who may have employed François Linke (1855–1946) when the young Czech first arrived in Paris (Payne 1981: 32–42). Siegfried Bing (1838–1905), owner of the "L'Art Nouveau" shop in Paris and one of several individuals responsible for introducing the art of Japan to Europeans, migrated to France in the 1850s from Hamburg, Germany.

MAKING

Machines and patents

Perhaps the most profound change in the making of furniture during the nineteenth century was the increasing utilization of machines, as opposed to the traditional hand tools of the individual furniture or cabinet maker. This development was accompanied, naturally, by greater efficiency in the production of woodwork and furniture, meaning more could be produced at lower costs. Another obvious consequence was that the items produced could be made to precise specifications without the inevitable variations introduced through human production. Although individual cabinetmakers were still very much in demand, and employed by both large, comprehensive, and small piece-making firms alike, the invention of more and more machines, which their creators purported made furniture production more convenient and standardized, influenced and went hand-in-hand with other developments in furniture making of the nineteenth century. These changes included the expanding role of the designer, the rise of the Arts and Crafts movement and the entry into the furniture making trade of new players such as department stores.

The Great Exhibition of 1851 is a prism through which to view many of the changes that characterize furniture of the nineteenth century and differentiate it from its predecessors of the eighteenth century. This is especially relevant when investigating the role of machinery. As Paul Greenhalgh has written, "The Great Exhibition, like virtually all its successors around the world, fetishised the machine, choosing exclusively to see in it a glorious past and the chance of a blemishless future" (1988: 13). Indeed, Ralph Nicholson Wornum (1812–77), the artist and art historian who later became keeper of the National Gallery in London, wrote in his prize-winning essay "The Exhibition of 1851 as a Lesson in Taste" that

> The specimens of Jordan's machine-carving are another promise of the unexampled facilities of the coming age in all mechanical resources, and if we can but establish the essential quality of all decoration, taste, the rising

> generation will have nothing to fear from the rivalry or the prestige of past ages. These specimens of machine carving, the most delicate touches only being given by hand, are quite equal to the general average of that executed wholly by hand; and where many examples of one design are required, as in church-carving, the saving of labour and expense must be enormous.
>
> (Wornum 1851: XIV***)

Wornum was referring, specifically, to a church screen made by Jordan's Patent Carving Machine (Figure 2.1), about which Nikolaus Pevsner (1902–83), the German-British architectural historian, wrote a century later:

> the many admirers of the machine-carved Screen ... would have argued something like this: It may be very difficult to carve a screen by hand and it might take three years to do. What a triumph of the human mind is it then to invent machinery which can do the same work in one hundredth of the time and in addition do it more exactly.
>
> (Pevsner 1951b: 32–3)

Yet, as Pevsner observes from the vantage point of the mid-twentieth century, despite these benefits,

> Our accepted argument is, and has been ever since Ruskin and Morris: ornament is valuable only in so far as it represents the imagination of the human mind and the skill of the human hand. To imitate it mechanically is too easy a substitute.
>
> (1951b: 31)

Pevsner supports this view through citing the authoritative German architect Gottfried Semper (1803–79), himself a refugee from the May Uprising of 1849 in Dresden, who had his own ambivalent feelings about the use of machines. He admitted that at some point in the future these developments would be used "to the benefit and honour of society," yet he was hesitant to applaud them without reserve. Semper comments that

> thanks to means borrowed from science, [capitalism] achieves without effort the most difficult and laborious; the hardest porphyry and granite can be cut like chalk, and polished like wax, ivory can be softened and pressed into moulds, metal is no longer cast or chased but by natural forces unknown until recently deposited galvanoplastically ... the machine sows, knits, embroiders, carves, paints and ... puts to shame all human skill.
>
> (Semper 1852: 9–10, quoted in Pevsner 1951b: 32–3)

FIGURE 2.1 Patent Wood Carving Company, London, Church screen, 1851. *Art Journal Illustrated Catalogue of the Exhibition of the Industry of all Nations*, p. 132. Photograph courtesy of University of Wisconsin Digital Collections.

Indeed, the introduction of machines could not be stopped, although during the nineteenth century they worked alongside rather than wholly replaced the human component in manufacturing. For example, while employing hundreds of traditional craftspeople, Jackson and Graham, one of the comprehensive furniture makers in London's West End, also installed a steam engine in the 1850s for simple sawing operations. Later, in the 1860s, the firm experimented with machine carving, something that even Morris and Company subsequently adopted (Aslin 1962: 83).

Accompanying the growing presence of the machine in furniture making was the increasing use of patents to protect innovations in design or production. This could be seen, for example, in the patents for the many uses of metal, including tubular metal, in the construction of furniture such as Cowley & James's Patent Iron Bedstead and Tomkin's Ornamental Iron Bedstead as well as the table and armchair in hollow wrought-iron tubes by A. Kitchelt of Vienna, all exhibited in London in 1851. Pevsner classes these under the "pride in ingeniousness which took the place of aesthetic appreciation in many of the exhibits of 1851" (1951b: 33–7). Metal furniture was not only patented but also used: Charles Dickens and his wife had an iron rocking chair in their dining room at 1 Devonshire Terrace, London, which may have looked something like the chair attributed to R.W. Winfield & Co. at the Victoria and Albert Museum (CIRC.20–1961). In the United States, George Hunzinger (1835–98) was known as well for his innovative patented designs. Patents, however, were taken out not only because of the use of new materials in furniture, but also for innovative designs, such as the metamorphic pieces and portable furniture falling under the category of "campaign furniture."

Portable "campaign" furniture found a ready market among officers of the armies and navies of various European states (Figure 8.4). Its development went back to at least the mid-eighteenth century, and it could be made of wood as well as metal and other materials. What was most important was that it could be taken apart and transported easily. In the nineteenth century, the number of makers in Britain alone creating such furniture, and often patenting it, numbered well over one hundred (Brawer 2001: 157–214). Perhaps one of the most well-known firms was Morgan and Saunders of London whose metamorphic library chair that converts into a stepladder for reaching books on upper shelves still regularly turns up in auctions and dealer inventories. The firm's history is illustrative of the highly competitive nature of the patent furniture-making business in London at the start of the nineteenth century, which saw many of the most significant manufacturers cluster around Catherine Street near the Strand.

Before founding their firm in 1801, Thomas Morgan and Joseph Sanders had both worked for another patent furniture maker in Catherine Street, Thomas Butler, a part-time Nonconformist (a Protestant who dissents from the Church of England) preacher. In 1801, instead of selling his business to the newly founded Morgan and Sanders, Butler sold it to Thomas Oxenham, whom he had originally engaged to value his stock. Morgan and Sanders claimed that Butler had promised them their business, and thus began several years of recriminations and rivalry between the two firms. Among other achievements, Morgan and Sanders had designed an "imperial" dining table and sideboard for Admiral Nelson's estate, Merton Place in Surrey. This commission may have been behind Morgan and Sanders renaming their premises "Trafalgar House." It must then have been a great day for the partners when, as announced in *The Times* of April 3, 1816, they acquired "a considerable part of Mr. Butler's late Ware-rooms adjoining their own" (Brawer 2001: 192–3; Plate 25). The victory, however, was short-lived for Joseph Sanders died in 1818 and the firm, now known as Morgan and Co., was acquired in 1820 by John Durham who had served as foreman for the company. Durham, in turn, declared bankruptcy in 1826 (169–71, 192–4).

Competition and comprehensive firms

Competition among cabinetmakers in the nineteenth century, and the taking over of a firm by its former employees and rivals, was an oft-repeated tale throughout the period. Perhaps one of the most famous London examples was that of Jackson and Graham (fl. 1836–85), a high-end comprehensive cabinetmaking firm founded at 37 Oxford Street around 1836 by Peter Graham and Thomas Charles Jackson. They expanded rapidly from 250 employees in 1855 to 600 by 1875 (Gere and Whiteway 1993: 289). The company won prizes at almost all the significant European international exhibitions until 1885 when it was absorbed by Collinson and Lock (1870–97). Both F.G. Collinson and George James S. Lock (1846–1900) had worked for Jackson and Graham. They left that company to work for Herring and Company (established in 1782) in Fleet Street in the 1860s. They eventually became the owners of the Herring business, establishing Collinson and Lock in 1870. In 1885 they amalgamated with their former employers creating the firm, initially, of Collinson and Lock and Jackson and Graham (Edwards 2012: 256–7). Their chief designer between *c.* 1885 and 1897 was Stephen Webb (1849–1933), who was later appointed Professor of Sculpture at the Royal College of Art. Webb designed, and Collinson and Lock made, a number of pieces incorporating Renaissance-inspired grotesque intarsia in ivory. A Georgian-form side table with this inlay is now in the Victoria and Albert Museum (W.32–1954). Collinson and Lock, too, eventually faltered and were absorbed, in turn, by Gillow in 1897. Gillow, however, was bought by Waring in 1903 becoming Waring & Gillow. This firm survived until 1962 (Aslin 1962: 84). Meanwhile, the Jackson and Graham partners continued independently of their original firm, possibly, at first, as Graham and Banks, decorators and manufacturers of chimneypieces, paneling, and furniture at 445 Oxford Street (*Architectural Journal* 1901). They certainly attempted to continue with an advertisement for the firm Graham and Biddle, described as the "only surviving partners of Jackson and Graham," appearing in *The Art Workers' Quarterly* of April 1905. Graham and Biddle also exhibited, at the Paris 1889 *Exposition Universelle*, a cabinet and flower stand by them that featured in the *Art Journal* review of the exhibition (*Art Journal* 1889: ix, xvi). Such complex genealogies existed for many of the London cabinetmaking firms. John Johnstone of New Bond Street, for instance, became, over the course of the nineteenth century, Johnstone, Jupe and Co., followed by Johnstone and Jeanes, and then Johnstone and Norman.

In describing businesses like those in the preceding paragraph, Pat Kirkham coined the term "comprehensive manufacturing firm," which she defined as the "organization within a single workplace of the main crafts involved in the production of furniture" (1988: 57). What this meant in practice is that alongside the creation of furniture, many large cabinetmaking firms also served as upholsters, decorators, and sometimes even funeral directors. Although Kirkham suggests the comprehensive firm was unique to London, these could be found elsewhere in Europe and the United States. In Belgium, for example, the Brussels firm Snyers, Rang et Cie described themselves as complete furnishers, upholsters, and decorators (*Exposition Universelle d'Anvers* 1894: 111).

In London, a number of these comprehensive firms dominated furniture production in the West End, an area that came to be associated with top-end pieces. Among these makers was Holland and Sons, founded in 1803 by Stephen Taprell and William Holland, the latter related to the architect Henry Holland. Another was the aforementioned Gillow in Oxford Street. Founded in 1769 by two cabinetmakers, William Taylor and Thomas Gillow, the firm was later acquired by the furniture maker Gillow of Lancaster, founded and owned by relatives of Thomas Gillow. As a general rule, only pieces made by the comprehensive firms were displayed and sold in their shops (Kirkham 1988: 63). That firms such as Holland and Son made everything in-house, probably even when working on large commissions such as the furnishing of the Palace of Westminster, is borne out by a study of the stamps the individual makers employed by the firm left on the furniture (Anderson 2005c: 221–3). The comprehensive firms were also regular exhibitors at international exhibitions, often competing to commission designs from the best artists as well. The "Pericles" sideboard, for example, was designed by Bruce J. Talbert (1838–81) for Holland and Sons for the 1867 Paris exhibition (Plate 12). Talbert produced a design for Gillows for the 1871 London exhibition (see below).

By mid-century, London's comprehensive furniture making firms began to feel pressure from two areas: the "linen-drapers," who developed into the furnishing and department stores later in the century, particularly those located on Tottenham Court Road such as Maple (founded in 1841), Shoolbred, and Heal; and the rise of the sweating or piecework system in London's East End, which was associated with lesser quality and in many ways made those retail outlets in Tottenham Court Road possible. In fact, later in the century Maple was investigated for "sweating" or pitting suppliers against one another in an effort to lower prices (Edwards 2011: 151–2). Tottenham Court Road, located between the West End "honourable" and East End "dishonourable" makers, had attracted important furniture craftspeople, including a number of immigrants, ever since the mid-eighteenth century. Retailers began settling there as well from the early nineteenth century and, with the East End suppliers only four kilometers away, this created the environment for a contracting system to develop (144).

James Shoolbred and Company, founded in 1817, had by the late nineteenth century become one of the better department stores in London. The novelist William Makepeace Thackeray (1811–63) includes a reference to Shoolbred's in his final complete novel of 1862 *The Adventures of Philip on his Way Through the World: Shewing Who Robbed Him, Who Helped Him, and Who Passed Him By*: "His artless wife and mine were conversing … upon the respective merits of some sweet chintzes which they had seen at Shoolbred's, in Tottenham Court Road, and which were so cheap and pleasant, and lively to look at!" (1862: 230). Their expanded furniture department opened in 1870, and in 1880 they even produced a replica of the "Pet" sideboard designed by Bruce Talbert and exhibited by Gillow at the 1871 London international exhibition. The original was acquired by the South Kensington (later Victoria and Albert) Museum (Sotheby's 2001: lot 134). Heal and Son had also opened their premises in Tottenham Court Road by at least 1818. They began as bedding manufacturers but by mid-century they were selling a broad selection of furniture as well. They adapted to changes in taste and the market better than Shoolbred, who ceased to trade in 1931, associating themselves with contemporary design. Heal's still exists today, in Tottenham Court Road and at other locations. Maple, Shoolbred, and Heal all had their own furniture workshops, although Maple continued to combine contract work with their own production into the twentieth century (Edwards 2011: 152–3).

Tottenham Court Road, and the cheap furniture coming out of London's East End, was often lampooned in the press and in literature. In *Our Mutual Friend*, for example, Charles Dickens uses the Veneerings as a means of poking fun at the pretensions of fashionable society:

> Mr. and Mrs. Veneering were bran-new people in a bran-new house in a bran-new quarter of London. Everything about the Veneerings was spick and span new. All their furniture was new, all their friends were new, all their servants were new, their plate was new, their carriage was new, their harness was new, their horses were new, their pictures were new, they themselves were new, they were newly married as was lawfully compatible with their having a bran-new baby, and if they had set up a great-grandfather, he would have come home ... French polished to the crown of his head.
>
> For, in the Veneering establishment, from the hall-chairs with the new coat of arms, to the grand pianoforte with the new action, and upstairs again to the new fire-escape, all things were in a state of high varnish and polish. And what was observable in the furniture, was observable in the Veneerings—the surface smelt a little too much of the workshop and was a trifle stickey.
>
> ([1865] 1997: 17)

Veneers are thin slices of often colorful, high-quality hardwoods that are applied to the main body or carcass of a piece of furniture. The carcass is frequently, although not always, constructed from less expensive, softer wood such as deal (fir or pine). Dickens is here referring to the cheaply made veneered furniture often originating in London's East End sweatshops and using it to make a comment on the outward show by the Veneerings of their high social status when in reality there is no real depth to it, just as the wood veneer is hiding a soft, lighter wood underneath. Furniture making in London's East End only really began in the first half of the nineteenth century and grew rapidly from the 1840s, providing more and more competition for the West End makers who employed highly skilled specialist craftspeople and more expensive materials, and therefore could not operate as cheaply. There was clearly a market for this less expensive furniture: London's population quickly increased from 900,000 in 1801 to 2,225,000 in 1840, with 6,400 new homes built for these predominantly "middle-" and "lower-"class individuals between 1839 and 1850 (Kirkham, Mace, and Porter 1987: 3).

Artists and artisans

The expanding use of machines to undertake furniture making, previously the preserve of human craftspeople, was accompanied in the second half of the nineteenth century by an equally enthusiastic appreciation of the work of the "hand, heart and soul."[3] As outlined elsewhere in this volume, the Arts and Crafts movement was occupied specifically with counteracting the negative effects of industrialization on traditional skills. In England it is most often associated with the theoretical writings of John Ruskin (1819–1900) and the activism and particularly the design work of William Morris (1834–96) as well as the circle around the latter. However, an interest in artisanal furniture was not exclusive to England. For some of his earliest furniture designs, the Scottish architect-designer Robert Lorimer (1864–1929) employed the Wheeler family of wheelwrights in Arncroach, near Kellie Castle, the Lorimer residence in Fife, Scotland. This early furniture often features marquetry utilizing different types of wood, such as that incorporated into an oak chest that Lorimer displayed at the 1899 Arts and Crafts Exhibition in London (National Museums of Scotland 1992 SVL16; Shen 1992 3–4, 12). Notably, this marquetry emphasized the natural colors and grains of the timbers used without, in general, tinting the wood or combining it with other materials as can be seen in many examples of French marquetry from the seventeenth and eighteenth centuries.

Contemporaneous with Lorimer's marquetry is that produced by the École de Nancy in France. It reflects the greater sway of Art Nouveau over design on the Continent during the late nineteenth century. Although well-known designers such as Louis Majorelle (1859–1926) and Émile Gallé (1846–1904), as well as the retailer Siegfried Bing in Paris, were at the forefront of this development, others were also involved (Ramond 2000: 71). The Alsatian Charles Spindler (1866–1938), for example, whose workshop in Saint-Léonard, Alsace, still exists today, trained and employed local residents in marquetry and promoted local art and culture (Loetscher 2005). In a somewhat similar vein, Lockwood de Forest (1850–1932) promoted Indian decorative arts among American clients in an effort to preserve artisanal skills on the Indian subcontinent. De Forest had established a woodworking workshop in Ahmedabad, India, where he had pieces for Associated Artists made (see below). He and John Lockwood

Kipling (1837–1911) organized an exhibition of work by the Ahmedabad Wood Carving Company in Lahore in 1881. After the association disintegrated, de Forest continued to patronize the Indian workshop for another thirty years, seeking to "preserve a threatened artisanal heritage by promoting Indian handcraftsmanship," echoing the efforts of William Morris and others in England who strove to promote traditional workshop skills (Mayer 1996: 2; Bryant and Weber 2017).

It was not, however, only a concern for the preservation of artisanal skills but also the growing importance of the "artist" within the decorative arts that prompted the making of one-off artistic furniture. The individuals creating these pieces were often trained as sculptors, and their pieces exhibit a very different approach from those of the carvers and wheelwrights, like those employed by Lorimer, who were practicing a craft. Indeed, sculptors had long been making bronze mounts for furniture and these sculptural elements, in the nineteenth century, could appear especially exuberant. The cabinet designed by Jean Brandely (active 1855–67) and made by Charles-Guillaume Diehl (1811–*c.* 1885) with mounts and a central plaque by Emmanuel Frémiet (1824–1910) is a monumental example of this (Plate 13).[4] As Claire Jones argues, in the second half of the nineteenth century there was, in France at least, a false separation of art from industry because sculptors played a role in the reform movement within the design of the applied arts. As she states, "sculptors literally shaped industrial art, both through their active engagement in the design and modelling of manufacturers' products, and through their involvement in associations organized to promote industrial art" (Jones 2014: 18). That sculptors could view involvement in the making of furniture as a legitimate means of artistic expression is borne out by the example of the French-Alsatian François-Rupert Carabin (1862–1932).

Carabin apprenticed as a wood carver for a furniture maker in Paris after having first apprenticed as an engraver. When he produced furniture, his approach was very much that of an individual artist rather than an artisan working in collaboration with others. His career path, therefore, led him to the "fine" as opposed to the "industrial" arts. For example, although he exhibited often, he did so through the salons rather than the international exhibitions, entering his first piece, a work of sculpture, in the 1884 Salon des Indépendants. Later, after being privately commissioned to produce a bookcase, which he completed single-handedly in 1890 (apart from the wrought iron pieces), he displayed the piece in his studio and then at the 1892 Société Nationale des Beaux-Arts exhibition in the *objets d'art* section (Figure 2.2). One critic hoped it signaled a new direction in the making of furniture that, among other things, would see artists engaging in work traditionally undertaken by artisans and vice versa. Carabin continued to produce furniture through 1908 (Jones 2014: 182–3). His work is incredibly distinctive, featuring nude women supporting

FIGURE 2.2 François-Rupert Carabin, Bookcase, 1890. Photograph courtesy of Sowa Sergiusz/Alamy.

and posed on his pieces of furniture with unusual motifs like bats in their hair (Merklen 1974).

Valentino Panciera Besarel (1829–1902), too, was an artist who created furniture, although his work clearly stemmed from a regional tradition. Besarel descended from a line of wood sculptors: his great-grandfather Valentino

(1747–1811), grandfather Giovanni (1778–1842), and father Giovanni Battista (1801–73) had all been wood sculptors before him. He also drew on a long regional tradition that dated back to before the time of perhaps the most famous Italian wood sculptor of the seventeenth and eighteenth centuries, Andrea Brustolon (1662–1732). Brustolon was from nearby Belluno in the Dolomites and his furniture can be seen today in the Ca' Rezzonico in Venice, among other places (see his mirror, Figure 8.2, in "Visual Representations" in *A Cultural History of Furniture in the Age of Exploration*). Indeed, Besarel created a suite of furniture heavily inspired by Brustolon for the Italian sovereigns at the Palazzo del Quirinale in Rome, one of his many commissions for European royalty (De Grassi 2002: 167–8). Besarel also showed his work, both furniture including cabinets, seating furniture, and sideboards and other more traditional sculptural creations, at many national and international exhibitions (240–3).

In this, he had a number of Italian contemporaries, perhaps the most famous of these being Luigi Frullini (1839–97) from Florence who exhibited at, among other fairs, the Paris *Exposition Universelle* of 1878 and completed commissions for numerous foreign middle-class clients.[5] Like Besarel, he belonged to a regional tradition; among some of the contemporaneous Tuscan sculptors and cabinetmakers being Angiolo Barbetti (1805–73) of Siena, who displayed his work to great success at the Great Exhibition in 1851 (Pavoni 1997: 39–43). Frullini enjoyed an immensely successful career and his long list of wealthy clients includes the owner of the Château-sur-Mer mansion in Newport, Rhode Island, George Peabody Wetmore (1846–1921) (Ames 1970: 299–300, 305). However, as Rosanna Pavoni has observed, while these craftsmen were "carrying forward a noble tradition and preserving a legacy of 'enduring value'," Italy's "privileged relationship with tradition" was both "a splendid opportunity for self-promotion" but also an "obstacle against attempts at renewal in the long term" (1997: 39). Although, for example, Frullini made a point of copying directly from nature and experimenting with tools to create the effects he sought, his grotesques, griffins, and other features ultimately belie a revivalist approach to Renaissance design (Plate 14).[6]

Osborne House on the Isle of Wight, the summer house and retreat built for Queen Victoria and Prince Albert between 1845 and 1851, holds examples of another regional tradition, Swiss "Black Forest" carving. Prince Albert championed it at the Great Exhibition. Albert had visited Switzerland in 1837, the same year that the woodworking studio of Michael Wettli (or Wättly) was founded in Bern. Wood carving in Switzerland had developed as a cottage industry early in the nineteenth century, particularly centered on the Bernese Oberland. By the end of the century it had become a staple industry of the region employing over one thousand carvers. Today the most famous products of "Black Forest" carving are the life-size bears fashioned in positions that allow them to be used for such things as umbrella stands. However, many other types of finely carved items were also produced. In 1842 Albert purchased from an agent in Bern what was arguably the most impressive Swiss exhibit at the London 1851 exhibition: a lady's *escritoire* (desk) of white wood made by Wettli to be used from either a sitting or standing position and decorated with scenes of "Alpine life." The desk was illustrated in John Tallis's *History and Description of the Crystal Palace and the Exhibition of the World's Industry in 1851* and is probably the same desk that now stands in the Swiss Cottage at Osborne House (Anderson 2005b: 50–8) (Figure 2.3).

FIGURE 2.3 Michael Wettli, Lady's Escritoire, 1851. *Art Journal Illustrated Catalogue of the Exhibition of the Industry of all Nations*, p. 307. Photograph courtesy of the University of Wisconsin–Madison Libraries.

Still, being a regional, artisanal product in the mid-nineteenth century, no matter how well made, did not guarantee appreciation. A sideboard made by Matthew Bland of Halifax, Yorkshire, and exhibited at the Crystal Palace in 1851 serves as a good example of how individual craftsmanship, despite the use of traditional materials and techniques, could fall far short of universal approval in an international context. The Royal Commission that oversaw the organization of the 1851 Great Exhibition also appointed regional committees throughout Britain to coordinate the presentation of locally made items alongside those from international and well-known exhibitors. The Bland sideboard was one of these regional exhibits. Enthusiastically described in the local press, the sideboard was surmounted by rich carving in the form of a vase, fruit, and vines, all inspired by the garden of one of the local stately homes, Hope Hall. Described as "a credit to Halifax" by the local newspaper, the sideboard, in particular its enthusiastic carving, was one of a number of regional British furniture exhibits that earned the scorn of the jury in London, their report being highly critical of furniture "too often crowded with unnecessary embellishment" ("Class XXVI" 1852: 544; Anderson 2005a).

Existing alongside these artistic and artisanal furniture makers and the "comprehensive" firms were more loosely structured decorating partnerships such as Louis Comfort Tiffany and Associated American Artists. Working with Tiffany (1848–1933) were Candace Wheeler (1827–1923), Samuel Colman (1832–1920), and Lockwood de Forest. The partners in the "association" each took responsibility for one area of production: Tiffany for glass, Wheeler for textiles and embroidery, Colman for the use of color, and de Forest for architectural woodwork. The partnership only lasted between 1879 and 1883 (Mayer 1996: 2). This is similar to how the Scottish architect Sir Robert Lorimer worked: he collaborated with a number of other craft and decorating firms, such as Scott Morton & Co. and Whytock and Reid for his furniture and woodwork, throughout his career (Savage 1980).

Reproductions and copies

Carabin's unique pieces were being produced at the same time that other French firms were focusing on producing copies of well-known eighteenth-century models, or specimens belonging to the late nineteenth-century "belle epoque" style that had clearly been inspired by the rich woods and gilt-bronze mounts of the previous century. Perhaps the most famous of the latter was François Linke, originally from the Czech Republic, who, after sojourns in a number of central and eastern European cities, arrived in Paris in 1875 (Payne 2003: 21–30). Together with the sculptor Léon Messagé (1842–1901), who was responsible for the exuberant gilt-bronze mounts, Linke created furniture that was not copied from eighteenth-century models but rather inspired by the lyrical rococo style mixed with the sensuality of Art Nouveau, adapted to furniture of dimensions and purpose more suitable to the needs and fashion of the late nineteenth and very early twentieth centuries (70–95). Among the pair's most significant and characteristic creations are a lady's writing desk originally intended for display at the 1900 *Exposition Universelle* (Payne 1981: jacket front cover; 2003: 156) and the Grande Bibliothèque that was actually exhibited in Paris in 1900 (Payne 2003: 120).

Before Linke, however, the copying of eighteenth-century French furniture held in public collections had been well established in Paris. Indeed, Linke himself was an accomplished copyist of French eighteenth-century furniture (and proficient in a number of other styles as well; his versatility, no doubt, accounting for his career longevity as a furniture maker). Among these makers who specialized in replicas was Louis-Auguste-Alfred Beurdeley (1808–82) who realized exact copies of French furniture in the Transitional (between rococo and neoclassical or Louis XV/XVI) and neoclassical (Louis XVI) styles. The Paul Sormani firm (fl. 1847–1934), alongside their exact copies of Louis XV and Louis XVI pieces, also made furniture in the style of André Charles Boulle (1642–1732) and in a freely interpreted "Louis" style. (English makers also copied the Boulle style, calling it "Buhl.") However, perhaps the greatest Parisian copyist of eighteenth-century French furniture was Henry Dasson (1825–96) who to this day enjoys a reputation for employing the highest quality materials and craftsmanship. For this reason, it is sometimes claimed that modern collectors are better off buying a piece by Dasson than an eighteenth-century original (Payne 1981: 32–42).

Although not a copyist, nor even a cabinetmaker, Ferdinand Barbedienne (1810–92), a bronze founder who created mounts for furniture, also influenced French furniture of the nineteenth century. Barbedienne and his partner Achille Collas (1795–1859) had established themselves as manufacturers of historical European sculpture reproductions in a variety of materials. In furniture, Barbedienne favored the Renaissance revival style, which can be seen in a gilt-bronze mounted bookcase he entered in the 1851 London Great Exhibition. The firm of Jackson and Graham acted as Barbedienne's London agents and showed the bookcase on their own stand, despite the Barbedienne firm having their own stand in the French section. The bookcase was ornamented with replicas of figures from Lorenzo Ghiberti's (1378–1455) *Gates of Paradise*, the bronze doors adorning the baptistery of Florence cathedral in Italy, as well as three of Michelangelo's statues in the Medici funeral chapel (Jones 2014: 43–7). The way in which the mounts had been applied, which enhanced the bookcase's architectural form rather than distracted from it, was praised by critics at the 1851 exhibition: "Here, in a completely new direction, is the beautiful application of mechanically worked bronze to furniture, with which it could be said to dissolve, rather than to be content with decorating it" (quoted in Jones 2014: 45).[7]

MATERIALS

Perhaps in no other area was nineteenth-century furniture production so innovative and forward-looking as in the utilization of materials. Consumers in the nineteenth century experienced a marked change in the range of goods available, triggered by an influx of previously unknown, exotic substances alongside the creative use of well-known materials. Not only unusual but sometimes also experimental furniture was displayed and proffered to the public. Coal, for example, a common household item, was transformed into furniture fit for the British royal household. The coal used for these specimens came from Wemyss in Fife, Scotland, where it had been mined since the seventeenth century. When burning, this particular type of coal makes a sound like the clicking of a parrot's beak, which explains its name, parrot coal. This material is also extremely hard, meaning it can be carved and withstand being highly polished. While this accounts for its ability to be fashioned into furniture, that it actually was used for this purpose can only be made clear through an understanding of the entrepreneurial spirit of the mid-nineteenth century. Parrot coal furniture was probably commissioned by the Wemyss Coal Company, established to exploit deposits on land belonging to the Wemyss family, to showcase the unusual qualities of the material. Thomas Williamson (1817–60), a local mason, carved much of it (Plate 15). The novelty caught on and he was listed in the 1851 census as Coal Carver to Her Majesty. In fact, Williamson carved a sofa from parrot coal that had been commissioned by Prince Albert and exhibited at the Great Exhibition of 1851.[8] A local Fife chronicler described Williamson as "an ingenious artisan [who] has of late chiselled a variety of massive and really beautiful articles from blocks of parrot coal ... Her Majesty has a sofa of his making, after an elaborate design ... and many of his vases, inkstands, cups and so on, find their way into the collections of virtuosi [knowledgeable collectors]" (Jones 1987a: 35–8; Phillips Edinburgh 1998, 1999). The sofa was eventually installed at Osborne House.

The Great Exhibition spurred several makers to experiment with other materials as unusual as coal, among them papier-mâché and gutta-percha, the latter a natural plastic derived from the sap of trees native to the Malaysian Archipelago. Papier-mâché, of course, was not a new substance, but its use as the basis for furniture was innovative. Perhaps the most well-known examples are chairs made by Jennens and Bettridge (fl. 1815–64), originally of Birmingham but later also with offices in London, Paris, and New York. These chairs were japanned and then gilt and decorated with mother-of-pearl. For the 1851 exhibition Jennens and Bettridge showed a particularly imaginative piece known as the "Day-Dreamer" chair (Figure 9.1). Papier-mâché furniture and interior decoration were also produced on the Continent, one maker, Paul Gropius of Berlin, showing a wall bracket at the Crystal Palace (Pevsner 1951b: 37–40).

At the time of the 1851 exhibition, gutta-percha had only recently been scientifically classified. It was, though, by no means unknown: John Tradescant described it in his 1656 "Rarities" catalog as "plyable mazer wood" that "being warmed in water, will work to any form." Nonetheless, not until 1842 did Dr William Montgomerie, in the service of the East India Company, recommend it be used for surgical splints, its first commercial application ("Popular Miscellany" 1884: 861). He later exhibited some specimens of it at the Royal Society of Arts in London in 1843 (Black 1983: 11). Shortly after this, the Gutta Percha Company was established. It was they who exhibited a naturalistic Elizabethan-style sideboard in London in 1851 in which, the *Illustrated London News* claimed, cracks and discoloration could be seen (Pevsner 1951b: 40–1).[9] Although it did not really prove practical in the end for large pieces of furniture, gutta-percha was greatly in demand for a number of other uses, especially the insulation of telegraph cables, which led to the trees from which it was tapped coming close to extinction by the end of the nineteenth century (Tully 2009: 560).

Illustrated sources on and the official catalog of the Great Exhibition provide invaluable information on a number of other materials being used in the production of furniture at mid-century including zinc, tubular metal, brass, cast iron, and bentwood (the bentwood chairs of Thonet of Vienna are discussed by Megan Aldrich in more depth in Chapter 1 in this volume). Examples of decorative furniture in carved bog yew also showcased a novel material, one closely tied to the history of Ireland where these items were made. Most famous among these was an armchair with busts of ancient Irish warriors and the ancient arms of Ireland produced by Jones of Dublin (Figure 2.4).

Another novel material for the making of furniture, lava stone, was featured in the 1827 edition of the Expositions des produits de l'industrie française (Exhibitions of the Products of French Industry), national French exhibitions that ran periodically between 1798 and 1849. These are recognized as the inspiration for and forerunners of the international exhibitions that began with the Great Exhibition of 1851 in London. The lava stone from Volvic in Auvergne, France, had already been quarried for many centuries, although by the early nineteenth century, the quarries were largely in disuse. Gilbert Joseph Gaspard, comte de Chabrol de Volvic (1773–1843), a French official, took up the cause, promoting both Volvic and its lava stone. Chabrol collaborated with chemists, among them Ferdinand Morteleque (1774–1844), who then developed a technique for painting in enamel on the stone, his first *tableau* and other pieces being entered in the 1827 exhibition (Morteleque 1830: 184–6). His technique, which, as David Oakey describes in Chapter 7 in this volume, was also tied to architectural innovations of the first half of the nineteenth century, was exploited by the firm set up by his son-in-law, Pierre Hachette, and the architect Jacques-Ignace Hittorff (1792–1867): Société Hachette et

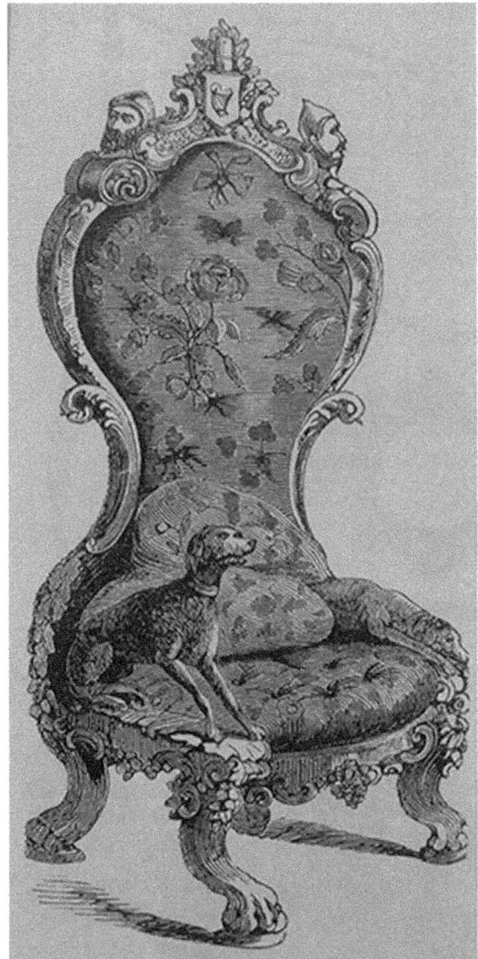

FIGURE 2.4 A.J. Jones, Armchair, *c.* 1850. *Art Journal Illustrated Catalogue of the Exhibition of the Industry of all Nations*, p. 263. Photograph courtesy of University of California Libraries/Internet Archive.

Companie. Perhaps the most famous outputs of the company are the tabletops that Hittorff sent to important government leaders around Europe in the hope of securing larger commissions for architectural projects, such as the one in Plate 29. Unfortunately, orders were not steady enough to make the enterprise financially viable and Hittorff, who ran the firm between 1832 and 1838, eventually abandoned it (Kiene 2015).

Cabinets also had porcelain plaques set into them as well as micromosaic, often produced in Rome, and painted enamel panels. Perhaps the most elegant example of this last is a cabinet made by the London firm Wright and Mansfield to a design by "Mr. Crosse" of a piece in the "Adam" style, referring to the late eighteenth-century Scottish architect-designer Robert Adam (1728–92). Made of satinwood, it harks back to the Sheraton-style furniture from the beginning of the nineteenth century. However, it does more than just revive a style, it actually updates one: the Wedgwood plaques replicate the use Robert Adam made of neoclassical motifs painted on the walls and ceilings of rooms he designed. They also relate to the French-style furniture made in England with porcelain plaques that look back to those commissioned by the *marchands-merciers* in eighteenth-century Paris (Sargentson 1997). The Minton ceramics manufacturing company based in Stoke-on-Trent produced porcelain in the Sèvres style in the mid-nineteenth century under the supervision of its art director, Joseph-François Léon Arnoux (1816–1902) (Jervis 1896: 19–20). A piano exhibited by Jackson and Graham at the international exhibition of 1862 had Minton porcelain mounts painted by Thomas Allen, who also executed the Minton staircase at the South Kensington (Victoria and Albert) Museum in London (*Art Journal* 1862: 146; Jervis 1896: 21). A more adventurous use of porcelain in furniture can be seen in the cabinets produced in Germany by the Meissen factory that, with the large percentage of porcelain used in all parts of the cabinet, provide an opportunity to showcase the porcelain rather than provide useful storage (Payne 1981: 336).

Innovations such as enameled lava stone tabletops could be exquisitely beautiful. However, items such as the gutta-percha sideboard show a kind of inventiveness that clearly aimed to highlight the possibilities, rather than desirability, of utilizing particular materials. Whatever judgments are made about taste in furniture in the nineteenth century, there can be no doubt that it was an exciting period in which to be experimenting with the materials and techniques of furniture making.

CHAPTER THREE

Types and Uses

CAMILLE MESTDAGH

There is an obvious permanence in furniture history: in general, furniture produced since antiquity has not undergone innovative development in a functional sense. An Etruscan barrel-shaped chair,[1] for example, fulfills the same basic requirements as a twenty-first-century chair. The Continental term for furniture derives from the Latin *mobilis* meaning movable, in contrast to the term for a building derived from *immobilis*, meaning immovable. According to this distinction, if a house was built for generations to enjoy, the furniture could be changed according to fashion, as could the textiles, considered together as part of the *fourniture* (French origin of the English words "furnishings" and "furniture"). Similarly, something like a *bureau plat* (writing table) by André Charles Boulle (1642–1732) or an Italian baroque console table could be moved from building to building, meaning it might be found in a Parisian *hôtel particulier* (a grand townhouse), an English country house, or a Russian palace.

The first international European furniture style, seen in the work and commissions of André Charles Boulle, developed as early as the late 1600s (Ronfort 2009). During the first decades of the nineteenth century, too, the "Empire style," referring to the growing French Empire under Napoleon, spread throughout Europe and across the Atlantic. Despite the international presence of this style, English neoclassical designs nonetheless continued to dominate the furniture industry in America and in the colonies of the British Empire throughout the century. Alongside these international styles, the nineteenth century also saw a large expansion of the production of goods and of their circulation with the development of international and national transportation systems, the organization of the international exhibitions, and the installation of a complex network of "courtiers" and representatives in most European capitals but also as far away as New York and Saint Petersburg. The archetypes of interior decoration thus also became international.

Nineteenth-century interiors, generally described as "eclectic," illustrate perfectly the relationship between permanence and mobility, or the mixing of old and new furniture of various styles and origins, as summarized by Simon Swynfen Jervis: "Late nineteenth-century conventions of interior arrangement are resistant to analyses, beyond the crudely functional ... it is easy to gain a general impression of studied informality, density and variety, but beyond this it is difficult to progress" (2005: 245). The preference of some individuals at this time to live with antique pieces alongside modern ones demonstrates that the functionality of a seventeenth-century dresser or a set of eighteenth-century chairs was perfectly adequate for modern usage. It also contributes to blur the boundaries between decorating and collecting, and as Anca I. Lasc concludes in her analysis of interior decorating manuals published toward the end of the century: "Rather than a superficial activity that resulted in random associations of objects in space, interior decorating in the age of historicism was a complex matter" (Lasc 2013: 17).

In the eighteenth century, furniture generally had to be "new" to be appealing, in contrast to the nineteenth century in which a desire for "antique" furniture developed. Many of those who had started out dealing in secondhand goods eventually became curiosity and antique dealers as their businesses experienced a great escalation during the first half of the century (Westgarth 2009). The royal courts began to employ such dealers. For example, Carlton House, the London residence of the Prince Regent, later George IV, and the prince's private apartments at Windsor Castle were partly furnished with antiques during the 1820s (Roberts 2001). A decade later in France, the Garde Meuble de la Couronne did business with no less than twenty *marchands de curiosités* (curiosity merchants) for the supply of furniture, light fittings, etc. in French royal palaces (Dion-Tenenbaum 2005). European royal patrons continued to commission furniture from cabinetmakers but fine antique pieces were also available and desirable. The latter were often less expensive than equivalent newly made pieces and they could be chosen to match the existing décor. As underlined by the German art historian Jakob von Falke (1825–97), "time has given it [antiques] a reconciling patina that allows an easier combination of different elements and the stylistically diverse" (1873). The influence of architects advising on interior decoration and in the process establishing contacts with the trade, also played a major role in this trend, as well as in the development of auction sales and catalogs.

Another determining factor for the furniture market was the concept of comfort as a result of progress. At the heart of domestic comfort too, furniture served as a manifestation of social and economic status. As such, the demand for new furniture remained strong. However, from the 1820s until the end of the century, the taste for antiques and historical objects inevitably pushed modern production toward the imitation or reinterpretation of historical styles. Furniture designed and/or made for the aristocracy and the wealthiest of clients was not only admired and imitated by members of the upper class, but also by those belonging to the middle classes. This became especially true with the increased exposure to the highest achievements in manufacturing represented in national and international industrial exhibitions, starting with the Great Exhibition held in London in 1851. By the 1860s, the establishment of public museums devoted to the decorative arts such as the South Kensington Museum in London, the frequent organization of exhibitions devoted to the decorative arts across Europe, and the development of specialized art and manufacturing publications had a crucial influence on the furniture industry and its clientele:

> Such exposure to historical products and artefacts had practical implications ... revivals included the production or reproductions of historical models, to satisfy the demand of the popular market, and also encouraged the development of personal collections so that individuals could satisfy and expand their interest and knowledge with examples of antique furniture or porcelain to decorate their homes.
>
> (Collard 2003: 35)

Commercial venues such as the newly established department stores in large European cities also encouraged this popular enthusiasm for interior decoration.

An increase in purchasing power among the middle class led to the emergence of the idea of a "democratization of luxury," despite an old principle "maintained long into the nineteenth century, [which] allowed for luxury for the aristocracy, comfort for the bourgeoisie and mere necessity for the working class" (Muthesius 2009: 16). The furniture industry was mostly interested in the richest sections of society and the upper-middle class. Following industrialization and the subsequent migration of rural populations to urban centers with an ever-increasing size and density, the working class was confined to very small dwellings, consisting of one or two rooms, usually rented furnished. Those classes were buying secondhand furniture of lesser quality but still considered a step in furniture ownership. Emile Zola describes this in *L'Assommoir* (1877) where the characters Gervaise and Copeau

> bought their furniture at a used furniture store ... There was a bed, a night table, a chest of drawers, a wardrobe, a round table ... and six chairs. It was all made of mahogany ... It was for them like a serious and definitive start in

> life, something that, by making them property owners gave them importance in the milieu of well-off people of their neighbourhood.
>
> (Auslander 1996: 267)

A great gulf divided different sections of society and the variations in furniture production reflected it. At an 1882 national furniture competition in Paris, for example, to be considered affordable "for a young couple" it was recommended that a bedroom set selling price should not exceed 500 francs. In addition, the price of a single luxury piece such as a vitrine or a side cabinet was set at a maximum of 6000 francs. The margin between production aimed at middle-class pockets and the luxury end of the market was still immense at the end of the century.[2]

The rise of the middle class is often considered synonymous with that of bourgeois taste. In Germany, Austria, northern Italy, and the Scandinavian countries the name Biedermeier, chosen to describe the style of furniture that developed from 1825 to 1835, was derogatory and considered archetypal of the bourgeois taste, glorifying the comfortable life of a secure middle class disinterested in politics.[3] Biedermeier can be seen as a simplification of the Empire style and, arguably, the aim of reducing forms was at the heart of various attempts to reform furniture and make it affordable throughout the century.

To a large extent, furniture typology was dictated by architecture, with the creation of rooms conceived for specific uses according to social conventions and furniture to complement these. In the second half of the century, typical Anglo-American upper-middle-class dwellings were suburban terraced houses, while on the Continent city centers were re-urbanized with large blocks of flats with balconies, as can be seen in Berlin, Vienna, or the Haussmann boulevards in Paris. They usually consisted of at least two living rooms and a few bedrooms and also included a study. With the development of railway connections, some could also afford a "villa" in suburbia, a typical reminiscence of the aristocratic country house but closer to the city (Favardin 1979).

In Loudon's *Encyclopedia* of 1833, an English house is described as containing an entrance hall or a gallery leading to a saloon. It is defined as "a sort of vestibule to the living-rooms" (1833). Loudon also states that two drawing rooms were necessary in a London house but not in a country residence where the library could be used as a sitting room. The dining room had to be the most formal and magnificent room with "two carved sideboards" (Cornforth 1978: 20). This makes an interesting comparison with the recommendations published in 1856 by a contributor to the journal *Le Moniteur de l'Ameublement*, which describes what a contemporary French apartment should include: an antechamber, a dining room, a reception room, a small sitting room or boudoir, a study, one to a few bedrooms, and a dressing room. A larger dwelling would also comprise a billiard room, an oratory, etc. In the case of a villa, it would in addition occasionally offer a conservatory. The antechamber should have an armoire and an umbrella stand; the dining room chairs and a large table, but also a sideboard. The reception room should be the most luxurious room in the residence, with a sofa, armchairs and chairs with upholstered backs, occasional chairs, a *causeuse* (love seat) near the mantelpiece, a *borne* or a *confidante*[4] (sofa with triangular seats at each end), an occasional table or a console, a small sideboard, and a games table. The boudoir or small sitting room was to be decorated by the lady of the house and furnished with a lady's desk, a small table, a knitting table, one or a few *jardinières*, a sideboard with shelves, occasional chairs, and a *causeuse* (Chabert 1865). The bedroom should be furnished with an *armoire à glace* (wardrobe with a mirror on the front), a dressing table, a jewelry cabinet, a bedside table, a prie-dieu (a desk for kneeling during prayer), a chest of drawers, and comfortable chairs. The office should include a desk, a bookcase, a table, armchairs, etc. This home arrangement seems typical of its time in Europe and America and varied only according the size of the dwelling. Therefore, this description is a good starting point to identify some of the archetypes of furniture commonly associated with the nineteenth-century domestic interior.

This analysis of characteristic nineteenth-century furniture types is organized according to basic forms and functions: seats, tables, cabinets, dining and bedroom sets. They will be illustrated with examples from museum collections, old photographs, depictions of interiors, and records from the international exhibitions and trade catalogs.

COMFORTABLY SEATED

"An Age of Sofas and Cushions"[5]

When intended to furnish formal rooms, seating furniture was often conceived in sets to create unity. From the first half of the eighteenth century, sets of padded back chairs intended for sitting rooms often comprised a number of chairs, armchairs, and sometimes a matching sofa. By the 1830s, "settees" or sofas had become extremely popular and systematically formed part of a salon suite. They were omnipresent in northeastern European Biedermeier interiors (Plate 16). Occasionally they were also placed in dining rooms such as the large divan veneered in mahogany from the dining room of Empress Carolina Augusta of Austria (Empress 1816–35) in the Hofburg palace in Vienna (Hofmobiliendepot, MD 72.390).

Although sofas were considered an essential requirement for most of the nineteenth century and even conceived as pairs for the grander salons, the form had been eclipsed earlier, in the Napoleonic Empire period, by the daybed inspired by antiquity. Madame Récamier (1777–1849) was portrayed by Jacques Louis David[6] (1748–1825) seated on such a daybed with out-scrolling ends called *méridienne*, whose shape is very similar to that of the *lit bateau*. Very similar daybeds with upholstered sides of equal size and no back also became fashionable across the Channel during the English Regency period. An example featured in Thomas Hope's (1769–1831) publication of his sketches of furniture *Household Furniture and Interior Decoration* (1807). *Méridienne*-type daybeds remained fashionable in the second half of the century as part of bedroom sets or intended for the boudoir.

Another type of settee, the sofa *en pommier*,[7] developed during the Empire period. It was upholstered all over and had a tilted back and two sides, one higher than the other forming the bedhead. On some examples the lower end could be reclined using a small mechanism to create a daybed. This was rapidly replaced by "sofa beds," the sides of which reclined when pushed. The most praised attempts that aimed for the middle market concerned "transformation" furniture and sofa beds were indeed a favored type: "this furniture is at a very reasonable price which allows use in less wealthy families ... in the modest homes where space is most often lacking" (*Exposition Universelle* 1856: 1126).

Another new form of sofa was the *borne* settee, also called the "drawing room ottoman," an early example of which is included in the architect John Nash's (1752–1835) view of the Grand Saloon at the Brighton Royal Pavilion (1826). It was made of different sections to create a circular seat, to be placed in the center of the room (Figure 3.1). It was fashionable for most of the century, as evidenced by examples displayed at the international expositions.[8] Although *bornes* were more commonly associated with formal interiors, they can be seen in domestic interiors on a smaller scale. In *The Apartment of the Comte de Mornay* painted by Eugène Delacroix in 1832 (Musée du Louvre, R.F. 2206), the *borne* was formed by a pair of couches with cushions arranged back-to-back. Mornay had just returned from an official visit to Morocco where he met Delacroix (1798–1863). The arrangement the room depicted followed the Near Eastern fashion, which generated, during the second half of the century, a vogue for casually draped furniture and loose cushions. This was rather informal and was mainly seen in smoking rooms, small sitting rooms, and artists' studios. Later in the century, a photograph of the French painter Louise Abbema (1853–1927) shows her sitting on a Middle Eastern-style couch in the Parisian apartment of the legendary actress Sarah Bernhardt (1844–1923).[9] In England, following the same fashion, "the cosy corner, a late nineteenth-century cushioned recess by the fireplace shielded with Moorish fretwork arches and heaped with oriental pillows, was ubiquitous in middle-class homes" (Cohen 2006: 110).

FIGURE 3.1 Left: Men seated on a drawing room ottoman, France, *c.* 1835. Right: Ladies seated on a *confidante* and an easy chair, in a Parisian salon, France, *c.* 1875. Album Maciet. Photograph © Bibliothèque des Arts Décoratifs.

Sitting to converse

The *fauteuil en gondole* (literally "armchair following the shape of the Venetian gondola") was an early example of seating furniture that changed the upright seating position. It was designed with a deeper and curved padded back, indicating that the *fauteuil* was comfortable. Introduced during the Napoleonic period, this form was successful and spread across Europe. Refined examples were made such as one incorporating metal inlay (at Neues Schloss in Baden-Baden), realized by the Munich cabinetmaker Franz Xaver Fortner (1798–1877), but many variations of this form of armchair were also conceived for middle-class interiors. By the 1830s and 1840s, the padded seats and the use of steel springs recently introduced in the chair industry became synonymous with increasing comfort and led to a large production of so-called comfortable seats. The armless version of the *fauteuil en gondole*, known as a "toad armchair," introduced the broader type of "easy chair," conceived without a frame and upholstered all over. On some examples the feet were covered by fringing and cord (Figure 3.1). These "easy chairs" were also made cheaper through the use of a metal understructure. As they became fashionable, their designs were adapted throughout Europe and America and have become icons of the nineteenth-century interior. They can be seen in living rooms across various sections of society, from the aristocratic to upper- and lower-middle-class. Again, industrial progress made textiles and upholstery more affordable and new methods developed to fasten the padding and the covers such as the *capitonné* or buttoning.

It was thought that the more comfortable the sitting position, the more entertaining the conversation would be. Following this trend, conversation seats were introduced in France in the 1840s and encountered worldwide success. The small sofa made of a pair of seats named *causeuse* or *tête à tête*,[10] developed into the *confidante* in the form of a "S" with a seat at each end, allowing for two seated guests to converse without having to turn their heads, and to the *indiscret*, similarly composed with the addition of a third seater (Figure 3.1).

In the last quarter of the century when eclecticism reigned, Charles Blanc defended the idea that the interior should be composed with a variety of colors and styles and wrote that gendered sitting rooms such as the boudoir, reserved for the lady of the house to receive guests, or the male equivalent, a "study" or "a smoking room," should not be arranged symmetrically. Furthermore, it "is not necessary for the chairs to be the same nor for the upholstery to match ... On the contrary, an impression of freedom is perfectly suitable in those intimate small salons" (Blanc 1882: 139).

Innovative chairs

Inventive designs were motivated by the development of technology and notably by new applications of metalwork. The use of cast iron began as a novelty and was not restricted to exterior use. Exploring the possibilities of this new material and techniques, The American Chair Company of Troy, New York, created the "centripetal" spring chair in 1849.[11] The chair is made of cast iron with an upholstered circular seat connected to four cast iron legs through a spring device that allows movement in various directions. The same company produced reclining seats that also enjoyed great popularity. In England, by 1878, Thomas Jeckyll (1827–81) designed a hall chair that was manufactured by Barnard, Bishop & Barnards in a single "pour" of cast iron (Nelson-Atkins Museum of Art, 2010.19.1).

The development of garden furniture also greatly encouraged the use of metal. As the hearts of cities were devoted to commerce, public parks and gardens developed and the need for commercial kiosks or cafés created a demand for outdoor furniture. On the domestic side, the addition of a "winter garden" and "veranda" in upper-class dwellings also encouraged the production of such furniture. At the 1855 Paris Exposition, most of the garden furniture shown was constructed of cast iron, which was regarded as a huge improvement over traditional wooden furniture. Chairs made of wicker (woven reed) or rattan (from a climbing palm) were still very common and suitable for a middle-class budget, but thanks to the use of metal, simpler and more interesting designs were introduced such as a suite of garden furniture designed by the architect Peter Herwegen (1814–93), manufactured by J.B. Kaltenecker & Sohn in Vienna (Ottillinger 1989: 235–49).[12]

Used inside or outside, the rocking chair is one of a few examples in furniture history that developed from working-class use and then became adopted by the upper classes. This form was extremely popular in the nineteenth century and many American and English manufacturers exported various versions of the famous chair, in wicker, wood, or metal. One model was produced by Peter Cooper in New Jersey in the 1860s, inspired by the example formed of tubular brass exhibited by the Birmingham firm of R.W. Winfield & Co. at the 1851 London Great Exhibition (*Exhibition of the Works ... 1851* 1852: 1106). The metal type was probably the most innovative design of the period until about ten years later when Michael Thonet (1796–1871) created his *Model #1* rocking chair in bentwood (Brooklyn Museum, 69.79.1). Thonet bentwood chairs are probably the most successful example of industrially made furniture in the second half of the nineteenth century (Figure 8.3).[13] In 1855, in Vienna, Thonet Brothers started producing steam-bent solid wood furniture (attaching a metal strip along its length). This was more efficient and less costly than using laminated wood. Their later so-called *bistro chairs* became very popular not only because the firm developed an international network of outlets but also because these chairs were perfect for use in public spaces at the time when cafés, restaurants, and hotels were booming in major European cities. As early as 1849, the Daum café in Vienna commissioned a large series of identical chairs known as Model No. 4 (Musée d'Orsay, OAO 940). The same chairs can be seen in a depiction of *Café Griensteidl* in Vienna (1896).[14] These chairs were light, hygienic (with a wood or cane seat), of neutral design, and could be produced in a series that reflected the idea of "uniformity" and "equality," an idea that had taken hold in the modern city. The chairs perfectly complemented commercial and public environments.

TABLES AS CENTERPIECES

Associated with the chairs in most sitting room arrangements, various kinds of small tables were already introduced in the middle of the eighteenth century, many of them light, moveable, and highly decorative. The success of these tables did not fade, on the contrary their presence and use became conventional.

Center tables

In her study of the French royal palaces and their furnishings, Colombe Samoyault-Verlet describes how during the early years of the French Restoration (1815–20s) it was important to place a piece of furniture in the center of the room. Large center tables, called *tables de famille*, became essential in the main sitting room or "salon" setting (Samoyault-Verlet 1991). These circular tables consist of a top with a leather surface above a large frieze, sometimes fitted with drawers and raised on a baluster support with four scrolling feet. Around the same time in England, Edward Holmes Baldock (1777–1845) supplied several comparable central tables, of octagonal form, veneered with floral marquetry and fitted with drawers.[15] One of these tables is now at Temple Newsam, originally sold to the 5th Duke of Buccleugh in 1840 (1806–84).[16] Like the *tables de famille* they have a leather top but the top section, fitted with drawers, revolves. They are usually described as library tables. Indeed, around 1830, libraries became a favored gathering room for families after dinner. The idea of devoting a room to sitting and reading or playing games together as a

FIGURE 3.2 *Le Hall*, 1882, Schommer, François (1850–1935). In grand houses the hall could be used as the main reception room. This picture shows the favoured pastimes such as piano playing, card games and painting. It is also furnished with a drawing room ottoman, numerous plant stands and jardinières for exotic specimens. Album Maciet © Bibliothèque des Arts Décoratifs.

family developed significantly in the nineteenth century (Plate 3.2). Even in the grandest homes, the central table became a major symbol of family togetherness. In the English *Encyclopedia* of 1833 the country residence is described as "containing a saloon and library, the latter would be used as the family sitting room on common occasions ... the seat furniture would be of great variety .... A large round table is usually placed in the middle of the room, in which are generally books, prints and other things to amuse the company" (Cornforth 1978). A watercolor of *The Drawing Room at 59 Seymour Street* (London)[17] shows that this arrangement had become archetypal in the furnishing of a sitting room in a middle-class home by the middle of the century.

These circular tables or *tables de salon* were also common in Biedermeier and southern European homes, intended for a middle-class market as, for example, the model seen in Ferdinand List's (active 1840–70) *Wiener Möbel Journal* (1852).[18] These center tables are, in fact, adapted from *guéridons* that were iconic in French First Empire interiors. As the most fashionable type of furniture in the Empire period, it was adapted to various designs and materials across the European continent. In Russia, for example, the famous architect Andreï Nikiforovitch Voronikhine (1759–1814) conceived the most luxurious examples of *guéridons*,[19] in gilt or patinated bronze.

In Italy as well, light wood veneered circular *tables de salon* were common in sitting rooms. They were related to luxurious seventeenth-century Italian tabletops, notably those with a *pietra dura* (hardstone) inlay. In the 1850s large center tables became a form favored by Italian furniture makers with which to compete in international exhibitions. Exhibition furniture, made especially for the event, consisted of *chefs d'oeuvre* conceived to impress wealthy clients and other visitors. Such a large rectangular center table is the one displayed at the Great Exhibition of 1851 and attributed to the Falcini brothers, Luigi (1794–1861) and Angiolo (1801–50).[20] Established in Florence they specialized in the making of center tables with "wooden mosaic" and mother-of-pearl decoration assembled to resemble a *pietra dura* composition, reviving a technique perfected during the seventeenth century. The Falcini table combines a *scagliola*[21] top with a composition that imitates a hardstone mosaic inlay, supported by a marquetry base of various woods and mother-of-pearl. At the various international exhibitions, the English manufacturers also showed many examples of circular center tables with refined marquetry such as the one presented by Holland & Sons in 1862 incorporating old Masters engravings within an inlay of contrasting woods, silver, and ivory (Plate 17). Center tables counted amongst those showpieces or *meubles d'apparat*, placed in the middle of reception rooms of a grand home they served as ornaments and could occasionally be used to display collectable objects.

Jardinières *and occasional tables*

Jardinières were prevalent in mid-nineteenth-century interiors as occasional containers for plants. Their production was encouraged by the broader availability of exotic house plants and the fashion for verandas and conservatories, partly initiated by the Great Exhibition of 1851 and its Crystal Palace. *Jardinières* were commonly formed of a table or console table (against a wall) with a top incorporating a box, often covered with a lid when empty. They were already fashionable in the first decade of the century, sometimes almost completely cast in bronze as seen in the famous example by Pierre-Philippe Thomire (1751–1843), where the intricate basket is supported by winged female figures (Musée du Château de Fontainebleau). Cabinetmakers continued to produce them at the end of the century and Emile Gallé (1846–1904) presented his exuberantly shaped *Flora marina Flora exotica* at the 1889 Paris *Exposition Universelle* (Musée de l'Ecole de Nancy, NV76). Undeniably, this fashion for interior plants and flowers, combined with the influence of the Arts and Crafts movement and Japanese art, contributed to the popularity of the Art Nouveau style in the last decade of the century. In more modest homes small circular tables were introduced as plant stands as a substitute for *jardinières* and were extremely common toward the end of the century. As stressed by Deborah Cohen: "a bamboo plant stand, dripping with fern pots, is more redolent of the late Victorian period than an elegantly streamlined tea service designed by Christopher Dresser" (2006: 15) (Figure 3.2).

The term "occasional" table generally describes those "light" moveable tables that were particularly appreciated in domestic interiors. Small tables scattered around the sitting room were essential to create a certain atmosphere as described in Loudon's *Encyclopedia* of 1833:

> As nothing gives a more dismal effect than an appearance of idleness, everything should be so arranged, both here [in the library] and in the drawing room, as if the persons using the rooms had been employed in some way or other. This effect would be produced by the daily papers, and some periodical works, and open letters received in the morning, on the principal tables ... The inkstands not thoroughly in order, with some unfinished writing and open books or portfolios, would give at least the appearance of industry.
>
> (Cornforth 1978)

Many forms of multiuse tables had already been introduced at the end of the eighteenth century. In England, sofa tables, designed with a small leaf at each end, were commonly placed behind the sofa or flanking it as a pair. As described by the English cabinetmaker Thomas Sheraton (1751–1806) "the ladies chiefly occupy them to draw, write or read upon" (1803: 305). Occasional and versatile tables continued to be particularly fashionable and were often designed with an element of surprise: a table may have several different functions not apparent at first sight that were activated by clever mechanisms. The number of patents for such systems rose greatly after the 1850s as legislation evolved in many European countries and the United States that encouraged this type of invention. Indeed, various types of multifunctional tables proliferated, such as reading tables incorporating revolving bookshelves and others with drawers opening to reveal folding music stands. Game tables and easels were also extremely common in middle-class interiors, complementing the most popular pastimes.

Writing tables and desks

If the etiquette was for women to use occasional tables to write and read, men often had their own study (Plate 3.3). It has been a long tradition to portray men with official functions in their study or *cabinet de travail*, next to their desks. Writing tables, or *bureaux plats*, sometimes comprising a small filing cabinet were the most commonly adopted. The pedestal desk, consisting of a table raised on two pedestals fitted with drawers became extremely popular in the nineteenth century. In England and America they even started to be produced for the mass market in the 1850s.

FIGURE 3.3 *Cabinet de travail* or study, *c.* 1874. Designed by Charles Hunsinger (1823–94), cabinetmaker, Paris. This room can also function as a small sitting room, with a couch and a vitrine cabinet to showcase small objects. It is placed next to an architectural bookcase following the archetype of a tall armoire or buffet. The then standardized pedestal desk is accompanied by a chair with a deep curved back. Album Maciet. Photograph © Bibliothèque du Musée des Arts décoratifs.

In the more commercial or public sphere, there was a certain democratization of the desk by the 1870s following a growth in demand for office furnishings, as banks and industries developed, increasing the need for administrative and accounting work. More office space was required to house these activities. The Brunswick Building, considered one of the first purpose-built office blocks, was constructed in Liverpool in 1841. By the end of the nineteenth century, large office buildings could be seen in all major cities of Europe and the United States. American furniture manufacturers were leaders in importing office furniture, often designed and adapted from English models. The firm Cutler & Son, founded in Buffalo, New York, in the late 1820s, was famous for their roll-top desks, also called *Cutler Desks*, of which examples were displayed at the 1876 Philadelphia Centennial Exhibition. Offering many pigeonholes above the writing surface, with filing drawers below, this form was an international success. The widest and most popular range of American roll-top desks, adopted in both the domestic and business markets, was the *Wooton desks*. William S. Wooton, from Indianapolis, obtained patents for his design in 1874. Soon the company established retail outlets in locations from Glasgow to Rio de Janeiro. The desk was mounted on casters for easy movement and was designed to occupy minimal space when folded shut; it offered a lot of storage space for an increasing amount of paperwork. The desk opened with a pair of doors to reveal a series of pigeonholes and shelves, centered with a fall front desk. This form was soon criticized because of its complexity. At the end of the century "the demise of the enclosed desk as a type was to occur .... With the intention of increasing efficiency, desks were soon reduced to tables with drawers" (Edwards 1995: 114).

Billiard tables and pianos

Billiard tables are not a nineteenth-century invention and some surviving tables made in the seventeenth century can still be seen, notably in England at Knowle and Boughton. Nevertheless, in the nineteenth century the game became very popular and many billiard halls opened in major cities. Grand domestic interiors also usually included a billiard room (Figure 3.4). At Beaufront Castle, near Hexham, Northumberland, built around 1836 as a "castellated" house by the architect John Dobson (1787–1865) for William Cuthbert, the most spectacular rib-vaulted billiard room counts as one of Dobson's best interiors. The room was initially decorated with armor, flags, and horns to give it a "baronial" aspect, which reflected the social and ceremonial importance of the game. At the international exhibitions billiard tables were included in the furniture section. As a jury reporter underlines, "a billiard is at the same time a piece of furniture and an instrument of precision" (*Exposition Universelle* 1856). At the 1851 Great Exhibition, the French Maison Bouchardet, for example, presented a billiard table in the Boulle style, with tortoiseshell and metal inlay, mounted with Sèvres

FIGURE 3.4 A billiard room, *c.* 1882. Designed by the architect Louis Bonnier (1856–1946). Album Maciet. Photograph © Bibliothèque du Musée des Arts décoratifs.

medallions and another in carved mahogany in the Renaissance style, both reflecting the leading trends in furniture production (*Exposition* 1854–73).

If having a room devoted to billiards implied a large dwelling, the game itself was not reserved for home owners from privileged sections of society. At Polesden Lacey in England, for example, there was a billiard table in the servants' quarters. The table was made by Burroughes & Watts, which was founded in 1836 in London and supplied billiard tables to the middle-class market (National Trust, NT 1245996). In the United States, billiard tables were also manufactured for upper-middle-class homes. In Hartford, Connecticut, the house of the American writer Mark Twain (Samuel Langhorne Clemens, 1835–1910) built in 1874 had a billiard room that served as his study as well as a place for social gatherings. His biographer wrote: "Every Friday evening, or oftener, a small party of billiard lovers gathered, and played until the late hour, told stories, smoked till the room was blue ... Mark Twain always had a genuine passion for billiards" (Paine 1912).

Like most upper-middle-class people of the second half of the century, Mark Twain also played piano and his daughter married a virtuoso pianist of the golden age. As with billiard tables, pianos could be manufactured as decorative pieces of furniture. An interesting example is the grand piano designed *c.* 1885 by the artist and designer Lawrence Alma-Tadema (1836–1912), with a pair of armchairs and two sofas *en suite*, all intended for the music room of Henry Gurdon Marquand's (1819–1902) mansion on Madison Avenue and 68th Street in New York City (piano: Sterling and Francine Clark Art Institute; one armchair: Victoria and Albert Museum [hereafter V&A], W.25:1, 2–1980; one sofa: Metropolitan Museum of Art, 1975.219a). It is thought to have been one the costliest purchases made by this important American collector. Displayed in the center of rooms, pianos had their place of honor in grand interiors and beyond their primary function, they were impressive pieces of "parade." If billiard tables were symbolic of male entertainment, pianos were also associated with women, as noted by Susan Lasdun, "the ability to play the piano and sing was expected from cultivated women in the nineteenth century" (1981). As such they were extremely common in domestic settings (Lasdun 1981). The Parisian photographer Eugène Atget (1857–1927) in his *Intérieurs parisiens* presents the small apartment of "Mme D., Bd du Port Royal, petite rentière," where the piano was placed in the dining room near the sideboard (Musée Carnavalet, Paris PH1563; Nesbit and Reynaud 1992). "Torfrida," a British lady writing for the journal *Lady's Companion* as a decoration advisor, reported that a sofa was beyond her means, though she had a piano on hire for purchase (Cohen 2006). Edward Burne-Jones (1833–98), a leading figure in the English art world of his day, designed and painted a new upright piano for his family use at the Grange, his own house in Fulham. He was interested in improving the appearance of pianos and, he reported, "I have always been wanting for years to reform pianos, since they are as it were the very altar of homes, and a second hearth to people" (Burne-Jones 1904: 111; Lasdun 1981: 125). A few years later, he received the commission of the decoration of a grand piano from his patron William Graham. He also designed the gesso decoration of the stained green grand piano supplied by Morris & Co. to Constantine Alexander Ionides (1833–1900) (V&A, W.23:1 to 4-1927). It was placed in the drawing room of the collector's house in Holland Park, London, and also exhibited at the first Arts & Crafts Exhibition in 1888. Grand pianos seem to have been preferred by those avant-gardes who wished to make a statement. For example, Louis Majorelle (1859–1926), in association with the artist Victor Prouvé (1858–1943), exhibited their piano entitled *Chanson du soir* at the 1904 Paris Salon (21522). Decorated with figurative marquetry, it was a typical work of the Art Nouveau style. The piano was kept by Majorelle in his villa in Nancy and given by him in 1919 to the Musée des Arts Décoratifs, Paris.

CABINETS FOR/TO DISPLAY

As the piano could be a central element of an artistic conception of the interior decoration, so were some prominent cabinets made to showcase or store objects.

Vitrine cabinets

As recently underlined by Deborah Cohen, "from Oslo to Boston, Marseille to Hamburg, late nineteenth-century interiors were crammed full of objects" (2006: 16). Indeed, the display of a large quantity of objects was considered a mark of social and economic status. Traditionally, collecting was a serious hobby associated with the aristocracy; the privilege of time and a discerning education that would lead to the knowledge of a chosen kind of object. This perception broadened in the nineteenth century as the distinctions of class evolved. With the development of specialized literature, exhibitions, and the formation of museums devoted to the decorative arts, collecting became a popular and approachable hobby: "Suddenly, a generation of artists, inspired by literature, was looking for fragments of the past .... This fad has won all social classes .... It descended to the people everywhere to become a common part of usual furnishings" (Roqueplain 1869; Charpy 2015). To showcase these objects in domestic spaces specific display cabinets were necessary. Thanks to the industrial production of glass, vitrines were not so expensive to make and glazed doors, glass sides, and shelves combined with a mirrored back were commonly in use in the second half of the century. As the Renaissance style dominated European furniture production in the 1850s, the first forms of freestanding vitrines can be comparable to those of sideboards and bookcases. They are architectural with a pediment above glass doors for the upper section and carved doors for the lower section. The firm Ribaillier exhibited a grand example of a freestanding vitrine cabinet with open shelves on the side corners at the 1855 Paris *Exposition Universelle*. Napoleon III acquired it.[22] Although it clearly functioned as a vitrine, this cabinet was described as a "buffet" by the jury in 1855. Indeed, it could have been used as a sideboard as it was similarly composed, indicating the preponderance of this archetype in the development and concept of other cabinets (*Exposition Universelle* 1856). However, twenty-one years later at the Centennial Exhibition in Philadelphia a carved "display cabinet," still in the Renaissance style but conceived as a tall armoire with a pair of glass doors and sides, was exhibited by E. Gijani of Florence (Smith 1876: 47). As the commercialization and consummation of decorative objects, old and new, developed, the production of these cabinets expanded greatly, especially for the burgeoning middle class. They were also described in trade catalogs as "china cabinets,"[23] because decorative porcelain objects, as opposed to those made of other materials, were most commonly found in middle-class homes. Small vitrines and *bijouterie* tables were also in great demand, used to display collections of small articles. Side cabinets fitted with glazed doors and sides were also used as vitrines, such as a finely carved example exhibited by Frullini of Florence at the Philadelphia Exhibition in 1876 (Smith 1876: 470). Side cabinets were extremely popular throughout the century, sometimes conceived in pairs. Indeed, they traditionally stood in galleries or sitting rooms where, because of their height, they displayed decorative or rare objects, such as porcelain vases or clock garnitures, leaving enough space above to hang a picture or a mirror.

The sideboard

In the context of the revivals, one of the most widely spread concepts in mid- and late nineteenth-century interior decoration was the Renaissance dining room: the sideboard, *buffet* in French or *Bufett* in German, became the standard piece to provide storage in the dining room, although the term was broadly used at the time to refer to various forms. The examples at Charlecote Park, England, are significant in the evolution of the sideboard types. In 1837, George Lucy (1789–1845) purchased for the dining room "a fine large carved oak sideboard"[24] with a rectangular top above a pair of cupboard doors surmounted by a shaped frieze from the London dealer Edward Holmes Baldock (Charlecote Park, National Trust, NT 532957). In 1858, this sideboard was moved to the great hall, displaced by James Morris Willcox's (d.1859) Charlecote buffet purchased that year for the dining room. The latter is much taller, as the lower section is surmounted by a very large pediment, highly carved with representations of the bounty of nature and the trophies of the chase, and surmounted by a female figure of plenty, a fisherman, and a hunter (National Trust, NT 532965). Both Charlecote sideboards only offered limited storage space but servants used the large horizontal surfaces to place dishes of food. During this period, another "open sideboard" type was popular. This model consisted of open shelves and compartments, often incorporating mirrors, raised on a stand with cupboard doors below. Such an example was presented by the American firm of Allen and Brothers at the Philadelphia exhibition of 1876 (Figure 3.5).[25] According to a period engraving, the back of the upper structure was all mirrored and fitted with shelves to the sides where numerous objects were displayed—cups, jars, silver plates, decorative urns, etc.

Sideboards were an international success. A noted article from 1974 by Kenneth Ames entitled "The Battle of the Sideboards" examines many examples of presentation furniture created as "showpieces" deducting that "by the middle of the century, they had become the prime exhibition piece" (1974). Indeed, the 1862 international exhibition jury reports "the London exhibition ... was studded with sideboards, perhaps the majority of them English." In 1851, the French designer Fourdinois was acclaimed for his gigantic "Renaissance style" sideboard (about six meters in height and width) but compared to other examples it did not offer much space for display, seemingly made for decorative rather than functional purposes. In 1876, Giuseppe Ferrari (1844–98), a relatively unknown wood carver and sculptor of Italian origin living in New

FIGURE 3.5 Allen and Brothers (maker), Sideboard, Walter Smith's *The Masterpieces of the Centennial International Exhibition*, vol. 2 (1876). Photograph courtesy of Digital Library for the Decorative Arts and Material Culture.

York, exhibited a carved cabinet entitled "Dante" (Philadelphia Museum) at the Centennial Exhibition:

> [The] piece was intended as a presentation piece, for while standing an imposing eight feet (nearly two and a half meters) in height, the marble surface above the drawers is but a mere eighteen inches (forty-six centimeters) deep, rather shallow for the display of plate, and another indication of the artist's intention to create a "showpiece" rather than a functioning piece of furniture.
>
> (Raizman 2013: 65)

In simpler dwellings, the dining room was also considered important, especially when there were no other living or entertaining spaces. In this context, the sideboard may have been a unique piece of furniture with decorative value and although exhibition pieces were far too expensive for middle-class pockets, furniture manufacturers offered a great variety of styles, sizes, and prices that were more affordable.[26]

Overmantels

Overmantels are architectural arrangements that can be compared to the upper section of many open sideboards. Traditionally in France, England, and the United States, fireplaces were surmounted by a mantelpiece and a large mirror. The marble shelf or top of a mantelpiece usually supported a clock garniture but in the second half of the century the fashion developed for independent overmantel structures incorporating many shelves for large displays of objects or ceramics (Plate 18). The interior decorating firm Herter Brothers (active 1864–1906) conceived a complex architectural overmantel arrangement for Mrs. Vanderbilt's Boudoir at William Henry Vanderbilt's (1821–85) house in New York City (Lewis, Turner, and McQuillin 1987). This upper structure was conceived with many niches and some vitrine cupboards where old glass, ceramics, and sculpture were displayed. A similar arrangement was also to be found in Mr. Vanderbilt's bedroom, incorporating a central mirror. In England, at Waddesdon Manor in the Smoking room, a comparable mantelpiece upper structure is still used as a display for some of Ferdinand de Rothschild's collection of Renaissance glass and ceramics. If these examples relate to some of the richest patrons and collectors of the time, overmantels can also be seen in photographs depicting drawing rooms from middle-class homes, especially in the United States and England.[27]

THE CONCEPT OF SETS

Furniture production flourished across the century, with an abundance of models from the past being referred to and inspiring revival forms, from

Gothic to neoclassical styles. As a result, a debate emerged from the 1850s regarding how these different styles and references of times and places could coexist in one private interior. Some decorative arts historians and critics recommended eclectic arrangements with a mixture of styles furnishing the same room while others defended the rule of unity, meaning that a single period style should be chosen for each room, in accordance to its function (Blanc 1882; Havard 1883). The development of sets certainly followed the last.

The dining set

In the second half of the century the idea for a predominant style in the dining room and bedroom became widespread. Therefore, if all pieces of furniture were to match a chosen style, it made sense to commercialize and acquire them together as a set. The crucial position of the sideboard has been discussed above, first associated with the adaptation of the Renaissance style dining room and designed individually as a showcase piece. This form became commonly associated with a dresser and/or an overmantel and, along with the table and chairs, they formed the main components of a dining set. In their *Series of furnished specimen rooms*, Hewetsons of Tottenham Court Road published illustrations of such dining room sets in their trade catalog (*c.* 1885). The typology of the dining room as an interior with integrated furnishings prevailed at numerous early twentieth-century exhibitions and in department store displays (Plate 19). It appears that it proved more productive to advertise and commercialize furniture as an ensemble rather than as individual pieces. In the 1900s, furniture reformers continued to promote the necessity of the dining room set. For their dining room conceived in the emerging Art Nouveau style, Pérol Frères designed both an open sideboard incorporating a mirror and a sideboard with glazed doors (Musée d'Orsay, OA 1482). Most of all, with the development of Art Nouveau and the greater employment of architects in the conception of interiors, rooms were planned in their entirety with furniture forming part of the architecture. Following this principle, the French architect Hector Guimard (1867–1942) designed shelves, cupboards, and vitrines that were completely integrated into the paneling for the *salle à manger* of his own house. Dated *c.* 1909, it was donated by Mrs. Guimard to the Musée du Petit Palais, Paris (PPO3674). Victor Horta's (1861–1947) Brussels house designed a few years earlier shows a similar symbiosis of architecture and furniture. In the dining room, the sideboard was centered in its lower part with a mantelpiece. It was built as a fixed structure and fitted perfectly in a purposely created alcove.

Although these ensembles were the work of architects rather than furniture makers and were in fact few in number, they demonstrate essential relationships between furniture and architecture, functions and forms.

The bedroom set

Another room for which the concept of sets greatly developed was the bedroom, unlike the seventeenth and early eighteenth century when it formed part of the reception rooms of which the focal point was the state bed or *lit de parade*, the bedroom was an intimate space in the nineteenth century.[28] Furthermore, as the concept of the "matrimonial" bedroom developed from the 1840s, a married couple, no matter which economic level, shared a bedroom. With this new idea beds came in both single and double sizes. According to Charles Blanc, the *lit bateau*, usually placed against the wall, was very popular during the first half of the nineteenth century and later because most houses did not have alcoves (Blanc 1882). Indeed, this new form of bed with out-scrolling ends, commonly described as boat-shaped, appeared around 1800 and was popular with all classes of society. This form, with solid curved ends, allowed for a separation of the sleeping area from the rest of the room without the addition of drapery, which had represented an added expense. Naturally, as with upholstered chairs, the decorative effects of beds relied greatly on the textiles, confirming the crucial role played by the upholsterer and decorator in luxury interiors. Textiles became more widely available and cheaper due to improved manufacturing techniques and the increase in imports from China and India. By the middle of the century, draperies were added to simpler beds, including the popular half-testers and more common brass beds.[29] Indeed, although metal was used for modern chairs, it was also utilized in the manufacture of beds, the latter fabricated in iron as well as the more expensive brass. In their catalog, Maple & Co. in London offered a number of choices and options.[30]

Even before the introduction of the dining suite, bedroom furniture was often conceived as an ensemble. During the first years of the century, for example, in the Napoleonic era, the typical Empire bedroom was composed of assorted pieces of furniture including a bed, a bedside cupboard known as a *somno*, a cheval mirror, and a dressing table. Sometimes even a *secrétaire*, opening with a fall-front, was added to the set. One of the earliest and fine examples of a dressing table was listed in the boudoir of Madame Bonaparte in the Palais des Tuileries (musée du Château de Malmaison). It consists of a table supporting a large mirror flanked by candelabras fixed to the table. Deriving from the dressing table, many forms of bedroom cabinets were created throughout the century. They were intended for ladies, incorporating a mirror and offering storage compartments for jewelry or clothing accessories.

Originally conceived *en suite* with the dressing table, the cheval mirror was popular during the Empire period but remained fashionable throughout the century. More commonly, the *armoire à glace* supplanted the cheval mirror.

During the 1840s, as most European countries experienced an enormous increase in the production and use of mirror glass, armoires began to be fitted with large sheet mirrors on the doors. The typical armoire consisted of a large central cupboard opening with a glass door, surmounted by a pediment and flanked on each side by an additional cupboard.

As evidenced by trade catalogs, the typology of the bedroom set had become standardized by the end of the century, almost systematically incorporating a bed, bedside cupboards (nightstands), a wardrobe, a dressing table, and a washstand.[31] The bathroom with running water and plumbed-in bathtubs did not appear until the end of the century and the washstand remained a common element of the bedroom set (Figure 3.6). In some examples, the basin was directly integrated into the dressing table. The bathroom represented a completely new kind of room in the middle-class apartment by the beginning of the twentieth century. Interestingly, a modern bedroom designed by Henry van de Velde (1863–1957) and photographed in 1904 included a bedside cupboard, a cheval mirror combined with a small chest of drawers, and a washstand.[32] This indicates that the concept of the set largely inherited from the mid-nineteenth century was still adaptable to modern design and conventions.

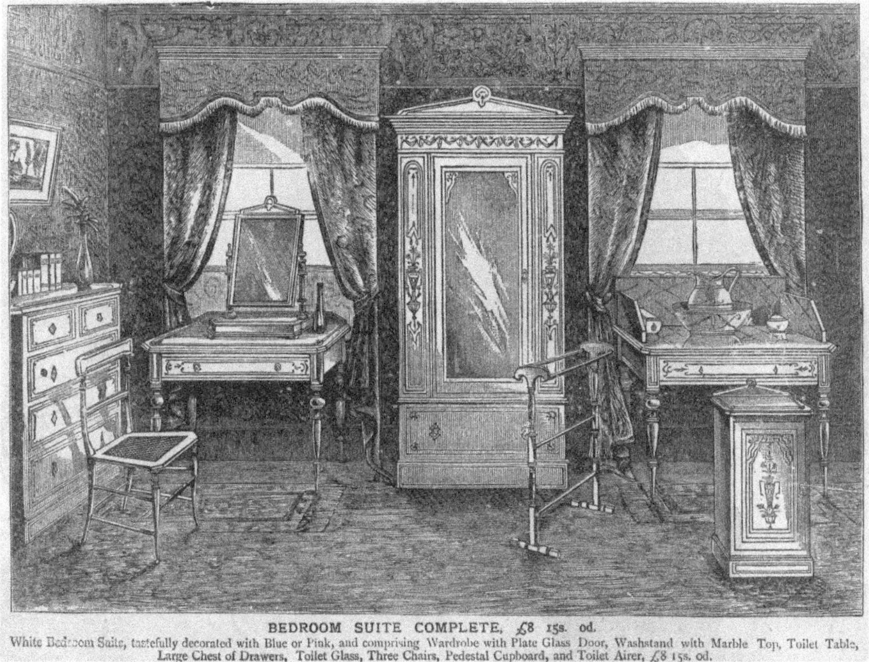

FIGURE 3.6 The Studley bedroom suite commercialized by Hewetsons, *c.* 1885. Photograph courtesy of Walker Art Library/Alamy Stock Photo.

CONCLUSION

Although domestic furniture remained traditional in form, the early nineteenth century saw the introduction and popularization of new types. These prevailed throughout the century, despite socioeconomic changes in European and American societies. Indeed, the nineteenth century was a period of great dissemination of style and form, from one country to another, through the international exhibitions, and from the upper classes to the middle classes. A capitalist economy established its roots and social consciousness grew. Consequently, a sense of ownership and decorum resonated throughout the domestic interior, while practicality hid behind the concept of comfort. In the domestic interiors of the wealthy, the primary role of furniture was to impress and fulfil the representation of an elite. As Daniel Roche stressed, furniture is instrumental in the affirmation of a social status: "Everywhere furniture is the means to express wealth; the trend is found even among the poor" (Roche 1997: 196). If class consciousness developed in various sections of society, so too did the concept of individualization in interiors through the collection of objects and the eclectic choices involved in mixing styles and old and new furniture. As such, the era is often categorized as "the Age of Bric à Brac." This new trend was very popular and did not encourage the idealistic vision of simplification of forms and uniformity in domestic interiors that was visible in public spaces.

Despite major developments in furniture making accompanied by an immense expansion of production in the Western world, the luxury goods market resisted mechanization and largely continued to rely on manual labor. At the end of the century, a fashion for so-called artistic furniture showed increasing sophistication, yet with the industry aiming for mass production to cater to demand, the result was imitation instead of the introduction of new designs. Thus, while many patents were granted for mechanisms and transformational furniture such as reclining seats, sofa beds, and multipurpose tables, these remained traditional in form. In the second half of the century, there was a new division in furniture production: "luxury" and "affordable." First described in the international exhibition catalogs from the 1870s the division into two distinctive groups became clear thereafter. This dichotomy was at the heart of the criticism emerging from visionary reform agendas such as that of the Arts and Crafts movement, which defended and promoted hand craftsmanship and medieval sources. Art Nouveau designers and architects, inspired by natural forms, also advocated for the concept of a "total work of art," where architecture and furniture are symbiotic. Both these movements insisted on the "artistic" conception of furniture whose realization, unfortunately, was limited to certain sections of society. Nonetheless, a fundamental characteristic of Art Nouveau furniture was that it was conceived in harmony with architecture;

therefore, it was almost systematically designed as sets for specific rooms. The furniture industry rapidly adopted the idea of these sets but the designs were still based on nineteenth-century archetypes: sideboards, *armoires à glaces*, dressing tables, etc. All those types were still at the heart of the furniture made for wealthy patrons and continued to dominate domestic models in the Art Deco style until the Second World War.

CHAPTER FOUR

The Domestic Setting

Self, Stories, and Furniture in the Nineteenth Century

AMY G. RICHTER

In the nineteenth century, furniture told stories. Chairs spoke of power and status within the family; sideboards depicted humans' place in the natural order; hall stands narrated the boundary between private and public life. This was of course a ventriloquist's trick: the furniture offering the words and ideas of human speakers. The illusion was compelling. Throughout the century, people imparted meaning to domestic articles and, in turn, used furniture to decipher character, define community, and assert authority. They believed the stories objects told—so much so that furnishing a room or outfitting a house became a way of narrating oneself and others.

In *Pride and Prejudice* (1813), for example, Jane Austen's readers and the protagonist, Elizabeth Bennet, first appreciate Mr. Darcy's true character only when they are shown his home, Pemberley. "The rooms were lofty and handsome, and their furniture suitable to the fortune of its proprietor; but Elizabeth saw, with admiration of his taste, that it was neither gaudy nor uselessly fine; with less of splendor, and more real elegance" (Austen [1813] 1988: 246). Led by Mr. Darcy's devoted housekeeper, the tour reveals a piano purchased for his sister as well as "a very pretty sitting-room lately fitted up with greater elegance and lightness ... to give pleasure to Miss Darcy" (250). Here, at a turning point in the novel, furnishings and artwork convey what Darcy could not divulge and Elizabeth could not previously detect: his good nature and generous heart.

Of course, not all furniture spoke as eloquently as Mr. Darcy's. In 1853 Samuel Raynor published *The Parlor* as part of the series New Books and True Books for the Young (Figure 4.1). The text made the case for furniture's didactic contributions to child-rearing, describing typical parlor furnishings and suggesting the lesson each item taught. Young boys were encouraged to appreciate the skilled labor that went into constructing a door. A simple hinge inspired curiosity: "Did you ever look at one to see how it moves?" An image of a sideboard, however, offered a more pointed moral. Having informed young readers that sideboards are made of mahogany and contain small cupboards for cutlery, the author noted that many people keep wine, liquor, and glasses in their sideboards. "Then they ask their friends to go to the sideboard and drink. But I would not have a drop of such bad things in the sideboard or the house. By one glass of liquor you may perhaps lead a person to become a drunkard. Liquor has ruined many a happy family" (Raynor 1853). Such heavy-handed moralizing broke the ventriloquist's illusion, revealing the human narrator in the hope that actual doors, hinges, and sideboards would continue to offer moral guidance long after the book was closed.

Despite the inelegance of *The Parlor*'s prose, its conceit of using furniture to embody and impart moral traits permeated nineteenth-century culture. In 1852, Harriet Beecher Stowe hoped to inspire her readers' sympathy when she introduced her long-suffering hero, Uncle Tom, and his wife, Aunt Chloe, with details of their domestic arrangements. Stowe let the furniture do the talking:

> In one corner of [the cabin] stood a bed, covered neatly with a snowy spread; and by the side of it was a piece of carpeting, of some considerable size. On this piece of carpeting Aunt Chloe took her stand, as being decidedly in the upper walks of life; and it and the bed by which it lay, and the whole corner, in fact, were treated with distinguished consideration, and made, so far as possible, sacred from the marauding inroads and desecrations of little folks. In fact, that corner was the *drawing-room* of the establishment. In the other corner was a bed of much humbler pretensions, and evidently designed for *use*. The wall over the fireplace was adorned with some very brilliant scriptural prints, and a portrait of General Washington, drawn and colored in a manner which would certainly have astonished that hero, if ever he happened to meet with its like.
>
> (Stowe [1852] 1962: 23)

When readers encounter Tom's proper domestic arrangements, they already know that his master, Mr. Shelby, has made plans to sell him. Nonetheless, Tom's furnishings—carpeting, a makeshift settee, a bed, prints and artwork—establish his standing as a moral Christian. Entering Tom's well-appointed cabin, readers are meant to feel the injustice of his situation. Even in slavery, he

A SIDEBOARD.

Sideboards are made of mahogany. They have small cupboards in them to hold plates, knives and forks, and what you choose.

Some people keep bottles of wine in them, and other liquors, with glasses to drink them in. Then they ask their friends to go to the sideboard and drink.

But I would not have a drop of such bad things in the sideboard or the house. By one glass of liquor you may perhaps lead a person to become a drunkard. Liquor has ruined many a happy family.

God has turned many drunkards to sober men. Let us thank him for it.

FIGURE 4.1 *The Parlor* (New Books and True Books for the Young, 1853). Photograph courtesy of the American Antiquarian Society.

and his wife approximate the respectability, privacy, and personal refinement more commonly associated with the "upper walks of life." How could this man be bought? How could he be sold away from this home and the values conveyed by its furnishings? Throughout the novel, domestic settings mark and measure individuals' morality—serving as shorthand for personal character and signposts on Tom's downward journey from his own humble cabin to Simon Legree's mansion of "coarse neglect and discomfort." In his final earthly home, Tom must live in one of several "rude shells, destitute of any species of furniture, except a heap of straw, foul with dirt, spread confusedly over the floor, which was merely the bare ground, trodden hard by the tramping of innumerable feet" (Stowe [1852] 1962: 395). Such were the domestic arrangements provided by a man who made his living buying and selling souls.[1]

Again and again throughout the nineteenth century, authors used domestic spaces and their furnishings to tell stories and deepen characters in both senses of the word. To Austen and Stowe add Charles Dickens, Henry James, Louisa May Alcott, Emile Zola, Kate Chopin, Charlotte Perkins Gilman, Edith Wharton, Stephen Crane, Theodore Dreiser, and many more.[2] The number and variety of authors and works is dizzying. Even today, it is difficult to imagine the impoverished gentility of Alcott's *Little Women* or the faded hopes of Dickens's Miss Havisham without picturing the rooms they inhabited. With the repetition of a simple rocking chair, Dreiser punctuated the power of Sister Carrie's dreams and the emptiness of her striving; and his readers understood that this familiar object was associated with children, the aged, the infirm—that it was appropriate for private repose rather than public display (Kaplan 1992: 144).

Thus, in a bourgeois culture that turned values into objects and objects back into values, furniture could speak to economic security or social climbing, cultural conformity or transgression, parochialism or cosmopolitanism, familial harmony or discord, moral integrity or hypocrisy and corruption. Literature from the period not only documents these values but also reveals that authors and audiences shared a high level of fluency in both furniture and its cultural meanings. In the latter half of the nineteenth century, German advice manuals encouraged women to embrace domestic duties and the uplifting influence of a well-ordered home by quoting Friedrich Schiller's 1800 poem, "The Song of the Bell," in which "a clean polished cabinet [collecting] the gleaming wools, the snow white linens" signifies the nation's homely virtues (Reagin 2007: 43). And in 1886, when the German writer Georg Hirth sought to describe the furniture of the 1820s and 1830s, he looked to a satirical character created by Ludwig Eichrodt and Adolf Kussmaul for a term that would also convey the conventional middle-class personality of the times: Biedermeier. The name, combining the protagonists of two poems, "Biedermann's Evening Comfort" and "Bummelmaier's Complaint" stuck as an apt description of central European furnishings from 1815 to 1848.[3] Such linguistic and cultural borrowing reveals how knowledge of furniture pieces and styles circulated broadly enough that they themselves operated as a type of lingua franca moving from text to lived experience and back again.

To convey the complexity of meanings imparted to and expressed by furnishings in the nineteenth century, this chapter will further consider how the give and take between words, furniture, and values transformed domestic items into a form of self-expression; suggest how nineteenth-century men and women gained and demonstrated fluency in the language of furnishings; and consider some of the stories they told with this rich vocabulary. This chapter is less interested in particular furniture styles (although these did convey specific meanings) but instead focuses on how domestic items conveyed notions of privacy, control, and refinement (Richter 2015). Although these ideals were often rooted in specific national contexts, the broad patterns (gender roles and the separation of private and public, for example) and historical shifts (changes in production, distribution, consumption as well as the growing awareness and impact of globalization) were shared among Western cultures.[4] As Kenneth Ames wrote of his own study of Victorian material culture, "The culture described here was lived in America, but extended beyond this country. Although it may have taken on a distinctive flavor here, much of it was either formulated elsewhere or created in response to external cultural forces" (Ames 1992: 4).

OBJECT LESSONS: LEARNING TO READ FURNITURE AND PEOPLE

Several related and mutually reinforcing trends coincided to give domestic furnishings a place of cultural prominence during the nineteenth century. First, new technologies of production and networks of distribution fueled the proliferation and specialization of furniture types and initiated an unprecedented expansion of print culture. The result was not only more goods and texts, but also broader markets for both. These markets were readily found in the emerging middle class, which despite its economic diversity shared ideals of domesticity, morality, self-restraint, and individual uplift. Furniture and texts mingled in the early decades of the nineteenth century as catalogs, advertisements, and design books presented new items to a growing middle-class audience (Figure 4.2). At the same time, a steady supply of magazines and prescriptive literature encouraged men and women of the expanding middle class to integrate these goods into their homes. Furniture, advertisements, advice, and ritual fed off of one another in entrance halls, parlors, and libraries, where bourgeois men and women signaled their status and character by demonstrating appreciation for and mastery of goods and their functions.[5]

If furniture was a type of language in the nineteenth century, Thomas Webster's *An Encyclopaedia of Domestic Economy* was an ideal primer.

FIGURE 4.2 Hennessy's Cottage Furniture advertisement, 1852. Photograph courtesy of Library of Congress, Prints & Photographs Division, LC-USZ62-53908.

Published in 1844 in London and reprinted in New York the following year, it addressed "those who are beginning house-keeping" and in need of outfitting their homes. It included descriptions and woodcuts of "furniture in use at present" so "that young housekeepers may acquire, by their means, such a general knowledge of the subject, as will be useful in enabling them to enquire after, and to select, those articles which are indispensable" (Webster and Parkes 1844: 213). What followed was an almost overwhelming catalog of domestic items that taken together reflect the middle class's commitment to classification. Webster acknowledged, "Perhaps almost all the articles we are about to describe may be known in a general way to most persons, yet it cannot but be useful to have them enumerated, classed, and brought before us, in one view, that attention may be drawn to them in a precise and methodical manner" (213).

Webster named tables for at least sixteen different uses: dining tables (square, telescoping, round, cottage, breakfast), library tables, pier tables, card tables, sofa tables, occasional tables, billiard tables, ladies' work tables (also work boxes and baskets), toilet and dressing tables, tea-poises, music stands, plant stands, cut-flower stands, and tray stands (Webster and Parkes 1844: 229–41). He explained that a "what–not is a whimsical appellation for a very convenient stand of several stories" (264), and extolled the virtues of rising tables with tops that could transform into three separate shelves and then back into an "ordinary side table that may always remain in the room" (269). Then noting, "Scarcely any article of furniture has undergone so many changes, and admits of such variety of forms, as chairs," Webster enumerated the current varieties of parlor chairs, easy or arm chairs, drawing room chairs, library chairs, reading chairs, hall chairs, and bedroom chairs (243–50). Significantly, he presented furniture not only by type but also by room. In this manner, he introduced the middle class to the range of goods available and implicitly argued for their necessity in respectable domestic life. For example, Webster advised that a properly outfitted entrance hall required doorscrapers and brushes, chairs, mats, cloak and hat stands, benches, a letterbox, floor cloth, lamps, and umbrella drains (288). These items managed the daily comings and goings of family members, guests, servants, and messengers.

While books such as Webster's described and depicted the number and variety of home furnishings, etiquette books, conduct manuals, and domestic guides highlighted their uses, placing them more squarely within social and cultural contexts. Although most prescriptive works discussed furniture as an essential component of domestic respectability and the separation of private and public spheres, there were subtle gradations of emphasis—like dialects within a shared language.[6] Etiquette books tended to emphasize issues of form, manners, and taste. Within their pages furniture set the stage for rituals of politeness, delineated public and private spaces within the home, and reinforced order by creating social hierarchies and encouraging bodily self-control. Eliza Leslie in *The Ladies' Guide to True Politeness and Perfect Manners*, for example, informed her readers that when ladies visit for tea, "The domestic that attends the door should be instructed to show the guest up-stairs, as soon as she arrives; conducting her to an unoccupied apartment, where she may take off her bonnet, and arrange her hair, or any part of her dress that may require change or improvement" (Leslie 1864: 31). Here a knowing and polite hostess must provide a toilet-table "furnished with a clean hair-brush, and a nice comb." Leslie continued in some detail:

> We recommend those hair-brushes that have a mirror on the back, so as to afford the lady a glimpse of the back of her head and neck. Better still, as an appendage to a dressing-table, is a regular hand-mirror, of sufficient size to allow a really *satisfactory* view. These hand-mirrors are very convenient, to be used in conjunction with the large dressing-glass. Their cost is but trifling. The toilet-pincushion should always have pins in it. A small work-box properly furnished with needles, scissors, thimble, and cotton-spools, ought also to find a place on the dressing-table, in case the visiter [*sic*] may have occasion to repair any accident that may have happened to her dress.
>
> (1864: 32)

While the guest prepares herself in privacy, the hostess waits to receive her in the parlor, the public face of a genteel home. Leslie advised that the guest should be seated "in the corner of a sofa, or in a fauteuil, or large comfortable chair." Like Webster, she taught her readers to appreciate the details and distinctions of furnishings. For example, if the visitor must take a place in a rocking-chair the hostess should provide a footstool because "the dizzy and ungraceful practice of rocking in a rocking-chair is now discontinued by all genteel people, except when entirely alone." Instead the author recommended stuffed easy chairs on casters. "Half a dozen of various forms are not considered too many" (Leslie 1864: 33).[7]

Although furniture styles and forms crossed national boundaries, their social meanings were often rooted in national cultures. With these nuances in mind, Mrs. Alfred Sidgwick offered her fellow English women insight into the private life of Germans. Of German parentage but born and raised in England, Sidgwick used the language of furniture to translate between the two cultures. For example, she noted that the layout of a German drawing room might seem old-fashioned to outsiders. "There was invariably a sofa and a table in front of the sofa, and a rug or small carpet under the table." But this particular arrangement was rooted in a system of deference in which "the sofa is considered the place of honour to which a hostess invites her leading guest" (Sidgwick 1912: 102). Where Leslie taught her readers to parse the variety of seating options, Sidgwick explained that German hostesses had to negotiate a complicated array of "absurd titles" to place the correct person on the sofa. (She likened the task to that of the British hostess who must organize guests properly at the dinner table.) In Germany, the simplicity of furniture forms belied a similarly intricate system of etiquette that demanded weighing guests' status and then placing them appropriately. To make her point Sidgwick told the story of an English girl who mistakenly took a place on the sofa. "The hostess promptly and audibly told [the girl] to get up, for she knew it was not an affair to pass off as a joke." Lifelong feuds had begun, "all turn[ing] on a *Kaffee Klatsch* and the wrong women on the sofa" (102–3).

As described in etiquette books, furniture provided both the context and means for polite social intercourse, enabling guests to manage their self-presentation, status, and decorum away from home and in turn permitting hosts to demonstrate their hospitality, attentiveness, and refinement in the private sphere. By contrast, domestic advice literature tended to underscore the importance of economy and the role of the home in shaping the moral character of its inhabitants. Offering advice on furniture construction and cleaning alongside information on cooking, child-rearing, and plumbing, these works emphasized harmony and practicality, often scoffing at those who valued ornamentation and display at the expense of a smoothly running household. Furnishings were meant to set the proper moral tone for family life and help create a respite from the corrupting forces of the public sphere. No less committed to gentility and civil social interactions than etiquette books and conduct manuals, domestic advice literature often calculated the financial and familial costs of perfect conformity to refined social rituals. To this end, they paid less attention to details of style, design, and ornamentation.

This attitude is well represented by Catharine Beecher's widely circulated 1845 *Treatise on Domestic Economy*.[8] For Beecher home was first and foremost the site of women's labor and a setting for uplifting family morals. Too much attention to the front of house endangered the smooth operation of the back of the house, particularly the kitchen. The result of such miscalculation was domestic disorder, cross housewives, and familial discord. Beecher advised:

> It would be far better, for a lady to give up some expensive article, in the parlor, and apply the money, thus saved, for kitchen conveniences, than to have a stinted supply, where the most labor is to be performed. If our Countrywomen would devote more to comfort and convenience, and less to show, it would be a great improvement. Expensive mirrors and pier-tables in the parlor, and an unpainted, gloomy, ill-furnished kitchen, not unfrequently are found under the same roof.
>
> (1845: 163)

Privileging show over comfort and convenience was "a weakness and folly" that compromised the honesty of home life.[9] According to Beecher, "Sometimes a parlor, and company-chamber, will be furnished in a style suitable only for the wealthy, while the table will be supplied with shabby linen, and imperfect crockery, and every other part of the house will look, in comparison with these fine rooms, mean and niggardly" (1845: 189). The home was not a place to put the needs of strangers over those of loved ones. Instead Beecher's *Treatise on Domestic Economy* and similar domestic advice manuals emphasized the role of furniture in safeguarding family comfort. While explaining how to sweep "a parlor with handsome furniture," Beecher specified the furnishings to be protected from dust. These included "sofas, centre table, piano, books, and [the] mantelpiece," the trappings of a typical genteel parlor. Likewise, she advised her readers to "dust ornaments, and fine books, with feather brushes, kept for the purpose" (306). Beecher even offered step-by-step directions for building a comfortable couch for chambers and common parlors. ("Have a frame made ... of common stuff, six feet long, twenty-eight inches wide, and twelve inches high. It must be made thus low, because the casters and cushions will raise it several inches.") Once a carpenter constructed the frame, the homemaker could make the cushions and pillows. Beecher endorsed the finished product, observing, "The writer has seen a couch of this kind, in a common parlor, which cost less than eight dollars, was much admired, and was a constant comfort to the feeble mother, as well as many other members of the family" (313). Economy and comfort were once again placed in the service of familial relationships.

Despite differences in emphasis, Leslie and Beecher expressed a shared appreciation for home's uplifting role, depicting it as a site of good conduct and pleasant social interaction sustained by carefully chosen furnishings and decoration. Affirming the separate spheres ideal that defined respectable middle-class culture, each author presented the home as a private space to be protected from the intrusions and compromised conduct of public life, albeit through different means. Likewise, both assumed women's morals, manners, and attention to the needs of others set the proper tone in the domestic sphere. Sometimes the authors imply that the selection and proper use of furnishings revealed refinement; at other times they suggest that furniture refined conduct and character. Together they reflect the complexity and contradictions that shaped home furnishings' role in nineteenth-century life. In short, etiquette manuals such as Leslie's and domestic advice literature like Beecher's treated furniture as both markers and makers of social and moral respectability. While a person might possess an innate character expressed in their home furnishings, the proper arrangement of domestic goods and decorations could, in turn, instill morals. An 1873 article on "The Domestic Use of Design" in the *Furniture Gazette* echoed this belief, noting:

> There can be no doubt that altogether, independently of direct intellectual culture, either from books or society, the mind is moulded and coloured to a great extent by the persistent impressions produced upon it by the most familiar objects that daily meet the eye .... That a carefully regulated and intelligent change of the domestic scenery about a sick person is beneficial is obvious, and yet there are few who correctly apprehend to how great an

> extent the character, and especially the temper, may be affected by the nature of ordinary physical surroundings.
>
> ("The Domestic Use of Design" 1873: 4)

Nor was this association of furniture with refinement, respectability, and character exclusive to a specific social class. Etiquette books and domestic manuals referred to their readers as "ladies," a term of often ambiguous meaning (Richter 2005). On the one hand, etiquette books seem to be advising leisured and accomplished women of an elevated social and economic status. On the other hand, home advice manuals addressed a class of women whose domestic labor was perfectly compatible with refined sensibilities and respectable conduct (Grier 1988: 67). In practice, the boundary between these groups of "ladies" was permeable. For example, Mrs. Sidgwick wrote of a German professor who claimed that the surest way to understand his nation's home life was by viewing his wife's linen cabinet: "an immense cupboard occupying the longest wall in the room ... [with] shelf upon shelf, pile upon pile of linen, exactly ordered, tied with lemon coloured ribbon, embroidered beyond doubt with the initials of the lady who brought it here as a bride" (1912: 109–10). Indeed for many middle-class Germans the linen cabinet was a national symbol, suggesting both refined living and the skill and frugality of the German housewife. In the words of a popular embroidery pattern that adorned many linen cupboards: "Sweet smelling, soft, snow white, protected lies herein, the most beautiful linens rewarding the industry of the faithful hands of the German housewife – her ornament and glory" (Reagin 2007: 44). No wonder Sidgwick noted that the professor's wife, a lady and celebrated musician, "had put up and made every blind and curtain, and had even carpentered and upholstered an empire sofa in her drawing-room" (1912: 110).

In the United States, the same rules of etiquette and domestic propriety presented to elite readers were reprinted in ten-cent pamphlets and circulated among working-class girls, immigrants, and African Americans. (Certainly, these shared sensibilities were confirmed by Beecher's acknowledgement that many women chose to have parlors even when they could not easily afford them as well as by her instructions for thrifty homemade alternatives.) Furniture manufacturers simultaneously contributed to and exploited this shared culture, producing and advertising goods of varied quality to accommodate a range of budgets. Design books often depicted variations of a single good in one sheet or plate, allowing the viewer to take in the range of ornamentation, quality, and price at a glance. In this way, like etiquette and domestic manuals, they drew and erased lines of status by simultaneously revealing socioeconomic distinctions and affirming shared values.

Once again nineteenth-century fiction provides rich examples of how furnishings were employed to confound and clarify the relationship between economic status, women's domestic labor, and respectability. Published in 1837, Catharine Maria Sedgwick's *The Poor Rich Man, and The Rich Poor Man* depicted domestic refinement among the urban poor. Although protagonist Harry Aiken's tenement flat is permeated by paid and unpaid labor, Sedgwick notes that he has "a conscience void of offence." His character and that of his wife, Susan, is reflected in their home where "the floor of the room was partly covered with a carpet, and the part visible as clean as hands could make it. It was summer, and the blinds were closed, admitting only light enough to enable the persons within to carry on their occupations" (Sedgwick 1837: 81). In the text as at home, small details spoke volumes; the Aikens's poverty did not exclude an appreciation for nice things or a desire for privacy. Almost sixty years later, in *Maggie a Girl of the Streets*, Stephen Crane paid similar attention to domestic details to separate his protagonist from the poverty and violence of her family. Maggie

> contemplated the dark, dust-stained walls, and the scant and crude furniture of her home. A clock, in a splintered and battered oblong box of varnished wood, she suddenly regarded as an abomination .... The almost vanished flowers in the carpet-pattern, she conceived to be newly hideous. Some faint attempts she had made with blue ribbon, to freshen the appearance of a dingy curtain, she now saw to be piteous.
>
> (Crane 1896: 47)

She carefully repairs broken furniture and applies a lambrequin to the mantelpiece in her tenement home only to have them torn apart by her drunken mother. The fate of these decorating efforts foreshadows Maggie's destruction.

The belief that furniture shaped and reflected character transcended prescriptive literature and fiction, finding a place in the politics and social science of the late nineteenth century. Harkening back to Harriet Beecher Stowe, activist and sociologist W.E.B. Du Bois used the language of domestic goods to catalog the disadvantages and accomplishments of African Americans in slavery and freedom (Figure 4.3). Recounting the living conditions of slaves, he wrote, "The African knew nothing of the little niceties and comforts of the civilized home—everything of beauty and daintiness had disappeared with the rude uprooting of the African home, and little had been learned to replace them" (Du Bois 1901: 492). The impact was detrimental and long lasting. More than forty years after the end of slavery, Du Bois observed "a curious bareness and roughness in the ordinary Negro home, the remains of an uncouthness which in slavery times made the home anything but a pleasant lovable place." He described homes with "few chairs with backs" that could be best described in terms of absent domestic amenities: "no sheets on the beds, no books, no newspapers, no closets or out-houses, no bed-rooms, no table-cloths and very

FIGURE 4.3 DuBois Piano Lesson. Photograph courtesy of Library of Congress, Prints and Photographs Division, LC-DIG-ppmsca-08779.

few dishes, no carpets and usually no floors, no windows, no pictures, no clocks, no lights at night save that of the fire-place." In sum, "little or nothing save bare rough shelter" (492). And yet, given the chance, many African Americans seized upon freedom to shape their domestic lives and reframe their futures.

Despite his concerns about slavery's impact on Black domesticity, at the 1900 Paris *Exposition Universelle* Du Bois presented images of the refined homes of African Americans as a rebuttal to white racism and as a measure of Black character. Like so many others he put his faith in domestic furnishings as a universal language of social respectability.

Culture is complicated, and it is dangerous to overstate the causation behind any particular system of values and meaning-making. Nonetheless, in the nineteenth century new processes in the production and distribution of both furniture and texts combined with a focus on the domestic sphere to create a broad audience of readers informed about furnishings and their cultural power. The meanings ascribed to furniture reflected the celebration of the private sphere as a site of moral and refined conduct associated with femininity and women's influence. To a considerable degree, the ability to conform to this domestic ideal was shaped by wealth and social class, and yet furniture conveyed something less tangible and more valuable than the economic means of its owners. A well-chosen piece of furniture communicated that one knew the proper rules of conduct and understood the needs and expectations of others. A properly outfitted home, a carefully decorated room, or even the possession of a few good pieces signaled knowledge of and conformity to a shared culture of genteel respectability and moral character. Taken together, works such as Webster's *Encyclopaedia of Domestic Economy,* Leslie's *Ladies' Guide to True Politeness and Perfect Manners*, and Beecher's *Treatise on Domestic Economy* educated readers to decipher the meanings behind the items in Uncle Tom's cabin or Maggie's tenement and, in turn, to use furniture to shape and reveal their own characters. Many, like Mrs. Alfred Sidgwick and W.E.B. Du Bois, turned the domestic sphere inside out to assert their fluency in a shared language of respectability and civility. Thus, with its meanings rooted in the private sphere, furniture also became a language of the public self.

MOVING STORIES: FURNITURE GOES PUBLIC

In 1879 William Marin and his parents migrated from Michigan to the Red River Valley in western Minnesota. Several years later when William decided to tell the story of his childhood on America's western frontier, he did so by focusing on his family's furnishings. Like so many of his contemporaries, he felt it necessary to catalogue his domestic fixtures in some detail:

> We had an organ, the only one in the neighborhood, and some of the old walnut furniture that we had saved from the hotel fire, including tall walnut beds and dressers and chairs of the U. S. Grant period. Of course there was a whatnot, and we had a rather fine old cherry center table on which reposed a pressed leather family album .... We also had rocking chairs, cane-seated

> dining-room chairs, and a sofa covered with large figured Brussels .... The pictures on the wall were chromos of the style of 1870 that might now be attractive to the amateur curio-seeker who believes that such specimens are valuable antiques.
>
> (Marin 1931: 138)

Echoing prescriptive literature and contemporary fiction, Marin used domestic goods to communicate his family's place in the world, giving it standing and differentiating him from his neighbors. All together the enumerated items intimated a certain level of refined living in an otherwise rugged setting. Marin noted that his home "was probably furnished much better than that of the average prairie pioneer" and that "many of the early settlers did not have the pretentious home, comparatively speaking, that we had." In addition to recounting his family's domestic items, he explained that "we lived each day as best we could using the entire house" rather than living in just one room as so many of his neighbors did (Marin 1931: 138, 139). By contrast, Marin noted that many settlers made do with homemade furniture—"a pine table, benches, beds, a trunk or two, a couple of chairs, and a wooden cupboard"—in a single room. The lowest level of domestic refinement was embodied by the "bachelor's hall," where a single man passed his days with just a bed, a pine table, benches, and a few shelves. To underscore the primitive life within such a home, Marin concluded, "The housekeeping particulars of such an establishment would not be at all edifying" (140).

A little over a decade after Marin's arrival in Minnesota, Frederick Jackson Turner delivered his famous paper, "The Significance of the Frontier in American History," at the 1893 World's Columbian Exposition in Chicago. In it Turner considered how the repeated settlement of "free land" had created a uniquely American character, as settlers encountered primitive conditions, were stripped of their civilized ways, and sought again to conquer the wilderness—a story that has long dominated the popular imaginings of the American West. Yet William Marin used the furnishings of his family and neighbors to tell a different story of life on the late nineteenth-century American frontier. The organ suggested a home filled with religious music; the center table connoted the propriety of a parlor; the whatnot conjured carefully displayed ornaments and souvenirs; and three different kinds of seating indicated an appreciation that household members and guests had varied needs for comfort and status. Despite their placement in a sod dwelling, these items offered a narrative of stability and continuity rather than reinvention.[10] The furniture, for both Marin and his readers, communicated that western settlers had successfully brought the material culture and values of civilized domesticity with them to the frontier—a self-conscious act that required perhaps as much will as conquering and settling an unfamiliar, wild terrain.

Variations of Marin's story abound in the nineteenth century, as furniture and its meanings enabled people to stabilize their surroundings and identities in new and unfamiliar settings, to place themselves in a shared culture of respectability. In German Southwest Africa, for example, housewives buttressed the efforts of imperial rule by outfitting their homes with the trappings of middle-class domesticity, washing, bleaching, ironing, and hanging white curtains. In this new context, the linen cabinet offered familiarity, comfort, and a sense of national and racial superiority (Reagin 2007: 65–6). Faced with the dislocations of migration and frontier living, men and women sought to remind themselves and their loved ones that they were essentially unchanged or perhaps changed for the better. They transported the markers of domesticity and respectability—books, pianos, furniture, table linen, and silverware. Along the Kansas frontier, Martha Farnsworth celebrated the happiness of her second marriage by recording her domestic arrangements in her diary: "I have one pretty Wolf rug, which I placed in front of a Bench, I made myself and covered, then I have a box, covered and two chairs. I got at [the] grocery common manila wrapping paper and made window shades, and we have our Piano, and we have music in our home and are happy" (Kwolek-Folland 1984: 34). Like Marin, many chose to expose the private goods of their homes to public view making a case for their public standing (Figure 4.4). In April 1871, Emily Combes reported on

FIGURE 4.4 David Hilton family, near Weissert, Custer County, Nebraska, *c.* 1887. Photograph courtesy of the Nebraska State Historical Society.

her new life in Manhattan, Kansas, "The houses are neat and pretty many being built of stone and furnished nicely – plenty of books, carpets, pictures, [and a] piano" (30). Such letters "back East" were often accompanied by photographs documenting domestic furnishings and serving as further evidence of refined living. Indeed many families carried their furnishings outdoors to ensure better quality of their photographic cataloging.

Nor was the reliance on domestic goods as a public presentation of self limited to the frontier. In 1889, when Jane Addams established the first settlement house in the United States, she used her furnishings to assert the respectability of herself, her mission, and her new neighbors on Halstead Street in Chicago. Recounting her earliest days at Hull House, Addams wrote that she and her cofounder, Ellen Gates Starr, "furnished the house as we would have furnished it were it in another part of the city, with the photographs and other impedimenta we had collected in Europe, and with a few bits of family mahogany." Downplaying the exceptional nature of their undertaking, Addams cast a groundbreaking act of social reform in a traditional light, echoing Catharine Beecher's description of a "handsome parlor." She concluded, "Probably no young matron ever placed her own things in her own home with more pleasure than that with which we first furnished Hull-House" (Addams 1910: 94). Addams used the furnishings of Hull House to tell a story of continuity and conventional gender roles even as she staked a claim to the new frontiers of urban life and women's political engagement.[11]

In Marin's and Addams's accounts, furniture is both object and metaphor. Embodying values of respectability and domesticity, it opened up new cultural spaces by rendering physical spaces—the frontier or an urban slum—comfortable and marking them as hospitable to refinement. This dynamic inspired some surprising furniture stories. For example, in November 1885, the *Railway Age* printed an article on the unlikely pairing of women's political rights and railroad furniture. According to the piece, the members of a recent women's rights convention in New York unanimously endorsed a measure involving railroad car seats. "The complaint was that the seats in ... public conveyances were constructed entirely for the use of men, and were consequently too high for the accommodation of most women" ("Women's Complaint about Car Seats" 1885: 722). Women's rights advocates understood that to enter into politics, they needed access to public spaces and thus required furniture that reflected and legitimized their presence. The women in the article called for lower seats, drafted a memorial to this effect, and circulated it for signatures. And they were not alone in noting the important and contested role of furniture in rendering men and women comfortable during train travel: almost a decade earlier, the *New York Times* chastised selfish male travelers who complained that parlor car seats were designed without arms or footrests to please female passengers and "satisfy the exigencies of feminine fashion" ("Arms and the Chair" 1876: 4). Certainly chivalry demanded such a sacrifice.

The debate over railroad car seating was a chapter in a larger nineteenth-century story that public spaces could be rendered "homelike"—a story few told better than the American industrialist George Mortimer Pullman. Inspired by etiquette books' portrayal of the parlor as a stage for respectable conduct, Pullman designed his luxurious railroad cars to reproduce the behavior, manners, and privacy associated with a well-appointed home. What better way to regulate a new and unwieldy social space characterized by intimacy, anonymity, and social heterogeneity? Pullman spent extravagantly on elaborate car interiors—putting his faith in fine woods, rich upholstery, and elegant rugs to bring the best elements of private conduct to public interactions (Figure 4.5). Like the authors of domestic advice manuals, he asserted that civility could be nurtured, and that the right furnishings would cultivate instincts for good manners and a harmonious public life. He explained, "I have always held that people are very greatly influenced by their physical surroundings ... Bring [a man] into a room elegantly carpeted and furnished and the effect upon his bearing is immediate" (Doty 1893: 23). In a finely furnished railway car, according to Pullman, no traveler "would expectorate on the surroundings and wipe his boots on the accessories" (Pullman Company 1893: 7).

So complete was the association between Pullman cars and domestic interiors that many popular stories of train travel became stories about furniture. Alongside descriptions of routes, sights, and engineering feats, railway guides offered travelers detailed descriptions of fine woods, elaborate hangings, rich upholsteries, and silver-plated metalwork. In an 1883 guidebook, the Passenger Department of the Savannah, Florida, and Western Railway Company boasted about the buffet in one of its sleeping cars: "The buffet's finish, both in woodwork and marquetry, corresponds with the interior of the car, [and] the effect is highly pleasing, suggesting in convenience and luxury an elegant sideboard in a richly appointed mansion" (Graves 1883: 11). Guidebooks and railroad brochures often listed the variety of decorating styles used in their cars alongside descriptions of the latest technological innovations. An 1853 article in *Scientific American* praised a new car on the Hudson River Railroad by noting that it was "furnished with a sofa, four chairs, a looking glass and a small center table" (Mencken 1957: 17). Moved onto the trains and into public life, the standard furnishings of a middle-class parlor connoted not only stability and gentility, but also progress.

ACTS OF TRANSLATION AND TRANSFORMATION

Somewhat ironically, the use of furniture and ornamentation in railroad cars became its own domestic style, influencing home decorating decisions—and not always for the better. Stories of railroad furniture may have started out as efforts to stabilize social and technological change, but something got lost (or perhaps gained) in translating furniture's domestic meanings to public life. In 1925,

Pullman Parlor Car.

FIGURE 4.5 Pullman parlor car, "Railway Passenger Travel," *Scribner's Magazine*, September 1888. Photograph courtesy of Amy G. Richter.

Charles Byers implored readers of the *Modern Priscilla Home Furnishing Book* to reject "the Early Pullman period of American home decoration ... when massive, ugly, battle-axe black walnut furniture was our heart's desire, and inflammatory color schemes in wall and floor coverings helped to make us a nation of color illiterates" (1925: 2). Advertisements, etiquette books, and advice literature had taught people, especially women, to furnish their homes in the service of family morality and social gentility. In turn, businesses and retailers appropriated furniture's domestic associations to make commercial settings respectable and inviting to female consumers. Public or commercial parlors permitted women to claim new spaces and roles while maintaining their association with the home. These spaces, however, exaggerated the details and ornamentation of domestic design, a point often lost on consumers who sought to incorporate the taste and trappings of public domesticity into their private homes.[12]

Byer's criticism suggests that the language of furniture was mistranslated when it crossed the boundary between private and public, home and market, and back again. In 1898, Stephen Crane poked fun at this cultural misappropriation in "The Bride Comes to Yellow Sky." When a newlywed couple encounters the opulent furnishings of a Pullman car for the first time, they are disoriented, swept away by the possibilities of such unfamiliar splendor. While the groom displayed "the pride of an owner," his wife's "eyes opened wider as she contemplated the sea-green figured velvet, the shining brass, silver, and glass, the wood that gleamed as darkly brilliant as the surface of a pool of oil." Imagining such luxury as "the environment of their new estate [...] the man's face in particular beamed with an elation that made him appear ridiculous" (Crane [1898] 1993: 80).

Transported and translated to the needs of commercial public spaces, furnishings disrupted the values of self-restraint, domestic labor, and propriety associated with the best kind of bourgeois home life. Perhaps no space embodied and manipulated this transformation more than the nineteenth-century department store (Leach 1984; Abelson 1989). Here, in spaces such as Paris's Bon Marché, elaborate ladies' lounges, public parlors, and domesticated touches lured women into commercial settings. In Emile Zola's *The Ladies' Paradise* (1883), furniture, staircases, fountains, rugs, fabrics, and trimmings compelled women to buy what they did not need and often could not afford. Looking at his store overflowing with female shoppers Octave Mouret, the book's protagonist, explained, "Oh! These ladies aren't in my shop, they're at home here" (Zola [1883] 2008: 248). By this he meant that they were comfortable and catered to in a space designed for them, but also that they revealed their flaws and weaknesses, overwhelmed by desire for the goods on display. Carried-away, female shoppers deceived themselves, lied to their husbands, and even shoplifted as they sought out the beautiful, the new, and the exotic. The drive to sell and consume uncoupled furnishings from their moral role in the home and taught them to speak a new language of desire.[13] Zola seemed to warn his readers that if furniture told stories, it could also mislead by confusing consumers and confounding the distinctions of status. In the right hands décor might shape character for the better, but in commercial settings it could also stir up emotion and overload the senses.

Despite Zola's concerns, or in confirmation of them, the elaborate displays and abundant goods of urban department stores oriented women to an expanding world of "cosmopolitan domesticity"—an ideal that merged foreign wares and decorating styles with the intimate self-expression of the bourgeois home (Hoganson 2007). By the end of the nineteenth century, furniture was routinely produced, marketed, and consumed in a self-consciously global marketplace. This sensibility reflected not only the growth and elaboration of local and international marketplaces, but also a new vision of domesticity and the values communicated through household furnishings. Western women had long looked to French and British furniture for fashionability and good taste, but now a new crop of decorating and home publications educated them to cast a wider net. British, American, and German women's magazines reported on the homes and furnishings of "Mongol, 'Gypsy,' Arab, Chinese, Ceylonese, Mexican, Egyptian, Burmese, Turkish, Indian, West African, and Eskimo women" (Reagin 2007: 55). Articles from *Decorator and Furnisher*, for example, offered details of "A Roman Studio" and "An Italian Renaissance Dining-Room" alongside "An Indian Room" and "Interiors in the Oriental Style" ("A Roman Studio" 1884: 87; "An Indian Room" 1889: 38; "An Interior in the Turkish Style" 1894: 69; "An Italian Renaissance Dining-Room" 1896: 69; "Interiors in the Oriental Style" 1896: 103). An article about "The Exhibition of Rooms at the Crystal Palace" included an image of an "Oriental boudoir or tea room" alongside a Louis Quinze bedroom and a Louis Seize drawing room ("The Exhibition of Rooms at the Crystal Palace" 1892: 97).

Unlike previous etiquette manuals and domestic advice literature that focused on the privacy of home life, late nineteenth-century publications emphasized the ways in which furniture could tell stories of engagement with the world. Rivaling the eclectic taste of George Pullman's parlor cars or the splendor of urban emporia, wealthy women and their decorators created homes with themed rooms to showcase the furniture styles of distinct countries and regions (Hoganson 2007). Beyond more rarefied social circles, women's magazines provided examples and simple instructions for introducing Asian touches into one's home.[14] "Cozy corners" were an easy, popular, and economical way to participate in this Orientalist trend, permitting women of limited means to convert a small part of a room into an Eastern oasis. A typical article from *Ladies' Home Journal* explained how to make a cozy corner inexpensively:

> Take a long, narrow mirror, framed as cheaply as possible, and fasten it firmly against the wall corner-wise, with a corner shelf above it; then have India drapery silk, plain figured, or the Oriental muslin imitation (the former is about seventy-five cents a yard–fifty cents if plain–and the latter fifteen cents), and festoon it across the top, tacking it to the edge of the shelf. On each side catch it here and there in a knot through which a tiny Japanese

> fan can be thrust, if you have tired of this style of decoration. Continue the drapery across the bottom, and in front of the mirror stand a small table holding a palm, in a handsome bit of pottery, a figure or a pretty photograph. On the top shelf have a large Japanese jar or a bright piece of bric-a-brac of some kind.
>
> ("Cozy Corners for Parlors" 1890: ii)

In 1904 William Martin Johnson's *Inside of One Hundred Homes* confirmed that ordinary American women had become fluent in the language of international goods. With photographs of modest homes and small flats from places such as Orange, New Jersey; Cleveland, Ohio; and Hartford, Connecticut, his photographs and text reveal typical interiors decorated with East Indian printed cottons, Bagdad (*sic*) curtains, China matting, Japanese parasols, and Oriental fans (Figure 4.6).[15]

FIGURE 4.6 Cozy corner, from William Martin Johnson's *Inside of One Hundred Homes* (1904). Photograph courtesy of Amy G. Richter.

A new generation of experts and advertisers encouraged consumers to use domestic goods to tell complex and contradictory stories that merged national identity and international knowledge. And so Charles Eastlake advocated a design aesthetic that looked back to English forms, incorporated Japanese and Middle Eastern styles, and proved very popular in the United States, where his *Hints on Household Taste* went through six editions between 1872 and 1883. The American editor of the 1874 edition explained, "Although Mr. Eastlake's book is addressed to Englishmen, there is hardly a sentence in it, apart from some local allusions, which may not be read by Americans as if directly intended for them" (Eastlake 1874: vii). This round-robin style of cultural borrowing permitted those who appropriated design elements from the East to feel an affinity with other Western women who engaged in similar acts. Even in her admiring depiction of German home life, Mrs. Sidgwick could not resist snickering at what passed for "English fashion" in Germany. "You see charming rooms in Germany nowadays, but they are never quite like English ones, even when your friends point to a wicker chair or an Eastern carpet and tell you that they love everything English" (Sidgwick 1912: 104). Furnishings now spoke with so many voices and accents that German housewives understood Eastern carpets as English and Americans embraced Japanese design as the gift of Mr. Eastlake.

Rather than conveying participation in a shared moral order or creating stability in the face of change, furniture now served as both means and evidence of individual identity and even reinvention. Writing of a Turkish-style interior in 1894, *The Decorator and Furnisher* explained:

> The great charm of such outré belongings is the agreeable sense of rest and change they impart to the mind as compared with our own home-made furnishings. The effect is somewhat similar to that of travel, in which the strangest things have the greatest charm. The average American cottage and its furnishings are hard, boxy and rectangular, and being as it were the automatic products of machinery they lack sentiment, whereas Eastern products being mostly hand-made, and by a slow-going people to whom machinery is not a necessity, a delightful irregularity, softness, and the play of human sentiment pervades both their conception and execution.
>
> ("An Interior in the Turkish Style" 1894: 16)

The cozy corner and "exotic" goods were not the only design elements capable of catalyzing and embodying self-transformation. Immigrant Mary Antin recounted her wonder at the American furnishings of her tenement home. In Russia, she and her family had been accustomed to "upholstered parlors, embroidered linen, silver spoons and candlesticks, goblets of gold, kitchen shelves shining with copper and brass." And yet, writing many years later she remained impressed by her first encounter with the simple wooden furnishings of her new home. After a dinner of canned foods, she and her siblings were introduced to "a curious piece of furniture on runners." Marking the difference between her old and new life, Antin explained, "One born and bred to the use of a rocking-chair cannot imagine how ludicrous people can make themselves when attempting to use it for the first time." For her becoming American meant conquering "the American machine of perpetual motion" (Antin 1912: 185). For still other immigrants of the time, American identity was embodied in the heavy, machine-made furnishings of the "Pullman style" that were falling out of favor with the middle class.[16]

By the century's end, furniture continued to tell stories, but the linguistic possibilities were more varied and personalized. Once imagined as a shared language of the private sphere, furniture's vocabulary and syntax had been expanded into public life, transformed and widely appropriated across lines of race, class, and ethnicity. Less focused on common values and character, furniture now spoke of identity and even personality.[17] Mrs. H.R. Haweis, in *The Art of Decoration* rejected "the fatal sheep-walk which the timid and the ignorant so soon beat out, the stereotyped house of the stereotyped art-decorator" (1881: 21). Likewise, an 1898 article in *House Beautiful* praised the "individuality of homes" and advised that furnishings must be lived "into shape, as it were, and [made to] adapt themselves to look like one[self]" (Abbott 1898). And the range of available choices was considerable. Advocates of the Arts and Crafts movement embedded a new language of morality into not only the aesthetics but the construction of domestic furnishings. But as they rejected the vulgarity and cheap opulence of machine-made goods, utopians and feminists sought to transfer the best aspects of industrial efficiency into the home, reframing the domestic sphere as a site of modernization.[18]Still others held on to an older vocabulary of good taste. Indeed just a year before *House Beautiful* celebrated domestic individualism, Edith Wharton looked to an earlier sensibility, recommending:

> If little can be spent in buying furniture, willow arm-chairs with denim cushions and solid tables with stained legs and covers of denim or corduroy will be more satisfactory than the "parlor suit" turned out in thousands by the manufacturer of cheap furniture, or the pseudo-Georgian or pseudo-Empire of the dealer in "high-grade goods."
>
> (Wharton and Codman 1897: 26)

It is easy to be overwhelmed by the details and distinctions of this turn-of-the-century advice, but the belief that furniture both revealed and shaped its owners permeated the various schools of thought. In many ways, this linguistic proliferation informs our contemporary furniture stories. Even today, when furniture speaks, our own lips move, mouthing the words "I am."

CHAPTER FIVE

The Public Setting

SYLVAIN CORDIER

As functional objects thought of primarily in domestic contexts, pieces of furniture are also useful tools in the staging of public space, in expressing varying degrees of authority and power, and in the organization of the social fabric. The conditions of their display establish them within a complex and varied language, providing points of reference and key readings on the relationships between different social participants. In this chapter, I will attempt to highlight, through a comparative analysis of mainly French and some British examples, the main issues in the nineteenth century relating to the use of furnishings in spaces considered as public, emphasizing those that served as seats of authority—especially that of the head of state, whether that be an emperor, king, or prime minister. The chapter will focus on furnishings outside of the private sphere, where they visually and practically participated in a discourse on societal reactions and relationships to authority. Having inherited numerous principles established in preceding centuries, it became necessary in the course of the nineteenth century to rethink and redefine the public's relationship to the social function of the arrangement and décor of these authoritative spaces.

FURNITURE AND THE NECESSITY OF AN ETIQUETTE

France: The construction of authority

Throughout the nineteenth century, the renewal of the palatial state apartments in France illustrates particularly well how furnishings were employed to characterize and organize public spaces. The *Etiquette du Palais Imperial* (Etiquette of the Imperial Palace) (1806) and the *Règlement pour l'ameublement des palais impériaux* (Regulations for the Furnishings of the Imperial Palaces) (Archives nationale de France, 02/240, 6 Theimida Year XIII, July 25, 1805) are two foundational texts that address the protocol of the Napoleonic court. For the administration of the Imperial Household, the most pressing question concerned how to furnish spaces that were to welcome guests to the palace according to their rank, to define and manifest the authority of the inviting sovereign. This concern reflects an intention to confer within the space of the court a grammar that expresses a hierarchy of honors and the use of seating to create a gradual progression toward the sovereign. Aesthetic concerns, the restoration of traditions, and the creation of new protocols were combined with a desire to support Parisian industries and artisans.

The *Etiquette imperiale* established a clear distinction between spaces of representation, or those open to the public of courtiers, military officers, diplomats, and their spouses that were furnished to receive and to set the scene of the progression toward the center of power, and the spaces reserved for the daily life of the emperor and empress. Within the palaces of Tuileries, Saint-Cloud, Fontainebleau, and Compiègne, those rooms known as the "State Apartments" were distinguished by protocol from a second type of space, called the "ordinary apartments of their majesties." A secondary distinction was imposed on these latter apartments that differentiated the more private reception spaces, called "apartments of honor," which adhered to the same rules that applied to the State Apartments, from the truly private spaces, where on the contrary, luxury was sought in practicality and comfort. For our purposes, it is the State Apartments that are of the greatest concern, as their furnishing were viewed by the public—that is, those who were invited or admitted within the walls of the palace.

The particular role played by the throne in manifesting monarchical authority in nineteenth-century French palaces, which will be discussed in greater detail later in this chapter, was not the only means by which furnishing represented the preeminent public figure of the sovereign. The state apartments consisted of, on paper, a concert hall, a first salon, a second salon, a throne room, a salon of the emperor or *grand cabinet*, and a gallery. The Apartments of Honor were comprised of a guardroom, two to three salons, a dining room, and another concert hall. The idea was to establish rigorously, through the arrangement and nature of the objects within these rooms, a hierarchical order of spaces. Each person who experienced the succession of apartments, accompanied by a chamberlain, would have realized the meaning of the progression, from the antechamber to the first salon, then from one salon to the next, through to the symbolic presence of the emperor in the throne room and the *grand cabinet*. The *Règlement pour l'ameublement* (1805) states:

> The antechambers and the first rooms were furnished with large benches and stools, covered in tapestry from the Savonnerie ... the second rooms, waiting

> rooms, music and game rooms, rooms of the princes and of LL.MM. [*sic*] are furnished with two armchairs only for LL. MM. And of a sufficient number of X-shaped stools upholstered and stuffed with silk ... Added to that are some consoles with candelabras.
>
> Room of the Council.[1] A grand round table covered in a rich carpet, a sole armchair for S.M., leather upholstered chairs around the table and X-shaped stool around the apartment.

Seating, in its various types, played a principal role in the hierarchy of spaces. In the first two antechambers, for example, the benches and simple stools that welcomed courtiers constituted the most humble degree of this scale of furnishing. Here, the effective presence of the sovereign is not in fact required by the protocol. This presence, which calls for more evident pomp, is envisaged in the second salon, through the sequencing of x-shaped stools, the curial piece of furniture par excellence, which is distinguished from the simple stool by the placement of its feet in an x formation. Either completely gilded or partially gilded and painted white, these backless seats were installed in sufficient numbers along the walls of this room, accompanying a pair of armchairs for the sovereign and his spouse. The decision to continue to use the x-shaped stool, one of the main characteristics that affirmed a court etiquette, seemingly contradicted, by its use, the republican spirit of the Revolution.

Therefore, regarding the rooms that led courtiers progressively toward the Throne Room, the *Etiquette du Palais imperial* prohibited, "as a general rule, the entering of the room where one finds the emperor and empress, no matter the visitor." If this rule is applied to the layout of furniture, this detail elucidates that the two armchairs, installed as a pair in the middle of the x-shaped stools, were not intended to accommodate actual meetings between the monarch and his subjects in this series of rooms, but rather were unoccupied but significant visual markers of the permanence of the imperial authority in each of these spaces. The imperial couple is signified as perpetually present because a pair of seats exclusively associated with them are found in these rooms, in view of everyone, and distinct from the rest of the furnishing, acting as small substitution thrones throughout the progression to the Throne Room. This symbolism is accentuated during the times when the emperor leaves the palace, an order given to turn around the two armchairs.

A letter of 1811, issued from the services of the Imperial Household, allows a glimpse of the particular adaptations necessary to accommodate the realities of life during these years and clearly confirmed the distributive function of the hierarchical arrangement of seats:

> In the apartments of honour and representation, armchairs will be reserved for the Emperor and Empress. The age of Madame [Napoleon's mother]

> must be considered; she will also sit on an armchair. All other people, comprised of princes and princesses of the imperial family will, in the event they are required to sit in the apartments of honour and representation, have chairs, or X-shaped stools, if there are no chairs. However, chairs with backs will be given to princesses of the imperial family who are pregnant ... In the ceremonies for which Their Majesties are on the Throne, or under a canopy ... only the Emperor and Empress sit in the armchairs. All other persons, princes and princesses, grand dignitaries, etc. will remain standing and placed according to their rank.
>
> (Archives nationale de France, 02/556, "Extrait des minutes de la Secrétairerie d'Etat, décision pour l'étiquette du palais," September 12, 1811)

It is clear that furniture functioned above all to reveal the segregation of each person's position, and that court life supposed a frequent "back and forth" of seats to adapt to various differences in formal situations. As such, the furnishing was more a permanent political spectacle than a utilitarian one.

After the fall of the empire in 1814–15, the kings of the Restoration and their administration judged the principles defined by the services of the Napoleonic court's Imperial Household legitimate and pertinent, despite their visceral contempt for the *aventure imperial* of "The Usurper Bonaparte." The commissions for the new seats and wall coverings made for the palaces of Louis XVIII (1815–24), and later Charles X (1824–30), were first motivated by a desire to forget, particularly at the beginning of the reign of Louis XVIII, not the forms of this protocol, but the heraldic presence of the crowned "N" and the imperial eagles. These Napoleonic symbols were replaced by the fleur-de-lis of the monarchy but most of the objects remained. Second, it was necessary to renovate or replace pieces in states of disrepair. In 1818, for example, the state of the furniture of the first room of the Tuileries' State Apartments, which had been delivered fifteen years previously, was judged "ridiculous" (Samoyault-Verlet 1991: 43). The cabinetmaker Pierre-Gaston Brion was commissioned to execute twelve new benches, thirty-six stools, and a chimney screen, which painstakingly respected the furnishing regulations of the first salon enacted under the empire (Langeois 2004: 210–15). Though a few changes were introduced in the etiquette, the spirit of the furnishing and notably the relationship between the type and structure of hierarchical spaces was rigorously maintained.

The ascension to the throne of Louis-Philippe in 1830 marked a change of this spirit in France. A telling example of this transformation is found in Eugène Lami's painting, *Concert given to Queen Victoria by the singers of the Comedic Opera, in the Gallerie des Guise at the Château d'Eu* (1844–8; Palace of Versailles) (Plate 20).[2] The scene depicts the great gallery in the royal residence of Château d'Eu, which had been refurbished for the occasion of the reception of the Queen of England and her husband. The artist was a favorite of the House of Orléans, who had commissioned the painting to commemorate the event. The work demonstrates a synthesis of the spirit of the July Monarchy and its conception for the furniture used for the reception of a head of state. The rupture between the court etiquette of Louis-Philippe and the formal regulations of the preceding monarchies of the Restoration and the empire is clearly translated through the choice of furnishings. Notably, a large family table, situated at the end of the gallery rather than at its center, greets the honored guests represented in the painting. Aside from Louis-Philippe and his wife, Marie-Amélie, Queen Victoria and Prince Albert, sitting on two settees of different heights and surrounded by French princes and princesses, are easily recognized. Two of the princesses—the Princess of Joinville and Princess Clémentine—are seated on two x-shaped stools, while their spouses are on chairs. One of them turns her back to the two royal couples to enjoy the concert better. The guests do not appear to be seated according to a strict hierarchical behavioral code, but rather are situated randomly, depending on their desires, sitting on what they wished. Also remarkable is the assumed eclecticism, none of the seats appearing as a coherent ensemble: the x-shaped Empire stools coexist with the neo-Louis XIV chairs, other seats are neo-Renaissance, while some are covered settees. However, it is nonetheless the very official context of a state reception, suggesting that this intimate familial setting was a political strategy, functioning at the service of court diplomacy. The regime assumed a relaxed character in the regal context where, in principle, the prestige of both households would be solemnly confronted by guests.

Louis-Philippe's regime was well acquainted with the people and the bourgeoisie. In insisting on opening the palaces to society's new elites, and in assuming for himself the image of the bourgeois king living a simple life, Louis-Philippe thought of his court with less ceremony, in contrast to preceding traditions. However, the question then arises of whether the traditional setting of regal power was being erased in favor of a more relaxed way of life, or whether, as reflected in the Lami painting, codes of behavioral familiarity were enacted as a renewal of the political symbol.

Within this context—the permitting of the public to access the private sphere of the new royal family—the role of the bed also took on new importance. Opening wide the doors of Louis-Philippe's bedchamber, it was necessary to demonstrate that the royal couple shared the same bed, thus no longer adhering to the traditional monarchical custom of distinguishing between a parade chamber and a private chamber, that is to say, between a consecrated place of rest for the sovereign's sacred body and a place for domestic life. With the issue of the royal bed now affirmed in the eyes of the public as that of an individual, Louis-Philippe's monarchy was attacking a very strong symbol: this "double bed" expressed not only a lifestyle of simplicity and geniality, but also, and especially, the reversal of the sacred mystery of the monarchy (Courtin 2014: 125–36). It was Louis-Philippe who took the responsibility of removing or, rather, consciously contradicting the bed's traditional impact on the public memory, to the benefit of the new image he intended to convey of the constitutional monarchy.

Napoleon III's ascension to the throne in 1852 raised the issue of the assumed return, in the apartments of the Tuileries Palace, of the décor established under Napoleon I, founder of the dynasty. This ideological concern had to consider, however, how mentalities had evolved since the beginning of the nineteenth century. If the court of the Second Empire drew upon the Napoleonic aesthetic, then it was also de facto heir to the innovations and simplifications introduced under Louis-Philippe, which contrasted significantly with the strict principles of the *Règlement pour l'ameublement* (1805). Therefore, in the State Apartments, armchairs were placed amongst x-shaped stools along the walls of the Grande Salle des Maréchaux (the Great Hall of the Marshals), the room that preceded the State Apartments, which had been intended by the First Empire only to be furnished with benches and stools. Imposed on top of the organizational logic of these hierarchal spaces were considerations regarding the comfort of the courtiers. Boulle furniture and rococo consoles are found in numerous rooms, confirming the triumph of a stylistic, but at the same time protocol, eclecticism over the rigors of the Empire style and its strict typological regulation.

In at least one location, although the French model was adopted, it was not fully understood. In the spring of 1817, the President of the United States, James Monroe, decided to order furniture for the Oval Room of the White House (Cordier 2012b: 131–6). The presidential residence had recently been restored after suffering severe damage during the Anglo-American War of 1812–14. Monroe had begun his career as a diplomat in France during the Consulat, the period of French government of France from the fall of the Directoire in 1799 until the start of the Napoleonic Empire in 1804, and had retained the particular Francophile sentiment. He thought that furniture suitable for what would be the public reception room of the official home of the young nation's head of state should be ordered from Paris. A congressional commission was formed to control the budget, the commissioners being responsible for finding a cabinetmaker worthy of the task. They chose Pierre-Antoine Bellangé (1757–1827), supplier to the Garde-Meuble of the French Crown. The correspondence exchanged regarding this commission indicates that the president stated his wishes fairly precisely regarding the seating he desired. Taking into consideration the size of the room, the White House expected a modest number of simple and elegant chairs and armchairs made of mahogany and decorated with the motif of an eagle, its wings outstretched. Imagine the surprise when they unwrapped the delivery from Paris to find a much larger than anticipated ensemble of furniture, which included a console, two settees, two wing chairs, eighteen armchairs, eighteen regular chairs, four x-shaped stools, six footed-stools, and two screens. All had been made with gilded wood rather than mahogany and adorned with an olive branch motif instead of the eagles. The United States officials accused the French of cheating them, as the final bill was of course much higher than expected. The response of the commissioners responsible for the exchange is telling: in Paris, the requests from the American president to furnish a reception room for the head of state had been judged too modest. Commissioning Bellangé, who normally worked for the Garde-Meuble, to execute the palatial order from the United States speaks volumes about the difference in customs on either side of the Atlantic Ocean, but it also reveals how important the furnishing of a public space as a symbol of political power was at this time. From the American point of view, the ensemble delivered was shocking. It revealed a strong will to compose a semblance of a throne room, certain people interpreting the presence of the pair of wing chairs among the armchairs and other seats as the chairs of a higher rank, destined for the presidential couple to distinguish themselves from the rest of the citizens. Tension also developed particularly around the presence of the four x-shaped stools that were associated with the idea of etiquette contrary to the republican spirit, prioritizing citizens who were supposed to be considered equal. The resulting debates about this suite of furniture were impassioned. In examining the list of furniture delivered by Bellangé from the perspective of French protocol, it is apparent, however, that in reality, this was an ensemble (the wing chairs, the numerous armchairs and chairs, and the small number of x-shaped stools) for pageantry, but was nonetheless very different from the official furniture of the salon of the State Apartments of a monarchical palace where one would find a large suite of x-shaped stools and two armchairs of representation. It corresponds more, in terms of typology, to a reception room of a powerful Parisian aristocrat such as a Napoleonic marshal or minister. The affair was eventually settled, and Bellangé's furniture for the White House was distributed among other rooms in the residence, the Oval Room being too small to contain such a vast ensemble. It was used until the 1860s, before being auctioned off and replaced.

THE THRONE: SEAT, ICON, FETISH

At the top of the typological hierarchy associated with function and symbol, monarchical thrones of the nineteenth century constitute an extensive corpus. They illustrate particularly well the manner in which the formal discussion of authority and power, from one generation to the next, and from one country to another, uses the furniture-object in the service of ideological discourse. To understand this dialogue in the nineteenth century, it is pertinent to begin our reflection with a Napoleonic example. In terms of staging the power of the

French court during the first decade of the century, the throne room of the main imperial palace, the Tuileries, played an essential role.

Ceremonies such as formal audiences, the presentation of the major state organizations, and tribute to civil servants occurred in the throne room. Napoleon (1769–1821) also used it to receive the Senate, the Conseil d'Etat, the Corps Legislatif, the Tribunat, the Cour de Cassation, or the representatives of these bodies. The award of the Legion d'Honneur was presented in the throne room. The room's function contrasted with those of preceding French monarchies and invented new codes. Whereas the royal court at Versailles focused on the activities of the monarch's person—in the most intimate room, the bedroom, courtiers were admitted by rank to watch the king eat and dress and undress—Napoleon shifted the emphasis from his person, to his position as emperor. In fact, the royal bedroom became Napoleon's throne room.

At the center of this setting, the throne itself—the State Chair—emerged as an effective symbol of the authority of the new sovereign, who had been brought to power by the contingencies of the French Revolution. The model for the throne, designed by Charles Percier (1764–1838) and Pierre Fontaine (1762–1853), became an emblem of the regime; it is therefore found in the majority of the state portraits commissioned to disseminate the official image of the emperor. A slightly modified version of this throne, though still easily recognizable, was also chosen to adorn the crosses of the new chivalric order of the Reunion,[3] instituted by Napoleon in 1811.

The inventories and archives in the Garde-Meuble, responsible for the management of the furniture and objects of art intended for the decoration of royal and imperial dwellings, related to these commissions offer a good idea of how the furnishing of this throne room was conceived (Samoyault 1987). The Napoleonic throne room functioned principally as a venue in which the emperor could receive public homage. The throne room, in conjunction with the adjacent room, the *grand cabinet*, represented in essence the culmination of the Imperial Household administration's attention and reflection, revealing, through the proper arrangement of the space, the place and moment where imperial dignity appeared in all its splendor. As with previous royal arrangements of rooms, Napoleon's court sustained a progressive enfilade of spaces, reinforcing the court's hierarchies. The throne room was preceded by two small antechambers and a large central hall, with the *grand cabinet* even further removed and more private than the throne room. Only princes, marshals, and cardinals were allowed into this inner sanctum.

In the throne room, the seats were distributed in the following way: around the throne itself, placed under a large canopy, were two armchairs of representation—one for the empress and the other for the mother of the emperor. In addition to these distinctive armchairs were six chairs for the princesses of the imperial family, that is, Napoleon's three sisters and three sisters-in-law. Thirty-six x-shaped stools were positioned along the wall. Each chair was luxuriously covered in damask. This numeric distribution—thirty-six/six/two—made each type of seat a multiple of a superior type, giving the impression of surrounding the emperor's throne, which stood alone and was unique. Notably, in the throne room, the emperor was enthroned alone; in contrast to the other rooms in the State Apartments, where the armchairs of representation were placed in pairs. In this room, the empress occupied a seat of a clearly lower rank.

As described in the inventories, this furnishing must, however, only be considered as an ideal plan. The surviving records, both visual and verbal, of the regime demonstrate, in effect, that the throne room was frequently empty of most of the required furniture; during ceremonies the members of the court instead stood around Napoleon's throne. Innocent-Louis Goubaud's painting, *Le deputation du Sénat romain offrant ses hommages à l'empereur* (The deputation of the Roman Senate offering its homage to the emperor),[4] depicts this well (Plate 21). Absent are the seats of representation, chairs, and x-shaped stools; there are also no women in the audience. The presence of chairs did not necessarily signify that the high-level officials concerned had the right to sit on them. The seat was in fact more of a signifier of imperial presence than a functional object that could be used by those in attendance.

This arrangement at the Tuileries became the principle example followed in the secondary imperial palaces of Saint-Cloud, Fontainebleau, and the palace of Monte Cavallo in Rome. Significantly, this organization, particularly effective in staging political power, was later copied by the Bourbons, enemies of the Napoleonic Empire, who returned to power after the fall of the imperial regime in 1814. Though the Napoleonic association of the actual chairs meant that they were not thought appropriate in serving the new Louis XVIII and his entourage, the Restoration did not question the principle of the typological hierarchy of the seating arrangement that had been conceived by the empire. The new king, therefore, did not seek to return to the practices in effect at Versailles before the Revolution. However, it was necessary to procure very quickly a new throne for Louis XVIII, something that could be truly his, along with a new ensemble of surrounding chairs—seats of representation, chairs, and x-shaped stools—to allow this arrangement to continue. It was in their ornamentation, and only there, that these new seats expressed remnants of the spirit that existed before the Revolution.

The court chose the well-established decorator, Jean-Démosthène Dugourc (1749–1825) to design the new throne, as well as the new furniture for the salon, which was to be comprised of seats of representation, chairs, x-shaped stools, and screens. François-Honoré-Georges Jacob-Desmalter (1770–1841), the same firm that had, ten years earlier, furnished the emperor's residence, realized Dugourc's designs. Begun in 1817, this decorative program was created over many years; it also involved the Beauvais tapestry manufactory and the Frères Grands silk company in Lyon (Gastinel-Coural 1991: 74–80). The design of the new throne was inspired by the one, possibly imaginary, that was depicted in the last official portrait made of King Louis XVI by Antoine-François Callet (1741–1823) (Musée National du Château de Versailles, MV 3890).[5] Dugourc, who, during the *ancien régime* worked for the former court of Versailles, sought to erase the revolutionary period by stylistically citing the ornament of this previous period. The new throne was used by Charles X (1757–1836, r.1824–30) in the throne room at the Tuileries, and then by Louis-Philippe (1773–1850, r. 1830–48) after the 1830 July Revolution. This second French Revolution, however, required the king to reconsider the chair's decoration, resulting in the removal of the fleur-de-lis. It was eventually destroyed during the Revolution of 1848 when insurgents who had seized the palace transported it from the rue de Rivoli to the Place de la Bastille, where it was burned as a symbol of the monarchy (Cordier 2008: 69–71; 2012a: 125–7).

The ascension, then affirmation, of the Second Empire at the beginning of the 1850s renewed, in its way, the discussion of political authority as expressed through furniture in a public setting. It is notable, for example, that the imperial throne of Napoleon III (1808–73) in fact became, with Napoleon's marriage to Eugénie de Montijo in 1853, two identical state chairs, copied from the model of the throne of the First Empire. Thus, there was one throne each for the emperor and empress, the wife seeing her role on the same level as that of the reigning monarch. She was no longer required to sit in the chairs surrounding the throne of her husband. Such an arrangement is an uncontestable revolution of the traditional protocol. Unthinkable under the *ancien régime*, it would also have been rejected by Napoleon under the First Empire.[6] It would not have been considered by the kings of the Restoration, Louis XVIII and Charles X, both being widowers, and it was not imposed by Louis-Philippe. The monarchy of Napoleon III was therefore that of a couple as joint heads of state, ostensibly sharing the honors and the duties, a principle that was perfectly reflected in the public setting of their state furniture. The sacred character of the throne, however, remained. This was demonstrated by the amusing testimony of the comtesse des Garets, a maid of honor of the empress, in 1868:

> I remember that one rainy day, the Prince [Napoleon III's only son] and his friends, being bored, dragged us, his cousins and myself, into their games, and we then organized a game of *chat perché* [tag] in the salons. Bold in his ardour, one of our group stormed into the Throne Room and was going to perch himself on the august chair! Our dear Tristan Lambert [Tristan, baron Lambert (1846–1929)] who had never been before a throne without showing due respect, was devastated; he was red with indignation and shook

> with great anger. The Prince and the rest of our group were the victims of his outburst, which was well-deserved; if General Frossard, governor of the Prince, had not been absent that day, we would have really been in trouble!
>
> (Garets 1928: 28–9)

As noted by Colombe Samoyault-Verlet, although this new throne arrangement for a couple was seen at Tuileries, the layout of the throne room at Fontainebleau remained as it had been during the First Empire, with only one principal chair, that for the emperor. Nonetheless, the 1864 painting by Jean-Léon Gérôme (1824–1904), the *Réception des ambassadeurs du Siam par Napoléon III et l'impératrice Eugénie* (Reception of the Ambassadors from Siam by Napoleon III and the Empress Eugenie) (Musée National du Château de Versailles, MV 5004) (Plate 22) does show one occasion, certainly exceptional, where there were two armchairs for the imperial couple in the Henri II Gallery at Fontainebleau in 1861. However, this was almost certainly a temporary arrangement.

Nineteenth-century France, throughout its turbulent institutional history, experimented with different types of rule and various expressions and settings of sovereign authority in the parliamentary context. Particularly subject to the imperial executive under Napoleon, the assemblies of legislative power, the Senate and the Legislative Body, had thrones placed within them to acknowledge the authority of the emperor. Two of these throne chairs are still known: that of the Senate and that of the Legislative Body. What catches the attention of the art historian is the particular way in which these seats differ from Percier and Fontaine's model of the palatial throne, distinguished by its circular back, which stood out as one of the emblems of the regime. The two "legislative" thrones, although both made by the cabinet workshop of Jacob-Desmalter, are in fact compositionally quite different from the "executive" ones. They are secondary thrones, materializing the subordinate place of the legislative chambers in comparison to the imperial palaces within the hierarchy power. The throne of the Legislative Body was delivered in 1805. Its square back is surmounted by a crowned pediment, flanked by two eagles; the armrests consist of two impressive chimeras carved in the round. The design was proposed by the architect of the Legislative Body, Bernard Poyet (1742–1824), who had been inspired by Ennio Quirino Visconti's so-called marble throne of Bacchus for the Museo Pio Clementino, which had been confiscated by the French armies and presented at the Musée Napoléon in Paris (Nouvel-Kammerer 2007: 154). Contemporarily, that of the Senate presents a décor in the same spirit, where two winged sphinxes in the round replace the protomes, or figurative busts, of the chimeras, and where the back is straight and rectangular (Samoyault 2009: 159).

After exploring the throne's function as an emblem of the public expression of authority, it is now necessary to elaborate on the complexity associated with the symbolism of the seat. In the regal context, there are two considerations regarding the furnishing of official spaces. The first, previously mentioned, addresses those furnishings that were used in a ceremonial context, while the monarch was in the space, and thus contributed to the visual association of the ruler within that space. The second, which stems from the first, and was equally essential to the aura of the monarchy, consisted in symbolically manifesting, outside of the ceremonial context, the perpetual presence of the ruler. Bestowed the greatest respect, the throne embodied the function of the monarch—the only person who had the right to be seated there. Unoccupied most of the time, and visible as such, a throne is in fact never empty. The furnishings of an official space that constituted a throne room or a high chamber of parliament needed to successfully reconcile and harmonize these two realities—that of the real temporary presence and that of the symbolic permanent presence of the sovereign.

A watercolor of the imperial throne in the Tuileries by Percier and Fontaine (*c.* 1804, private collection) indicates that these two architects, responsible for the decoration of Napoleon's throne, included in their design a heavy wooden gilded balustrade in the middle of the stairs leading to the throne (Samoyault 1987: 188). French protocol imposed an essential element in the staging of power, by distancing the seat (and therefore the body) of the sovereign with respect to the rest of the room—that is to say, not only from the highest subjects of the court but indeed from the rest of society. The presence of this balustrade is certainly interesting. Perhaps we should see it, as Jean-Pierre Samoyault did, as the fruit of a clumsy confusion on the part of the architects—the former regime had used the balustrade in the parade chamber of the king to define a symbolically impassable space for the royal bed, considered the principal center of the sovereign's sacred body. Alternatively, could it not have been a deliberate way to reveal the regime's transition from the bed to the throne as a symbol of power and authority? Nonetheless, the balustrade, ordered from Jacob-Desmalter at the same time as the other elements of the throne, was never installed in the room, a sign that the opinion on this subject had changed.[7]

The practice of evoking the absence of the sovereign through an empty seat takes on a particular meaning in the French political context of the second half of the nineteenth century, of which the artificial throne room at the Château de Chambord is a revealing example. Henri d'Artois, Count of Chambord (1820–83), last Bourbon claimant to the Crown of France after the fall of his grandfather Charles X, spent the majority of this life in exile while remaining the owner of the immense Château de Chambord built by François I in the Loire Valley. D'Artois was very attached to the château, which he used to manifest his presence in the eyes of those he considered, under the July Monarchy followed by the Second Empire, as his legitimate subjects. Although the Legitimist pretender to the throne "Henri V" resided in Austria in the castle of Frohsdorf, he spared no expense to embellish his French residence over a forty-year period. Conscious of the role played by museums in the narration of national history, he opened the doors of Chambord to the public, which he intended to use as an ideological platform. Its throne room is therefore a room of the absent, with a staging program that justified the destruction of the historic room, the old bedroom of the Grand Dauphin, son of Louis XIV, that it replaced. A carved oak throne was made for the space (Musée National du Château de Chambord 2011: 292) (Plate 23). The style of the throne borrowed its vocabulary from the French Renaissance. Its silhouette evokes an immense *cathedra* chair and the height of the back, flanked on both sides by fleurs-de-lis in the round, presents a large adorned low-relief panel, between which are two cornucopias and a laurel wreath, and a fleur-de-lis shield surmounted by the royal crown. Though it corresponded to the fashion of the time and the palace's architectural spirit, its décor also encouraged, especially to the visitor of Chambord, the immemorial character of the royal institution. Although brand new, the throne had nonetheless expressed the illusion of an ancestral seat, awaiting the return of its legitimate owner, who had been expelled by the upheavals of contemporary history.

As the symbol of the monarchy and thereby garnering respect even if vacant, the throne even personified the monarch. In this it could be associated with a specific individual and no longer only with the regime or with an institutional authority thought of as permanent. This is frequently perceptible in the application and positioning of the cipher of a particular sovereign, such as Napoleon's "N," surrounded by laurels and placed on his regal furniture.

These associations between the personal and the perpetual, though, also reveal the ambiguity of using a seat to receive and symbolize the function, the physical presence, and the legitimacy of the monarch or head of state. In this respect, the example of the arrangement of the throne for Alphonse XII, who reigned in Spain from 1875, deserves discussion. Throughout the nineteenth century, the throne room of the royal palace in Madrid maintained the décor that had been conceived in the 1760s for the accession of Charles III Bourbon (1716–88). The throne room suite was composed of twelve consoles with high pier glasses and a throne consisting of a canopy and drapery of Genoese velvet brocaded in Naples, four lions in gilded bronze, and a chair of sculpted wood by the Neapolitan Gennaro di Fiore. This *barocchetto* Neapolitan style furniture, lighter in form and palette than classical baroque designs, but not as active or organic as the rococo, was delivered to Madrid in 1766, where it was gilded in 1772 (Patrimonio Nacional, Royal Palace, Madrid) (Sancho 2011: 282). At its creation, this seat had been adorned with a portrait medallion of the king, enclosed in a thick garland of laurels and roses. This personification seems to have given Charles precedence over all other dynastic symbols. Charles III's throne, replaced during the reigns of his successors, found a new function at the end of the nineteenth century, when a Madrid artisan was commissioned to create a faithful copy, replacing the ancestral portrait with that of the reigning sovereign, Alphonse XII. This practice of placing the current reigning monarch's portrait on the throne became a tradition in the next century and, in fact, persists to the present day. This visual representation therefore coexists with the affirmation of the permanence of the monarchy that is symbolized by the presence of the throne.

Within the context of diplomatic settings, the embassies of monarchical nations in the nineteenth century counted among their ceremonial rooms a throne room in honor of their head of state. An old photograph representing the embassy of Prussia's throne room—it became the German Empire in 1871—in Paris provides a good example of this.[8] Considered the throne room since 1867, the room was home to an armchair delivered by the workshop of Fourdinois in 1864 (Gabet 2011: 294). In the photograph, datable to the first years of the twentieth century, the chair has been turned toward the wall and the canopy, under which is an immense portrait of William II. A seat reserved for a sovereign, it is his image and his alone that the chair faces. It respects as such an eighteenth-century practice of the German state of the Holy Roman empire (Sander 2004: 121–38).

BRITAIN: FURNISHING THE POLITICAL SPACE FROM ROYAL PALACES TO PARLIAMENT

The examination of British customs in terms of furnishing regal spaces within monarchical residences puts into focus the comparison between the courts of the two nations at the beginning of the nineteenth century. It clearly demonstrates that English settings were simpler and more flexible in the kinds of furniture used from one room to the next than French examples.

This difference in approach is due to the fact that Great Britain had not undergone any fundamental political transitions that were comparable to that of the French Revolution. The first half of the nineteenth century did not question the natural heredity of the monarchs from the eighteenth century. While Napoleon had to reconstruct and rethink the framework, notably the visual framework, of a legitimate monarchical sovereign, the British royal household at the beginning of the nineteenth century saw the continuation of the Hanoverian monarchy, the nature of its political regime, and the permanence of its institutions. Many of the king's palaces had originally been designed for the Stuart monarchy and their spaces, in light of developments in both France and England, appeared chastened by the spirit of the times. As such, one cannot think of Windsor or Hampton Court as functioning under the same criteria as the Tuileries or Saint-Cloud. The erasure of the real power of the king to the benefit of the cabinet, amplified at the turn of the century by the illness of George III, revealed that although the symbolic value of spaces remained, the British court had already evolved toward greater modesty during the eighteenth century.

Consequently, the state apartments, as a manifestation of the monarch's authority, appear to have been soberly conceived at the end of the reign of George III, as a result of monarchical power having been displaced during the course of the preceding century. Indeed, as we will examine later, power was expressed less in the palace of a sovereign than it was in the solemn and complex space of the parliament. Moreover, nineteenth-century royal residences, by virtue of this constitutional distancing, became a privileged place to exhibit the royal family's extraordinary collection of art and, as such, as a sort of first private house and private collection of the country. The furnishings are only soberly involved as an ideological discourse. The situation is thus the inverse in France, where the principal treasures of the Crown collections had been, since the end of the eighteenth century, in the public museum at the Louvre, leaving to the palace space itself the responsibility of staging symbols of political power, rather than providing a place to showcase the personal taste of the sovereigns.

A particularly interesting publication in this regard, *The History of the Royal Residences* by W.H. Pyne, appeared in London in 1819. It was the essential guide to the Crown's extraordinary collections of paintings; yet, despite its title, it said nothing about the political nature of staging such places, in general remaining silent on the description of the furnishing of the rooms. However, the very rich illustrations within the Pyne publication provide a clearer picture and allow us to draw certain conclusions.

Deducing from the illustrations, the State Apartment at Windsor still reflected seventeenth- and eighteenth-century thought. It was organized around two main rooms: the Audience Chamber and the Presence Chamber. The first was a central point of the ceremony and appeared as a throne room. The throne with its footstool, of gilt wood and blue velvet upholstery, was placed on a platform, under a canopy. A pair of stools were placed on either side, symbolically destined for the Queen and the Prince of Wales. Benches and other stools placed along the walls made up the rest of the furnishings, the stools being the same model as those used for the queen and the heir to the throne on the platform. The expression of hierarchies, revealed by the relative positioning of these seats, is therefore not defined by different seating typology.

The Audience Chamber, the room dedicated to formal presentations to the sovereign, was followed by the Presence Chamber, which by its furnishings was a second throne room, and the function of which expressed, in the official space of the State Apartment, the sacred character of the royal person. At Windsor, its furnishing was more sober than that of the Audience Chamber. The furniture was made of mahogany, undoubtedly employed to match the tone of the paneling. The upholstery was red velvet. The throne here was also composed of three seats: an armchair for the king surrounded by two stools, placed on a platform and under a canopy adorned with the initial of George III. The remainder of the furniture was comprised of stools from the same set. Notably, the space of the state apartments retained the state bedchamber, which was no longer used in the court of France after the abolition of the royalty of the *ancien régime*. At Windsor, the furnishing hailed from the beginning of the eighteenth century, translated through Queen Anne's bed from the 1710s, which was separated from the rest of the room by a curious long grilling screen, the position of which is reminiscent of the European tradition of the balustrade that distinguished the sacred body of the monarchy from the rest of society. The same reuse of furnishings was retained at the other monarchical residences, including Hampton Court.

It was only at Carlton House, which provided the lavish residence for the prince regent, later to become George IV, that the protocol was altered. This, however, may have been due to the position of the regent rather than a change in the organization of the household. The interiors were striking for their magnificence and their perfect adherence to the fashion of the time. However, they also reveal that, although part of a royal residence, the private taste of the prince came before the regal character of the building's function. The only exception is that the residence possessed a throne room with furnishings revealing the particular constitutional situation in Britain at the time. The throne was placed under the canopy, surmounted by the emblem of the Prince of Wales. Yet, the most important position in the room was occupied by a large table, around which sixteen armchairs were placed with a sumptuous antique chair at the end of the table, a characteristic object of Regency fashion, but also reminiscent of the seats of the *intelligentsia* of Greek society—thus a throne room, certainly, but one at the time of the Regency. The ceremonial seat is not that of a king, but of his son, and appropriate to the placement of the furniture of the space of a powerful delegate, in the name of the sovereign.

While the British monarchy established conventions within royal places not so very different from those in France, a very different consideration of the staging of political authority took place in the true ceremonial nature of English power. The monarchy was becoming increasingly symbolic, in terms of its authority, and therefore it is within the parliamentary precincts where the most interesting questions arose concerning the relationship between furniture and power in nineteenth-century England.

The neo-Gothic Palace of Westminster or Houses of Parliament, the building of which began in 1840 on the ruins of the previous medieval building destroyed by fire in 1834, was designed by Charles Barry (1795–1860) with the assistance of A.W.N. Pugin (1812–52), who conceived the interiors. It is undoubtedly within the parliamentary space, of which the monarch is an essential component, that the true throne of the British monarchy resides. In particular, it is in the furnishing of the House of Peers that one can witness the manner in which

PLATE 1 "The transept from the Grand Entrance." *Souvenir of the Great Exhibition*. Published by Ackermann & Co., 96 Strand. Day & Son, lithographers to the Queen. 1851. Photograph courtesy of the V&A Museum/Wikimedia Commons.

PLATE 2 The Medieval Court of the Great exhibition, 1851. From: Dickinson's Comprehensive Pictures of the Great Exhibition of 1851; Joseph Nash, artist; Dickinson Brothers, publishers, 1854. Hand-colored lithograph. Gift of Bessie Potter Vonnoh, 1941/the Metropolitan Museum of Art. Photograph courtesy of the Metropolitan Museum of Art.

PLATE 3 Auguste-Emile Ringuet-Leprince and Michel-Joseph-Napoléon Liénard, Cabinet en console, 1851. Philadelphia Museum of Art: Purchased with the Walter E. Stait Fund and the John D. McIlhenny Fund, 2016, 2016-6-2a,b. Photograph courtesy of Philadelphia Museum of Art.

PLATE 4 Cradle carved in boxwood from Sir Matthew Digby Wyatt's *The Industrial Arts of the Nineteenth Century (1851–1853)*. Photograph courtesy of Hamza Khan/Alamy Stock Photo.

PLATE 5 Armoire. Deigned by A.W.N. Pugin; manufactured by John Gregory Crace; Carved oak with painted decoration and brass; designed 1850. Photograph courtesy of the V&A Museum/Wikimedia Commons.

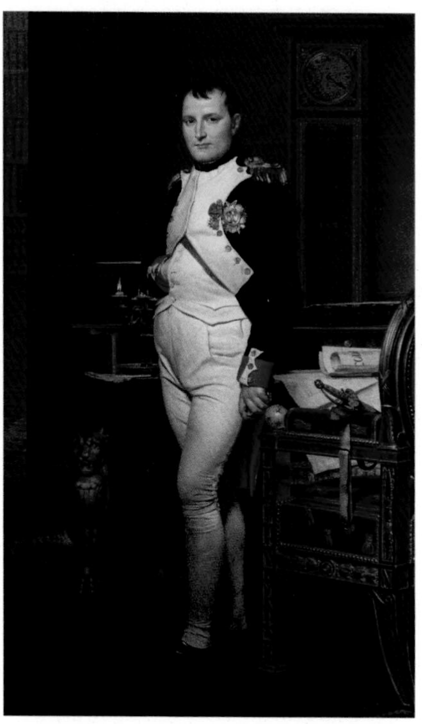

PLATE 6 Jacques-Louis David, *The Emperor Napoleon in his Study at the Tuileries*, 1811. Photograph courtesy of the National Gallery of Art, Washington, DC.

PLATE 7 Commode cabinet, 1855. Designed by Alexandre Eugène Prignot; Manufactured by Jackson and Graham. Marquetry of various woods, Hillwood, porcelain plaques and marble inlay with mirror. Photograph courtesy of the V&A.

PLATE 8 Designed by Philip Webb; painted by William Morris; manufactured by Morris, Marshall, Faulkner & Co.; Painted and gilded mahogany, pine and oak. Victoria and Albert Museum 341:1 to 8-1906. Photograph © Victoria and Albert Museum, London.

PLATE 9 A Pair of ladderback chairs, *c.* 1900. Designed by Ernest Gimson; made by Edward Gardner. Ash and beech. Photograph by Abbey Studios courtesy of Paul Reeves of London.

PLATE 10 Card table, 1817. Made by Charles-Honoré Lannuier. Mahogany veneer, white pine, yellow poplar, gilded gesso, vert antique, and gilded brass. Gift of Justine VR. Milliken, 1995/Metropolitan Museum of Art. Photograph courtesy of the Metropolitan Museum of Art.

PLATE 11 Slipper Chair, *c.* 1855. Made by John Henry Belter or J. H. Belter & Co. Rosewood, ash. Gift of Mr. and Mrs. Lowell Ross Burch and Miss Jean Mclean Morron, 1951/Metropolitan Museum of Art. Photograph courtesy of the Metropolitan Museum of Art.

PLATE 12 Sideboard, also known as the Pericles Dressoir, 1866. Designed by Bruce J. Talbert; manufactured by Holland & Sons. Oak, inlaid with ebony, walnut, boxwood, amaranth, carved and gilded; brass fittings. Purchase, Gift of Irwin Untermyer, by exchange; Romano I. Peluso, Ada Peluso, William Lie Zeckendorf, Lila Acheson Wallace, Malcolm Hewitt Wiener Foundation, Carol Grossman, Patricia Wengraf Ltd., Anonymous, Henry Arnhold, Marilyn and Lawrence Friedland, Irene Roosevelt Aitken, Andrew Butterfield and Claire Schiffman, Jason Jacques, Anne Rorimer, and Ian Wardropper and Sarah McNear Gifts, in honor of James David Draper, 2015. Photograph courtesy of the Metropolitan Museum of Art/Wikimedia Commons.

PLATE 13 Cabinet, 1867. Designed by Jean Brandely; woodwork made by Charles-Guillaume Diehl; mounts and large central plaque by Emmanuel Frémiet. Oak veneered with cedar, walnut, ebony and ivory; silvered-bronze mounts. Purchase, Mr. and Mrs. Frank E. Richardson Gift, 1989. Photograph courtesy of the Metropolitan Museum of Art.

PLATE 14 Luigi Frullini (carver), Armchair, 1876, Florence, Italy. Through prior gifts of Emily Crane Chadbourne, Edna Olive Johnson, Mr. and Mrs. Joseph Regenstein, Sr., and Mrs. Gustavus F. Swift, Jr.; purchased with funds provided by Kenilworth Garden Club and Mr. and Mrs. Bruce Southworth; Richard T. Crane, Jr., Endowment; European Decorative Arts Purchase Fund. Photograph courtesy of The Art Institute of Chicago.

PLATE 15 Centre table, *c.* 1850. Made by Thomas Williamson. Wemyss parrot coal. Photograph courtesy of Peter Petrou London.

PLATE 16 Jakob Alt (1789–1872), A Biedermeier sitting room, *c.* 1821. The room is furnished with a typical sofa showing a curved back, a sofa bed, and a circular table. Photograph courtesy of Heritage Image Partnership Ltd./Alamy Stock Photo.

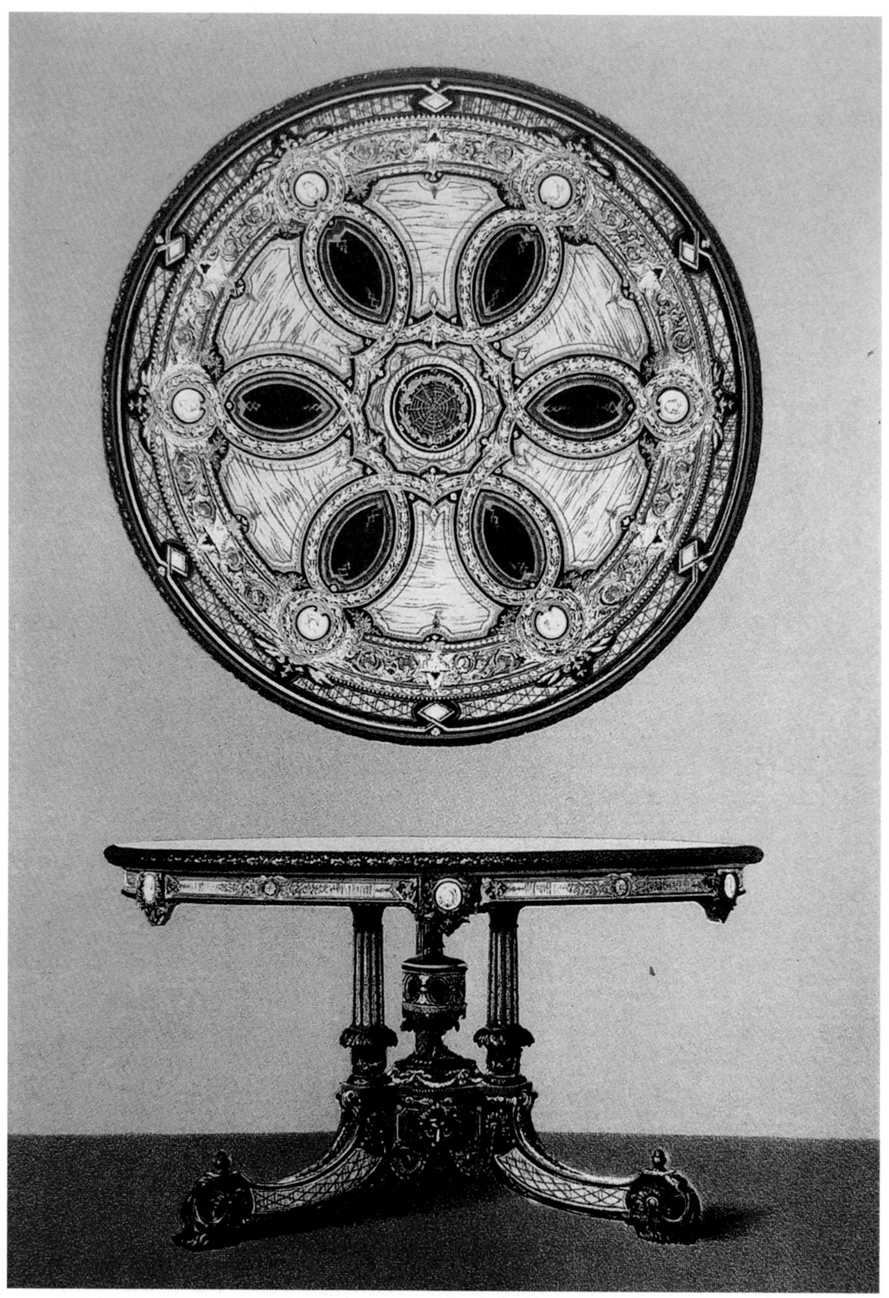

PLATE 17 Centre table with marquetry, *c*. 1862, Manufactured by Holland and Sons. Image courtesy of Smithsonian Libraries and Archives.

PLATE 18 Left: Overmantel in "Mrs Vanderbilt's boudoir," *c.* 1881, designed for William H. Vanderbilt's house, New York. Designed by Herter Brothers. From Strahan, Edward. 1883–84. *Mr. Vanderbilt's house and collection.* Right: Aublet, Albert. *Bibelots chinois*, Paris, *Paris illustré*, 1887, numéro 30, couverture. Photographs © Bibliothèque du Musée des Arts décoratifs.

PLATE 19 Dining room, Pavillon du Printemps. Paris Exposition Universelle 1889. Album Maciet. Photograph © Bibliothèque du Musée des Arts décoratifs.

PLATE 20 *Concert given to Queen Victoria by the singers of the Comedic Opera, in the Galerie des Guise at the Château d'Eu*, 1844–8. Painted by Eugène Louis Lami. Oil on canvas. Musée national du Château de Versailles. Photograph courtesy of Fine Art Images/Heritage Images/Getty Images.

PLATE 21 *La Députation du Sénat romain offrant ses hommages à S. M. l'Empereur et Roi, 16 novembre 1809 (The Deputation from the Roman Senate paying homage to Napoleon 1 on 16 November 1809)*, 1810. Painted by Innocent-louis Goubaud. Oil on canvas. Château de Fontainbleau. Photograph courtesy of Christophel Fine Art / Universal Images Group/Getty Images.

PLATE 22 *Reception des ambassadeurs du Siam par Napoléon III et l'impératrice Eugénie*, 1864. Painted by Jean-Léon Gérôme. Oil on canvas. Château de Versailles. Photograph courtesy of the Museum of the History of France/Wikimedia Commons.

PLATE 23 Throne. Oak. Musée national du Château de Chambord. Photograph courtesy of Hervé Lenain/Alamy Stock Photo.

PLATE 24 Proposed Decoration for the Senate Chamber of the Original Parliament Buildings. Architecture designed by Augustus Laver and Thomas Stent. Photograph courtesy of Library and Archives Canada, Acc. no. 1935–149–1.

PLATE 25 "Messrs. Morgan and Sander's Ware-room, Catherine Street, Strand," *Ackermann's Repository of Arts*, vol. 2, series 1 (August 1809), plate 11, p. 122. Harris Brisbane Dick Fund, 1942/Metropolitan Museum of Art. Photograph courtesy of the Metropolitan Museum of Art.

PLATE 26 Jewel cabinet made for empress Josephine, known as the Grand Ecrin, 1809. Designed by Charles Percier, made by François-Honoré-Georges Jacob-Desmalter, with mounts by Pierre-Philippe Thomire. Mahogany, amaranth, yew, ebony and mother of pearl with gilded bronze. Musée du Louvre. Photograph courtesy of Album/ Alamy Stock Photo.

PLATE 27 *Fragments on the Theory and Practice of Landscape Gardening*, 1816. Designed by Humphry Repton. Photograph courtesy of the Getty Research Institute/ Internet Archive.

PLATE 28 Chair, 1835. Designed by Karl Friedrich Schinkel. Cast iron. Photograph courtesy of Jürgen Hans.

PLATE 29 Centre table, 1833. Designed by Jacques Ignace Hittorff. Enamel on lava with mahogany and ormolu base. Photograph courtesy of the Chrysler Museum of Art.

PLATE 30 Dining chair for Scarisbrick Hall, Lancashire, *c.* 1838. Designed by A.W.N. Pugin. Oak, upholstered in imitation leather. Photograph © Victoria and Albert Museum, London.

PLATE 31 Cabinet, *c.* 1845. Designed by A.W.N. Pugin; manufacture attributed to George Myers; with hardware by John Hardman & Co. Carved, painted, and gilded oak with brass fittings. Purchase funded by the Barrie and Deedee Wigmore Foundation, art Fund and the Friends of the V&A. Photograph © Victoria and Albert Museum, London.

PLATE 32 Side Chair, *c.* 1857. Designed by Alexander Jackson Davis, Possibly made by Burns and Brother. Black walnut; replacement underupholstery and showcover. Gift of Jane B. Davies, in memory of lyn Davies, 1995/Metropolitan Museum of Art. Photograph courtesy of the Metropolitan Museum of Art.

PLATE 33 Desk, *c.* 1886. Designed by Arthur Heygate Mackmurdo. Oak with brass. Photograph courtesy of Granger Historical Picture Archive/Alamy Stock Photo.

PLATE 34 *Meubles et Objets de Goût,* *c.* 1801–31. Designs from Pierre de la Mésangère. Photograph © Spencer Collection, New York Public Library.

PLATE 35 Design for a *chaise longue, Le Garde Meuble*. Design and publication by Désiré Guilmard. Photograph courtesy of the Smithsonian Libraries and Archives.

PLATE 36 Table, *c.* 1851. Made by George J. Morant & Son. Carved, painted and gilded mahogany and lime wood with cast plaster and metal and molded leather decoration with painted glass top. Photograph © Victoria and Albert Museum, London.

FIGURE 5.1 The Bishop of Peterborough addressing the House of Lords, London. Illustration from Robert Wilson's *The Life and Times of Queen Victoria*, vol. 4 (London: Cassell and Company, 1900). Photograph courtesy of The Print Collector/ Alamy Stock Photo.

the nineteenth-century British Parliament addressed this question (Figure 5.1). Barry himself describes the general interior décor of the room in this way:

> Without doubt the interior of the House of Lords is the finest specimen of gothic civil architecture in Europe; its arrangements and decorations being perfect. Entering from the Peers' Lobby, the effect of the House is magnificent; the length and loftiness of the apartment, its finely proportioned windows, with the gilded and canopied niches between them; the Throne, glowing with gold and colors; the richly carved paneling which lines the walls; the roof, most elaborately painted; its massy [*sic*] beams and sculptural ornaments, and pendants richly gilded; all unite in forming a scene of Royal magnificence.
>
> (Barry and Ryde 1849)

The room is arranged like a chapterhouse, the seats of the lords placed on either side of a central space running the length of the room. This seating arrangement did not differ in principle from the arrangement in the previous building, before the fire in 1834, which itself was centuries old. In both the new and old House of Lords, the seats consisted of five ranks, situated in tiers; the four central ranks furnished with backbenches without armrests and upholstered in red velvet. All were identical, with the exception of the first bench on the left side that was outfitted with armrests and was intended for the Spiritual Lords, denoting their superior status as ecclesiastical officials. These benches expressed equal rights among peers, who were invited to sit together in a communal spirit. This parliamentary logic responds to that of the monarchy. The throne is situated on the south wall. Its immense carved wood baldachin, elevated by three registers, is described by Barry as follows:

> The centre of the southern end of the House is occupied by the Throne, and on either side of it, below the Gallery, is a doorway leading to the Victoria Lobby. The Throne is elevated on steps, the central portion having three, and the sides two steps, covered with a carpet of richest velvet pile. The ground color of the carpet is a bright scarlet, and the pattern on it consists of roses and lions alternately. A gold-colored fringe borders the carpet.
>
> The canopy to the Throne is divided into three compartments; the central one, much loftier than the others, is for her Majesty; that on the right hand for the Prince of Wales, and that on the left for Prince Albert ... The paneling at the sides, on either hand of the Chair of State, consists of two rows of open-worked arches, with elaborate tracery, and above them other panels filled with floreated [*sic*] enrichments of the most exuberant fancy ... Her Majesty's State Chair is particularly splendid in its enrichments; in general outline it is similar to the chair in which the Sovereigns of England have been wont to sit at their coronations, but in detail it differs widely from its plain prototype ... The State Chairs for the Prince of Wales and Prince Albert are exactly alike in form and general details, the only variations being the embroidery on the velvet backs; and the monograms. The backs are circular-headed. The velvet backs are most magnificent specimens of embroidery, and in design command unqualified praise, ornament and appropriateness being so happily blended.
>
> (Barry and Ryde 1849)

The State Chair was particularly impressive in its dimensions and abundance of sculpted, painted, and gilded ornament. Barry underlines its formal relationship with the throne of Saint Edward, which was preserved in Westminster Abbey and used during coronation ceremonies. In other words, the sovereign was invited to preside over the Chamber or House of Lords, because it had been here, symbolically, where he or she had been crowned on the ancestral throne. The furnishing of the Lords' chamber, then, is understood as an affirmation of the role of this sacred ceremony that initiates the reign and validates the legitimacy of the monarch to exist and act in the legislative process. As such, the neo-Gothic vocabulary of the parliamentary palace finds ideological justification: the style of Westminster is appropriately medieval because of the supreme authoritative process of the medieval tradition.

The places reserved on either side of the throne—one for the heir and the other for the consort—merit attention, as the staging of the monarchy in this way clearly isolated the immediate family of the reigning sovereign, while giving them an official place as witnesses to parliamentary activity during the Royal Speech. The rest of the time, when these seats were empty, they connoted a legitimate symbolic presence: this arrangement associates and hierarchizes the sovereign and her/his successor, clearly expressing the permanence of the royal institution.

The British, as in the French imperial and royal tradition, distanced the throne in the House of Lords. Dickinson and Foster's late nineteenth-century painting, *The Home Rule Debate in the House of Lords* (1893, The House of Parliament Collection, WOA 2945), depicts the position of a gilded metal security railing between the throne and the chamber. The scene, however, shows a certain number of parliamentarians not hesitating to cross this barrier, some even sitting nonchalantly on the steps. The balustrade thus serves primarily as a symbolic distancing of the sovereign, rather than as a true and strict prohibition to penetrate the royal space.

Protocol reinforced the distinction and relationship of the throne and the legislative members. With no one authorized to take the place of the sovereign, the chair remained empty in their absence, its display serving to materialize the otherwise remote monarch while affirming their authority. This principle is well illustrated in the context of colonial Britain in the Victorian age, when the sovereign did not reside in her dominions, the states where she was, in fact, Head of State. The Canadian parliament in Ottawa, built twenty years after the palace at Westminster, demonstrates these principles particularly well. Erected in the new capital in 1865, replacing the first parliament in Montreal that had been destroyed by fire in 1849 and that of Quebec City that was abandoned in the mid-1850s, it undoubtedly represented the "Victorianization" of Canadian institutions. This occurred a short time before the end of the colonial system and the official creation of the Canadian Confederacy, in 1867, in the form of a dominion composed of provinces. One of the first projects put forward for the Legislative Council's building—which would become the Senate—was the proposition by the architects Stent and Laver of a fairly accurate interpretation of the parliamentary building in London (National Archives of Canada, NAC 18033) (Young 1995: 48) (Plate 24). At the time of Confederation, the Legislative Council had been furnished with simple armchairs from the old parliament in Quebec. The throne had been placed at the center of the room, situated under a large neo-baroque canopy;[9] it was quickly replaced by a new ensemble that embodied the principle of absence—or rather non-residence—of the sovereign. Thus, the throne of Victoria, Queen of Canada—which could be used by her governor general—was neo-Gothic in style, but made with carved Canadian maple, situated on a platform elevated by three stairs, under a canopy. This seat was made in 1878 for the Governor General, John George Edward Henry Douglas Sutherland Campbell, 9th Duke of Argyll,the Marquis of Lorne (1845–1914), with a second, smaller seat for his wife, Queen Victoria's fourth daughter Princess Louise (1848–1939). Designed by the Chief Architect's office in the Department of Public Work, it was carved by the Toronto firm, Holbrook and Mollington.[10] This throne and its companion were inspired stylistically by the British throne, probably the one made in 1808 by Tatham and Bailey and installed during the reign of William IV in Saint George's Hall at Windsor Castle (Roberts 1989: 46–7). The custom was to associate these seats with a third chair, the style of which was also Gothic, though it was smaller in size, for the Speaker of the House (*The Governor General's Throne and Speaker's chair in the Senate, Ottawa,* National Archives, NA PA9230) (Figure 5.2).[11] Always placed in front of the throne, this seat was moved next to the throne during ceremonies that implied the effective presence of the monarchy.[12] This setting asserted the perpetual presence of the Crown, respectfully relegated to the back of the three-seat configuration. These related thrones, one behind the other, materialized the de facto remoteness of the queen, to the benefit of the head of the chamber and its proceedings.

CONCLUSION

This chapter has focused on the furniture that conveyed political authority and privilege, especially related to the monarchies and the parliamentary spaces of France and Britain. During the nineteenth century, however, tremendous transformations occurred within the public sphere. More public and civic buildings were constructed and needed furnishings. Municipal buildings, whether city halls or courthouses, needed furnishings and occasionally these were drawn up by noted architects and designers (see Frank Furness in Philadelphia; Henry Van Brunt in Boston for American examples). The advent of the railroad throughout the world necessitated train stations and these were often extravagant structures with waiting rooms for the different classes of riders. Even small towns had train stations and these were supplied later in the century with mass-produced furniture. The trains too had seating for different riders as well as dining and sleeping cars. By the mid-nineteenth century, public libraries also populated both large and small cities, again, usually furnished with mass-produced seating furniture and shelving. Universities became accessible to more students and new research and halls of residence were constructed and furnished. Elaborate theaters were built, especially at the end of the century, that could cater to a wide variety of audiences from vaudeville to opera—each furnished to match the building's interiors. Restaurants also became

FIGURE 5.2 The Governor General's Throne and Speaker's chair in the Senate, Ottawa. Photograph courtesy of Library and Archives Canada, Acc. No. 1935-149-1.

increasingly popular as the middle class grew to have more disposable income and restaurants of different styles and types developed around the world. As the century advanced, so did the specialization of form, the variety of public gathering places, and the sheer quantity of furnishings manufactured. This period saw an enormous growth in these arenas, such that would set the stage for more growth and refinement in the coming century.

CHAPTER SIX

Exhibition and Display

CATHERINE L. FUTTER

The nineteenth century ushered in the great age of the public display that saw the promotion of furniture as never before. Motivating factors for this increase in exhibition were numerous. The growth of the middle class with both more disposable income and leisure time allowed more consumers to both purchase goods but also visit exhibitions and shops. The rise of nationalism and its corollary, the promotion of nationalistic pride in goods fabricated in the country or region or the marketing of natural resources or finished goods from colonial territories, also informed this elevation of the display of furniture. Design educators and critics sought to improve the taste of designers, manufacturers, craftsmen, amateur makers, and consumers through the exhibitions and publications. There were also movements that sought to demonstrate that furniture and other decorative arts were the equal in style, skill, and beauty to painting and sculpture. Napoleon III hoped to unite the fine and decorative arts, and in 1853, proclaimed that traditional separation of the arts should be dissolved. In 1855, the annual French Salon exhibition of paintings and sculpture was held at the same time as the Paris international exhibition (Hiesinger and Rishel 1978: 30). Later in the century, the design reform movement hoped that exhibitions would eradicate the delineation between fine and decorative art. The displays at the expositions of the second half of the century certainly combined furniture with ceramics, lighting, and textiles to convey a complete or unified interior.

During the early years of the century, national and regional exhibitions such as the Expositions des produits de l'industrie Française and those of the British and American Mechanics Institutes, such as the 1839 Leeds Public Exhibition of Works of Art, Science, Natural History and Manufacturing Skills, allowed craftsmen and manufacturers to exhibit their wares and survey and assess the range of furniture and its processes. These fairs and displays in turn gave rise to the international exhibitions, expositions universelles, and the world's fairs that characterize this period. For the first time, natural resources and goods from around the world were on view for the appreciation of manufacturers, the general public, and students. In addition, there were also exhibitions of furniture—both antique and modern, some solely for display, others for sale. Purchases from exhibitions by royalty or the patronage of towns and districts for presents to royalty to commemorate events, were also important catalysts in the production and sale of furniture. Consumers could shop at stores of individual manufacturers or retailers or browse through the department stores that were established beginning in the 1850s. For the first time the most internationally sourced and widest selection of furniture was available at a wide variety and number of venues. Not until the advent of the internet did the diversity of opportunities to view and purchase furniture change.

PRIVATE COLLECTIONS, GALLERIES, AND MUSEUMS

With increased numbers of railroad lines, improved roads, and more expendable wealth facilitating travel, the upper and upper-middle classes, especially in Britain and those who traveled from the United States, were more likely to explore their region or even farther afield. Guide books became indispensable companions, focusing not only on historical sites, landscapes, architecture, and the fine arts but also often on important or significant furniture. *Galignani's New Paris Guide* of 1838, for example, directed visitors to the fine furnishings on display at the various royal sites, including the Palais Royal, the château of Meudon and the château at Neuilly where the apartments of the Queen and Duke of Orleans "are remarkably elegant; ... their furniture is of the most tasteful and luxurious description" (Galignani and Company 1838: 173, 471, 473). The English Reverend John A. Clark, in his *Rome, and its Wonders, and its Worship* of 1840, furthermore, extolled the virtues of visiting the Borghese palace for "the furniture of the splendid suite of rooms is exceedingly beautiful" (1840: 127). Meanwhile, Americans traveling through 1870s Europe were encouraged to look at the furniture in great houses and palaces open to the public. This included Schönbrunn in Vienna, where it "will occupy several hours to examine all its antique furniture, its carvings in wood and stone" (Fetridge 1873: 361). Guides to the country houses and monuments of Britain such as *Bembrose's Guide to Derbyshire* of 1869, moreover, described the furniture at Chatsworth pointing out two chairs "in which William IV and Queen Adelaide were crowned" as well as furniture in the Wellington Bed-room (Hicklin and Wallis 1869: 102, 123).

Alongside visiting historic homes and palaces, visitors could see displays of furniture in private residences that were opened to the public as art galleries. One of the most well known, the home of the antiquarian collector and designer Thomas Hope, opened in London in 1804. The public were allowed to view his spectacular installations with tickets on special viewing days when they were encouraged to look at the furnishings as well as the antique vases and sculptures. Thomas Hope's *Household Furniture and Interior Decoration* (1807) documented the interiors with his distinctive furnishings inspired by Egyptian, Greek, and Roman models (Figure 6.1). Likewise, by 1828, visitors to the Galleria Pubblica in Florence could view the treasures of the Medici family, including a collection of ancient Egyptian furniture that had been acquired by the Austrian chancellor to Alexandria, Egypt, and subsequently purchased by the Italian king (*Guida della città di Firenze* 1828: 249).

By the middle of the century, private individuals leased spaces to hold public exhibitions of furniture. Some exhibitions had works for sale, while others did not. In 1843, for instance, William B. Langdon published a catalog of an exhibition of Chinese works of art at St George's Place in Hyde Park Corner, London. The exhibition seems more impressive for the variety of works on

FIGURE 6.1 The Egyptian Room, from Thomas Hope's *Household Furniture and Interior Decoration* (London, 1807), plate 8. NAL Pressmark 57.Q.1. Photograph courtesy of V&A/Wikimedia Commons.

view and its ambience or effect, rather than for any inclusion of great works of art. Included, for example, were mannequins in the costumes of a "Mandarin," priests, "Chinese lady of rank," and actors. There were dioramas of a "Chinese gentleman's summer residence," which included a small selection of furniture (Langdon 1843: 50).

What we consider traditional museum displays of furniture began when the British Museum opened in 1753, exhibiting works of ancient furniture in the Egyptian and Bronze Rooms (British Museum 1850: 56–7, 88–9). It was not, however, until the founding of the Museum of Manufactures, later called the South Kensington Museum and, in 1899, renamed the Victoria and Albert Museum, that historical, modern, and global furniture was exhibited critically, with a purely educational mission. Men who sought to elevate the quality of design in British manufacturing and the education and taste of consumers founded the museum in 1852 following the tremendous success of the London 1851 Great Exhibition of the Works of Industry of All Nations. They determined to establish a museum with a permanent collection of the history of industrial production alongside contemporary examples. By making works of art available and accessible to all, they sought to educate the laboring class and to inspire improvement in the production of British designers and manufacturers. In keeping with the tenets of accessibility, the museum had free admission three days a week.

John Hungerford Pollen's *Ancient & Modern Furniture and Woodwork in the South Kensington Museum* (1874) is an invaluable resource and guide to the museum's collection of furniture and woodwork in our period. A visit to the South Kensington Museum allowed visitors of all classes and ages to be exposed to the finest cabinetry and manufacturing. The museum's collection grew from the acquisition of objects from several sources: international exhibitions, private donations, and even reproductions of noted examples of historical furniture.

From the international exposition, the museum acquired pieces by major British and French designers and cabinetmakers, including an armoire in the French Gothic style designed by A.W.N. Pugin exhibited in 1851 and a pair of ivory armchairs with matching stools in the Rococo Revival style (Victoria and Albert Museum [hereafter V&A], 001216(IS), 01219(IS)) shown in Paris in 1855. Keepers even ventured to acquire from foreign expositions, such as a large needlework screen designed by Walter Crane (1845–1915) executed by the Royal School of Art Needlework (V&A, T.774 to D-1972), and exhibited at the Philadelphia Centennial Exhibition of 1876. Private donations of furniture were also important to the development of the collection to exhibit masterworks by the leading craftsmen of the past. Significant gifts included the Soulages collection of Italian and French Renaissance objects, acquired between 1859 and 1865, and the bequest of the John Jones collection in 1882, which supplied important pieces of French eighteenth-century cabinetwork. This last gift included works by Jean Henri Riesener (1734–1806), Jean-François Oeben (1721–63), André Charles Boulle (1642–1732), Bernard van Risenburgh (*c.* 1730–67), and Martin Carlin (*c.* 1730–85). In addition to original works, the museum supplemented its acquisitions with reproductions of important cabinetry, as in 1868, when it acquired twenty-three works by Giovanni Franchi and Son of Clerkenwell, London, of electroformed copper and electroplated silver copies of furniture designed for Knole in about 1660.

As in the acquisition of historical pieces, museum leaders also embarked on a program of exhibitions that also demonstrated a commitment to educating manufacturers, the public, and students through the display of good design. The first and probably largest exhibition included over nine thousand works of paintings, sculpture, etc. from over five hundred lenders was the Special Exhibition of Works of Art of the Medieval, Renaissance and More Recent Periods held in 1862. Queen Victoria was one of the lenders of seventeenth- and eighteenth-century French furniture, which certainly added to the cachet and attraction of the exhibition (Collard 2003: 36). This was followed by an exhibition of Spanish and Portuguese decorative arts in 1881 and one of recent acquisition of antique French Gothic and Renaissance woodwork and cabinetmaking in 1895 (Robinson 1881: 133–4; "French Woodwork at South Kensington" 1895: 25–9).

If you were not able to travel to London, in 1855 the South Kensington Museum created an outreach program for loan exhibitions that traveled to most of the principal towns in England, Scotland, and Ireland. It was hoped that the exhibitions would "raise the taste of the country" and inspire the formation of local museums. After 1864, the museum made short-term loans of its collections for public exhibitions at the schools of art, free libraries, and museums. The project seems to have been a huge success ("History of the Kensington Loan Collection-I" 1881: 268–9).

Other decorative arts museums, usually modeled on the South Kensington Museum, were established during the nineteenth century, further illustrating the dedication to design education. In 1890, Countess von Krackow, writing in *The American Architect and Building News*, cited the success of the program at the Berlin Industrial Museum, exclaiming "how considerable it is for students, artists and artisans on one side, and, on the other, for the general public!" She continued that the evening hours allowed the museum to be filled with "lights and audiences; the aim being to prepare consumers of a quality fit for appreciating the producers whom the industrial schools of the country educate and inspire" ("The Winter Exhibition of the Berlin Industrial Museum" 1890: 174). New institutions in Europe included the Deutsches Gewerbe-Museum zu Berlin (Berlin Industrial Museum) in 1868, which became the Kunstgewerbemuseum in 1879; the Vienna Museum für angewandte Kunst (MAK), founded in 1863;

and the Hamburg Museum für Kunst und Gewerbe, founded in 1874. Three design museums opened in Norway during the nineteenth century: the Museum of Decorative Arts and Design in Oslo in 1876; the West Norway Museum of Decorative Art in Bergen in 1877; and the Nordenfjeldske Kunstindustrimuseum in Trondheim in 1893. In 1890, the Danish Museum of Art and Design in Copenhagen was founded, while in New York, the Cooper-Hewitt Design Museum opened in 1896.

SALES AND AUCTIONS OF FURNITURE

Sales and auctions were another public venue for the exhibition of furniture. In an 1819 advertisement in *The Literary Gazette*, William Bullock announced that the Egyptian Hall in Piccadilly had become an exhibition space as well as the "Mart for the disposal, either by private contract, or public auction of ... furniture of every description" (October 9, 1819: 655). The following spring Bullock exhibited for sale, "Buhl, Ebony, Rosewood and India Japan Cabinets, Commodes and Skreens [*sic*] ... useful and ornamental furniture" (*The Literary Gazette*, April 15, 1820: 255). These sales were accompanied by catalogs.

An exhibition that combined county fair with propagandistic zeal was the Anti-Corn Law League Bazaar, held in Covent Garden, London, in the spring of 1845. Although the majority of goods were memorabilia emblazoned with sheaves of wheat, textiles, and even dresses, other items including furniture were displayed and sold at the bazaar (Gurney 2006: 385–405). What set the Anti-Corn Law League Bazaar apart from the other commercial enterprises were two important factors: it supported a political and economic cause, free trade, and it was organized by the wives and daughters of the national and local leaders of the League. Women were not only the consumers but also the organizers (392–5).

The French Revolution put a great number of eighteenth-century goods on the market, including important case furniture with marquetry, ormolu-mounted, and inlaid surfaces by well-known makers. Buyers, many in England, incorporated the pieces into interiors that also included modern copies of eighteenth-century furniture or new designs. The Prince of Wales, Empress Eugénie, the Rothschilds, and the collector John Bowes[1] were just some of those that amassed collections of eighteenth-century French furniture after the Revolution (Samoyault-Verlet 1978: 75).

In nineteenth-century Paris three auction houses (Druot, Petit, and Charpentier) sold fine furnishings, mostly from the previous century (Auslander 1988: 378–9). Most of the furniture they sold was of the highest quality. For example, the Paris sales catalog of a "riche mobilier" in 1833 included mahogany *fauteuils* with an accompanying console, armoire for the salon and mahogany bookcases, chairs, and tables with their luxurious upholstery (*Catalogue d'un*

Riche Mobilier 1833: 16–18). Of course, the great English auction houses, such as Christie's, Sotheby's, and Phillips & Son, also displayed and sold furniture in numerous sales throughout the century.

SHOPS

Traditional furniture showrooms

During the nineteenth century, consumers experienced shopping and the display of goods in completely new ways. Although shops and warehouses presented furniture by type or function throughout the century, by the last decades furniture was displayed in pseudo room settings so that consumers could see how seating furniture, tables, and cabinets could be integrated with carpets, lamps, wallpaper, and even other decorative objects. In addition, although the stand-alone furniture showroom remained integral to the shopping experience, there was, by the 1860s, a new dimension: the department store. Window-shopping became a leisure activity and the display of goods, including furniture, was transformed.

Until the 1840s, shopping for furniture meant going to workshops—some composed of a single woodworker who manufactured all the components of a piece of furniture, while others allowed for a division of labor and more specialization of forms. Often these workshops had showrooms for their drop-in customers to view and purchase premade works (Plate 25). An 1866 advertisement for the London firm of Jackson and Graham publicizes "that they have recently made great additions to their former extensive premises, which render their establishment the largest of its kind in this or any other country. The Spacious Show Rooms and Galleries are filled with an unrivalled stock, the prices of which are all marked in plain figures at the most moderate rates for ready money" (Edwards 1998: 238–65). In 1884, Henry B. Wheatley in *The Decorator and Furnisher* described the firm's windows: "The work of the autumn begins now to be apparent in the shop windows, where many novelties are being shown. Messrs. Jackson and Graham have exhibited some handsome furniture, prepared by them for the Imperial Palace of Japan. Much of it is very elaborate in character, and the gilt cornices are singularly gorgeous" (Wheatley 1884: 139).

The greatest center for London showrooms catering to the growing middle class was located in Tottenham Court Road (Figure 6.2). There, one of the most renowned furniture manufacturers and retailers was Heal and Son, established as purveyors of feather dressers and bedding in 1818. Although the firm was known for beds and bedding accoutrements, in the 1850s it added other types of furnishings (Figure 6.2). The company also determined that storefront architecture was important to attract customers and, in the mid-1850s, designed a

FIGURE 6.2 Nineteenth century advertisement, for 'Maple & Co', chairs; England; 1892. Photograph courtesy of World History Archive/Alamy Stock Photo.

new frontage to the store (Edwards 2011: 17). According to an 1865 description of the interior of Heal's: "The entire stock is arranged in eight rooms, six galleries each 120 feet long and two large ground floors" (18).

In 1895, a visitor to Hewetson's, one of Heal's most serious rivals in the neighborhood, exclaimed at the variety of the wares on view:

> Behind the huge windows facing Tottenham Court Road there was a splendid mass of furniture, tapestries perfect in coloring, cretonnes copied from good last century designs, but of genuine old oak there was little. However, I walked in and looked round the vast showrooms full of specimens of good modern English work, admired bedroom suites of white enamelled wood, graceful in outline, and dainty in appearance, sideboards of massive mahogany, drawing-room cabinets, à la Chippendale, luxurious couches and charming furniture in oak, stained green ... I was taken across Store Street to a different building, and found that the collection was so large that it had been necessary to house it in other premises. It would be difficult not to grow eloquent over the collection that Messrs. Hewetson's have got together. It is chiefly old English, though Wales is well represented.
>
> ("The Artistic Home" 1895: 43)

Both the West and East End London firms supplied not only furniture, carpets, and other furnishing textiles, but often they sold other decorative objects such as ceramics, metalwork, etc., so that the customer could complete a comprehensive interior with one stop.

Although Union Square was the metropolis's shopping center, furniture showrooms and warehouses were spread throughout nineteenth-century New York City. *History and Commerce of New York 1891* enumerates, probably through paid announcements supplied by the business owners, a number of furniture dealers. In the northern part of the city, T.D. Blight announced his credentials as "a dealer in fine furniture," being an Englishman with eleven years' experience with the Newcastle upon Tyne department store Bainbridge & Co. and time with W. & J. Sloan and Owen Jones & Sons, prominent New York dealers. Some dealers stocked both modern and antique furniture, while others touted their familiarity with "artistic" furniture. Adolph Finkenberg on Avenue B advertised that he could supply "all grades, from cheapest to the finest and most elaborate in magnificent parlor suits, upholstery goods, chamber sets, hall sets, kitchen furniture, bedding, mattresses, etc. are carried in abundant profusion." He boasted that his shop was two floors and was 30 × 70 feet (9 × 21 meters) with "the main salesroom on the first floor, with the warerooms overhead." These New York makers advertised their personal histories, listing where they were born (Germany, England, and Ireland), and worked with some of the biggest names in the New York furniture trade, including Herter Brothers, Pottier, Stymus & Co., and Alexander Roux (*History and Commerce* 1891: 15, 109, 114, 124, 133–4, 136, 165) Ernest F. Hagen, the well-known and documented cabinetmaker and dealer in antique furniture, is included in this compendium: "At his spacious and well appointed store will be found a large assortment of antique furniture, of which Mr. Hagen makes a specialty, handsomely carved and superbly finished, elegant cabinets, beautiful bookcases, chiffoniers, wardrobes, desks, etc., while furniture is made and upholstered to order in new and original designs in the highest style of art and at short notice" (136).

Imported goods from Asia, especially from Japan, also enjoyed great popularity, although it was not until the third quarter of the century that Asian makers began to produce furniture for American and European markets.[2] In 1866 Ashley Abraham Vantine (1828–90), opened his first store in New York with Japanese goods, mainly novelty items. An article in the *New York Times* from 1867 mentions writing desks and silver-mounted cabinets (cited in Yamamori 2008: 99). In 1871, Vantine also stocked Chinese and Indian crafts and Turkish rugs, sometimes staging large auctions of this material in East Coast cities. At the end of the century, some department stores, too, included Asian objects and even Asian departments. In 1891, the Almy, Bigelow, and Washburn Department Store in Salem, Massachusetts, advertised that it had a shipment of goods from Asia arranged by Bunkio Matsuki (1867–1940) (Chen

2010: 19–46). Sadajiro Yamanaka (1866–1936) also worked to import and disseminate Asian art through auction catalogs and sales. Although the majority of the goods provided by Matsuki and Yamanaka seem to have been prints, pottery, and textiles, both Japanese entrepreneurs appear to have stocked some Chinese and Japanese furniture.

A REVOLUTION IN DISPLAY: THE COMPLETE INTERIOR

While traditional showrooms prevailed as the most popular approach for the display and sale of furniture for the retail market, a new mode of presentation took hold: that of a fully furnished space that conveyed to the consumer how they could live and what furnishings they required to achieve the latest fashions in interior design. These shops developed into the earliest art galleries dedicated to decorative arts—supplying for their clients works in a variety of materials. They also prompted new styles in design and the work of specific designers. By the end of the century, they were international in focus, bringing together furniture by French, Belgian, and English manufacturers with metalwork from England and even glass from New York.

In Britain, one of the most noted and innovative firms of the mid- and late nineteenth century was Marshall, Faulkner & Co. (later Morris, Marshall, Faulkner & Co., and still later, in 1875, Morris & Co.). Although the company was better known for its textiles, wallpapers, and stained glass, some of the firm's designs and products included furniture. In the spring of 1861, the artist, critic, and entrepreneur William Morris (1834–96), joined with fellow artists Peter Paul Marshall (1830–1900), Ford Madox Brown (1821–93), Edward Burne-Jones (1833–98), architect Philip Webb (1831–1915), and friend and mathematics tutor Charles Faulkner (1833–92) to set up a studio and showroom at 8 Red Lion Square in Holborn. The company initially focused on ecclesiastical commissions, and within a year Morris and his partners were exhibiting at the 1862 International Exhibition, where they won awards for stained glass and furniture. The furniture produced by Morris, Marshall, Faulkner & Co. reflected Morris's interest in English and French Gothic furniture and architecture.

In 1877, Morris & Co. opened a showroom at 264 (later 449) Oxford Street—close to rivals Liberty's and Heal's. Morris had two lines of furniture available to his clientele: the "state furniture," often designed by Webb, usually substantial sideboards and cabinets, constructed of oak, stained black or green, often decorated with lacquered or painted panels or inserts of stamped leather. The other lines, considered "work-a-day," were designed by Madox Brown and Dante Gabriel Rossetti (1828–82), usually inspired by English country examples. When customers visited the Oxford Street shop they were able to purchase the entire Morris & Co. line from hand-printed wallpapers, textiles, and furniture to complementary ceramics by William de Morgan, glass by James Powell, and lighting devices by W.A.S. Benson (1854–1924). Morris & Co. also had agents in the United States, Europe, and even Australia. Morris's participation in the Arts and Crafts Exhibition Society also allowed potential customers to see where "design and handicraft are encouraged in their best forms, and the furniture exhibited bears the names, not only of those who draw the designs, but also those who carry out the work, so that credit due to each is distinctly seen" (L.H.S. 1893: 1143–4).

In 1895, the dealer Siegfried Bing (1838–1905) opened his famous Paris gallery, La Maison de l'Art Nouveau, which promoted not only Japanese designs but, more importantly, furniture, ceramics, glass, textiles, and jewelry in the new organic style, which came to be known as Art Nouveau after Bing's shop. The Belgian architect and designer Henry van de Velde designed the interior of the gallery, with stained glass by the American Louis Comfort Tiffany.

Another example of a gallery that displayed fully furnished interiors was the Galeries des Artistes Modernes at the Rue Caumartin. Here, in 1896, five designers exhibited their works; of those, three provided furniture: Alexandre Charpentier (1856–1909),[3] Charles Plumet (1861–1928), and Jean Dampt (1854–1945), all of whom were "united in their aims, in addition to being allied by community of ideas and mutual ambition. Their desire is to show the public work not designed to be unique, but such as can be executed in the ordinary course of labour—articles of everyday use, that is, within the reach of all" (Mourey 1897a: 119–25; 1897b: 55–6). Reviewing an exhibition of decorative arts at the Salon du Champ de Mars in 1897, the same critic was highly critical of the displays of furniture, which he claimed showed "eccentricity" and were "distorted and ugly, and heavily overcharged with ornamentation" (Mourey 1897a: 36–47). Mourey continued to promote Les Six to English-speaking audiences, writing a very positive review of their second exhibition at the Galerie des Artistes Modernes in the Rue Caumartin from 1898, featuring several illustrations of furniture in a restrained Art Nouveau idiom by Plumet (Mourey 1898: 81–91).

In Berlin, the Hirschwald gallery carried furniture by Charles Plumet, Louis Majorelle (1859–1926), Gustave Serrurier-Bovy (1858–1910), William Morris and Edward Burne-Jones, and Tony Selmersheim (1871–1971); metalwork by W.A.S. Benson and Charles R. Ashbee (1863–42); and textiles by a number of designers and craftsmen (see "Studio–Talk" 1898: 118–20; 1899b: 136–9). Illustrations indicate that this international display allowed visitors to encounter a number of the most avant-garde designs of the late nineteenth century ("Studio–Talk" 1899b: 139). The same year, Messrs. Keller and Reiner opened a "Salon" in Munich, which featured an entrance hall designed by Henry van de Velde and several rooms displaying paintings and applied art by an international group of artists, including the French Impressionists, and designers ("Studio–Talk" 1899a: 286–7).

THE NEW SHOPPING EXPERIENCE: THE DEPARTMENT STORE

Radical developments in retail businesses, especially in France after the Revolution, set the stage for the first department stores. While cabinetmakers that specialized in custom-made furniture continued to produce and retail their works with little change and small exclusive galleries or shops such as those of Morris and Bing emerged with a new form of sales, they were, by the end of the century, almost overwhelmed by the large department stores. In Europe, England, and the United States, the stores that emerged from the dry-goods emporia of the 1820s eventually included furniture in their merchandise. While the discussion of the origins of the department store are complex, it appears that nationalism prevails with American, French, and British historians all claiming that the first department store was opened in their country. For these historians, the origins of the department store in each country are consistent with the transformation of a dry goods or drapery store into a multi-departmental store that accommodated all of the customers' needs—from fabrics, clothing, and linens to other household goods. According to Leora Auslander, the effect of the department store on the furniture industry was minimal as the bulk of store sales were from less substantial investments, such as lengths of cloth, not heavy wooden furniture (1988: 411–12). She suggests that the specialized furnishing stores, which offered a range of services, continued to be the primary locus of the expenditure on furniture throughout the nineteenth century.

In Paris, the *magasins de nouveautés* set the stage for a revolution in retailing. Originally drapers and stores specializing in the sales of textiles had fixed prices, extended credit, easy return policies, and allowed shoppers to peruse the goods without any obligation to buy. The *magasins de nouveautés* started about 1824 with *La Belle Jardinière*, followed by the establishment of *Aux Trois Quartiers* (1829) and *Le Petit Saint Thomas* (1830). These shops were the forerunners of the department store, which also had the same policies we now take for granted—posted prices, easy return policies, and easy perusing.

Another model set the stage for the department store in England. In 1831, the London Pantechnicon opened in fashionable Belgrave Square. This new shop was for the "convenience" it would afford to the "higher classes." Part of the establishment was devoted to the sale of carriages and "to the housing of furniture of every description," meaning that those that did not own their own houses in London could store their furniture from one fashionable "season" to the other. Pantechnicon included The Warehouse Bazaar where furniture and other goods could be stored or sold. In addition, there was a large auction room attached to this department that covered over an acre in surface area (*Mechanics' Magazine* 1831: 390–1: *The Atheneum* 1831–2: 199).

Other prototypes for the department store were bazaars. In 1829, a bazaar (fair or marketplace) was built in Cincinnati in the *arabesque* style "combining the airy lightness of Grecian with the sombrous gravity of the Gothic taste." Wares included clothing, stationery, china, and "ornamental household furniture" (*Cincinnati Directory* 1829: 175). The Manchester Bazaar, established by John Watts in 1831, is also credited as being a forerunner of the department store. As with other early stores, Watts' emporium developed from a drapery business.

One of the most compelling descriptions of the transformation of Paris and shopping in the early to mid-1850s can be found in Emile Zola's *The Ladies' Paradise*, published in 1883. In this work, the reader feels that Zola is accompanying them on walks through Paris, first visiting the old-fashioned, small, dark, and even dank shops that sold only one or a limited range of goods. The counterpoint, where the book's hero and heroine work, is the gleaming new department stores filled to the ceilings with gorgeous displays of textiles and clothing and, on the upper floors, furniture. Zola captures the excitement of a new form of leisure—shopping—as well as the piles of goods in innovative displays that captured the imagination and purses of the Parisian women of all classes.

> A compact mass of heads was surging through the arcades [of the fictional department store the Ladies' Paradise], spreading out like an overflowing river into the middle of the hall. A real commercial battle was developing; the salesmen were holding an army of women at their mercy ... The great afternoon rush-hour had arrived, when the overheated machine led the dance of customers, extracting money from their very flesh.
>
> (Zola [1883] 1995: 108)

Furniture departments were not one of the initial departments, as textiles and then lingerie, gloves, etc. were, in these large stores; they were added over time. Zola details the demise of independent, old-fashioned furniture dealers, as "the success of the rival department promised to be tremendous." The protagonist, Octave Mouret, was "alone" in "putting the carpet and furniture departments on the second floor, for in those departments customers were rarer, and their presence on the ground floor would have created cold, empty gaps" (Zola [1883] 1995: 218, 236).

The 1840s saw a surge of development of department stores on both sides of the Atlantic. In the United States, one of the first was A.T. Stewart's "Marble Palace," which opened in 1846 on New York's Broadway and Chambers Street in Lower Manhattan. The large Italianate multistory store presented a larger range of goods in a regimented and organized manner. As with other department stores, it was not until the very end of the century that furniture became integral to the goods on offer at Stewart's. Three years after Stewart's opened, in Britain,

Bainbridge's of Newcastle upon Tyne was founded in 1849, claiming to be the first department store in the world. It was started in 1838 with the partnership of Emerson Muschamp Bainbridge and William Alder Dunn, when they opened a drapery and fashion shop. By 1849, Bainbridge's had twenty-three separate departments, with weekly profits recorded by department. By the 1870s, there were more than forty retail departments and, when Bainbridge died in 1892 and his sons took over, the staff numbered over six hundred with floor space of over 3,250 square meters.

Urban department stores, such as Printemps and Bon Marché in Paris, Wanamakers in Philadelphia, Macy's in New York, Marshall Field's in Chicago, and Eaton's in Toronto, are well documented and have been studied from a variety of viewpoints, employing gender and/or consumer methodologies (Figure 6.3). Department stores were not, however, restricted to the large city centers and could be found in smaller cities throughout the United States, Britain, and Canada (Howard 2008: 457–86). Often, as in the large urban areas, they developed from drapery shops.

THE EXHIBITION

In addition to new developments in shopping, nineteenth-century consumers were able to see and sometimes even purchase furniture at exhibitions. Until 1851, exhibitions were limited to regional or national displays. From the 1820s, educational institutions, private or trade societies organized exhibitions—often with the premise of educating a range of audiences. We know of many of these exhibitions because of the published catalogs that advertised the displays, the manufacturers, the juries, and the industrial supporters of these popular and often expensive affairs. Being able to exhibit at an exposition was often the result of who you knew on the organizing committees. Today, we look at these published documents for a variety of reasons: not only the introduction or popularization of a process or style, but which manufacturers used these enterprises to promote their products to national or international audiences. Examining the medal winners often reveals a highly political system of rewarding those on committees. In addition to the official catalogs of the expositions were articles in trade and even art magazines usually praising the products of the manufacturers from their own country of origin.

Visitors read about the fairs in journal and newspaper articles as well as catalogs with steel engravings—a practice that promoted the fairs but also allowed those who could not attend to visit vicariously. Catalogs and articles became customary for the international expositions that took place throughout the century around the globe. They were published in a great number of languages for a wide variety of audiences—from trade journals, to ladies'

FIGURE 6.3 Grands Magasins de Nouveautés au Printemps. Illustration for *The Illustrated London News*, October 18, 1884. Photograph courtesy of Look and Learn, London.

magazines, to art journals and even guide books—promoting the exhibitions as major events that would appeal to all levels of society with a great range of interests. Below is an examination of the regional and local exhibitions and those that brought together international exhibitors and audiences.

REGIONAL AND LOCAL

In France, the national exhibitions started at the end of the eighteenth century. The Seconde Exposition Publique of 1801, which displayed "les Produits de l'Industrie française," included two gold medal winners for furniture, the Parisian firms of Lignereux and Jacob Frères. Both workshops were characterized by an aristocratic clientele and extolled for their "elegance and richness" and "the accuracy and the completeness of the exterior and interior elements." Jacob Frères was commended for "their style ... of great character and most difficult details of sculpture are executed with perfection" (*Seconde exposition* 1801: 14–15). Both firms received gold medals in 1803 and Jacob continued to garner prizes, even as it became Jacob-Desmalter.

The 1824 French exposition included a great number of furniture manufacturers, probably a sign of the recovery of the French economy following the Napoleonic Wars. In the exposition catalog's introduction, the section on *ébénisterie* and *menuiserie* describes the diversity of woods used in the decoration of the furniture, these replacing in popularity mahogany, which was now considered a bit somber. The writer commends the makers for the elegant forms that are functional, yet display a wise use of ornament (*Rapport* 1824: 415). At the 1842 fair of French Manufactures Royales, the displays were limited to Sèvres porcelains, and Gobelins and Beauvais tapestries, with some furniture incorporating elaborate scenic porcelain plaques.

National expositions were held throughout Europe during the nineteenth century. Most in France were held in Paris, but there were other exhibitions that included displays of furniture, especially in the 1830s; one was held in Lyon in 1837. In addition, an 1828 fair in Geneva included the work of various *ébénistes* while *La Belgique industrielle de l'exposition des produits de l'industrie en 1835* exhibited eleven manufacturers of furniture executed in mahogany and other precious woods (*Exposition des produits* 1835: 47). Designs of a commode and a secretary by the gold medal winner Pelseneer of Brussels, published with illustrations in the 1836 reports, were extolled for their architectural elegance and good taste (Faure 1836: 176–80). Holland was not to be outdone by fairs, and held an exposition générale of objets d'art in Haarlem in 1825, with makers from Haarlem, Amsterdam, Ghent (in Belgium), and other centers.

While Continental Europeans were holding national and regional fairs, Americans and British were presenting fairs at mechanics' institutes. Mechanics' institutes were established to disseminate scientific knowledge to members, usually manufacturers or mechanics, promote industrial developments, and at the same time, protect the social welfare and safety of their membership (Price 2000: 270–1). The institutes provided lectures on art, industry, and "natural philosophy," aiming to educate their membership and promote self-improvement.[4] The institutes also published technical journals and staged exhibitions. The first mechanics' institute was established in Edinburgh in 1821; a second Scottish institute was founded in 1823; and the first English institutes opened the same year in Liverpool and London. Soon these organizations spread throughout the English-speaking world, with some in Australia established by the late 1820s. In the United States, the Franklin Institute of Philadelphia held the first fair in 1824, followed by those of the American Institute in 1829 and the first Mechanics' Institutes of the City of New-York fair in 1835. These fairs displayed the machines that produced goods such as hats, boots, furniture, and numerous other objects (278).

By 1831, the Seventh Exhibition of Domestic Manufactures, held at the Masonic Hall in Philadelphia, attracted over forty thousand visitors who saw textiles, stoves, writing paper, and Britannia ware (a pewter alloy). The notice in *Hazard's Register of Pennsylvania* noted that there was

> great improvement in the taste of the manufactures ... in the chaster and more graceful forms of the cabinet ware, most of the pianos ... the good workmanship of which often suffered much formerly by the abuse of ornament. Even now we occasionally observe forms too massive, or inappropriate to the uses expected of the goods—colors too gaudy or inharmonious—gildings too lavishly spread upon objects of furniture.
>
> (*Hazard's Register* 1831: 305–8)

One of the exhibitors included the well-known French immigrant cabinetmaker Anthony Gabriel Quervelle (1789–1856).

Even after the establishment of a series of international expositions, national exhibitions, or those that focused solely on furniture, continued to be presented. One model presented contemporary furniture together with antique examples or copies of such. In Leeds in 1881 and the Agriculture Hall in Islington (London) in 1883 modern examples of British manufacturing were shown alongside genuine antiques or those manufactured to imitate them ("Sketches" 1883: 6236). Queen Victoria's Jubilee of 1887 served as the impetus for numerous exhibitions, including one in Newcastle.[5] In London, during the 1880s a series of Building Exhibitions included extensive displays of furniture. At the Second Annual Furniture Trade Exhibition, for example, were the wares of well-known manufacturers such as Gillow & Co. and the Austrian Bent Wood Furniture Co. ("Furnishing Items at the Building Exhibition" 1882: 197). *The Furniture Gazette* of 1881 declared that such a London exhibition benefited various audiences: manufacturers could be satisfied with their work and dealers could compare products by competing makers side by side ("Forthcoming Furniture Exhibition" 1881: 295).

TRADE AND SOCIETY EXHIBITIONS

By the 1880s, a number of European, British, and American organizations presented expositions of designs as well as finished projects, by professionals and amateurs. *The Furniture Gazette* documented a great number of exhibitions in 1881 devoted to decorative arts in general and furniture in particular. In the spring, there was an *Exhibition of Decorative Art* at the Albert Hall in London. Most of the furniture on display, however, was French in origin, probably to continue to emphasize the superiority, at least in the minds of many British critics, of French design over British. There were several English exhibitors, including Gillow & Co., who displayed part of a boudoir that the firm had exhibited at the Royal Pavilion at the Paris exhibition of 1878. Gillow's showed an "Adams style ... center table, decorated with painted flowers and classical subjects." The doors of the boudoir were also singled out for their use of satinwood with marquetry and low-relief carving. Liberty & Co. also participated in this exhibition with Japanese carved-wood panels ("Exhibition of Decorative Art" 1881: 361). In the same volume an exhibition of designs for furniture and decoration at the Royal Academy was harshly criticized for the absence of works by major designers such as William Burgess and Richard Norman Shaw, for the scarcity of drawings for individual cabinetry or seating furniture, and for the styles representing imitations of earlier styles rather than "modern" designs ("Designs for Furniture" 1881: 362).

Important exhibitions of objects, including furniture, were held by l'Union centrale des beaux-arts appliqués à l'industrie in Paris. Established in 1864, the Union centrale emerged from two industrial arts exhibitions held in Paris in 1861 and 1863, sponsored by the Caisse de Secours des Inventeurs et Artistes Industriels, a private organization founded in 1844 by the Baron Isadore Justin Séverin Taylor (1789–1879). The textile designer Édouard Guichard (1815–89) presided over a committee of manufacturers, designers, artists, and critics to plan small exhibitions. The exhibition of 1864, sponsored by the newly created Union centrale and organized by the industrial designer Amédée Couder (1797–1864), the sculptor Jules Klagmann (1810–67), and Guichard, promoted good design and reinforced the necessity of private industry working hand in hand with artists and designers. Soon the Union centrale not only sponsored exhibitions, but also a museum, similar to the South Kensington Museum, a library, lectures and courses, and competitions, all for their membership. The proceeds from the membership subscriptions acquired works for the museum and library (Hiesinger and Rishel 1978: 32). Financially successful exhibitions were held in 1865 and 1869. By 1864 the museum and the library were open, with access given to artists and industrial workers. Both the museum and the library were free of charge and open so that workers could come after completing their day's labors. The 1865 exhibition included displays of historical design from private collections (*Rapports 1865*, cited in Hiesinger and Rishel 1978: 33). Schools of art from all parts of France held competitions to educate designers, workers, and the public. In 1865, for instance, there was a special professional competition "for bedroom furniture of moderate price," which the organizers hoped would improve the goods offered to the public (Hiesinger and Rishel 1978: 33). By 1869, the competition was restricted to designs for goods that had been manufactured, rather than speculative ideas. In 1896, one English critic, however, decried the Union centrale:

> Its object—to judge by its high-sounding title—is to unite, to centralize, the decorative arts. As a matter of fact, it is quite unconcerned with anything of the sort. It neither unites nor centralizes anything whatsoever, and its gallery is simply stuffed with a mass of incongruous rubbish, without value, and absolutely without originality. No truly new and original work of art has ever been seen therein, for they detest freshness and novelty, and are entirely bound up in superannuated academic traditions.
>
> (Mourey 1896: 211–12)

The Union centrale also sponsored exhibitions of art that served to inspire designers. Emile-Auguste Reiber (1826–93), a designer for the French silver and metalwork firm of Christofle, visited an 1869 exhibition of Asian works of art, from which he would derive designs for clocks, candelabra, and other objects (see Musée d'Orsay OAO 1360; Minneapolis Institute of Arts, 96.72A,B).

In 1882, the Union centrale sponsored its seventh exhibition, *Les Arts du bois, des tissus et du papier* with a retrospective installation of historical and modern furniture. The catalog includes a history of furniture and the various techniques in the decoration of wooden furniture. It also included a "salle orientale" with examples of Chinese decorative arts and furniture from the collections of Siegfried Bing and the first director of the Union centrale, Antonin Proust (1832–1905), among others. Modern furniture on view included the famous electroplated corner cabinet in the Chinese-Japanese-European style designed by Reiber for Christofle, displayed at the Paris 1878 exposition (now at the Musée des arts décoratifs, Paris, Inv. 27662); cabinets exhibiting pastiches of French early neoclassiscism and Japanese design by Auguste-Hippolyte Sauvrezy (1815–84); and traditional Renaissance revival works by Henri Fourdinois (*Les arts du bois* 1883). The Union centrale and its efforts to emulate the South Kensington Museum would culminate in the establishment of the Musée des arts décoratifs.

In addition to the Union centrale exhibitions, Paris also hosted the Annual Industrial Exhibition in the Palais de l'Industrie. One of the expositions took place in 1879 and included mainly French manufacturers, although the writer C.H.B. commented that most of the furniture was "not very interesting" ("Correspondence: The Paris Industrial Exhibition" 1879: 134).

Other exhibitions were more specialized and targeted to makers. An exhibition of models, drawings, and specimens was organized by the Carpenters' and Joiners' Companies in London in 1884 with over 140 exhibitors and about 500 works. The most highly praised aspect of the exhibition was the display of examples of carving. The audience for the exhibition was members of the guild rather than the public. The Clerk of the Carpenters' Company gave opening remarks citing that exhibitions of this sort allowed craftsmen and the public access to ancient and rare works and supported a greater understanding of the skill and artistry of the craftsmen's labors ("Exhibition of Works in Wood" 1884: 449). Other guilds, research, collecting, or academic societies also staged exhibitions, such as the 1897 *Exposition artistique et rétrospective* in Montauban, near Toulouse, France, presented by the Société archéologique de Tarn-et-Garonne (*Exposition artistique* 1897: 56–65).

Finally, there were public exhibitions of furniture that were political events. The most noted of these during the period under discussion was the display of the cradle commissioned by the City of Paris to receive the new infant of Emperor Napoleon III and Empress Eugénie in 1856 (Musée Carnavalet, Histoire de Paris, MB249). The cradle, of rosewood with gilded silver, silver, and enamels displayed the skills of designer, *ébéniste*, and *fondeur-ciseleur*, but more importantly proclaimed the establishment of the imperial dynasty and the stature of Paris as the center of power and prestige in the empire. Civic and imperial symbols abounded. Displayed in the throne room of the Hôtel de Ville, March 13–14, 1856, 25,000 visitors paid tribute to the empire (Samoyault-Verlet 1978: 94–6).

In London, the Arts and Crafts Exhibition Society held a number of displays of decorative and fine arts in 1888, 1889, and 1890 and then every three years until the 1950s. The designer and illustrator Walter Crane (1845–1915), founding president of the society, stated in 1905: "We desired first of all to give opportunity to the designer and craftsman to exhibit their work to the public for its artistic interest and thus to assert the claims of decorative art and handicraft to attention equally with the painter of easel pictures, hitherto almost exclusively associated with the term art in the public mind" (Crane 1905: 22). A writer in the *American Architect and Building News* from November 1888 condemns the separation of the designer from the customer. He praises a London exhibition for trying to remedy this situation, that there is an "extraordinary difference, between the exhibits and the ordinary show articles in the shop windows. One has been done for the love of the thing, the other to sell, one is full of artistic interest, the other is mechanical, lifeless" ("London" 1888: 231).

INTERNATIONAL EXPOSITIONS

Although the first international exposition did not take place until 1851, the threat of French superiority in manufacturing had been well noted in the British press and among critics and design reformers. In an article following the 1819 French national exhibition, one British critic stated that the British diplomat (Henry Stephen) Fox "expressed in the most marked way, his astonishment at the progress of French industry. He particularly noticed the excellence, manufacture and extreme cheapness of the workmen's tools. The exhibition of the present year affords incontestable proofs of the eminence to which France has risen in many branches of manufacturing industry" ("Exhibition of the Produce of French Industry" 1819: 681). By the 1840s, the author, critic, and entrepreneur Henry Cole was concerned that the French were outstripping British manufacturers and would soon dominate the international market place. In 1850, the Conseil supérieur de perfectionnement des manufacturers nationales staged an exhibition of the products of the national manufacturers (Sèvres, Beauvais, and Gobelins) who had been encouraged to work with artists for their designs. The Conseil noted that the best designs shown at the national expositions were those where industry worked hand in hand with art (Hiesinger and Rishel 1978: 31).

The first international exposition, the Great Exhibition of the Works of Industry of All Nations, took place in London's Hyde Park, from May 1 to October 11, 1851. Organized by a group of industrialists and critics and members of the Royal Society for the Encouragement of Arts, Manufactures and Commerce, headed by Cole and Prince Albert (1819–61), husband of Queen Victoria, it had about six million visitors. The exhibition was housed in what was to be called "The Crystal Palace," designed by Joseph Paxton (1803–65) with interiors by architect and designer Owen Jones (1809–74) and a central Medieval Court designed by Augustus Welby Northmore Pugin (1812–52) (Figure 6.4). Although the intention was to highlight British industry—through its own manufacturers and those of its colonies and dependencies—the exhibition also included goods and industrial products from forty-four European and American "foreign states" in over thirteen thousand exhibits. The displays were characterized by great numbers of goods, whether raw materials, such as cotton or grains, or completed industrial products, such as chairs, stacked high and crowded into booths. The natural light of the glass building allowed visitors to see a great deal as they ambled along the aisles.

In addition to displaying the goods of the British Empire, the organizers of exhibitions also hoped to elevate public taste. Ticket prices allowed for the general public to attend, thus exposing industrial workers and consumers of all classes to a great range of goods. Napoleon III, president of the imperial commission for the 1855 *Exposition Universelle*, encouraged the working

FIGURE 6.4 Interior of the Great Exhibition of the Works of Industry of All Nations in 1851 at the Crystal Palace in London. Photograph courtesy of Rijksmuseum/ Wikimedia Commons.

class to attend. At these great events, "the spectacle of the progress achieved by industry in every part of the globe, and the comparative study of the improvements in techniques and methods are in effect a powerful means of professional education" (*Rapports universelle de 1855* 1856 cited in Hiesinger and Rishel 1978: 32). The French imperial commission made it possible for nearly one thousand workers and craftsmen to visit the London 1862 exposition, providing for travel expenses (Hiesinger and Rishel 1978: 32).

The first international exhibition in 1851 was immediately answered in 1855 by a similar fair in Paris, which was then followed by another in London in 1862, and a subsequent fair in 1867 in Paris. Each fair grew in the number of exhibitors, although most lost considerable funds. The Paris 1867 *Exposition Universelle* is notable for the change in architecture—no longer a single building—the introduction of the national pavilions, and the first time that the Japanese participated as a nation (at the London 1862 International Exhibition, Sir Rutherford Alcock, British Minister to Japan, curated an exhibition of Japanese goods). Although goods at the 1851 exhibition were not for sale, visitors could easily learn where they were made and available for purchase. Later fairs served as market places, where the public (and even museum directors) could purchase goods directly from the manufacturers.

Prizes selected by juries—often made up of exhibitors!—were another aspect of the international expositions. Prizes were awarded in many categories and allowed the exhibitor to proclaim their superiority in advertisements and in subsequent fairs. Occasionally, exhibitors from outside the circle of the jury and hosting nation were awarded a medal, as in the gold medals presented to James Lamb of Manchester and Collinson and Lock of London at the Paris 1878 *Exposition Universelle* ("English Furniture" 1878: 198–9). At the same fair, Messrs. Jackson and Graham were awarded the grand prize "for their beautiful marquetry." The writer in *The American Architect and Building News* correctly suspects that the craftsmen of this award-winning marquetry was executed by "French and Italian workmen ... and it is known that the finest inlaid cabinet was designed by a Frenchman" (198).

At least fifty-one international expositions took place during the nineteenth century in over eighteen countries. These ranged from ones held in smaller towns, such as Dunedin, New Zealand, to those in larger industrial cities, such as Chicago. Organizers selected almost any political, commemorative, or industrial anniversary to use as the focus or rationale for an exhibition. The Philadelphia Centennial Exhibition of 1876 commemorated the hundredth anniversary of the Declaration of Independence, while the Paris Exposition of 1889 celebrated the hundredth anniversary of the French Revolution. There were a number of exhibitions in Australia and New Zealand during the late 1870s and 1880s, probably to draw attention to the local natural resources and to attract economic development. All these international expositions emphasized competition between manufacturers and rivalry between nations. Nationalism was promoted and encouraged. At the same time, delegations of manufacturers, designers, and workmen visited the fairs to study, learn, and imitate.[6]

Throughout the century, the displays of the furniture at the international exhibitions were criticized for their lack of ingenuity or inspiration. Ralph Wornum, in his review of the industrial designs at the 1851 exhibition commented: "There is nothing new in the exhibition in ornamental design: not a scheme, not a detail that has not been treated over and over again in ages that are gone" (Wornum 1851 cited in Ames 1974: 2). Manufacturers exhibited case and seating furniture that imitated Gothic, Renaissance, baroque, and rococo models. In addition, the majority of the exhibits were pastiches of many of these styles, which drew great criticism! Not only were the styles and forms borrowed from earlier periods, but the materials were too: ebony with hardstones, inspired by French Renaissance precedents—or gilt-metal mounts applied to the surface of eighteenth-century French examples of case furniture covered with marquetry. Yet, sometimes the critics could be enthusiastic about works that derived their form, design, and decoration from earlier sources. Henri Fourdinois's sideboard, exhibited at the 1851 exhibition, was praised by English and French writers. Fourdinois looked at French Renaissance and Mannerist designers such as Jean Goujon, Vredeman de Vries, and others for his design (Ames 1974: 2–3). Daniel Alcouffe's statement that the large bookcase exhibited by the French maker Louis-Auguste-Alfred Beurdeley (1802–82) at the 1867 exposition was not a pastiche, is undermined by his detailed description of the sources of elements from a number of different, mainly eighteenth-century furniture and interiors designed for Marie-Antoinette at Fontainebleau and Saint-Cloud (Alcouffe 1978: 96–7).

The display of furniture radically changed beginning with the Philadelphia Centennial Exhibition of 1876 and the Paris *Exposition Universelle* of 1878. The hitherto ubiquitous jumble of furniture was replaced with interiors that displayed rooms in coherent styles with woodwork, furniture, textiles (both window treatments and floor coverings), and lighting, all harmoniously installed with complementary decorative arts such as vases, etc. Visitors—potential customers—were able to envision what these items would look like in their own homes.

In an article on the furniture of the British section at the 1876 Philadelphia Centennial, the author finds "the British exhibition of furniture is the most complete and meritorious in the building ... we have ascribed this great work to the efforts of a coterie of architects ... but here come seven solid, substantial well-to-do British firms, who lay out a feast from which we cannot reject the smallest dish." The author does, however, declare that the display "would have been far more complete had they brought over examples of what they produce at moderate cost ... The London shops display hideous deformities as disgrace the present American exhibit. But either those who make them have had the good sense to keep them away, or the British Commission has had the good taste to reject them." The writer continues that American manufacturers will benefit from seeing good designs by makers such as Collinson and Lock, especially, as "it is doubtful if many of these goods will be sold" ("Decorative Fine-Art Work" 1876: 372). The British furniture was mainly in eighteenth-century styles, the Queen Anne and "Free Jacobean." Of particular interest was the way the furniture was exhibited. Each of the firms seems to have displayed furniture in room settings with paneling, wallpaper, completed ceilings, decorated with carpets and decorative objects. For example, James Shoolbred displayed "six furnished apartments," including an oak dining room. "The wealth of objects of art in pottery, metal, and embroidery, displayed by this firm in connection with its own manufactures, is an exhibition in itself." The Collinson and Lock display was the most elaborate with a large oak sideboard set with panels of Bacchus and Venus, and an oak and walnut bedroom, ebonized furniture inlaid with a variety of woods, stamped leather for the walls and a variety of ceramics by Doulton, Minton, and Brown-Westhead (372–3). Cox & Sons was the only firm to exhibit Gothic Revival examples, both as ecclesiastical and domestic goods. Unusually, Cox "has given liberal employment to the best architects of England, and invariably has given them full credit for their work." It was also commended: "one lesson taught by this exhibit is that what we waste on finish, the English put into perfection of workmanship and honest construction" ("English Furniture" 1876: 389–90). Another of the exhibitors, Wright & Mansfield, included genuine eighteenth-century furniture mixed with the display of their original designs (396–7).

In Paris at the 1878 exposition, "Collinson and Lock showed charming examples in Mr. [Richard Norman] Shaw's Queen Anne cottage, Rue des Nations ... The dining-room has seventeenth century panelled dado and ceiling, and the robust though comfortable character is carried out by the sturdy side-board, and its projecting cupboard with small brass-set panes. The room complete was offered for £1,700" ("English Furniture at the Exhibition" 1878: 198). At the same 1878 fair, Gillow & Co. decorated the Prince of Wales pavilion with a dining room, library, bedrooms for the prince and princess, and a drawing room. The furniture of the library, which incorporated Japanese-style motifs, is praised for "beautiful execution, but surcharged with colonnettes and bevels, and injured by futile effort to give a Japanese *cachet*" (198). The journalist saves his most damning criticism for the drawing room:

> I was particularly curious to see what English style would be used for the drawing room, but I found a stiff little Marie Antoinette boudoir, the walls covered with pale blue silk panels. Two nondescript chairs and two small stands formed the scanty furniture. It was an apology for a drawing-room, and with nothing English about it ... the small sitting room of the Prince of Wales is for sale at £5,000, for which figure an exquisite French drawing-room may be had.
>
> ("English Furniture at the Exhibition" 1878: 198)

Finally, the author condemns the English displays for neglecting the furnishings for drawing rooms, "there is hardly a piece exhibited which does not smack of slippers and dressing gown" ("English Furniture at the Exhibition" 1878: 198).

At the Glasgow International Exhibition of 1888 were the "royal reception rooms" decorated by Messrs. Wylie and Lochhead of Buchanan Street, Glasgow, in the "Moresque style" (Figure 6.5). The same firm also displayed a dining room in the "Scottish baronial style" with "plainly carved" oak furniture. The author does, however, criticize the Scottish furniture makers, writing that "we require, however, a little dash of genius in the designs, a little more genuine creative power on the part of the designers" ("The Glasgow International Exhibition 1888" 1888: 14). Clearly, competing styles and a lack of coherent nationalistic or even period style struck critics as both over- and underwhelming.

FIGURE 6.5 "Moresque style royal reception room by Wylie and Lochhead, Glasgow," from *The Art Journal* special supplement for the Glasgow International Exhibition, 1888, insert between pp. 8–9. Photograph © CSG CIC Glasgow Museums and Libraries Collection: The Mitchell Library, Special Collections.

Although the Paris international exposition of 1889 was noted for the Eiffel Tower, writers for national journals such as *The American Architect and Building News* focused on the displays of their countrymen. The critic took to task American exhibitors of what he considered an "ingenious and amusing" Derby roll-top desk and "too complicated" works by the American roll-top desk specialty firm from Buffalo, New York, A. Cutler & Son ("Paris" 1889: 181–2). English and Belgian furniture is also summarily dismissed as being "without much originality," while the Italian "pieces are generally imitated after our own, but with a super-abundance of detail, sculpture and decoration absolutely in bad taste." The Stabilimento Quartara, nonetheless, is praised for a "cabinet of natural pear-wood, very richly carved, and showing much cunning of hand in execution" (181–2). Only a few of the French manufacturers garnered accolades, among these Gabriel Viardot & Co., "whose furniture is particularly elegant and distinguished. It is Japan with a Parisian accent and originality of feeling." Emile Gallé's designs are commended as they "are artistic, not commonplace, but having a characteristic stamp" (Brincourt 1889: 39).

During the first fifty years that international expositions were held there was no international commission to establish where the fairs would be held.

Therefore, sometimes there were multiple fairs the same year, or even season. A notable year was 1897, when Nashville, Tennessee; Brisbane; Stockholm; and Brussels all held exhibitions. For the study of furniture, the most important of these 1897 fairs was in Brussels, which included a special complementary fair, the *Exposition Congolaise* held in conjunction with the Exposition Internationale de Bruxelles, in Tervuren. The *Exposition Conglaise* was an elaborate promotion of King Leopold II's private enterprise of forced labor, extraction of natural resources, and exploitation in the Congo Free State. Leopold hoped, through the display of extraordinary works fabricated from the natural resources of the Congo, including ivory and Congolese mahogany, to quiet the extremely unfavorable reports of the treatment of native peoples and to encourage Belgian and other foreign manufacturers and artists to employ these materials. The Belgian architect and designer Paul Hankar received the commission to design the interiors of the *Exposition Congolaise* pavilion. By studying works of native art, Hankar was inspired to design some anthropomorphic furniture, called, at the time, *le style congo*. Some of the seating furniture, although illustrating a more reductive vocabulary than fully developed Belgian Art Nouveau, explicitly derived from African models. The silhouettes of both Hankar's chairs and benches recall African figures and masks (Figure 6.6).

FIGURE 6.6 Paul Hankar, Bench in the Exposition Congolaise, Tervuren, at the Exposition Internationale de Bruxelles, 1897. Photograph courtesy of Wellcome Images/Wikimedia Commons.

Exhibitions held in British colonies were considered invaluable marketing for British manufacturers. A notice about the Melbourne Exhibition of 1881 observed that "Australia is one of the best foreign customers for English furniture, well-nigh half the cabinet goods shipped from this country finding a market on that continent." Furthermore, according to the article, Australian manufacturers had learned new techniques of display and manufacture from the English displays at the Paris 1878 international exposition. Messrs. W.H. Rock & Co. of Melbourne now "grouped their furniture in a room suitably decorated. The casual visitor is thus enabled to form a far more correct opinion as to the merits of the articles shown than when they are thrown together pell-mell, and arranged with no regard to the general *coup d'oeil*" ("Furniture Shown" 1881: 124).

CONCLUSION

The exhibition and marketing of furniture changed radically during the nineteenth century as opportunities for display escalated through improvements in transportation, manufacturing, and marketing. Travelers could visit more private and public collections; guide books helped them make arrangements and knowledgeably conducted them through the history and finer points of furniture. The first museums to build collections and exhibit permanent and temporary exhibitions of furniture began in the 1850s, establishing a venue for the education and pleasure of experts and novices. With increased wealth came more buyers for a proliferation of goods. There were new types of shops and shopping experiences. The furniture workshop became a factory and goods were sourced from warehouses and shops and, after the middle of the century, new splendid department stores with a greater variety of furniture types. Although the public still did not avail themselves of the occasion to purchase furniture from department stores, it was another opportunity to see different styles to help in the selection of goods. The most radical development in this period was the progress in the display of furniture, its tools of manufacture, processes, and raw materials as the national and, especially, international expositions or fairs took place. Visitors to these extravaganzas also saw a transformation in the exhibition of furniture, which before 1876 consisted of booths of single furniture manufacturers displaying dozens, if not hundreds, of styles and objects. At the Philadelphia Centennial Exhibition of 1876, these overcrowded presentations were transformed into room settings combining the goods of multiple manufactures. Companies no longer marketed only their wares but, as the century advanced, increasingly a lifestyle. In addition, although Europe continued to play an important role in the establishment of style in furniture and its display, increasingly other areas of the globe became centers: the United States, Australia, etc. Shops established outposts in these new markets and international and national exhibitions were staged—bringing the goods to the public. These exciting displays also served as catalysts for the dissemination of styles and technologies as manufacturers saw firsthand the models, materials, and manufacturing processes of their competitors. The international expositions had an added benefit of exhibiting goods from foreign lands stimulating cross-pollination and creating demand for ever-changing styles and motifs. The result was a furniture market with a cacophony of styles, materials, and models, where multiple styles were popular simultaneously. The nineteenth century was truly the age of the exhibition.

CHAPTER SEVEN

Furniture and Architecture

DAVID OAKEY

In the final years of the eighteenth century Thomas Sheraton's (1751–1806) *The Cabinet Makers and Upholsterer's Drawing Book*, published in instalments between 1791 and 1793, with a second edition in 1794 and revised in 1802, emphasized the architectural character of furniture. It contained diagrams outlining the proportions of the different classical orders; a plan and section of a fashionable drawing room; instructions on the use of draperies and curtains and the insertion of an alcove bed and a "turkey sofa" into a room; and directions for the placing of a commode beneath a pier glass. The book demonstrated that at the beginning of the nineteenth century the furniture maker's remit had already moved beyond simply making chairs and cabinets, and reminded its approximately six hundred subscribers to consider the architectural setting for their furniture, albeit still within the strict stylistic framework of the eighteenth century.

Fashionable furniture at this time was nearly always architectural in its inspiration. Neoclassicism, largely based on ancient architecture, was the unchallenged stylistic language of the early nineteenth century. A scarcity of genuine pieces of ancient furniture that could serve as examples for makers meant architectural sources were frequently used. Additionally, there was now a new search for archaeological accuracy in the style. The French Empire style referenced the archaeology of ancient Rome and emphasized the new Emperor Napoleon Bonaparte's imperial ascendancy; ancient fragments from Italy, Greece, and Egypt, architectural or otherwise, gathered during the emperor's military campaigns and installed in his Musée Napolèon provided a ready body of source material. The emperor's favored designers Charles Percier (1764–1838) and Pierre-François-Léonard Fontaine (1762–1853) both trained as architects; their first joint publication in 1798, *Palais, maisons, et autres édifices modernes dessinés à Rome* (Palaces, Houses and Other Modern Buildings Drawn in Rome) was an architectural one. It was this publication that originally motivated the Empress Josephine to employ the pair to work at her home, the Château de Malmaison in 1800, where they designed interiors of influential sumptuousness and coherency. Resulting from the success of this project, their publication of 1802, *Recueil de decorations intérieures comprenant tout ce qui a rapport à l'ameublement* (Collection of Interior Decorations Including Everything Relating to Furnishing), was an all-encompassing work focusing on furniture design that featured individual pieces as well as demonstrating the correct placement of objects within interiors. In the introduction, the authors announced that the book was intended to provide all the necessities required by someone of fashion to decorate and furnish an interior, while simultaneously disregarding everything that had come before as "petty, false and insignificant" (Percier and Fontaine 1801: 3). Over the course of fifteen years, Percier and Fontaine issued a number of books, a preoccupation with publishing that contrasts starkly with architects of the previous generation. The widespread popularity of their publications suggests that the importance of a designer who could produce architecture and corresponding furniture in small and large projects was recognized by a broadening section of society. Percier and Fontaine most successfully collaborated with the great furniture-making dynasty, the Jacob family, producing pieces of extraordinary inventiveness that borrowed extensively from their architectural repertoire, such as the magnificent jewel cabinet made for the Empress Josephine in 1810, the *Grand Ecrin* (Plate 26).

In Britain, the Prince of Wales, the future king George IV (1762–1830), also desired a more archaeologically correct classical style for his famous London home Carlton House. In 1790, his first architect Henry Holland (1745–1806) sent his best young draftsman, an eighteen-year-old Charles Heathcote Tatham (1772–1842), to Italy to source architectural fragments and casts, and make drawings of classical architecture that could be used as the basis for decorations and furnishings. The resultant drawings became available to a wider audience in 1799 when Tatham published them as part of his *Etchings, representing the best examples of Ancient Ornamental Architecture; Drawn from the Originals in Rome and Other Parts of Italy*. The book was enormously influential and was republished in 1803, 1810, and 1836 (and in German in 1805) (Riddell 2004). In 1806, Tatham followed it with a further volume, *Fragments of Grecian and Roman Architectural Ornaments*. Tatham was able to apply the designs in a number of different ways in his own architectural work, but they were also applied to furniture; he came from a furniture-making family and his brother Thomas was a senior partner in the furniture company Marsh and Tatham, later Tatham and Bailey, which supplied a prodigious amount of furniture to

Carlton House. The prince paid them £30,000 in just two years from 1808 to 1810 (de Bellaigue 1991: 38). Undoubtedly, a major ingredient in the remarkable impact of Marsh and Tatham's furniture is the application of their kinsman's Italian drawings to pieces such as the magnificent carved and gilded griffin pedestals, supplied to the Prince in 1813 and based on an architectural fragment illustrated in *Architectural Ornaments*, which remain in the British Royal Collection. This enormously successful mode of applying architectural detail was not just confined to Carlton House: Charles also used his brother's furniture at other English country houses such as Southill Park, Brocklesby Hall, and Castle Howard. These productions set a new precedent for the integration of architectural motifs and sources into English furniture design and confirmed that London makers could produce architecturally inspired furniture that rivalled that of their French competitors.

The designer and collector Thomas Hope (1769–1831) was not an architect, but like Percier and Fontaine and the Tathams, he employed architecture and archaeology as sources for his interior and furniture designs. His 1807 publication, *Household Furniture and Interior Decoration executed from Designs by Thomas Hope*, drew upon his far-flung Grand Tour in Greece, Turkey, and Egypt, looking to examples of ancient Greek and Egyptian architecture, rather than Roman, as sources of inspiration. The publication had a profound and lasting impact on nineteenth-century English and American furniture production and included a series of interior views of his London home in Duchess Street, which Hope used as a showcase for his collections and designs. Hope singled out Percier and Fontaine for praise in the introduction of *Household Furniture*, and in a similar tenor to the Frenchmen, denigrated the "wretched ideas and trivial conceits" produced by other designers (1807: 1). He was not complimentary to London furniture makers or "the race of draftsmen and of modellers, that of carvers of wood and stone, and of casters in metal and composition." He claimed that only two London craftsmen, the Flemish carver Peter Bogaert (d.1819) and the bronze caster Alexis Decaix (d.1811), could "in some measure confide the execution of the more complicate and more enriched portion of my designs" (10). Hope stated that he wanted to influence public taste, although his success in doing so was limited; his designs were too lavish for anyone of modest means. But a year later in 1808 the furniture maker George Smith published his own, cheaper, interpretations of Thomas Hope's designs in his similarly titled *Collection of Designs for Household Furniture and Interior Decoration, in the most Approved and Elegant Taste*.

Rudolph Ackerman's *Repository of the Arts*, which appeared monthly from 1809 to 1829, illustrated the work by many leading furniture makers and designers of the period, including a young Augustus Welby Northmore Pugin (1812–52) and John Buonarotti Papworth (1775–1847), both of whom would later work as architects. Pugin would become arguably the figure of greatest influence on mid-nineteenth-century architecture and design (discussed in greater detail below), but Papworth was also a remarkably flexible designer, who devised furniture both for his own projects and for other commercial firms, often under the influence of Percier and Fontaine. Another regular contributor to the *Repository* was George Bullock (1782–1818), who enjoyed an especially fruitful relationship with architects William Atkinson (1745–1839) and Richard Bridgens (1785–1846). He would collaborate closely with the former on the design and furnishing of the residence used by Napoleon during his period of exile on Saint Helena beginning in 1815 (Levy 1998). With the latter Bullock worked on projects such as Battle Abbey, producing furniture in a style designed to harmonize with the house's medieval interiors, examples of which survive in the collection of the Victoria and Albert Museum (W.53–1980; W.56–1980; W.17–1981). In 1838 Bridgens published *Furniture with Candelabra and Interior Decoration* that included examples clearly based on Bullock's furniture in the Grecian, Elizabethan, and Gothic styles, signaling a growing diversity that would become a central feature of the subsequent decades.

The contribution an architect could make to the design of furniture was increasingly recognized during this era. John Soane (1753–1837), who like C.H. Tatham, had trained in Henry Holland's office, declared in one of his earliest lectures at the Royal Academy in 1815, that "the same feeling that is produced by the first sight of a building, should be preserved even in the inferior Offices; nay the Furniture itself should partake of the Decorative Character of the building" (Watkin 2000: 185). A few of his furniture designs survive in the Sir John Soane Museum, including Gothic furniture made for the library at Stowe in 1805 (Ward-Jackson 1984: 28). An interesting example, this cabinet was not in keeping with the decorative character of the Palladian house but related more closely to the Marquis of Buckingham's collection of Saxon manuscripts that it was built to contain. In 1827 the English antiquary and author J. Britton echoed Soane's sentiments in his *The Union of Architecture, Sculpture and Painting* to complain, "unfortunately for good taste, Furniture, although forming so essential a part of decoration and effect, has been considered as not coming within the province of the architect or artist" (Britton 1827: 22).

The Romantic movement, a defining phenomenon of the early nineteenth century, placed a new emphasis on personal expression and individuality, affecting all modes of artistry and creativity. The movement was partially responsible for a new informality in social interaction, which was evident in the layout and furnishing of domestic spaces. In 1816 the landscape designer Humphry Repton (1752–1818) made his now-famous visual comparison between the old-fashioned formal Cedar Parlor and the modern, open-plan Living Room (Plate 27) in his *Fragments on the Theory and Practice of Landscape Gardening, Including Some Remarks on Grecian and Gothic Architecture* of 1816. The following rhyme accompanied it:

No more the Cedar Parlour's formal gloom
With dullness chills, tis now the Living Room;
Where Guests to whim, or taste, or fancy true,
Scattered in groups, their different plans pursue.

(Repton 1816: 58)

The comparison of spaces makes it clear that a conscious break from the formality and stiffness inherited from the eighteenth century was underway. Repton stated that it was necessary for both furnishings and architecture to change to suit contemporary life. This modification also precipitated a decline in the taste for classicism, which was in its essence also highly formal. Instead, the Gothic Revival, which in its early years had been, as espoused by aesthetes such as Horace Walpole (1717–97) and William Beckford (1760–1844), a highly romantic and idiosyncratic style of narrow appeal, grew in popularity. In 1811 the Prince Regent unveiled his astonishing Gothic conservatory at Carlton House designed by Thomas Hopper; not only was it Gothic, it was made entirely out of the modern materials of cast iron, specially reformulated concrete and glass. The style would now be the subject of increasing scrutiny and intellectual enquiry. In 1835 the architect and antiquary Thomas Rickman (1776–1841) published *An Attempt to Discriminate Styles of English Architecture, from the Norman Conquest to the Reformation*, differentiating the developing stages of architectural style during the medieval period. T.F. Hunt's 1830 publication *Exemplars of Tudor Architecture Adapted to Modern Habitations, with Illustrative Details Selected from Ancient Edifices and Observations on the Furniture of the Tudor Period* evinced a new interest in sixteenth-century architecture and furniture that became a new tangent of the Gothic Revival. The success of the so-called Elizabethan style's use at houses such as Charlecote Park, seat of the ancient Lucy family in Warwickshire, help to explain its growing popularity. This genuinely Elizabethan house, which had been visited by Queen Elizabeth I, survived with its magnificent Great Hall but otherwise had many of its defining period features removed in the seventeenth and eighteenth centuries. In 1829, work began to return it to its sixteenth-century splendor under the supervision of Benjamin Dean Wyatt (1775–1852), although largely executed by a lesser-known Warwickshire architect Charles S. Smith. There were no attempts to integrate older elements; everything was remade new in an "Elizabethan" style, including the paneling, stained glass, and wallpaper. The positive reception of Charlecote helped to encourage the adoption of the Elizabethan style by architects such as Sir Anthony Salvin (1799–1881), who employed the style in furniture created for Mamhead Park and Scotney Castle in the early 1840s, pieces of which survive in the Victoria and Albert Museum (W.5:1 to 5–1973). Joseph Nash's *Mansions of England*, a four-volume work with many highly romanticized illustrations, published between 1839 and 1849, focused on antiquated interiors and the manner in which furniture, both new and old, could be deployed in them.

In 1820, the Prince of Wales ascended the throne as King George IV. With the assistance of his architect Jeffry "Wyattville" Wyatt (1766–1840), George IV rebuilt and redecorated Windsor Castle, executing one of the most important sets of interiors in Britain during the early decades of the century. These spaces featured a mixture of contemporary French-inspired neoclassicism, Gothic Revival, and elements of the new Rococo Revival style. The Gothic areas featured bespoke furniture designed by the young A.W.N. Pugin, examples of which survive in the British Royal Collection, such as a pair of magnificent rosewood chairs (Royal Collection Trust, RCIN 29881). The Grand Reception Room integrated original eighteenth-century French carved wood panels or *boiseries* bought at auction in Paris. Just a year or so before the Windsor project, Elizabeth Manners, Duchess of Rutland, had installed French panels from the home of Louis XIV's morganatic wife Madame de Maintenon, at her home Belvoir Castle under the supervision of Jeffry Wyattville's cousins Benjamin Dean and Matthew Coates Wyatt (Robinson 1979: 107). This reuse of salvaged wall panels in interiors would become popular again later in the century.

The successful mixing of architectural styles here would prove prescient. In 1836, the botanist and garden designer John Claudius Loudon (1783–1843) published an *Encyclopaedia of Cottage, Farm and Villa Architecture and Furniture*, in which he confirmed a broadening of the available stylistic spectrum. He stated the range of styles now included:

> The Grecian or modern style, which is by far the most prevalent; the Gothic or perpendicular style, which imitates the lines and angles of the Tudor architecture, the Elizabethan style, which combines the Roman or Italian manner and the style of the age of Louis XIV or the florid Italian, which is characterized by curved lines and excess of curvilinear ornaments.
>
> (Loudon 1836: 1039)

As well as this expanding stylistic repertoire, the 1830s and 1840s witnessed the development of novel techniques that could be applied both to architecture and furniture. A primary example is cast iron, which despite being used in bridges since the late eighteenth century, was first widely applied in architecture and furniture from the 1840s. The great German polymath architect Karl Friedrich Schinkel (1781–1841) was especially instrumental in its wider adoption. He benefited from support and encouragement from the government of Prussia, which was eager to develop its domestic iron industry after the devastating effects of the Napoleonic Wars (Steffens 2003: 43). The Königlich-Technische Deputation für Gewerbe (Royal Technical Committee for Trade) was founded in Berlin in 1810 and distributed Schinkel's compendium of designs in cast iron, titled *Examples for Manufacturers and Craftsmen*, free of charge. It gave clear models for makers to follow, and thus Schinkel held considerable influence over the country's stylistic development. Examples of cast iron furniture made to his designs survive, such as an armchair at the Victoria and Albert Museum (Plate 28) and a pair of torchères in the Metropolitan Museum of Art (2007.188.1,.2). The use of cast metal in furniture would affect taste later in the century, not least in the Art Nouveau period.

The French architect Jacques Ignace Hittorff (1792–1867), a pupil of Charles Percier, pursued another unusual application of a new architectural technology to furniture. Hittorff is best remembered for designing much of nineteenth-century Paris and, not coincidentally, was an exponent of cast iron in architecture. In 1830, Hittorf published *Architecture Polychrome Chez les Grecs* (Greek Polychrome Architecture), which claimed that ancient Grecian temples and civic buildings had been brightly colored, both on their interiors and exteriors. Hittorff wanted to apply color to contemporary buildings in the same way, citing the potential of enameling and its application on large-scale construction to achieve this end. With the assistance of scientists he developed a technique for enameling lavastone and, in 1833, oversaw the production of a report submitted to the French Free Society of Fine Arts that discussed the new technique and its application in both fields. He hoped that the method "would testify to the advancement in our intelligence and art" (Mirault 1834: 12). From 1832 to 1838 Hittorff worked as director of Hachette et Cie, a firm established to create decorative pieces for sale in Paris and abroad utilizing the new technique to design tabletops, fireplaces, ornaments, plaques, column bases, candelabra, and mosaics. Pieces of this furniture survive in museum collections such as the tabletop in the Chrysler Museum of Art in Norfolk, Virginia (Plate 29). Hittorff was in contact with other exponents of color in architecture and furnishings, including Prince Albert's artistic advisor Ludwig Grüner (1801–88) in London, and Schinkel in Berlin. Grüner undertook his own experiments with colored furniture for Queen Victoria and Prince Albert, as shown by the pair of bronze-mounted inlaid stone side tables he designed, still in the Royal Collection (Royal Collection Trust, RCIN 41007) which were shown at the Great Exhibition of 1851. Their supports are clearly based on cast iron designs expounded by Schinkel a decade or so earlier.

The rise of Romantic nationalism combined with the development of the nation-state in the nineteenth century led to new and grand national architectural projects on an ambitious scale, which involved a wider range of designers than ever before, and which heightened discourse on style and decoration in the national consciousness. The arguments and debates in Britain during the 1830s and 1840s relating to the rebuilding of the Palace of Westminster in London, which had been destroyed by fire in 1834 save for the medieval Westminster Hall, is the most famous example. The initial point of contention was over whether the new palace should be built in a classical or Gothic style. To the modern mind, the Gothic was perhaps an obvious choice, but as recently as the 1820s John Soane had built a series of extensions to the palace in a classical style; some of his Palladian extensions to Westminster Hall survived until the 1880s. No other major public project had been built in the Gothic style before, and the decision to do so was more revolutionary than it might appear in retrospect; indeed, arguably it was among the greatest watersheds in British nineteenth-century architecture and style. This decision was in no small part owing to the activities of one designer-architect-critic, A.W.N. Pugin, a polemicist with a conservative religious agenda and a negative view of the modern age. He was the first to apply the moralistic dimension that would become such a defining feature of the mid-nineteenth-century discourse on architecture and design. In 1836 he published *Contrasts, or a Parallel between Noble Edifices of the Middle Ages and Corresponding Buildings Showing the Present Decay of Taste*, a book that, as the name suggests, relied on a succession of side-by-side visual comparisons between classical and medieval buildings. Published privately, it was viciously critical of classicism, which it branded as soulless and pagan. The book signaled the end of the classical monopoly on taste, and played an important part in the decision to rebuild the Palace of Westminster in the Gothic style.

Once finished, the palace was greeted as a triumph of cohesion between architect Charles Barry (1795–1860) and Pugin, acting as a designer and decorator. As mentioned above, Pugin had been involved in the design of furniture from a young age, perhaps explaining his clear abilities in harmonizing his furniture with architecture in a way that was immensely influential. This was particularly the case with the Westminster project: the palace required several suites of furniture, most of which remain in use to this day (Atterbury 1995: 322). The various types of chair designed by Pugin for the project are especially illustrative of the context-specific nature of the palace's furniture; some of the more rudimentary examples were clearly based on the simple *back-stools* of the fifteenth and sixteenth centuries (simply stools with backs), available for general use by visitors, officials, and other staff, while more complex versions were devised for the senior House of Lords, created by the more high-end maker, John Webb of Bond Street. Webb also fabricated sixteen exceptionally carved x-frame chairs for the lobby outside the House of Lords chambers based on sixteenth-century designs. The chair of state made for Prince Albert to use during the opening of the new House of Lords in 1847 also displays the influence of sixteenth-century sources. Other pieces of furniture included desks, notice stands, and clocks. All of them were cleverly contrived to harmonize with the grand architectural settings, and they were undoubtedly a crucial ingredient in the near-universal acclaim that greeted the project.

The correct execution of furniture was always a priority for Pugin; as early as 1829 he established his own workshop at 12 Hart Street, Covent Garden where he "determined to have all carved work, wherever possible, executed under my own eye" (Atterbury 1995: 163). He poured scorn on earlier medievalism and was especially dismissive of eighteenth-century picturesque Gothic, but was also critical of more recent attempts, especially in the realm of furniture, which he argued had consisted of inaccurate application of detailing to modern forms. In his later career he did much to bring authenticity and gravity both to neo-Gothic architecture and furniture. One of his most important advances was an emphasis on the honest construction of furniture, whereby every part served a purpose, with no extraneous or useless decoration, a concept that had its origins in his understanding of Gothic architecture. Pugin's first steps toward this can be seen in his chair for Scarisbrick Hall in Lancashire from about 1838, now at the Victoria and Albert Museum (Plate 30); a related design appears in his *Gothic Furniture in the Style of the Fifteenth Century* of 1835. His arguments were further developed in his 1841 publication *The True Principles of Pointed or Christian Architecture*, which championed "convenience, construction and propriety" in furniture (Pugin 1841: 1). Pugin's "structural tables," developed at this time, are almost entirely based on architecture, and clearly show his emphasis on function and form over decoration. The tables were also intended to be affordable. In 1849 Pugin wrote to John Gregory Crace (1809–89): "the great sale will be to the middling class ... I am anxious to induce a sensible style of furniture of good oak and constructively put together that shall compete with the vile trash made and sold" (Atterbury 1995: 171). In a similar vein was his so-called Glastonbury Chair from *c.* 1840, which although based on an original medieval chair from the Bishop's Palace at Wells, displays a striking, almost modernist starkness in its design, a primary example of Pugin's "revealed construction."

The working relationship between Pugin and the interior decorator and designer Crace was crucial to the former's success. It was predictive of the "design companies" that would come to dominate architecture, interior decoration and furniture design in the later century. The relationship was symbiotic in character: Pugin provided Crace with excellent designs and links to clients, while in return Crace turned Pugin's ideas into commercially appealing products. The pair frequently disagreed, often over Pugin's desire for simplicity in his furniture. In later years, as Pugin's own projects reduced in number, he came to rely on Crace, taking on the role of interior designer more than architect. One of their most accomplished later redecorations was the Grand Salon in Eastnor Castle from 1849, which included specially designed walnut furniture with extraordinary marquetry decoration. The room was further embellished with wall paintings, Minton tiles, brass elements such as the andirons designed to resemble lions, and an enormous stone fireplace. The magnificent cabinet in the Victoria and Albert Museum from around 1845 designed by Pugin for his home in Margate, the Grange, and most likely made for him by George Myers with elaborate mounts by Hardman of Birmingham, is also illustrative of this later style with fulsome carving based on actual medieval objects from Pugin's own collection (Plate 31). However, it is notable that the carved decoration is restrained so as not to disavow Pugin's fundamental tenet that "all ornament should consist of enrichment of the essential construction of a building" (Pugin 1841: 1). Many of his furniture designs manufactured by Crace survive; the firm continued producing them long after his untimely death in 1852 at the age of forty. There is little doubt that Pugin's activities induced a turning point in the creation of architectural furniture due to his relationship with Crace and, perhaps more importantly, his emphasis on the "honest structure" of architecture and furniture, which was adopted and developed further by the next generation of designers.

Pugin's activities also had considerable impact beyond British shores, especially in America. Architects such as Alexander Jackson Davis (1803–92), who designed and built more state capitols and government offices than any other architect in the United States, were heavily influenced by Pugin. Davis is most notable for popularizing the Gothic Revival in America, for example, building and designing the first secular Gothic building in New York City in the mid-1830s. Davis was an enthusiastic designer of furniture for his architectural projects and examples designed by him survive in the collection of the Metropolitan Museum of Art in New York (Plate 32). Much of his decoration was based on the published designs of Pugin, and in a similar vein to his British counterpart he excelled when working at a domestic scale. His greatest house, Lyndhurst, in Tarrytown, New York, built for the lawyer and politician William Paulding in 1838, remains one of the most complete examples of nineteenth-century neo-Gothic Revival architecture in the United States.

Pugin was one of the highest profile creative figures to be associated with the mid-century definitive event: the Great Exhibition of 1851. His Medieval Court was subject to fierce dispute, being equally celebrated and denigrated (Piggott 2004: 17). It would also be his last great work; he died the following year. The exhibition and its successors in Britain, France, and America were enormously stimulating in terms of design, but perhaps more so in terms of related debate and discourse, and seemed to galvanize middle-class awareness in these fields. Reports on the highlights of the 1851 exhibition were best-sellers, such as Matthew Digby Wyatt's (1820–77) *Industrial Arts of the Nineteenth Century* and Owen Jones (1809–74) and Christopher Dresser's (1834–1904) *The Grammar of Ornament* of 1856. Such publications broadened the available design sources for both architecture and furniture, increasing interest in, for example, the Middle East and Asia as sources of inspiration. The 1862 London International Exhibition is perhaps less well known, but was arguably yet more influential. This exhibition saw the arrival in Europe of genuine objects produced in Asia, which were perceived as having a greater authenticity than the Western objects made in Asian styles displayed there. After viewing the Japanese exhibit there, the architect and designer William Burges declared "truly the Japanese Court is the real medieval court of the Exhibition" (Burges 1862: 11). The exhibition was especially important in forming the so-called Art Movement whereby not only architects but artists too became involved in the designing of every aspect of a building inside and out, including the furniture and decorative objects. Dresser encouraged designers to look at surprising sources for inspiration in his 1870 *Principles of Decorative Design*, where he singled out Sir Gardiner Wilkinson's 1837 book *Manners and Customs of the Ancient Egyptians*. Wilkinson's book included illustrations of actual pieces of Egyptian domestic furniture from Thebes that had been accessioned by the British Museum from 1829 to 1835. The Pre-Raphaelite painter William Holman Hunt (1827–1910), working with John Crace, produced chairs in an Egyptian style in 1853; this was followed by another design by Ford Maddox Brown (1821–93) with William Morris in 1861. They became popular and struck a resonance with the growing taste for Japanese furniture; both styles shared a striking and novel elegance. Dresser became a major promoter of Japanese style, noting how the objects at the 1862 exhibition coincided with Pugin's preoccupations: they showed their construction, and made decorative elements of their functional rivets and fastenings. The Islamic style was consummately executed by George Aitchison (1825–1910) in the house he designed for the artist Frederick Leighton, especially in the extension built in 1877–81, which contained the famous Arab Hall. Although not all the fixtures and fittings of the house have survived, nineteenth-century photographs show impressive bookcases and an enormous sideboard for the dining room, which were designed by Aitchison according to the accounts of their manufacturer Gillows of Lancaster.

The dominant French architect of the period, Eugène-Emmanuel Viollet-le-Duc (1814–79), was a major progenitor of the Art Movement. Whilst an exponent of the Gothic Revival, in contrast to Pugin he embraced the new technological advances of the age with enthusiasm and explored the idea of applying modern materials such as cast iron to Gothic architecture. He also worked within the decorative fashions of the regime of Napoleon III (1848–70), characterized by the adaptation and evolution of preexisting styles into something new and different. Viollet-le-Duc's 1858 *Dictionnaire raisonné de l'architecture* (Complete Dictionary of Architecture) and 1864 *Architecture privée de Paris et des environs sous Napoleon III* (Private Architecture of Paris and Surrounding Areas under Napoleon III) had a profound impact in the realms of architecture. Likewise, his enormous *Dictionnaire raisonné du mobilier français* (Complete Dictionary of French Furniture) showed a complete mastery of both historic and contemporary styles. Here, in a similar fashion to Pugin, Ruskin, and Morris, he claimed that true French furniture dated from before the classically dominated reigns of Louis XIV, XV, and XVI, or the "age of absolutism" as he derogatorily termed it; namely, the Renaissance and medieval periods (Auslander 1996: 261). We are left in little doubt about the importance he placed on the architect's involvement in furniture: "during the sixteenth and seventeenth centuries architects not only paid attention to internal arrangements, but subordinated the designs for the exterior to them" (Viollet-le-Duc 1877: 381). Viollet-le-Duc also betrays some appreciation of the arguments of Pugin and Ruskin, especially in his support of the importance of honesty in structure if not in decoration. In 1863, Napoleon III commissioned him to design furniture for his country home, the Château de Pierrefonds, using the broad knowledge from his *Dictionnaire* to create a remarkable suite of revivalist, antiquarian pieces. The project was never completed owing to the disastrous Franco-Prussian War of 1870–1, in contrast to the Château de Roquetaillade, a private commission for the Leblanc de Mauvesin family where a more complete scheme was executed. This interior included furniture made by Tricot and Jeancourt of Paris in a "medieval" style to Viollet-le-Duc's designs.

William Burges (1827–81), arguably one of the most inventive architects of the 1860s and early 1870s, was inspired by a visit to Viollet-le-Duc's Pierrefonds in 1867 (Aldrich 1997: 216). Burges's influence on furniture design was as significant as on architecture; his new "reformed Gothic," characterized by color and angularity, impacted profoundly on both areas. He worked with many major figures in English architecture and design during the 1840s and 1850s, including the establishment architect Edward Blore (1787–1879) and Matthew Digby Wyatt. Although Pugin was a major early inspiration (Burges presented his son with a copy of *Contrasts* for his fourteenth birthday [Banham, MacDonald, and Porter 1991: 75]), Burges did not adopt Pugin's moral stance, instead allowing a more light-hearted approach to permeate his work, anticipating the emphasis on aesthetic enjoyment that would come later in the century. Additionally, Burges was increasingly heterogeneous in his inspiration, collecting prints and developing an enthusiasm for Asian, especially Japanese art. He was fortunate in having an indulgent patron, John Crichton-Stuart, the 3rd Marquis of Bute (1847–1900), who shared his vision and commissioned his magnum opus Cardiff Castle, where Burges harmonized the multicolored decoration of the architecture with the simply constructed rectilinear furniture, a project that would run from 1868 until his death in 1881. In 1856 he began to create painted furniture. The *Yatman Cabinet* of 1858, also at the Victoria and Albert Museum (CIRC.217:1, 2–1961), illustrates the seamless assimilation of useful furniture, decorative design, and architecture: the form of the cabinet derives from a Norman castle, the painter Sir Edward John Poynter (1836–1919) decorated it with scenes of the origins of writing and printing. A related cabinet by Burges from 1857, now in the Manchester Art Gallery (1979.132) and constructed by William Gualbert Saunders, shares many similar aspects of its design and decoration. Although Burges was not commercially successful, he is recognized as having influenced other designers such as Bruce James Talbert (1838–81) and J.P. Seddon (1827–1906). Seddon's 1867 publication *Gothic Forms Applied to Furniture, Metal Work and Decoration for Domestic Purposes* and Charles Eastlake's (1836–1906) 1868 decorating manual *Hints on Household Taste in Furniture, Upholstery and other Details* both borrowed from Burges's designs and were especially influential in America.

At the beginning of his career, the architect-designer Edward William Godwin (1833–86) looked to new sources such as Japanese art. Like Burges, he first noticed it at the London 1862 International Exhibition and his furniture designs for Dromore Castle in County Limerick Ireland in the late 1860s saw a rejection of historicist models in favor of a vocabulary that was inspired by Japanese art (Weber Soros 1999: 76). This striking furniture was executed to his designs by William Watt's Art Furniture Company. Around the same time, Godwin designed a sideboard for his home in a similar style, which is still in the Victoria and Albert Museum (CIRC.38:1 to 5–1953). Striking in its modern and reductive form, even to our twenty-first-century eyes, several versions of these distinctive cabinets were subsequently made and sold by Godwin over a period of twenty years. Thomas Jeckyll (1827–81), of the same generation as Burges and Godwin, was an architect who become adept at combining Japanese and Old English elements in his work. His earliest work of this kind may have been a suite of seat-furniture designed for the home of the industrialist Edward Green at Heath Old Hall in Wakefield in 1867–8. These may be the earliest pieces of furniture to be designed in this style in the late nineteenth century (Weber Soros and Arbuthnott 2003: 173). Jeckyll's most famous interior was at a house designed by Richard Norman Shaw for the shipping magnate Frederick Richards Leyland in 1875–6 in Kensington London, which would later become known as the Peacock Room. It was intended that the house would become a "Palace of Art": the room was to house Leyland's Asian ceramics collection while serving as the dining room. The room spliced Old English Jacobean style with Japanese in a way that did not prove especially popular with contemporary critics; Godwin, for example, claimed it was "a trifle mixed." However, Jeckyll's furnishings were better received: in particular the beautifully designed and carved shelving was praised in the *Furniture Gazette*. It was slightly later that the artist James McNeil Whistler (1834–1903) painted the walls with his magnificent blue and gold peacocks, which garnered considerable press attention and ensured it was Whistler who was remembered as the designer of the room, rather than Jeckyll. There is some argument over which of them designed its sideboards; however, it is certain that Jeckyll is responsible for the sunflower andirons, which have achieved near iconic status (Figure 7.1). The whole room can be seen as a particularly compelling embodiment of the Anglo-Japanese interior and the Aesthetic style in interior design. In 1919 it was moved to the Freer Gallery of Art in Washington, DC, where it remains today. Jeckyll built up an especially fruitful relationship with the cast iron company Barnard, Bishop & Barnards, designing their pavilion for the Philadelphia Centennial Exhibition of 1874 from cast iron. He then subsequently used his newfound skills to design andirons, fireplaces, gates, and garden furniture (Weber Soros and Arbuthnott 2003: 234).

The explosion of styles during the third quarter of the nineteenth century was not always seen as a positive development; some twentieth-century scholars have dubbed it the "Victorian design crisis" (Doordan 1995: 174). It was an era that would be defined by a constant search for novelty, but contradictorily often by looking to the past for inspiration. The repeated revivals of every

FIGURE 7.1 James McNeill Whistler, Harmony in Blue and Gold: The Peacock Room, 1876–1877, Gift of Charles Lang Freer, Freer Gallery of Art, F1904.61. Photograph courtesy of the Freer Gallery of Art.

architectural and decorative style from Romanesque to Robert Adam's neoclassicism can be seen as symptomatic of an age that was struggling to find its own identity. In 1858 George Gilbert Scott (1811–78), one of the great architects of the later century, professed to be in a constant search for "a style which will be pre-eminently of our own age" (Banham and Harris 1984: 125). In addition, compounding the anxiety was the onset of technological change and an intensification of the Industrial Revolution. John Ruskin (1819–1900), the leading nineteenth-century British art critic and thinker, stated in a lecture to the Royal Institute of Architects in May 1865:

> All lovely architecture was designed for cities in cloudless air; for cities in which piazzas and gardens opened in bright populousness and peace, cities built that men might live happily in them and take delight daily in each other's presence and powers. But our cities, built in black air which, by its accumulated foulness, first renders all ornament invisible in distance, and then chokes its interstices with soot ... for a city or cities such as this no architecture is possible—nay, no desire of it is possible to their inhabitants.
>
> (Ruskin and Hobson 1899: 345)

Ruskin is often referred to as an "art and social critic," which indicates how closely these two fields had become. Much of his work built on ideas first proposed by Pugin, yet Ruskin added weightiness and academic sophistication encouraging the taste for Romanesque and Venetian Gothic. He published the first philosophical and academic text to deal with the phenomenon of the Gothic Revival in May 1849, *The Seven Lamps of Architecture*. The "lamps" mentioned in the title were a series of principles to guide architectural revivals, including sacrifice, truth, power, beauty, life, memory, and obedience. This was followed by a more ambitious work, *The Stones of Venice*, which appeared in three volumes from 1851 for which Ruskin spent two long winters in Venice, making a close study of its architecture. Ruskin criticized industrialization for removing man from his environment: "we blanch cotton and strengthen steel, and refine sugar, and shape pottery; but to brighten, to strengthen, to refine, or to form a single living spirit, never enters into our estimate of advantages" (1964: 180). His writings set the tone for much of the stylistic development in the later century, largely owing to the designer-activist William Morris (1834–96), who was instrumental in extending these ideas into the production of furniture and decorative objects. On reading the preface to "The Nature of Gothic," a chapter of *The Stones of Venice*, Morris later wrote, "it seemed to point out a new road on which the world should travel"; that is, toward a situation where "art is the expression of man's pleasure in labour" (Leon 1949: 178). In other words, Morris believed that for an object to be enjoyable to view or use, it was fundamental that it had been satisfying and rewarding to make. This idea of moral significance in design and architecture was largely a legacy of Pugin, but was also a symptom of the age; an attempt to find order in an increasingly confused world. Both Morris and Ruskin supported the idea that decorative art was on a par with the fine arts; "get rid, then, at once, of any idea of decorative art being degraded or a separate kind of art" (Greenhalgh 1993: 5). Rather like Hope and Pugin before him, he also repeatedly complained about the quality of the furniture of the time claiming "it is a shoddy age; shoddy is king. From the statesman to the shoemaker, all is shoddy" (Flestrin 1892: 8).

Although Morris himself was never an architect, he trained within that setting, was vociferous about the necessary harmony between buildings and their contents, and was associated with many others who worked in both fields. His friends and compatriots who were architects, many of whom were based in London and were influenced directly by Morris, encouraged the progression of the broader Arts and Crafts movement. Morris began his career in 1856 in the office of George Edmund Street (1824–81), one of the leading Gothic architects at the time. Street was also a major exponent of Pugin's "revealed construction" in his experiments with furniture design, examples of which survive in the collection of the Victoria and Albert Museum and at Cuddesdon College, Oxford. In Street's office, Morris met his lifelong friend and collaborator Philip Webb (1831–1915). In 1861, he founded his own company, initially called "Fine Art Workmen in Painting, Carving, Furniture and the Metals," a title contrived to demonstrate his belief that furniture and furnishings should present artistic sensibilities to the same extent as fine art. It would later evolve into the more familiar and succinct Morris & Co. Founding members included Morris, Webb, and the Pre-Raphaelite artists Ford Madox Brown (1821–93), Edward Burne-Jones (1833–98), and Dante Gabriel Rossetti (1828–82). This company, which produced architecture, furniture, fine and decorative art brought a new cohesiveness to interiors of the period. Morris's "Red House" in Bexleyheath in southeast London, begun in 1859 and designed by Webb, who also provided much of the furniture, formed an early manifesto for the company. A member designed every aspect of the Red House's interior decoration. The group's display at the 1862 London exhibition attracted much attention, and included the St George Cabinet (Victoria and Albert Museum, 341:1 to 8–1906), painted by Morris himself in a similar style to Webb's furniture for the Red House. Webb was as important as Morris in many respects and designed more furniture, such as the Backgammon Cabinet, also shown at the 1862 International Exhibition. The founding of this design company would be an innovation that was widely copied, and would come to dominate the interaction between furniture and architecture in the latter part of century. This development was very deliberate; as Morris stated, "I shall say that among ourselves, the men of modern Europe, the existence of other arts is bound up with that of architecture" (2012: 241).

By the 1880s the popularity of the Gothic Revival was in decline, accelerated by the deaths of many followers of Pugin, such as Street, Burges, Jeckyll, and Godwin. Architects such as Richard Norman Shaw (1831–1912), William Eden Nesfield (1835–88), and John James Stevenson (1831–1908) championed a new style; the Queen Anne Revival which largely replaced Gothic style in architectural taste. Although it did indeed borrow design motifs from the reign of Queen Anne in the early eighteenth century, it also drew from a range of late seventeenth- and eighteenth-century sources and even older sixteenth-century motifs. In a sign of the style's popularity, Norman Shaw designed a Queen Anne style house for use as the British pavilion for the Paris 1878 *Exposition Universelle,* which received a gold medal and near universal approbation (Bergdoll et al. 2008: 15). The style, characterized by red brick contrasting with paler stone detailing, feature windows, asymmetry, strapwork decoration, and corner towers, dominated the domestic and official architecture of the 1870s and 1880s, and is still much in evidence in many British and American cities today.

This stylistic shift is discernible in the output of the architect Alfred Waterhouse (1830–1905), who designed many pieces of furniture, some for the Manchester firm of Doveston, Bird & Hull. His drawings can be found at the Royal Institute of British Architects (RIBA) in London. His designs for Manchester Town Hall, built in the 1870s, were in a full-blown Gothic style and echoed Pugin's remit at the Palace of Westminster in their scope. On moving to London in the early 1880s, sensing that the fashion for the Gothic style was waning, Waterhouse seems to have quickly come under the influence of Richard Norman Shaw and the new Queen Anne style, applying it to furniture designs for such commissions as Blackmoor House in Hampshire (Cunningham and Waterhouse 1992: 53). George Gilbert Scott Jr. (1839–97) designed furniture for his architectural projects in a similar fashion to Waterhouse. In 1874 he established his own architectural and interior design company, Watts & Co., with two other architects, George Frederick Bodley (1827–1907) and Thomas Garner (1839–1906), all three of whom specialized in ecclesiastical architecture. The company mainly worked in the Queen Anne style, but also produced examples of furniture and decoration inspired by the art and architecture of the seventeenth and eighteenth centuries. Gilbert Scott Jr. personally designed metalwork, wallpaper, and furniture, of which some drawings survive at RIBA. When working on the overall interior decoration of his projects, however, Gilbert Scott frequently used elements from the rival firm of William Morris and sometimes, the two designers collaborated on church furniture. Importantly, and in opposition to Ruskin and Morris who championed the importance of craftsmen in furniture manufacture, Gilbert Scott believed that during the medieval period whole building schemes, including the architecture, furniture, and decoration, were supervised by architects (Stamp 2002: 265). Thus, Gilbert

Scott thought that it was not only essential for him to have control over every aspect of a commission to achieve his artistic vision, but also that such a way of operating was entirely authentic and in a centuries-old tradition. He may have been influenced in this belief by the publication in 1859 of the designs by the thirteenth century French medieval architect Villard de Honnecourt, which contained designs for the architecture of cathedrals, alongside choir stalls, lecterns, and building machinery such as cranes.

In America, the economic boom from 1870 to 1900 became known as the "Gilded Age." A wealthy new elite rose in prominence with a generation of designers and architects, from both America and abroad, available to fulfill their desires. Architects at this time built fruitful relationships with furniture makers, perhaps the most famous of these being between A.H. Davenport & Company and the Boston-based architect H.H. Richardson (Farnam 1979: 80). In 1885, indicating the value Davenport placed on the architectural input for their designs, the company hired Francis H. Bacon (1856–1940) from Richardson's office to produce exclusive pieces, including a chair in the Hepplewhite style (now in the collection of the Metropolitan Museum of Art [1993.75]). Jules Allard and Sons, an interior design firm originally based in Paris, opened a New York branch in the mid-1880s and became one of the most successful such companies in America. Allard was important for encouraging the fashion for "period rooms" in private residences employing genuine antique paneling and furnished with historically appropriate furniture (Harris 2007: 119). This period also saw single residences, always for the very wealthy, with individual rooms and furnishings in a variety of styles, such as a Renaissance revival dining room or a Gothic library. The French Salon at Petit Château, residence of the industrialist William K. Vanderbilt built from 1878 to 1883 on New York's Fifth Avenue, was one of the earliest of these period interiors. Competitors to Allard were the Herter Brothers and Louis Comfort Tiffany's Associated Artists. Tiffany (1848–1933) and his company in many respects defined this gilded age. The Associated Artists were a group of highly skilled specialists including painters, glassmakers, stonemasons, mosaicists, wood carvers, cabinetmakers, potters, and weavers that could be considered a more ostentatious version of the "Guilds" formed by British designers in the 1880s and 1890s (see below). Such a range of skill sets enabled Tiffany, as overall designer, to turn his interiors into total works of art and he occasionally acted as an architect, designing, for example, his own home, Laurelton Hall, in Long Island.

In Britain, the closing decades of the century saw the wealth of the previously preeminent aristocratic classes devastated by the agricultural depression of the 1880s. Partially because of this, the British architectural discourse became increasingly concerned with smaller-scale domestic architecture preferred by industrialists, entrepreneurs, and members of the middle class. Although Morris and Pugin remained influential, a simplified version of their style became progressively more prevalent, and their moral agenda declined in favor. The melding of architecture, furniture, and decoration was further achieved by the rise of societies and so-called guilds, founded in the 1880s, which encouraged cross-fertilization among different media. In 1883, Arthur Heygate Mackmurdo (1851–1942) and Selwyn Image (1849–1930) founded the Century Guild of Artists. Both men had been students of Ruskin at Oxford and believed fervently that architecture could be a catalyst for bringing the fine and decorative arts together. Although Mackmurdo was an architect first and foremost, he was responsible for a number of highly influential furniture designs, such as his desk of 1886, now in the William Morris Museum in Walthamstow (Plate 33). In 1884 two of Philip Webb's followers, architects W.R. Lethaby (1857–1931) and George Jack (1855–1931), established the Art Worker's Guild, and in 1888 Charles Robert Ashbee (1863–1942) founded the Guild of Handicraft. Ashbee was especially interested in Morris's social agenda, and his concept of the "noble craftsman." He opened workshops in East London to provide work for poverty-stricken locals, and a retail space in Mayfair to sell their products to rich clients (Crawford 2005: 220). Ashbee would later exhibit his work at the Vienna Secession's eighth exhibition in 1900 where it was well received. These societies were also important for their publishing activities; in 1893, for example, *The Studio: An Illustrated Magazine of Fine and Applied Art* was first published. This journal was instrumental in broadening the international fame of several British designers, especially Charles Rennie-Mackintosh (1868–1928) and Charles Voysey (1847–1941). The Century Guild produced their own stylish publication, *The Hobby Horse* between 1884 and 1894. In 1887, the founding of the first Arts and Crafts Exhibition Society signaled renewed organization in the movement. They held their first exhibition in London in 1888, displaying every aspect of interior design and fomenting a renewed confidence among the movement's exponents. Publications such as Robert William Edis's (1839–1927) *Decoration and Furniture of Town Houses* of 1880, originally presented in a series of lectures to the Society of Artists, encouraged the artistic ethos in furnishing. Art furniture, like art ceramics, flourished in the later decades of the century and often made use of a designer who worked in a number of different media. Large stores such as Heal's and Liberty's became popular places where designer furniture could be obtained.

In 1890, Ernest Gimson (1864–1919), Sidney Barnsley (1865–1926), and three other architects, Reginald Blomfield (1856–1942), W.R. Lethaby, and Mervyn Macartney (1853–1932), established the furniture design and manufacturing company Kenton and Co., aiming to improve standards of craftsmanship (Comino Greensted 1982: 49). Although the firm only lasted two years, Gimson and Barnsley persevered, establishing a workshop on their own, which would later evolve into the Cotswold School of Furniture where they would be joined by Sidney's architect brother, Ernest Barnsley (1862–1926).

Gimson and Sidney Barnsley originally came to London during the late 1880s to pursue careers as architects in the studios of Norman Shaw and John Dando Sedding (1838–91). Writing later, the German architect, critic, and anglophile Hermann Muthesius claimed that Sedding "formed the first bridge between the architects' camp and that of handicraft proper" (Richardson 1983: 71), a step beyond simply linking architecture and furniture. In his work throughout the British Isles, Mackay Hugh Baillie Scott (1865–1945) designed small, rural residences and their furnishings, such as Blackwell in Cumbria from 1898–1900. The Arts and Crafts phenomenon took on increasingly international dimensions, growing in popularity in Europe and America as the end of the century approached. In America, some makers pushed the boundaries beyond what would have been acceptable in Britain. Gustav Stickley (1858–1942), for instance, championed the style but mass produced his furniture using mechanical methods, evolving it into a new form called the American Craftsman style. Like his British counterparts he disseminated his ideas via publications, producing *The Craftsman* from 1901 to 1916. Even the early furniture designs of the architect and designer Frank Lloyd Wright (1867–1959) display a clear Arts and Crafts sentiment.

Belgium saw the flourishing of a number of great designers who were particularly notable for developing the Art Nouveau style in both furniture and architecture. Like Louis Comfort Tiffany, Henry van de Velde (1863–1957) originally trained as a painter. He designed the interiors of Siegfried Bing's Paris art gallery "Maison de L'Art Nouveau" in 1895, which would give the movement its name. Significantly, although he adhered to the prescriptions of Ruskin and Morris, van de Velde rejected the reinterpretation of historical styles entirely and aimed to produce something that was completely new. Later, van de Velde would become a member of the Deutscher Werkbund (German Association of Craftsmen) on its foundation in 1900, which primarily aimed at improving links between designers and industry, and which would later kindle the new Bauhaus. Another great Belgian Art Nouveau innovator Victor Horta (1861–1947) built his masterpiece the Hôtel Tassel in Brussels in 1893–4, when the new style was not simply applied to the architecture and interior decoration, but to every object, fixture, and fitting, including the furniture. Horta was an innovator in the use of cast iron, applying it to great effect in both the building and objects he designed, and allowing its malleable qualities to influence the way wood was used in his furniture and interiors, creating interiors where architecture and furniture meld into one continuous organic line.

The success of projects by the great Scottish designer Charles Rennie Mackintosh was largely owing to his remarkable ability to combine architecture and furniture design. He created over four hundred pieces of furniture between 1893 and 1919 (Billcliffe 1979a: 9), all of which were intended for specific interiors and architectural projects. Maintaining control over every detail of his buildings, Mackintosh differed from earlier Arts and Crafts designers in that he rarely used the same furniture design for more than one of his projects. He was inspired by his native Scottish furniture tradition alongside his years at the Glasgow School of Art. The School's director Francis Newbery (1855–1946) was a major advocate of Arts and Crafts ideologies, inviting many of the prominent figures of the movement to lecture at the school, including Morris and Voysey. Mackintosh's all-encompassing approach also had much in common with the international Art Nouveau movement. The display of his productions at the Vienna Secession Exhibition in 1900 were greeted with intense acclaim, the angularity and occasional severity of the pieces being predictive of later movements including modernism and functionalism.

CONCLUSION

It is clear that during the course of the nineteenth century architect-designers were consistently at the forefront of stylistic and technological developments in furniture design. New market conditions, in which men and women of varying social backgrounds became consumers of furniture fabricated according to philosophical and stylistic principles, placed renewed importance on the input of designers and architects. Additionally, although the mid-century saw a proliferation of styles and a cheapening of manufacturing processes, the reactionary return to honesty, usefulness, and craftsmanship also gave a new impulse to design-led production, which architect-designers could provide. This newfound respect for the craftsman and designer enabled the proliferation of design companies and specialist retailers in the later century. By its end, the divisions between architecture, furniture, and indeed art had become blurred, and the concept of "design" was fully appreciated and present in every room in the homes of every social class in some form or another. Baillie Scott summed up the situation in 1895:

> It is difficult for the architect to draw a fixed line between the architecture of a house and the furniture. The conception of an interior must necessarily include the furniture which is to be used in it, and this naturally leads to the conclusion that the architect should design chairs and tables as well as the house itself.
>
> (Kornwolf 1972: 28)

CHAPTER EIGHT

Visual Representations

CAROLINE MCCAFFREY-HOWARTH

INTRODUCTION

A "visual representation" is a means of communicating information between an image and its viewer, essentially creating a dialogue. This dialogue reveals certain ideas about the cultural paradigm to which the representation belongs. Illustrations of furniture can be understood universally: they rise above language or cultural barriers and have the ability to disseminate fashionable styles to international audiences. As a form of decorative art, furniture carries a strong locational value, thus it represents the place in which it was produced and can be viewed as a manifestation of its contemporary culture (Schoeser and Boydel 2002: 4–9; Scott 2005: 137). Furniture that was designed, produced, and retailed in the nineteenth century was thus predetermined by its sociocultural context and the changing political fabric of society. Adrian Forty has emphasized that a design can only be successful as long as it embodies the cultural ideas that are held by its target audience (Forty 1992: 245). Therefore, to fulfill its purpose the visual representation needs to satisfy the expectations and desires of a consumer, while simultaneously responding to changing social, economic, geographic, and gender value structures. This chapter will explore how the visual imagery of furniture in nineteenth-century Europe and America represented and responded to these changing cultural values. By focusing on visual representation this chapter considers its ability to transcend verbal statements. It also aims to establish how furniture illustrations were created not only to be aesthetically instructive, or to prove commercial viability and secure market dominance, but also to construct, inspire, and influence taste.

In light of a growing consumer-driven society, furniture makers and retailers needed to increase the amount of visual material available in the commercial sphere to compete with fellow makers and satisfy the needs of the consumer while also securing future customers. Within this context, a piece of furniture was manufactured, recorded visually, and intended to be purchased by a potential nineteenth-century consumer. In terms of quantity, the magnitude of visual representation from the nineteenth century superseded that of the eighteenth century. Ranging from printed pattern books, periodicals, trade catalogs, international exhibition catalogs, and interior decoration manuals to visual recordings of furniture in prints, paintings, and by the end of the century, photography, these sources enabled an impressive dissemination of designs and encouraged the consumption of fashionable furniture throughout the social classes. As the nineteenth century progressed advances in printing technology, aided by the emergence of steam-powered cylindrical presses, lithographic techniques, and the use of color chromolithography, enabled a marked rise in the availability of printed visual sources (Margolin 2014: 188). Additional commercial growth and the dissemination of fashionable taste both within and outside of Europe was facilitated by images that were often eye-catching, colorful, detailed, and not reliant on textual literacy. Distributions of furniture design also benefited from an improvement in transport routes on an international scale, thanks to steamboats and better railroad construction. This was further encouraged by the cultural shift resulting from the French Revolution from 1789 onward with an increase in overseas travel by collectors and dealers in 1802 during the Peace of Amiens and again at the end of the Napoleonic Wars in 1815.

This chapter will demonstrate that, as the nineteenth century progressed, visual representation gravitated toward increased specialization and novelty that frequently embraced mechanical ingenuity, regularly presenting furniture targeted at a particular profession, category, gender, or social class. Underlying sociocultural structures undoubtedly influenced how a maker or retailer chose to record each piece visually. Concentrating on the role of printed illustrations in the European and American tradition, it seeks to give particular attention to the cultural history of pattern books, journals, trade catalogs, exhibition catalogs, and decorating manuals. The final section examines the way in which furniture was represented visually in correspondence and working drawings amongst colleagues and clients, often as an expression of ideas.

PATTERN BOOKS

To the furniture historian, the pattern book is surely one of the richest visual sources of furniture design. Traditionally, it was a book or pamphlet consisting of designs for various types of furniture, and by the beginning of the nineteenth century it already existed as an established concept. Earlier pattern books were published mainly by individual designers, often architect-designers or furniture-making entrepreneurs with prominent examples including Matthias Lock's *Six Sconces* (1744), *Six Tables* (1746), and *A New Book of Ornaments* (1752); Thomas Johnson's *Twelves Girandoles* (1755) and *A New Book of Ornaments* (1758); Thomas Chippendale's *The Gentleman and Cabinet-Maker's Director*, first published in 1754; and Robert Adam's *Works in Architecture of Robert and James Adam* produced in 1773. Nineteenth-century examples followed an established order of contents: first instruction on geometry and perspective, then practical observations on construction techniques and the suitability of particular woods, and finally, a collection of furniture illustrations.[1]

These visual representations provided practical information on styles and techniques for decorators, cabinetmakers, and architects, rather than for the general public. Usually drawn in black and white as scaled outlines, they gave several alternative designs for one object, such as a variety of chair legs or chair backs. Such illustrations enabled an individual designer to communicate a variety of ideas to a cabinetmaker or potential client, simultaneously allowing the maker to interpret and modify the designs at their own discretion. While this is not to say that pattern books were not commercially viable, essentially they belonged to an eighteenth-century paradigm, which was limited to aristocratic or wealthy patrons and did not cater to the emerging middle classes. By the 1850s, some pattern books adopted a more commercially driven strategy, notably Blackie's *Cabinet-Maker's Assistant* of 1853, which featured a trade catalog in the final section.

From the beginning of the nineteenth century there were a number of influential European furniture pattern books that followed the model established during the eighteenth century, including: Charles Percier and Pierre-François Léonard Fontaine's *Recueil de Décorations Intérieures* (1801), Thomas Sheraton's *Cabinet Dictionary* (1803), Thomas Hope's *Household Furniture and Interior Decoration* (1807), George Smith's *A Collection of Designs for Household Furniture and Interior Decoration* (1808), Peter Weber's *The Cabinet-Maker's Guide to the Whole Art of Dying, Staining, Varnishing, and Beautifying of Wood* (1809), James Baron's *Modern and Elegant Designs of Cabinet & Upholstery Furniture* (1814), Rudolph Ackermann's *A Series Containing Forty-Four Engravings in Colors, of Fashionable Furniture* (1823), John Taylor's *The Upholsterers and Cabinet Makers Pocket Assistant* (1825), George Smith's *Cabinet-Maker and Upholsterer's Guide* (1826), Thomas King's *The Upholsterer's Accelerator* (1833) and *Working Ornaments and Forms* (*c.* 1840), and H.W. and A. Arrowsmith's *House Decorator and Painter's Guide* (*c.* 1840).

From the 1830s onward, the number of German publications increased and comprised Marius Wölfer's *Modell-und Musterbuch für Bau-und Möbel-Tischler*, which was published in several editions between 1826 and 1836. Stylistically, this publication did not concentrate on the Biedermeier aesthetic and instead featured revival baroque, Gothic, and Renaissance historicist styles. In 1828 Wölfer produced another pattern book, *The Carpenter and Cabinetmaker*, while the German Carl Matthaey's *Designs and Descriptions of the Newest Styles for Artists and Craftsmen* was published in three volumes from 1831 and 1835, and Matthaey's *The New Teaching, Pattern*, and *Ornament Book for Cabinetmakers and Carpenters* appeared in 1840. Other notable pattern books were *Model and Patternbooks for Carpenters and Cabinetmakers* (1832), the *New Patternbook for Wood, Horn, and Bone Turners* (1841), and the *New Idea Magazine for Luxury, Furnishings, and Draperies* (1841). These pattern books were dominated by historicist revival styles and also emphasized neoclassical forms. Toward the middle of the century, the production of pattern books decreased somewhat, although Wilhelm Kimbel's *Journal for Cabinetmakers and Upholsterers* promoted several rococo revival designs and appeared from 1835 until 1853, D. Freudenvoll's *Neuestes Mainzer Moebel-Journal* from 1846 onward, and Thomas King's *The Upholsterer's Guide* was published posthumously in 1848.

The interest in Greek, Roman, and Egyptian antiquity was influenced by designers who traveled and recorded their observations visually, including Charles Heathcote Tatham's *Etchings of Ancient Ornamental Architecture* from 1799 and, most importantly, Baron Dominique-Vivant Denon's *Voyage dans la basse et la haute d'Egypte* (1802). In both Europe and America, a supremacy of such antique fashions, which continued eighteenth-century fashions, was demonstrated by several pattern books including *Recueil de Décorations Intérieures* by Percier and Fontaine from 1801 onward, Thomas Sheraton's *The Cabinet-Maker, Upholsterer, and General Artist's Encyclopedia* of 1804–6, and George Smith's *Collection of Designs for Household Furniture and Interior Decoration* in 1808, later followed by his *Cabinet Maker and Upholsterer's Guide* in 1826.

Napoleon, who championed Denon's work and invited him to accompany his expedition into Egypt in 1798, was determined to connect France with the great ancient empires of the past, while creating a decorative style representative of his new cultural and political regime, thus establishing a more authentic neoclassicism for the nineteenth century (Kisluk-Grosheide et al. 2006: 220). Denon believed that Egypt was the stylistic predecessor to Greece and Rome, and therefore its antiquity and decorative motifs "acquired equal celebrity" (Denon 1802: 266). Napoleon's chief designers, Percier and Fontaine, embraced Denon's illustrations in their adoption of antique motifs, notably ancient Grecian ornament that they thought represented ideas of political democracy (Nouvel-Kammerer 2007: 106). Generally referred to as *le style empire*, furniture and interiors from Napoleon's residences such as Malmaison were represented in Percier and Fontaine's *Recueil de Décorations Intérieures* (1801). This pattern book first appeared in installments, and was then reprinted in a more available single volume in 1812. Presented in black outlines the designs in *Recueil de Décorations Intérieures* both recorded furniture designs in the traditional manner as solitary pieces, as well as in complete interiors, giving the total visual concept. Smaller decorative scenes based on antique ornament alongside the design are also illustrated (Figure 8.1). Percier and Fontaine's motivation for placing authentic ancient ornament alongside their own interpretation is probably twofold: firstly, they may have intended to educate the reader in how to use such ornament appropriately, and secondly, it enabled them to assert their own authority and expertise. Notably, Percier and Fontaine's pattern book is thought to be the first known use of the phrase "interior decoration," which suggests that they envisioned that such designs could provide a complete decorating scheme for the reader. Their knowledge of the historical past is particularly apparent in citations of original sources for inspiration. Perhaps the designers believed that their furniture was more authentic in comparison to other, competing European designers.

This particular use of visual language in *Recueil* also influenced English pattern books, which embraced similar designs in a Greek Revival style. These celebrated antique ornament with an archaeologically authentic style of neoclassicism, such as Thomas Sheraton's *Cabinet Dictionary* (1803),

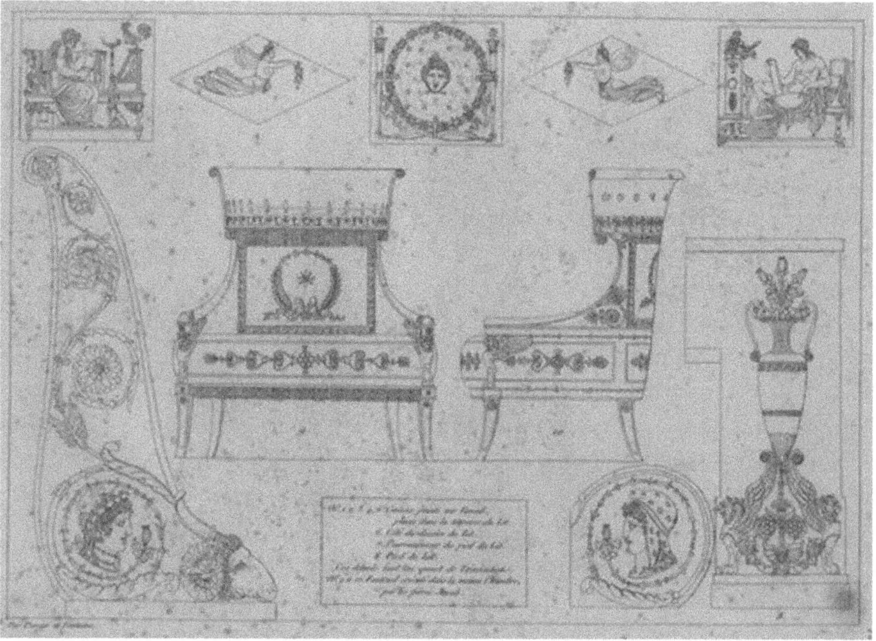

FIGURE 8.1 "Design of a Scrolled End of a Bedstead," from Percier and Fontaine's *Recueil de Decorations Intérieures* (1801), plate 15. Harris Brisbane Dick Fund, 1928, Metropolitan Museum of Art. Photograph courtesy of the Metropolitan Museum of Art.

Thomas Hope's *Household Furniture and Interior Decoration* (1807), and George Smith's *A Collection of Designs for Household Furniture and Interior Decoration* (1808). Although other styles of historicist design had begun to ascend, in J.C. Loudon's 1833 pattern book *Encyclopedia of Cottage, Farm and Villa Architecture and Furniture* he maintained that Grecian was still the most fashionable style. Loudon was correct in his observations, as demonstrated by illustrations found in various pattern books published by Thomas King between 1822 and 1848, and Peter and Michael Angelo Nicholson's *Practical Cabinet-Maker, Upholsterer and Complete Decorators* in 1826.

Loudon's *Encyclopedia* was one of the first pattern books whose target audience was not just limited to fellow cabinetmakers and designers. The publication highlights the increasing scope of pattern books toward the middle of the nineteenth century. Aimed at a wider audience, Loudon presents an informative guide with a variety of furniture from utilitarian mechanical press beds, to luxurious easy-chairs with buttoned upholstery and coiled springs, to nursery furniture, which encouraged better posture. Loudon was aware of the increasing means of the lower classes and tailored his furniture illustrations to target all ranks of society. This was evidently well received, as Loudon's *Encyclopedia* was reissued several times after 1833, and as late as 1867.

In Britain, despite the Napoleonic Wars, French fashion greatly influenced furniture design throughout the Regency period, which can be seen as lasting stylistically from 1793 to the 1830s (Morley 1993: 13). The assimilation of French design into British furniture demonstrates that fashionable taste transcended political situations. In England, the French style was championed by several members of the aristocracy, including the prince regent, the future King George IV, who had previously employed the French *marchand-mercier* Dominque Daguerre to work alongside the architect Henry Holland at Carlton House in London. Notably, Diana Davis has considered this growing taste for French decorative arts as a celebration of the "Anglo-Gallic interior" (Davis 2020: 2). George IV's furniture and interiors were recorded visually through paintings, such as portraits executed by Sir Thomas Lawrence, and Charles Wild's watercolors in the 1818 publication *The History of Royal Residences*. Thomas Sheraton's pattern book *Cabinet-Maker and Upholsterer's Drawing-Book* (1793–4) also contained visual reproductions of interiors at Carlton House, including the chinoiserie drawing room, thus producing a variety of visual sources for royal furniture that could be imitated and copied by other British and European designers.

Nineteenth-century pattern books indicate that numerous styles remained fashionable at the same time, with a prevailing interest in historicist revivals. These styles, which included Elizabethan, Italian, Renaissance, Grecian, "Louis Quatorze" or rococo and Gothic, dominated cabinetmaking throughout this period. Such historical styles reflect an overriding interest in Romanticism, historical objects, and antiquarian activity, as seen in novels by Sir Walter Scott and William Beckford. Visual representation of furniture helped to promulgate this historicism within cabinetmaking across Britain and further afield. Many historicist styles featured in several English pattern books from the 1830s onward, which not only contained illustrations of antique furniture but also outlined their historical context (Westgarth 2005: 32). These pattern books include Thomas Hunt's *Exemplars of Tudor Architecture ... and Furniture* (1830), A.W.N. Pugin's *Gothic Furniture in the Style of the Fifteenth Century* (1835), Sir Samuel Rush Meyrick and Henry Shaw's *Specimens of Ancient Furniture* (1836), which appeared as separated illustrated sheets between 1832 to 1835, Richard Bridgen's *Furniture with Candelabra and Interior Decoration* (1838), which included sixty plates of illustrated antique furniture without any text, Joseph Nash's *Mansions of England in the Olden Time* (1838–49), Matthew Lock's *Collection of Ornamental Designs ... and the decoration of rooms in the style of Louis 14th on 24 Plates* (1838), and Thomas King's posthumous *Specimens of Furniture in the Elizabethan and Louis Quatorze Styles* (1845).

The increasing number of visual representations in pattern books was indispensable in communicating, on an international scale, designs, forms, and proportions that were both manifestations of and vehicles for fashionable taste. By the early nineteenth century, an established tradition of disseminating styles and furniture designs internationally through pattern books existed, notably as we have seen between France and Britain. In Germany, pattern books such as the *Berlinner Möbel Journal* also included French designs by Percier and Fontaine and Pierre de la Mésangère. This spread of furniture design was sustained further by the many European cabinetmakers who immigrated to America during this time (see Chapter 2 in this volume). Although pieces of furniture were exported to the United States, supply was disrupted regularly due to political factors. Thomas Jefferson's 1807 embargo, for example, affected luxury goods, particularly metal mounts, and as a result, American cabinetmakers increased their production of furniture and may have become more dependent on printed visual sources (Aaseng 2002: 42). Consequently, their manufacture continued to be inspired by European designs thanks to the transmission of visual sources. Often American nineteenth-century furniture is an interpretation of European forms, styles, and decorative motifs (Fennimore 1981: 49). Of noted interest is Denon's *Voyage dans la basse et la haute d'Egypte*, which was published in English in New York as early as 1803. Denon was elected as an honorary member of the New York Academy of Arts in 1804, presumably due to the success of his pattern book, thus suggesting it was read widely (Oliver 2014: 34). European pattern books were also acquired by individuals, public libraries, and sold by American booksellers. Thomas Sheraton's *The Cabinet Dictionary*, which was first published in London in 1803, was already available in Philadelphia by 1805. It was offered by the bookseller William Duane and the Library Company of

Baltimore held a copy. The Library Company of Philadelphia also owned copies of Sheraton's *The Cabinet-Maker and Upholsterer's Drawing Book* (1793–4) and Hope's *Household Furniture and Interior Decoration* (1807) (Fennimore 1981: 54). As European pattern books were available to purchase and consult, conceivably they were used as reference by local cabinetmakers and American furniture firms took inspiration from the visual representations found within them.

Chair designs that are attributed to the manufacture of Duncan Phyfe, a New York cabinetmaker, indicate knowledge of such European visual representations. Good examples of this are two sketched designs for chairs by Phyfe (Figure 8.2) that may have been sent to the Philadelphia businessman Charles Bancker in around 1815 (Kenny 2011: 103).[2] A mahogany example of one of these chairs, now at the Metropolitan Museum of Art in New York, indicates that Phyfe accurately followed his sketched designs. The first design with saber-shaped legs on the left in the sketch is clearly based on the Greek *klismos* chair featured in pattern books by Hope, Smith, and Percier and Fontaine. At the same time, the "x frame" or curule legs on the second design can be linked directly to a design of a *tabouret ordinaire* or low stool by the Frenchman Pierre de la Mésangère (Plate 41) and plate 3 from the 1808 supplement to the *London Chair-Makers' and Carvers' Book of Prices.*

Were cabinetmakers simply responding to consumer demand or shaping taste through the furniture they produced? It is difficult to ascertain whether the American consumer was interested in emulating London and Paris fashions to remind themselves of their colonial European identities, or merely because they

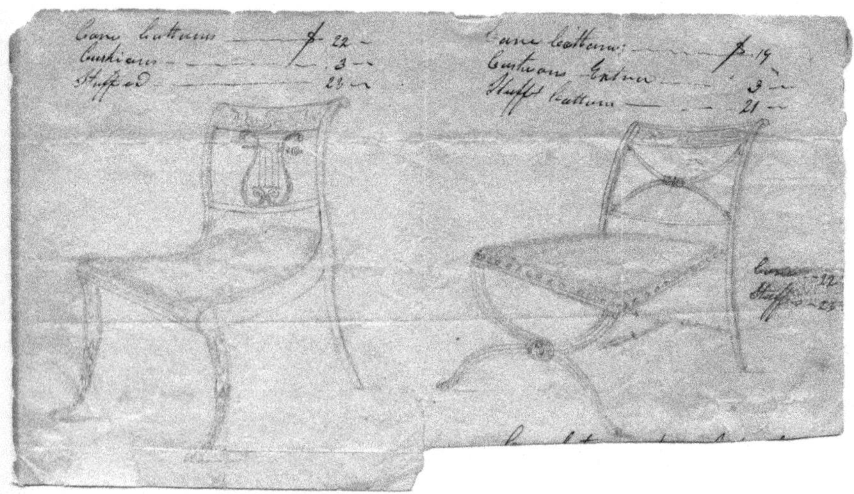

FIGURE 8.2 Sketch of two chairs attributed to Duncan Phyfe, 1815–16. © Joseph Downs Collection of Manuscripts and Ephemera, Col. 313, Winterthur Museum.

wanted to be fashionable. Many of Phyfe's designs embraced motifs such as the harp and lyre that were based on European neoclassical models. Similar decoration also appeared in *The New-York Book of Prices for Manufacturing Cabinet and Chair Work* published in 1802, with a second edition following in 1817, which only differed from the first in the addition of two pages (Apicella 2008: 141). Such few additions could suggest a lack of demand for novelty and innovation in New York furniture production, or more likely a continued desire by consumers for furniture that they deemed as fashionable. While in Europe many cabinetmakers produced pattern books, such a custom does not seem to have occurred as frequently in America; notably Phyfe and his competitors, such as Charles Lannuier, did not generate pattern books.

One of the earliest examples of an American furniture pattern book is *A Table of Prices for Cabinetwork in Hartford, Connecticut* (1792). Price books with illustrations, more so than pattern books, appear to have been preferred; including *The New-York Book of Prices for Manufacturing Cabinet and Chair Work* (1802 and 1817), *The Philadelphia Cabinet and Chair Makers' Union Book of Price* (1828), and *The New York Book of Prices for Manufacturing Cabinet and Chair Work* (1834). American furniture was also influenced heavily by the influx of German cabinetmakers and woodworkers from the 1810s to the 1850s, particularly to Philadelphia, who brought with them a Biedermeier aesthetic (Walker 1964: 35). Biedermeier designs were available through American booksellers, who sold German pattern books and developed connections with several German publishers, including Leipzig and Stuttgart (Beckerdite 1998: 80). The German-born cabinetmaker Charles Freudenvoll, whose father was the writer of *Neuestes Mainzer Moebel-Journal*, arrived in Philadelphia in the 1830s. Freudenvoll sold lithographic furniture designs, from his father's pattern book, marketed as the *New Magazine for Cabinet-Makers and Upholsterers*, at his store at 9 Gaskill Street; these designs illustrated both Biedermeier furniture and more Rococo Revival designs (74).

Towards the middle of the nineteenth century British visual representation of furniture shifted to a focus on the improvement of design education and standards of taste. This was, in part, instigated by an 1838 report by a parliamentary committee set up to evaluate the state of the art and manufactures industry in Britain. The report stated that British goods were lower in standard in design, overly ornamental, and lacking in manufacturing quality in comparison to European and American counterparts.

Unsurprisingly, pattern books began to address these issues. Richard Brown's *The Rudiments of Drawing Cabinet and Upholstery Furniture* from 1835 contained black-and-white illustrations showing furniture from different perspectives that made it easier for a designer to accurately copy the forms, thereby increasing their understanding of geometry and ability to design and manufacture three-dimensional shapes. Similarly, the preface to Henry

Whitaker's *The Practical Cabinet-Maker and Upholsterer's Treasury of Designs* stated that "public eye and taste may be improved at the same time" by his pattern book (1847: Preface).

A preoccupation for design reform was also coupled with an upsurge of interest in national identity and appreciation for Britain's rich design heritage (Broun et al. 1998: 2). By the latter half of the century this was promoted in publications. In 1878 J.W. Small published a pattern book of carefully measured drawings of Old Scottish furniture called *Scottish Woodwork of the Sixteenth and Seventeenth Centuries.* As a pattern book it was embraced by Scottish furniture designers, including Sir Robert Lorimer, George Walton, and Charles Rennie Mackintosh later in the century, seeking a vernacular design tradition that took inspiration from materials and construction based on past illustrations (Carruthers 2013). Small included a meticulously executed illustration of an old caqueteuse chair from Holyrood Palace as plate 42.[3] In 1904, Lorimer interpreted this form for the Earl of Crawford at Balcarres, thus revealing the long-lasting appeal of Small's pattern book; twenty-five years later its illustrations still inspired contemporary Scottish design. Lorimer's example was constructed in local timber with Scots oak, and used similar elaborate carving on the back and crest rail, much of which was derived from Small's illustration. Similarly, in Ireland, designers sought a national style that could express Irish heritage while also promoting good craftsmanship. Notably the furniture firm and maker Arthur Jones constructed chairs from Irish bog oak with harp, tower, and wolf motifs, an example of which is now at the National Museum of Ireland (Knight of Glin and Peill 2007: 195). By producing an illustrated catalog in 1853 entitled *Description of a Suite of Sculptured Decorative Furniture Illustrative of Irish History and Antiquities* Jones ensured that his national design spread throughout Ireland and beyond. Such Scottish and Irish examples suggest a pervading desire for late nineteenth-century furniture to achieve a traditional and national style that could evoke a sense of nostalgia and appreciation for the past.

COMMERCIAL PUBLICATIONS

While furniture designs featured in both eighteenth- and nineteenth-century pattern books varied from designs that had already been realized in existing interiors, to more fantastical examples, commercial publications, especially trade catalogs, often needed to offer a ready supply of the pieces they published visually. Visual representations of furniture found in printed publications such as journals, trade and exhibition catalogs, and decorating manuals, were one of the driving forces behind the consumption of furniture in the nineteenth-century commercial world. These publications served to satisfy individual consumer needs, catered for a wide range of social classes, and were produced more frequently than pattern books.

Journals

As printing advanced technologically, fashionable periodicals and journals emerged across Europe and the United States to gratify the demands of a society fascinated by the latest novelties and styles. While pattern books and trade catalogs grouped together stylistically heterogeneous furniture, journals tended to include only a select number of representations of a variety of styles. They were published more regularly and could reflect changing tastes and fashions at a greater frequency. Some notable journals that illustrated furniture were, in Britain, Rudolph Ackermann's *The Repository of Arts* and *The Belle Assemblée*; in France, *Journal des Dames et des Modes* and *Meubles et Objets de Goût*, both by Pierre de la Mésangère, Désiré Guilmard's *Le Garde Meuble*, Eugène Piot's *Le Cabinet de l'amateur* and Victor Quetin's *Le Magasin de Meubles*; in Germany, the *Journal des Luxus under der Moden* and J.W. Hanke's *Neues Journal für Möbelschreiner*; and, in America, *Graham's Magazine*, *Godey's Lady's Book*, and *Frank Leslie's Lady's Magazine*.

Journals aided the transfer of fashionable furniture designs across regions and countries. In 1809, the German-born Rudolph Ackermann, who owned a print shop on the Strand in London, initiated the monthly journal *The Repository of Arts* featuring hand-colored engravings of furniture. During the first year alone Ackermann registered approximately three thousand subscribers (Banham [1997] 2015: 6). Presumably many of these were located outside of Britain as Ackermann offered free posting to "New York, Halifax, Quebec and any part of the West Indies" (*Ackermann's Repository* 1813: Contents Page). Regularly journals looked to each other for inspiration and new sources of design, and as a result many visual representations of furniture were repeated in several different publications. In the January 1811 issue, Ackermann included an engraving of a circular sofa attributed to Morgan and Sanders, a London-based furniture firm. Actually, the design had been copied from an illustration in *Meubles et Objets de Goût* by the French designer Pierre de la Mésangère (Morley 1993: 280) (Plate 34). Mésangère is noted for having published a journal of ladies' fashion known as the *Journal des Dames et des Modes*; from 1802 to 1835 he also produced *Meubles et Objets de Goût. Meubles* was circulated widely throughout Britain and America and stylistically complemented Percier and Fontaine's decorative vocabulary. Although the concept of plagiarism in the nineteenth century did not have such negative connotations as it does today, it is puzzling as to why Ackermann or Morgan and Sanders did not give credit to Mésangère. One reason could be Ackermann's personal dislike of the French and the anti-Gallican spirit that remained prominent in English society despite the Prince Regent's preference for French fashion (Snodin 1984: 16). Primarily, this example sheds light on the idea that visual representations of furniture in journals were conditioned by subjectivity and, ultimately, Ackermann and Mésangère alike had the autonomy to include or omit whatever they so wished.

Concepts of comfort and convenience featured constantly in Ackermann's journals and were important elements of furniture design, often coupled with a greater novelty in design. For instance, in December 1811 Ackermann chose to publish a "newly invented" sofa table with folding flaps (Agius 1984: 28). Sofa tables were a response to the more informal and comfort-driven attitude of the nineteenth century. Used as an occasional table it could be adapted to any purpose, was easily moveable due to casters, and could therefore be tucked away in the corner of a room when no longer in use. Notably the architect Humphry Repton included a visual comparison between an old-fashioned *Cedar Parlour* and the *Modern Living Room* of 1816, which depicts a social environment with soft and comfortable furnishings that can be easily moved for various recreational purposes, thus increasing the informal atmosphere (Repton 1816: 58).

Additionally, this tendency to rearrange furniture is recorded visually in paintings of existing domestic interiors. In particular, the bourgeoisie and aristocratic interiors depicted by British artist Mary Ellen Best and Austrian architectural painter Rudolf von Alt exude a relaxed and sociable ambiance of the nineteenth-century domestic space. By seeing furniture represented visually in such paintings, the furniture historian is able to deduce how furniture was used, valued, and arranged within the interior, and this can lead to an investigation of how furniture interacted within the domestic sphere, with other decorative art, and with its owner or user. For example, Best's *Drawing Room at Howsam Hall* (*c.* 1830), *Miss Crompton's Room* (*c.* 1840), and *The Blue Room of Princess Elizabeth at Prinz-Karl-Palais* (1849) feature light furniture with colorful soft furnishings on wheels, along with display furniture that is often used to present porcelain and other artworks. In particular, Best represents furniture that harmonizes with the color and texture of the curtains, carpets, wallpaper, and paintings, to create balanced and *en suite* interiors, thus capturing how furniture was presented in the domestic interior at this time.

Pattern books followed this move toward greater informality, with Désiré Guilmard, a French designer, publishing furniture designs for use in more comfortable and sociable settings in his journal *Le Garde Meuble*, which was published bimonthly from 1844 to 1855. Guilmard illustrated predominantly Rococo Revival furniture, including several *fauteuils* and *chaise longues.* His use of lithography allowed for detailed, hand-tinted, colorful illustrations, which themselves exuded quality and luxury (Plate 35). From the 1830s, most seating furniture in France and Britain benefited from use of the coiled spring patent of 1828, based on the Viennese upholsterer Georg Junigl's experiment with iron springs, for which he received a patent in 1822 (Oates 1998: 174). Guilmard's designs would have included these new inventions and he made particular use of curved spring seats with additional padding, and this thick tufting is suggested through the illustration (Coffin 2008: 198).

Guilmard cleverly structured his furniture illustrations into separate guilds to pay homage to the *ancien régime* of the eighteenth century.[4] Each issue of Guimard's journal included nine loose lithographs: three *meubles*, three *sièges*, and three examples of drapery.[5] Presumably, the title of Guilmard's journal refers to the furniture guilds that were established by King Louis XIV in 1663, which essentially separated the *menuisiers*, who dealt primarily with carved furniture including chairs and beds, from the *ébénistes*, who focused on case furniture. Contemporary Parisians would have recognized this reference to the past; therefore, Guilmard's periodical not only promoted his designs but also captured contemporary interest and nostalgia for the *ancien régime*. In this way, he promoted the style embraced by Napoleon III (1808–73), the new president and, in 1852, emperor of France, and his consort, Empress Eugénie. The empress was particularly fascinated by the nostalgic and tragic figure of the eighteenth-century French queen Marie Antoinette (Pincemaille 2002: 168). Guilmard, as well as other French designers and furniture companies, including Allard and Sons, and Maison Leys, responded to this cultural attitude by providing consumers with furniture based on French eighteenth-century examples.

A dual purpose existed for visual representations of furniture in journals: on the one hand, they were included to guide the reader toward current fashionable trends; on the other hand, they responded to public demand, technological advances, and changes in social structures. As such, there was a significant growth in the diversification and specialization of furniture demonstrated visually in journals. Indicative of the technological advancements in furniture making, mechanical patents were taken out during the nineteenth century in increasing numbers. Ackermann featured several examples of mechanical furniture including a royal patent invalid chair in November 1810, and a luxurious Pocock reclining chair in March 1813. Ackermann's decision to represent different examples of furniture designed specifically for invalids in the *Repository* demonstrates a growing societal appreciation and commercialization for medical comfort. He also illustrated utilitarian mechanical furniture with space-saving attributes. Such portable furniture was usually destined for consumption by the lower classes who had less habitable space, by traveling workmen, and by those embarking on military or colonial campaigns. Ackermann's diversity of models confirms his awareness that it was necessary to cater to a wide range of social situations and audiences, who craved the latest fashions and most innovative designs. Such novelty continued to dominate furniture throughout the century, and patented furniture featured prominently in journals. By the 1890s, notably, the British journal *Furniture and Decoration* included a regular section entitled *Novelties*, featuring various illustrations of mechanical furniture, including several American inventions, such as a patent drawer equalizer to prevent drawers from sticking (*Furniture and Decoration* 1890: 18). Such a specifically designed piece of mechanical furniture reinforces the high level of specialization that consumers had come to expect by the end of the nineteenth century from commercial publications such as *Furniture and Decoration*, which were required to highlight a different novelty every week.

As the large majority of journal readers were most likely women, visual representation of furniture needed to satisfy individual needs in accordance with gender. This encouraged a proliferation in gender-specific furniture, tailored to the nineteenth-century woman. Designs that specified gender in furniture dated from the late eighteenth century, yet due to increasingly controlled gender roles that confined women to the domestic interior of the private sphere, it was the cultural rubric behind the production and advertisement of such gendered furniture that changed during the nineteenth century. Women were typically regarded as the arbiters of taste within the private space of the domestitc interior while men kept to the more "public" areas of society (Habermas 1991: 3). Consequently, careful reading of visual sources during this period demonstrates gender distinctions, which are socially constructed and representative of contemporary desires to define and segregate male and female domains. In particular, in the *Repository* several visual sources were targeted directly at women: Morgan and Sanders featured a lady's toilette set in 1809, a lady's worktable in June 1811, and a ladies' toilette dressing case with five mirrors in April 1812. This specialized furniture also enabled great luxury and convenience; of interest is the "Harlequin Pembroke" table featured in Sheraton's *Drawing-Book*, which had several purposes as a writing desk and a breakfast table, all to be used by a woman in her boudoir or particular living space.

Stricter gender roles conditioned such specialization of form and function, yet decorative arts also allowed nineteenth-century women to express their own particular tastes, identity, and status (Cohen 2006: 118). Loudon, in his 1842 pattern book, emphasized the necessity of considering the potential consumer's gender in an illustration of a wardrobe with a beam that has two armholes for ladies' dresses, allowing dresses to be examined and taken off more easily "without in the slightest dress creasing or otherwise injuring them" ([1836] 1883: 1,084). Journals such as the *Repository* and *Le Garde Meuble*, and Loudon's pattern book therefore included visual representations of furniture for women in response to their desire to self-fashion identity. Nineteenth-century furniture differentiated between genders, and often visual representations were aimed predominantly at women. This must have further reinforced their role as tastemakers within the home, and perhaps also made them feel valued as customers, as designers attempted to accommodate their various needs.

Trade catalogs

Knowledge of the furniture industry in the nineteenth century is heavily informed by visual sources found in trade catalogs. In comparison to the limited number of vivid colorful illustrations in journals, trade catalogs provided a more diverse range of furniture with numbered black-and-white illustrations. Trade catalogs can be viewed as vehicles for projecting the public image of the firm, as illustrations were employed to promote specific and existing pieces of furniture to consumers. Visual recording of furniture was therefore a commercial marketing strategy that enabled firms to target and to satisfy a large range of potential customers, while contending with other competitors. Due to the diversity of illustrated furniture, consumers could choose pieces tailored to their personal needs and compare price, style, and material, all within the comfort of their own homes. Normally free of charge, trade catalogs appealed to a wide audience and were not limited to those in society who could afford to purchase fashionable journals on a regular basis. This facilitated the dissemination of products to less affluent customers. Notably, the London firm of Heal's posted catalogs free on application and several firms, including Hewetsons, also located in London, did not charge for the catalog if an order was made or the catalog was returned within three weeks. Moreover, visual representations showed ready-made furniture that could be purchased and delivered almost instantaneously; by 1889, the London firm of Maple & Co. advertised that they had ten thousand ready-made bedsteads made from brass and iron in stock (Maple & Co. Furniture 1889).

Smaller furniture firms often struggled to afford the production costs of trade catalogs; instead they produced smaller pamphlets, trade manuals, or illustrated broadsheets. As early as the 1830s Joseph Meeks & Sons in America advertised furniture on hand-colored, lithographed broadsheets. Broadsheets permitted large numbers of images and information to be conveyed visually to the public on just one single page. In 1873, the German company the Thonet Brothers, who advertised their furniture internationally, also produced a furniture broadsheet with seventy-seven examples of their work (Figure 8.3). Originally based in Germany, Thonet Brothers opened in the 1830s when Michael Thonet successfully managed to use steam to bend beechwood rods into the components for chairs (Oates 1998: 166). The firm's widely distributed broadsheet, with its wide variety of examples, indicates that by the 1870s Thonet furniture was both diverse and highly desired. Consumers were motivated by the affordability, durability, and fashionable appearance of such bentwood furniture.

In later decades the printed process of trade broadsheets remained popular for regional furniture makers. One such firm is Edwin Skull of High Wycombe who, in 1860, printed a broadsheet illustrating 141 designs for chairs (Skull 1860). Illustrated advertisements and catalogs were therefore not limited to large industrial cities. Regional firms also embraced the fashion for trade catalogs to advertise their pieces to wider audiences. Often regional firms needed to accommodate local consumers or produce vernacular furniture characteristic of a particular area. By the end of the century, Scottish furniture firms

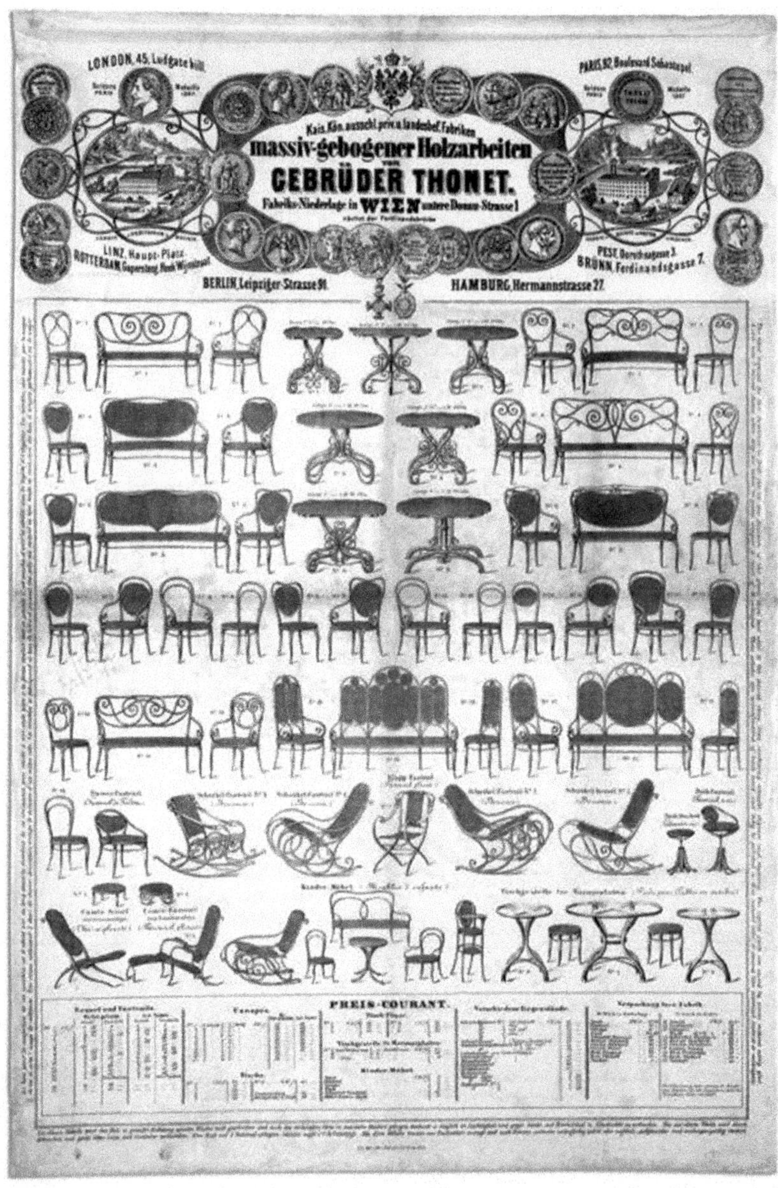

FIGURE 8.3 Thonet Brothers Advertising Broadsheet, 1867. Photograph © Thillman Collection.

produced illustrated catalogs to compete with London-based retailers. These included Christie & Miller of Falkirk in about 1880 and Bow's Emporium of Glasgow (Jones 1987b: Preface). The development of these local trade catalogs could be seen as a response to a boom in late nineteenth-century tourism throughout the Lowlands and Highlands of Scotland (Jones 1987b: Preface). Tourism encouraged the building of temporary vacation homes, especially in the Highlands, and owners and visitors demanded ready-made and affordable furniture to decorate these seasonal dwellings. Regional firms responded to these socioeconomic changes thus allowing consumers to acquire furniture locally without relying on shipping furniture from London-based firms. Here, furniture can be viewed as a manifestation of culture as Scottish trade catalogs were required to attract and satisfy tourists due to underlying geographical and economic cultural changes.

Ever-increasing consumer expectations also led to the creation of specialist furniture trade catalogs. In America, the 1850 publication of *School Architecture* featured a section dedicated to school furniture, while in Britain, *The School Builder's Guide* and *School Furniture Pattern Book*, both of 1852, addressed school furnishings. Both latter catalogs highlighted furniture that promoted hygiene as well as physical issues such as posture, thus encapsulating increasing cultural awareness of health and hygiene practices. As early as May 1854, Heal's produced an *Officers Portable Furniture Catalogue* with articles that were "invented for and used during the Peninsular war," including innovative iron bedsteads that folded into armchairs (Heal and Sons 1854: 14). In the catalog Heal's promoted the officer's furniture with an engaging and memorable illustration of a horse carrying all of the portable furniture easily on its back (Figure 8.4). The full set included a trunk that could transform into a table or a chair, and a separate bedstead with curtains. The striking image highlights the practicality and portability of Heal's furniture.

Toward the end of the century, trade catalogs for the furnishing of churches, as well as ones catering to housekeepers and children appeared. By 1888, Liberty & Company began producing Christmas catalogs that presented furniture appropriate for the festive season; and in 1896 Heal's printed illustrations of furniture suites especially designed for servants. Trade catalogs further reflected the diversification of furniture by dividing their furniture illustrations into specific categories: from babies' cribs, children's furniture, and cast-iron beds to articles especially for ladies and gentlemen. Although catalogs provided consumers with a great selection of pieces, through the process of specialization readers were still limited in their choices. One could argue that due to the categorization of furniture, consumers were relegated into certain groups. For instance, a male-dominated furniture trade determined the articles that were categorized as suitable for women, and many firms, including William Smee and Sons, indicated which furniture was "superior," thus reinforcing distinctions between social hierarchies. As furniture trade catalogs responded to changing cultural values and consumer expectations, it would appear that they simultaneously intensified social and gender classifications through the categorization of their furniture illustrations.

FIGURE 8.4 Officer's Equipage for Campaigning, Officers Portable Furniture Catalogue Heal's, 1854. Photograph courtesy of Caroline McCaffrey-Howarth.

By the later decades of the century it was standard practice for most trade catalogs to illustrate suites of furniture in imagined room settings, frequently in revival historicist styles, advising customers how to furnish whole interiors. While some furniture firms such as Wright and Mansfield engaged in a somewhat authentic reproduction of such designs, particularly a neoclassical Adam style, many others adapted the original designs in a much freer manner. In 1874, the London-based James Shoolbred & Company's catalog showed a bedchamber in the "Adam's Style," referencing the architect-designer Robert Adam and a drawing room in the "Louis Seize Style," which were both simplified interpretations of late eighteenth-century decorative schemes. This suggests that a proliferation of visual representation caused furniture design to become somewhat stagnant in its tendency to repeat familiar styles, yet it also indicates society's conservatism, especially as this was a period of economic upheaval. As such, perhaps it is not surprising that manufacturers catering to the middle and lower classes were not producing innovative, bespoke pieces but objects that could be mass-produced easily and interior decoration schemes for any type of residence. By the early 1900s Heal's still illustrated suites in the "Sheraton Style," reinforcing this culturally conservative attitude and reliance on extant fashions.

Since a reliance on industrial mass production existed, one could assume that the likes of Heal's and Maple's were preoccupied solely with targeting the middle-class market, yet this would limit an understanding of their commercial strategies. In reality, both London firms attracted all levels of society as clients, and this was in part, due to how they represented their furniture visually. In 1870, for example, Maple & Co. furnished the royal residence in Richmond Park for the Prince of Wales, Queen Victoria's eldest son (Barty-King 1992: 17). Notably, Smee and Sons intentionally labeled their best-quality furniture as "Superior" to guide more affluent clients in their trade catalog *Designs for Furniture* that was published between 1850 and 1855 (Joy 1977: xxix). Therefore any individual, no matter their social status, could examine a trade catalog and discover a piece of furniture that was best suited to their personal needs and price range.

By the 1870s, photography was used to great effect in representing furniture in trade catalogs. In 1874, J.W. Mason & Company of New York embraced the use of photolithographs in their trade catalog, stating in the preface that they are "very accurate" (J.W. Mason & Company 1874: Preface). Such technical advances were expensive processes but they allowed consumers to visualize furniture more realistically. In this catalog, one of Mason & Company's extension chairs can be seen in three separate states; a standard engraving might not have properly captured the piece in all of its positions. Here, it can be viewed clearly as a piece of furniture that is utilitarian while fashionable, which could be folded easily and put away when no longer required. Likewise, in 1874, Shoolbred embraced photolithography in a 38-page trade catalog. Shoolbred aspired to be high-quality furniture makers, which was highlighted by their use of freelance designers such as Owen Davis, who they commissioned to design imaginative interiors. The use of a more expensive printing process also emphasized the firm's reputation for elevated standards. Shoolbred's catalog and use of photolithography evidently led to great success and commercial viability as, by 1889, they produced a trade catalog with over four hundred pages of photo-illustrated furniture. In this regard, such companies paved the way for the proliferation of trade catalogs, comprised of photographs, which would come to dominate the early twentieth-century market.

Exhibition catalogs

An increasing number of international exhibitions surfaced by the latter half of the nineteenth century, and acted as an important marketing platform for furniture firms and designers. These exhibitions and world fairs took place predominantly in capital cities across Europe and America and were opportunities for countries to showcase technical innovation and ingenuity in design (Meyer 2006). While these exhibitions were only temporary, exhibition catalogs enabled a permanent visual record of the pieces that were displayed. Several books popularized furniture displayed at exhibitions such as the Great Exhibition of the Works of Industry of All Nations of 1851 and the Paris *Exposition Universelle* of 1855, including Blackie's 1853 pattern book, Henry Lawford's *The Cabinet of Practical, Useful and Decorative Furniture Designs* (1856), Matthew Digby's *Paris Universal Exhibition, Report on Furniture and Decoration* (1856), and John Braund's *Illustrations of Furniture from the Great Exhibitions of London & Paris* (1858). Braund's catalog listed only 110 subscribers to his publication, significantly fewer than the great number who visited these exhibitions. During the Philadelphia Centennial Exhibition in 1876, for example, ten million people passed through the doors during its six-month duration (Donnelly 2001: 91). Periodicals and journals published in England, France, Germany, and the United States, among others, often sent critics and published special sections on the fairs, especially the international exhibitions, such as the *Decorator and Furnisher*, the *Furniture Gazette*, and *The Studio* in Britain; *Revue artistique et littéraire* and *Le Musée artistique et littéraire: Revue Illustrée* in France; the *American Architect and Building News Furniture* and *Illustreret Tidende* in Denmark. The *Art Journal*, with a wide and aesthetically minded readership, illustrated select examples of exhibition furniture, including a meticulously engraved sideboard made by Gillows for the 1851 Great Exhibition, which demonstrated its detailed form and construction (*Art Journal Illustrated Catalogue* 1851: 203) and a number of bentwood chairs, a bench, and a table exhibited at the International Exhibition of 1862 (*Art Journal Illustrated Catalogue* 1862: 291). Several of these international exhibitions intended not only to promote good design, particularly the supremacy of national designs, but to educate visitors culturally, due to overriding interests in principles of design reform and morality, and the idea that household goods could shape moral character (Cohen 2006: 24).

Decorating manuals

Toward the latter half of the nineteenth century a plethora of printed advice manuals encouraged the public to decorate their domestic interiors in particular ways. Periodicals that promoted design appeared in several countries, including *Furniture and Decoration* in Britain, *Dekorative Kunst* and *Innendekoration* in Germany, and Francois Thiollet's *Nouveau Recueil de Menuiserie et de Décorations Intérieures* and Guilmard's *L'Ameublement et l'utile* in France.

Many decorating manuals gave everyday advice on furnishing the home through an abundance of visual sources that illuminated the instructive text at hand. More often than not, these were targeted at women who, along with their husbands, continued to play a significant role in the interior decoration of the private domestic sphere. Of marked interest is the British manual *The Englishwoman's Domestic Magazine*, which from 1852 gave advice on furnishing the domestic interior, even suggesting what color of dress complements a particular type of furniture. In one instance yellow is promoted as "it goes well with the mahogany furniture, and is very lively" (*The Englishwoman's Domestic Magazine* 1862: 63). In *The Englishwoman's Domestic Magazine*, a limited number of furniture examples were depicted as color engravings; often included in *The Fashions* section alongside changing styles in dress. For example, in November 1876, an illustration of a fashionable domestic interior indicates what type of furniture suited the stylistic trends of the moment. A lady dressed in vibrant purple with gold trimmings leans against a richly colored mahogany or rosewood gilt-metal mount cabinet with oval cartouches; both dress and furniture exude elegance, fashionable taste, and accompany the other perfectly (*The Englishwoman's Domestic Magazine* November 1876).

In Britain, appropriate interior decoration was also encouraged by Isabella Beeton's *Book of Household Management* (1861), and weekly periodical *The Queen*. In America Miss Leslie's *Lady's House Book* (1854), *Frank Leslie's Ladies Journal*, *Domestic Monthly*, and *Ladies' Home Journal* offered similar advice, making use of a select number of color as well as black-and-white engravings to illustrate their recommendations. Such manuals appealed to a wide audience of ladies from all social classes. In particular, the *Ladies' Home Journal* published in America from 1883 onward reached a circulation of 200,000 readers by 1885, and 400,000 by 1888 (Smeins 1999: 162). The illustrations within these manuals, which often depicted completely furnished interiors, could be used as a point of visual reference when the reader came to redecorate or reimagine their own domestic interior.

Decorating manuals did not focus solely on country houses or larger homes; instead examples such as Mrs. Orrinsmith's *Drawing Room*, published in 1878, addressed interiors found in houses of all levels of society (Logan 2001: 62). Chapter VI in *Drawing Room* is dedicated to furniture, with over sixteen lithographs executed by Clay, Sons, and Taylor, which illustrate Orrinsmith's various instructions regarding furniture styles and positions within the home, including: "A Jacobean Chair" (Orrinsmith 1878: 87), "A 'Sheraton' Sofa" (94), and a "Chinese China Case" (107). The "China Case" depicted a china cabinet on stand, displayed with china and positioned between two "picturesque chairs," which Orrinsmith states are "admirably illustrated" so as to demonstrate to her readers "what may be done by good use of straight lines" (106–7). If one was simply reading Orrinsmith's notion of achieving linearity her intention may not be transparent, but by aligning her instructions with illustrations the reader can understand that furniture which is straight-lined must be accompanied with complementary pieces to achieve a cohesive interior, which according to Orrinsmith suits the drawing room.

One of the most influential decorating manuals from this period was Charles Eastlake's *Hints on Household Taste*, first printed in 1868, and then again in 1872 when it was reissued twice in London. It was also printed in America for the first time in 1872 in Boston by Osgood and Company, with an added editorial introduction, addressing American consumers directly. Following the American Civil War from 1861 to 1865, the consumption of luxury goods in American declined rapidly. Eastlake's design manual signified a new era, one that rejected the sumptuous interiors of the pre-Civil War period and sought to promote better hygiene, less ornamentation on all decorative arts, and a new way of living that accommodated greater movement between the social classes. Aesthetically, Eastlake's designs were inspired by the Gothic Revival as envisioned by A.W.N. Pugin; they related to the tenets of design reform and favored a style that was honest, practical, and with ornament that was employed judiciously and indicated function. Through numerous visual representations of furniture in *Hints on Household Taste*, Eastlake illustrated "the character of design" (Eastlake 1868: xxiii), including woodcut designs that were later engraved in a more expensive photographic process by C. Hancock, based on original sketches by Eastlake and other designers (xxiii). Although the illustrations lacked color, photographic printing processes gave greater accuracy and were easily copied, thus encouraging the dissemination of Eastlake's aesthetic. Eastlake's designs procured a significant influence on furniture designers and consumers alike. While visual sources were copied or interpreted frequently by designers and firms throughout the nineteenth century, a significant amount of Eastlake's work was plagiarized, most notably by the American architect Henry Hudson Holly (Madigan 1975: 6). Publishing in *Harper's Monthly*, Holly featured illustrations and passages that were lifted directly from Eastlake's *Hints*, including a bedroom suite of furniture (*Harper's New Monthly Magazine* 1876: 358).

By the late 1860s, the Art Furniture Company in London advertised that they supplied pieces of furniture based on "designs by C.L. Eastlake." Eastlake appears to have adopted an interdependent relationship with furniture firms who he allowed to utilize his designs. By the fourth London edition of his book, he included illustrations of furniture designed not by himself, but by other London-based companies. Prominent companies include Jackson and Graham, who in turn produced furniture inspired by Eastlake's designs. Presumably this was a reaction to public fascination with Eastlake's book. By including illustrations of furniture from other designers and firms, Eastlake entered into partnerships, which superseded the traditional idea of self-promotion and instead used visual imagery to promote a particular decorative style.

WORKING DRAWINGS AND CORRESPONDENCE

Visual representation of furniture in working drawings and correspondence can be viewed as an expression of ideas between individuals. Ranging from faintly sketched pencil drawings to more detailed ink or watercolor designs, such illustrations had the potential to create a dialogue between designers, craftsmen, and their clients. As design historian Penny Sparke has commented, designs have the ability to express identity and ideas on an international level, "whether for personal, political or commercial ends" (2013: 6). The conveying of certain ideas and thoughts through this type of visual process suggests a belief in the transcending power of designs over words.

Working designs remain the only means by which some furniture companies recorded their furniture production visually during the nineteenth century. One of the best examples of this is Gillows, an English furniture firm with branches in Lancaster and London, which as Lindsay Boynton has identified, never published any books of furniture illustrations, presumably as they exercised caution over others taking their ideas (1996: 15). The only known means by which Gillows communicated visual representations of their furniture can be found in the Estimate Sketch Books that were circulated within the company (*Gillows Estimate Sketch Books, Letters and Waste Books*, Westminster City Archives, London). These estimate books highlight the diversity of Gillows' furniture production while also providing a fascinating visual record of the variety of their clientele. The restrained manner and lightness characteristic of Gillows furniture appears to have satisfied the taste of a wide spectrum of consumers. Drawings from these books were used predominantly internally, first and foremost to keep a record of the designs and their prices, and secondly, to create a dialogue between workers in Lancaster and the London office, who presumably sent designs back and forth to each other. Under the condition that they would never allow anyone else to view the drawings, these illustrations were sometimes distributed externally and entrusted to potential or existing clients (Boynton 1996: 20). Gillows' guarded approach to their furniture design may have bestowed consumers with a sense of exclusivity, but their decision not to produce an illustrated trade catalog or pattern book could have severely threatened their position commercially.

Individual furniture designers also created portfolios comprising working furniture designs. Most German cabinet makers notably carried their own personal visual source books with them when they immigrated internationally across Europe and America. Known as a *Meisterstück*, these were composed of innovative, working drawings and represented the final examination required for the rigorous German system to be considered as a master craftsman (Himmelheber 1983: 105–7).

Visual records of furniture in correspondence were also useful instruments for individual designers to communicate with patrons and existing clients. In a letter to a client named Mrs. Gough written in June 1830, the English Gothic Revival designer A.W.N. Pugin incorporated an ink drawing of a Gothic sideboard to give "an idea of my intentions" (Pugin 2001: 4). In the letter, Pugin maintains that it is a hastily done sketch yet it still creates a visual dialogue that enables him to explain his use of ornament and composition in a way that could be visualized easily by Mrs. Gough. Pugin states that he took the "liberty of making another design of a sideboard in a totally different composition which I am of opinion would be preferable in the situation" (Pugin 2001). By including an illustration, Pugin advised and satisfied the specific needs of his client by communicating the new design visually, which had changed from the original concept discussed. Here, the visual and verbal representation of furniture worked together to complement each other for Pugin to communicate his ideas successfully to his client.

The Scottish architect and furniture designer Sir Robert Lorimer incorporated visual representations of furniture into his correspondence constantly when writing to his friends and colleagues. In particular, Lorimer's lifelong correspondence with fellow architect Robin Dods, who immigrated to Australia, gives an invaluable insight into how visual representations of furniture can be used to express new ideas in letters. In August 1897, Lorimer wrote to Dods about the Scottish Arts and Crafts circle and sketched a caqueteuse chair with a trapezium rush seat by George Walton (Figure 8.5). Lorimer wrote that Walton designs "furniture in the furniture manner, that I like ... you feel the thing has been designed" (Robert Lorimer, Correspondence with Robin Dods, August 2, 1897, MS2484, University of Edinburgh Special Collections). The illustration enabled Dods to understand Lorimer's artistic viewpoint and simultaneously kept him apprised of advances in furniture design and styles in Scotland at this time.

Furthermore, in Lorimer's various commissions as an architect and interior designer, he presented sketches of furniture to his craftsmen, who sought his advice throughout the realization of a commission, and together they created the final product. A large proportion of the furniture that Lorimer designed was produced by the Edinburgh-based firm Whytock and Reid, which he often presented with hastily drawn pieces of furniture on rough notepaper (Cumming 2007: 90). Lorimer's use of visual representation of furniture enabled him to establish an interdependent relationship with his craftsmen whereby he quickly conveyed his intentions and thoughts in a manner that was more successful than verbal comments. It also reveals his Arts and Crafts tendencies as he believed that "separation of the designer from the craftsman was wrong" (Lorimer 1897). To Lorimer, therefore, the process of designing a piece of furniture was

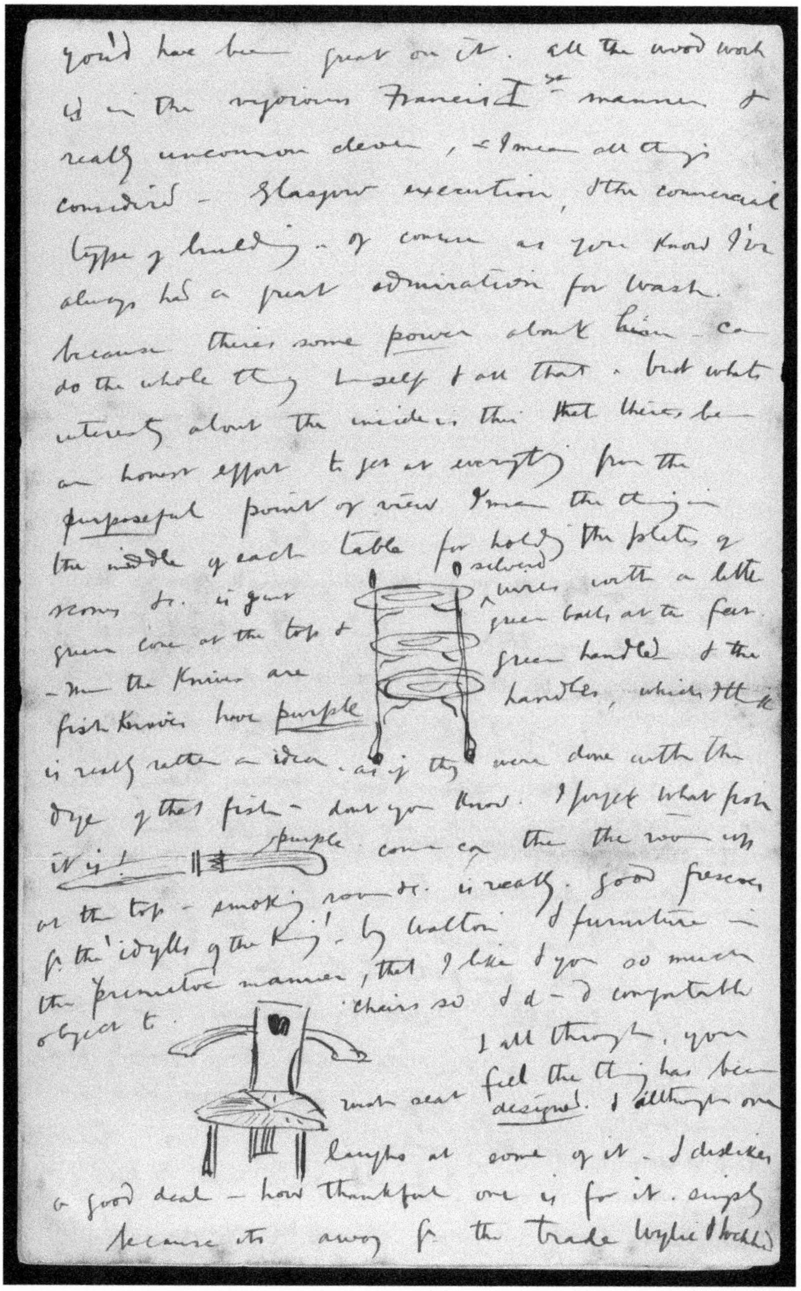

FIGURE 8.5 Portion of a letter from Sir Robert Lorimer to Robin Dods, August 1897. Photograph © CC by Edinburgh University Library.

collaborative; visual illustrations enabled him to transfer not only his aesthetic ideas but also his artistic beliefs, which included respect for craft-making traditions, honesty of construction, and use of local materials.

Antique furniture also featured in correspondence between collectors of furniture and their dealers or agents. For example, among the remaining Hertford Mawson letters, there is an instance where the 4th Marquess of Hertford sketched a pier table in black ink corresponding to an auction lot he forgot to ask his agent Samuel Mawson to purchase for him (Hertford 1981: 32). Hertford adopted a visual language to enable a successful communication between himself and his agent, which words presumably could not achieve.

While this chapter has not dealt with the collecting of antique furniture, it is worth mentioning briefly that visual illustrations also played their part in the antique furniture market. They were found increasingly in printed auction catalogs during the nineteenth century and from 1817 onward when the use of the term "antique furniture dealer" emerged (Westgarth 2009: ii). Elizabeth Pergam and Malcolm Baker have both written about the increasing use of illustrations in European auction catalogs, although Pergam notes that it was quite late in the nineteenth century when the art trade realized the potential of such visual depictions (Pergam 2014: 24). Antique furniture appeared in auction catalogs by firms such as Christie's and George Robins, notably the frontispiece of the 1842 Strawberry Hill Sale, which features some of the furniture and decorative arts offered for auction. The Stowe Sale of 1848, the Ralph Bernal Sale of 1855, and the Hamilton Palace Sale of 1882 also made significant use of illustrations within the text of the auction catalog. Overall, the use of visual representation of furniture in auction catalogs functioned to advertise key lots within a sale, presumably to increase competitive fervor between potential buyers.

CONCLUSION

While sometimes verbal text accompanied images, for the most part designers, cabinetmakers, and furniture firms in the nineteenth century relied on the universal power of illustrations to convey information and create dialogue with potential consumers. Advances in printing and transportation led to a greater dissemination of furniture design on an international level, with styles and interior decorating schemes often repeated by several different markets. As this chapter has demonstrated, by the end of the nineteenth century it became easier than ever before to circulate images of individual pieces of furniture, as well as fully furnished interior decorating schemes. These visual representations developed agency over the consumer and often influenced their decisions. Images of furniture therefore not only guided fashionable taste, but were shaped by and responded to changes in contemporary culture. The intrinsic link between visual representations of furniture embodied the complex social hierarchy and cultural paradigm of the nineteenth century. As we have seen, visual representations in printed material and private correspondence successfully encapsulated the changing value structures of nineteenth-century European and American society; namely, the growth of the middle classes, an increasingly consumer-driven society who needed to be seen to be fashionable, changing gender roles, and a desire for novelty, innovation, and technical ingenuity. Only by exploring how and why these visual sources were used, whether for aesthetic, instructive, or commercial purposes, can we appreciate fully the importance of visual representation of furniture during the nineteenth century and its ability to transcend words.

CHAPTER NINE

Verbal Representations

Writing Tables and Reading Chairs—Verbal-Textual-Intertextual Representations of Furniture

EMMA FERRY

INTRODUCTION

> *Furniture, whether useful or merely ornamental, at once reveals its own story of the degree of talent and the length of time devoted to its execution; all connected with it, to use a homely phrase, is plain and aboveboard, and the eye cannot be deceived by false appearances nor lured to admire by the display of glittering colours, as is the case in many other operative arts.*
>
> —*Art Journal Illustrated Catalogue* (1851: 79)

These comments from the *Art Journal Illustrated Catalogue of the Industry of All Nations 1851* are among the most famous verbal or, perhaps more properly, *textual* representations of furniture published during the nineteenth century. As this was "one of the first periods in furniture history for which there are overwhelming written sources" (Agius 1978: 19), the pioneer curators and connoisseurs who established nineteenth-century furniture as a subject worthy of serious scholarship were also able to draw upon many types of texts associated with furniture designed during this era; very often assessing their value as historical sources.[1] For instance, writing in 1962, Elizabeth Aslin (1923–89) categorized several different types of documentary evidence, each written or published with different intentions and aimed at different groups of readers. These included: the business records of leading manufacturers;

dated designs for specially commissioned pieces of furniture; the Patent Office Register of Designs (founded 1839); pattern books; trade catalogs; catalogs published for international exhibitions; and "the wealth of text and illustrations in periodicals," which she described as "the most useful information and ... certainly the most prolific" (Aslin 1962: 23). Ten years later, Jeremy Cooper also discussed the Victorian textual sources that furniture collectors and historians might draw upon, aiming to indicate "the nature of the information traceable in the many publications" and to provide "an account of the various stylistic changes evident in furniture design" (Cooper 1972: 115). While Aslin listed eight types of documentary evidence, Cooper organized his "bibliography" into five main groups; these also included "Pattern Books and Guides," "Trade Catalogues," and "Journals and Periodicals." In addition, focusing on printed materials rather than unpublished archival sources, Cooper listed "Books on Taste and Style" and "Critical and Factual Works on the Contemporary Arts" and pointed out that the texts in these two groups sometimes overlapped. Cooper also noted that Clive Wainwright (1942–99) at the Victoria and Albert Museum was then "engaged in compiling a general bibliographic survey of the period" (120); a survey that later formed the basis of the *Pictorial Dictionary of British Nineteenth Century Furniture Design* (1977). Published by the Antique Collectors' Club as a "Research Project" with an introduction by Edward Joy (1909–81), whose study of *English Furniture 1800–1851* was issued in the same year, the aim of the *Pictorial Dictionary* was "to show the complete range of Victorian furniture in illustrations drawn from contemporary sources" (Joy 1977: ix). Accordingly, the emphasis was placed upon presenting *visual* information rather than offering any analyses of the *texts* from which the images were reproduced: the illustrations were organized typologically and chronologically to show stylistic changes and innovations in furniture designs throughout the nineteenth century. Although focused on visual evidence, the *Pictorial Dictionary* also included a biographical section on "The Designers and Design Books" and a list of "Contemporary Sources," namely, pattern books, trade manuals, and catalogs, which ranged from Sheraton's "Appendix" to *The Cabinet-Maker and Upholsterer's Drawing Book* (1802) to Morris & Co.'s *Catalogue of Furniture* (1900). This list, which has provided subsequent generations of scholars and collectors with a useful starting point for further research, also demonstrated an important change in the purpose of textual representations of furniture published during the nineteenth century; from texts that discussed the *production* of furniture to those more concerned with its *distribution* and *consumption*—from pattern book to catalog. This is a shift mirrored by recent developments in the work of furniture historians, which has moved beyond the simple identification and discussion of designers, makers, materials, and popular styles to much closer examinations of the methods and systems of distribution and forms of consumption; here often focusing on the nineteenth-century construct of "home." Many studies have relied upon analyses of different types of verbal-textual representations of furniture published in the nineteenth century. This wealth of textual representations of furniture, didactic, descriptive, and/or disparaging, provides the critical reader with invaluable research material. Explained in pattern books, praised in exhibitions catalogs, or critiqued in trade journals, very often the same item of furniture can be considered from multiple synchronic viewpoints; while a diachronic analysis of its appearance in subsequent texts can chart the decline, fall, and revival of its appreciation and of nineteenth-century furniture more generally. Perhaps an example would be helpful; let's return to the Great Exhibition.

THE TALE OF PUGIN'S "BOOKCASE"

Described in the second volume of the *Official Descriptive and Illustrated Catalogue of the Great Exhibition of the Works of Industry of All Nations, 1851*, "Furniture" was exhibited in Section III, Class 26 along with "Upholstery, Paper Hangings, Decorative Ceilings, Papier Mâché and Japanned Goods," where the appearance of the entire class bespoke "a high degree of national prosperity" (*Official Descriptive and Illustrated Catalogue* 1851: 729).

The exhibits included a wide range of furniture types produced in a multitude of popular styles by 528 exhibitors[2] as well as the more unusual patented inventions and extraordinary virtuoso objects, often made on a gigantic scale or covered with elaborate decoration, created to attract maximum attention at the Crystal Palace (Plate 1). Indeed, the *Official Descriptive and Illustrated Catalogue* noted that "many of the decorative objects appear better to become the apartments of a palace than those of persons from the ordinary walks of life" and deemed "the amount of ingenuity, of contrivance and arrangement," which had been "expended upon furniture ... scarcely conceivable" (1851: 729). Objects such as the painted and gilded mahogany and limewood table made by George Morant & Son (Plate 36) with its naturalistic stork supports of cast plaster and metal; gilded leather bulrushes, flowers, and lily leaves; and a circular plate glass top painted in imitation of Florentine mosaic appeared in the *Official Catalogue* (plate 34), *Dicksinson's Comprehensive Pictures* (plate 17), and in the *Art-Journal Illustrated Catalogue*, where it was praised as one of three "elegant objects" exhibited by Morant (1851: 34). Yet, much of the furniture designed and described in the mid-Victorian period quickly came to represent "a depressing picture of the progress of taste in furniture" (Jervis 1968: 13). Well before the end of Queen Victoria's reign, the decorative arts of the period, including its furniture, had become "an aesthetic no-go area whose vast multiplicity of surviving artefacts were either beneath contempt or merely objects of derision" (Wainwright 1986: 9). Morant's Stork Table, which had been "widely criticised for the over naturalistic character of the base" (Victoria and Albert Museum [hereafter V&A], W.34:1, 2–1980), was silently put into storage. Even items of furniture approved of by the designers and theorists associated with the British "Design Reform" movement, who with government support sought to establish official Schools of Design *and* to improve the taste of the consuming public, would suffer serious neglect and an uncertain future. Perhaps the best known, and most fitting example for a chapter on verbal-textual-intertextual representations of furniture in the nineteenth century, is the tale of Pugin's "bookcase," a cabinet designed in the Gothic Revival style by A.W.N. Pugin (1812–52) and manufactured by Crace of London (Plate 5).

Exhibited among other items of furniture in the Medieval Court, "one of the most striking portions of the Exhibition," which Pugin had himself designed and superintended, the "cabinet bookcase, in carved oak, with ornamental brass work" (*Official Descriptive and Illustrated Catalogue* 1851: 761) was described by the *Art Journal* as "one of the most important pieces in the Medieval Court" (1851: 317). Despite anti-Catholic grumblings in the popular press (Teukolsky 2009: 88–91) and Ralph Wornum's assessment of the Medieval Court as "simply the copy of an old idea; old things in an old taste" (Wornum 1851: V***), the cabinet was the first piece of British furniture acquired for the new Museum of Ornamental Art based at Marlborough House (V&A: 25:1 to 3–1852). Costing £154 (an RPI equivalent of £17,110 in 2021), it was praised for the quality of its construction and carved details (Department of Practical Art 1852: 48). By the 1930s, however, when "official appreciation of the Gothic Revival was at its lowest" (this despite the publication of Kenneth Clark's *Gothic Revival* in 1928), the "disposal" of the cabinet was being considered.[3] Saved for use as an office bookcase at the Bethnal Green Museum, its importance went unrecognized for another twenty years, until it was included in an exhibition of *Victorian and Edwardian Decorative Arts*.

Held at the Victoria and Albert Museum in 1952 to "commemorate the centenary of the Museum of Ornamental Art" (Ashton in *Victorian and Edwardian Decorative Arts* 1952: 2), this exhibition marked an important turning point in the appreciation of nineteenth-century furniture as part of a wider "Victorian Revival."[4] Even so, the exhibits were chosen "in accordance with Pevsnerian orthodoxy in which special emphasis was placed on what was regarded as sincerity and originality" (Watkin 1980: 174). Indeed, Peter Floud (1911–60), Keeper of the Circulating Department at the Victoria and Albert Museum, who had organized the exhibition, noted in his introduction to the catalog:

> We have deliberately eliminated what was merely freakish or grotesque. At the same time we have purposely left out a whole host of Victorian designers whose work was unashamedly based on the copying of earlier styles.
>
> (Floud in *Victorian and Edwardian Decorative Arts* 1952: 5)

Unsurprisingly, there was no sign of Morant's stork table![5]

Fortunately, in a postmodern age such fascinating objects are of much more interest and prompt many more questions. Times and tastes have changed and since the serious revival of interest in Victorian culture in the mid-twentieth century, historians and collectors have been steadily reevaluating and rediscovering the furniture designed, manufactured, distributed, acquired, and used during the nineteenth century.

While both Pugin's "bookcase" *and* Morant's table survived to be displayed in the British Galleries at the Victoria and Albert Museum in London, other items were not so fortunate. At best "disregarded as merely old-stuff with only second-hand value" (Agius 1978: 19), at worst, for instance Jennens and Bettridge's papier-mâché "Day-Dreamer" chair, they have disappeared (Figure 9.1). But all is not entirely lost; many examples of nineteenth-century furniture have survived, if only on paper, as textual representations. For instance, the entry for the "Day-Dreamer" chair, in the *Official Descriptive and Illustrated Catalogue*, which included a full-page illustration, also offered a detailed explanation of its symbolic decoration:

> The "day dreamer",—an easy chair, designed by H. Fitz Cook, and manufactured in papier mâché, by the exhibitors. The chair is decorated at the top with two winged thoughts—the one with bird-like pinions, and crowned with roses, representing happy and joyous dreams; the other with leathern bat-like wings—unpleasant and troublesome ones. Behind is displayed Hope, under the figure of the rising sun. The twisted supports of the back are ornamented with the poppy, heartsease, convolvulus and snow-drop, all emblematic of the subject. In front of the seat is a shell, containing the head of a cherub, and on either side of it, pleasant and troubled dreams are represented by figures. At the side is seen a figure of Puck, lying asleep in a labyrinth of foliage, and holding a branch of poppies in his hand.
>
> (*Official Descriptive and Illustrated Catalogue* 1851: 748)

This additional textual representation enables the reader (both past and present) to decode the complexities of its design and to marvel at the technical ability of its manufacturers, who have given form to fantasy if not function.

In *Eminent Victorians* (1918), Lytton Strachey (1880–1932) famously warned future generations about the impossibility of writing the history of the Victorian age. Blaming the "vast quantity of information" that had been poured forth and accumulated about the period, he offered a solution to this embarrassment of textual riches:

> It is not by the direct method of a scrupulous narration that the explorer of the past can hope to depict that singular epoch. If he is wise, he will adopt a subtler strategy ... He will row out over that great ocean of material, and

6, Halkin St. West, Belgrave Square, London; and Birmingham. 7

"THE DAY-DREAMER CHAIR" IN PAPIER MÂCHÉ,

DESIGNED EXPRESSLY FOR THE GREAT EXHIBITION, BY H. FITZCOOK, ESQ., AND MANUFACTURED BY

JENNENS AND BETTRIDGE.

The Figure at top, crowned with roses, is intended to represent joyous dreams, and the one with bat-like wings, troublesome imaginings. Behind the figures is displayed the rising sun, suggestive of Hope. In front of the Seat is a Shell containing the Head of a Cherub; the Twisted Supports of the Back are ornamented with the Poppy and other Flowers emblematic of the subject.

FIGURE 9.1 Jennens and Bettridge (maker), The "Day-Dreamer" chair, 1851, papier-mâché. Photograph courtesy of the Winterthur Library/Internet Archive.

lower down into it, here and there, a little bucket, which will bring up to the light of day some characteristic specimen, from those far depths, to be examined with a careful curiosity.

(Strachey [1918] 2009: 5)

Just over a hundred years later, and mindful of the overwhelming amount of textual sources available, which in an age of digital humanities seems to have expanded exponentially, I have confined the contents of my "little bucket" to printed materials. Sadly, this excludes the unpublished archives of leading furniture manufacturers, for example, the famous *Estimate Sketch Books* (1784–1905), "the most frequently consulted series records" of Gillows. Held at Westminster City Archives these are a "factual record of the furniture produced by the firm and provide valuable information about furniture designs, the cost of materials, workmanship, sometimes the craftsmen responsible and the client for whom the piece was made" (CWA: 344). Fortunately, Susan E. Stuart's magnum opus *Gillows of Lancaster and London, 1730–1840* (2008), draws extensively upon the estimate sketchbooks, thus making "available vast swathes of previously unpublished material from what is unquestionably the most important surviving archive of any English cabinet-maker" (Levy 2009–10: 212).

Westminster City Archives also hold other frequently consulted collections that relate to furniture manufacturers and retailers, including the archive of Liberty of London, while the archives of the Crace Family (1692–1992), Holland & Son (1821–1968), Heal & Son Holdings plc (1810–2009), and E.W. Godwin are part of the Victoria and Albert Museum Collections held at the Archive of Art and Design.[6] These unpublished sources are, of course, significant textual representations of furniture that have been the subject of detailed investigations.[7] Many studies have drawn upon other unpublished texts kept within these archives such as diaries and letters written by furniture designers, makers, sellers, and customers, which are also invaluable forms of textual representation that provide evidence of the relationships between producers, distributors, and consumers and which offer descriptions of furniture. Again, however, for practical reasons, this type of unpublished handwritten material has also been deliberately denied a place in my bucket.

Pragmatism aside, the historical and cultural context of the nineteenth century provides further justification for this possibly contentious decision. As Richard Altick's pioneering book, *The Common Reader* ([1957] 1998), has demonstrated, the nineteenth century witnessed a massive expansion of print culture. Driven by technological developments in both print and paper production, improvements in systems of distribution (from the railways to the circulating libraries) were able to feed a rapidly growing mass-market of literate consumers who were hungry for print in all its forms. Indeed, due to important social changes including Foster's Education Act (1870), census data show that while the population rose from 7.8 million in 1801 to 30 million by 1901, so too did male and female literacy rates, which reached 97.2 percent and 96.8 percent, respectively, by 1900 (Altick [1957] 1998: 171). Inevitably, a growing population stimulated the demand for housing. Again, census figures show that in 1831 there were over 2.5 million houses in England and Wales increasing to over 6.25 million by 1901; houses that of course needed furniture. As Henry Mayhew (1812–87) noted in the third volume of *London Labour and the London Poor*:

> Since 1839 there have been 200 miles of new streets formed in London, no less than 6,405 new dwellings have been erected annually since that time; and it is but fair to assume that the majority of these new homes must have required new furniture.
>
> (1861: 223)

Strachey's choice of biographical subjects was ostensibly determined "by simple motives of convenience and of art" (Strachey [1918] 2009: 5), however, in considering the "new furniture" referred to by Mayhew, the second part of this chapter has been organized using a model of Production-Consumption developed by John A. Walker in *Design History and the History of Design* (1989). Presented diagrammatically, Walker divided the processes of design into four sections each representing a different phase: the production of designs; the manufacture of designed goods—in this case furniture; the distribution of those goods through marketing and retailing activities; and finally, the consumption and use of the goods including their customization, resale, collection, recycling, and/or destruction (Figure 9.2). I have applied this same principle to my classification of the primary publications discussed throughout the chapter, which in turn relate to the *production* (both design and manufacture), the *distribution*, and the *consumption* of actual furniture during the nineteenth century. This allows for a consideration of textual representations in terms of authorship *and* readership; here asking who wrote these texts, why they were written and published, and how they might have been understood by their intended readers.

The first part examines publications that relate to the design and manufacture of nineteenth-century furniture written *by* cabinetmakers and upholsterers, architect-designers, and design-educators *for* those working in the trade. These texts include cabinetmakers' price books, drawing books, instruction manuals, and treatises written by professional designers. The next section considers the range of publications issued as a means of marketing and distribution, including trade and exhibition catalogs written by or about manufacturers, and aimed at potential consumers. This section will also examine examples of domestic design advice literature; a valuable source in the history of furniture, which "is

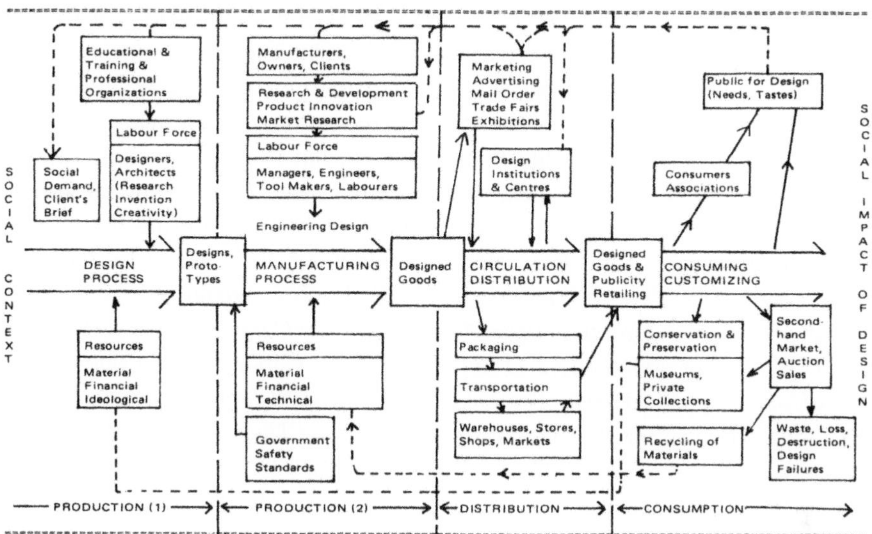

FIGURE 9.2 John A. Walker's model of Production-Consumption from *Design History and the History of Design* (1989). Photograph courtesy of John A. Walker/Pluto Publishing. Reproduced with permission of Pluto Books Limited (company number – 04740976) through PLSclear.

situated firmly within the category of mediation, operating as it does between the realms of production and consumption" (Lees-Maffei 2003: 3). Finally, the chapter will consider textual representations that relate to the consumption of furniture including published accounts of the collections amassed by patrons of designers, manufacturers, and furnishers, and descriptions of furniture within homes, both rich and poor, that were published in nineteenth-century books, reports, and magazine articles. Here I shall also consider descriptions of furniture found in the nineteenth-century novel, which although fictional rather than factual examples, are nonetheless, textual *representations* of furniture.

So now, with my life-jacket fastened and my little bucket ready to be lowered, I shall "row out over that great ocean of material" and, while afloat, I shall endeavor to bring up to the light of day some characteristic [textual] specimens about the design, manufacture, distribution and consumption of furniture that were published in the nineteenth century.

NINETEENTH-CENTURY TEXTS: THE PRODUCTION OF FURNITURE

A wide range of publications that relate to the production of furniture were issued in the nineteenth century demonstrating the shift from the *verbal* to the *textual* representation of furniture. Indeed, as Sheraton noted in his *Drawing*

Book, "a master cannot possibly convey to the workman so just an idea of a piece of furniture by a verbal description as may be done by a good sketch" (Sheraton 1802: 178). From furniture pattern books to the periodicals that eventually replaced them (Long 2002: 116), this tsunami of texts is just as Strachey warned. For instance, the number of English-language journals that contained discussion and descriptions of furniture originally published for the professional artist-designer, decorator, furniture maker, architect, and builder during the course of the nineteenth century is staggering. These include, chronologically: *The Art Union* (1838–49), *The Art Journal* (1839–1911), *The Builder* (f. 1843), *The Journal of Design and Manufacturing* (1849–52), *The Cabinet Maker's Assistant* (f. 1853), *The Building News* (1855–1926), *The Cabinet Maker's Monthly Journal of Design* (f. 1856), *The Decorator* (1864), *The Architect* (f. 1869), *The Workshop* (1869–72), *The House Furnisher and Decorator* (1872–3), *The Furniture Gazette* (1872–93), *The Art Workman* (1873–83), *The British Architect and Northern Engineer* (f. 1874), *The Magazine of Art* (1878–1904), *The Artist* (1880–92), *The Artist and Journal of Home Culture* (1880–94), *The Cabinet Maker and Art Furnisher* (1880–1902), *Decoration in Painting, Architecture, Furniture etc.* (1880–93), *The Journal of Decorative Art* (1881–1937), *The Art Designer* (f. 1884), *The Hobby Horse* (1884–8), *Art and Decoration* (1885–6), *Furniture and Decoration* (1890–98), *The Studio* (f. 1893), the *Journal of the Royal Institute of British Architects* (f.1893), *The Architectural Review* (f. 1896), *The House* (1897–1902), and *The Furnisher* (1899–1901). This long list, for which I apologize, is intended to highlight the breadth and depth of this great textual ocean and the potential for overfilling my little bucket with professional and trade magazines alone.

Since the 1950s, furniture historians have drawn upon a wide range of nineteenth-century texts that focus upon the production of furniture, or more properly the *design* of furniture. There are many significant monographs and articles that have effectively recovered the biographies and oeuvre of many British architect-designers, often with a focus on the works of the "Progressive"; notably: A.W.N. Pugin (1812–52), William Burges (1827–81), Christopher Dresser (1834–1904), Bruce Talbert (1838–81), C.F.A. Voysey (1857–1941), C.R. Ashbee (1863–1942), and Charles Rennie Mackintosh (1868–1928).[8] Besides the studies of leading nineteenth-century furniture manufacturing and furnishing companies including Gillows (f. 1730), Crace (f. 1768), Holland & Son (f. 1803), and Heal's (f. 1810), several scholars have used company archives to investigate the other London-based firms including the cabinetmaker George Bullock (fl. 1777–1818), Collinson and Lock (f. 1782), Charles Hindley & Sons (fl. 1817–92), Jackson and Graham (f. 1836), Maple & Co (f. 1870), and William Watt & Company (f. 1874).[9] The overabundance of texts about Morris, Marshall, Faulkner and Co., would probably fill an entire chapter, but there are several studies that focus upon specific pieces of furniture including the famous Sussex chair range or the "Morris Adjustable-Back Armchair"[10] designed and made by the well-known original members of "the Firm," Ford Madox Brown (1821–93), Dante Gabriel Rossetti (1828–82), and Philip Webb (1831–1915), as well as the later designs by George Jack (1855–1931).[11] Where records have survived, the work of smaller provincial firms of cabinetmakers has also been examined in articles published in the *Journal of the Regional Furniture Society*.[12] The work of "Ruskinian" Guilds,[13] and the Cotswold-based craftsmen associated with the Arts and Crafts movement have also received a great deal of attention.[14] Finally, driven by an interest in social and labor history since the late 1960s, the organization of the furniture "industry" has also been examined including the emergence of trades unionism; the division of labor within the "comprehensive manufacturing firms"; the "dishonourable" trade in London's East End; and the chair-making capital at High Wycombe in Buckinghamshire.[15] These studies have all been based upon a careful examination of nineteenth-century texts. So, what should I bring up to the light of day to examine with "careful curiosity"? Walker's diagram offers a solution, suggesting texts written *for* the labor force involved in the production processes—design and manufacture—*by* practitioners, educators, and professional organizations.

While the illustrated pattern books, discussed elsewhere in this volume, were published by individual cabinetmakers and upholsterers to disseminate fashionable designs for a wide range of furniture types, the Society (later Union) of London Cabinet Makers issued their own books of *Prices and Designs of Cabinet Work*, which "collectively form a factual compendium of incomparable richness for everyone seriously interested in furniture history" (Gilbert 1982: 15). First published in 1788, price books were prepared by a Committee of Masters and Journeymen, but unlike the "lavish pattern book intended to enhance the prestige and advertise the business of an individual firm," this type of publication was instead "a practical handbook for regulating and calculating the labour charges or piecework rates when making specific cabinet wares in common production" (11). Price books reveal a great deal about the economics of the furniture trade; as Martin Weil has commented, their "very existence suggests the need to establish stable and uniform prices which in turn suggests that the trade was disturbed by competitive pricing practices" (1979: 175). However, aimed at working cabinetmakers and intended for daily use in the workshop, they also contained long and detailed specifications for all types of furniture. The following description from the 1811 edition of the *London Cabinet-Makers' Union Book of Prices* gives the dimensions for, and cost of making, "A Cylinder-Fall Writing Table":

> All solid.—Three feet long, one foot nine inches wide, the upper framing ten and a half inches deep, the lower framing six and a half inches ditto, one drawer in front, cock beaded, &c.: four inches deep) outside, the inside fast;

> three small drawers and six letter-holes in ditto; the edge of the top and the sweep part of ends square; on plain Marlbro legs; the standing-board solid and made fast, and a front edge of inch stuff under ditto, to receive a mortice lock; the bottom rail of inch and quarter stuff; without any mouldings; the cylinder to run on four iron pins, or with wood tongues; the upper back of mahogany, screw'd in; partition edges faced with mahogany.
>
> (1811: 99)

Published without an accompanying plate, the language of the text indicated the technical knowledge required by the cabinetmaker; as Weil has also noted, price books are "especially useful for the insights they provide into the terminology used by the craftsman himself as opposed to the terminology invented in subsequent years by collectors and dealers" (1979: 175). The London Price Books were revised until 1866, with supplements issued for "work not included in the union book" and for specific items such as "improved extensible dining tables."[16] Versions were also published beyond the metropolis in towns and cities across England and north of the border in Scotland: they were also compiled in America, thus offering information about regional and national variations in popular designs.[17]

The price books, written for the skilled master, journeyman, and apprentice, focused upon the costs and specifications associated with the production of furniture; however, other texts published in the nineteenth century offered additional instruction for the cabinetmaker or upholsterer in a range of technical skills, particularly drawing. Akiko Shimbo has noted that many authors "stated that apprenticeship did not provide enough training" and that "there was demand among craftspeople for more advanced, sophisticated and practical knowledge of ornamental and perspective drawing" (2015: 50). Several early pattern books, for example, George Smith's *The Cabinet-Maker and Upholsterer's Guide, Drawing Book and Repository* (1826) included instructions on perspective and ornamental drawing and geometry "sufficient to make any one a draftsman in his own person" (1826: vi); detailed drawing exercises were also included in several furniture pattern books. In the "Preface" to the 1835 edition of *The Rudiments of Drawing Cabinet and Upholstery Furniture* (first published in 1822), Richard Brown drew attention to the shortcomings of his better-known predecessors and justified the need for his own publication:

> The writers on the subject of cabinet furniture have been comparatively few; and the books hitherto published containing merely designs for furniture, and not rudiments, gave rise to the present work. It is true that Chippendale and Sheraton have given rules for drawing; but the ideas of their trivial compositions being taken from the models of the French school of about the

> middle of the last century, now obsolete, has entirely discouraged cabinet-makers from investigating the principles employed in their delineations.
>
> (Brown 1835: iv)

Writing in 1847, Henry Whitaker also drew attention to the importance of drawing skills for designers in his snappily titled *The Practical Cabinet-Maker, Upholsterer and Decorator's Treasury of Designs in the Grecian, Italian, Renaissance, Louis-Quatorze, Gothic, Tudor, and Elizabethan Styles, Including Designs Executed for the Royal Palaces and for Some of the Principal Mansions of the Nobility and Gentry, and Club Houses*:

> With the pains that are now taken by the Government Schools of Design, to imbue all classes with a knowledge of drawing, ... we hope yet to see the day when England will stand as pre-eminent for excellence of design, as it does for the execution of every article that employs the hand of man, and contributes to health, comfort, or refinement.
>
> (Whitaker 1847: 5)

The Government Schools of Design, funded by the Board of Trade, had been established ten years earlier after the Parliamentary Select Committee on Arts and Manufactures (1835–6) reported on the poor standard of British-manufactured goods and their story has been discussed elsewhere.[18] The aim was to improve the standard of design education in Britain, and although Pugin famously dismissed the first School of Design at Somerset House as a "mere drawing school" ("Mr Pugin on Christian Art" 1845: 367), several architect-designers and artists (the so-called Design Reformers) associated with what became known as the "South Kensington System" produced a wide range of texts on furniture design during this period. These design-focused texts, which included treatises, instruction manuals, essays, published lectures, and articles in the professional and trade journals, indicated the growing division of labor in the production of furniture between what John Moyr Smith (1839–1912) described as "the department of design and ... that of practical workmanship" (1887: iv).

Some of these publications were written for an intended readership of designers and craftsmen directly involved in the production processes; for instance, William Bell Scott's *The Ornamentist or Artisan's Manual of the Various Branches of Ornamental Art* (1845). Other works, such as Christopher Dresser's *Studies in Design* (1876), were aimed at a wider possible audience, being

> intended to help the decorator and to enable those who live in decorated houses to judge, to an extent, of the merit of the ornament around them. It will also, it is hoped, aid the designer and the manufacturer of decorated objects, by suggesting to them useful ideas.
>
> (1876: Preface)

Christopher Dresser studied at the Government School of Design where he was influenced by the men leading the design reform movement: Richard Redgrave (1804–88), Henry Cole (1808–82), Owen Jones (1809–74), and Matthew Digby Wyatt (1820–77). Appointed Professor of Artistic Botany at the Department of Science and Art, South Kensington in 1855, Dresser contributed designs from "Leaves and Flowers from Nature" to Owen Jones's *Grammar of Ornament* (1856) (Newton 2005). He also wrote several books on design, including *The Art of Decorative Design* (1862), *Principles of Design* (1873), *Studies in Design* (1875), *Japan: Its Architecture, Art and Art-Manufactures* (1882), and *Modern Ornamentation* (1886) and he was the editor of the *Furniture Gazette* from 1880 to 1881. Dresser was among several authors who combined the roles of critic and practitioner in this period. Writing about E.W. Godwin (1833–86), who was "lead writer, editorial consultant and occasional graphic designer for the *British Architect and Northern* Engineer (1878–85)," Juliet Kinchin has commented that his "direct contemporaries such as Bruce Talbert, John Moyr Smith, Christopher Dresser and William Morris all heightened their visibility through committing themselves to print" (2005: 22).

Dresser's *Principles of Design* (1873), a text addressed to "working men," included a chapter on "Furniture," which was based upon three articles on "Art Furniture" first published in *The Technical Educator* (Dresser 1870: 311–13, 376–8, 403–6). A close reading of this work suggests that it is also an excellent example of *intertextuality*, which refers to many other contemporary texts. In fact, this single chapter incorporates textual representations of furniture including exhibition reports, trade catalogs, pattern books, professional journals, museum guide books, and advice manuals.

The construction of furniture was the key theme of Dresser's chapter: "for unless such works are properly constructed they cannot possibly be useful, and if not useful they would fail to answer the end for which they were contrived" (1873: 50). His opening remarks included a well-known quote from Richard Redgrave's *Supplementary Report*[19] on "the general state of design as applied to the fabric and manufactures in the Great Exhibition" (1852: 708):

> "Design", says Redgrave, "has reference to the construction of any work both for use and beauty, and therefore includes its ornamentation also. Ornament is merely the decoration of a thing constructed".
>
> (Dresser 1873: 50)

Next, Dresser considered "the structure of works of furniture" and focused upon wood "the material from which we form our furniture" (1873: 51). Here, having commented upon the grain and strength of different types of wood, he referred his readers to the *Catalogue of the Collection illustrating Construction and Building Material* in the South Kensington Museum and the manual of

Technical Drawing for Cabinetmakers by E.A. Davidson (51). Moving on to discuss the design and construction of chairs, Dresser complained that he saw "but few chairs in the market which are well constructed" (52). To illustrate this point he referred to, and "borrowed" images from, the popular domestic advice manual *Hints on Household Taste* (1868) by Charles Locke Eastlake (1836–1906). Dresser commented in a footnote:

> *It is well worth reading, as much may be learned from it. I think Mr. Eastlake right in many views, yet wrong in others, but I cannot help regarding him somewhat as an apostle of ugliness, as he appears to me to despise finish and refinement.
>
> (1873: 52)

Consequently, he reused an image of a chair recommended by Eastlake as an example of "good taste in furniture" to illustrate what Dresser considered "essentially bad and wrong" (Figure 9.3). He continued:

> Were I sitting in such a chair, I should be afraid to lean to the right or the left, for fear of the chair giving way. Give me a Yorkshire rocking-chair, in preference to one of these.
>
> (Dresser 1873: 53)

Instead he offered his own illustrations of chairs in a range of styles as examples that "show how I think chairs should be constructed":

> Fig. 30 is an arm-chair in the Greek style, which I have designed. Fig. 31 is a lady's chair in the Gothic style; Fig. 32, a lady's chair in early Greek. These I have prepared to show different modes of structure.
>
> (Dresser 1873: 55)

Dresser also discussed and illustrated a Greek-style "chair shown by Messrs. Gillow and Co., of Oxford Street, in the last Paris International Exhibition" (1873: 56), an event that he had reported on in *The Development of Ornamental Art in the International Exhibition* (1862). Alongside the "admirably constructed" Gillows chair Dresser placed an illustration "from Mr. Talbert's very excellent work on 'Gothic Furniture'" (56). Other designs for a settee and a sideboard from Talbert's pattern book *Gothic Forms Applied to Furniture, Metal Work and Decoration for Domestic Purposes* (1862) were also included and approved:

> Although Mr. Talbert is not always right, yet his book is well worthy of the most careful consideration and study; and this I can truly say, that it compares favourably with all other works on furniture with which I am acquainted.
>
> (Dresser 1873: 58)

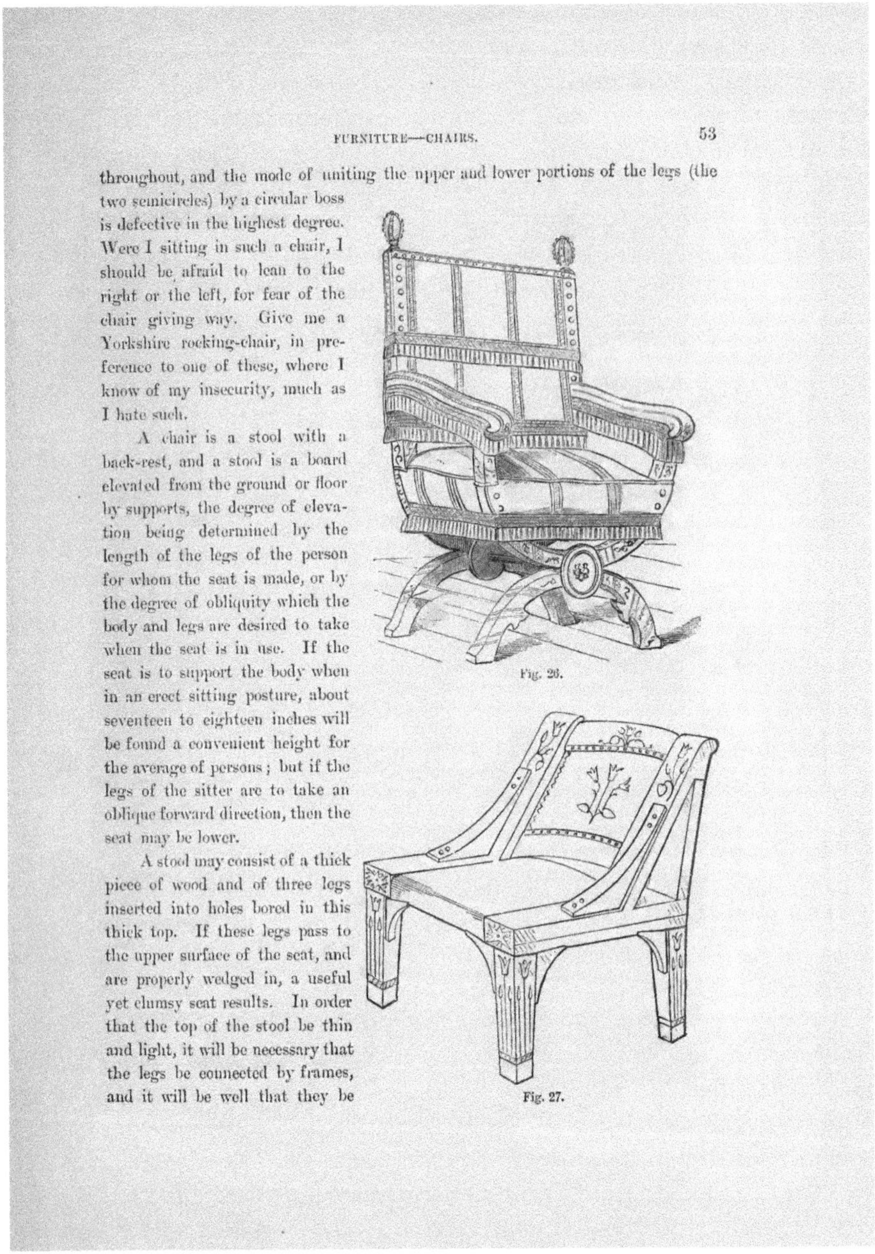

FURNITURE—CHAIRS. 53

throughout, and the mode of uniting the upper and lower portions of the legs (the two semicircles) by a circular boss is defective in the highest degree. Were I sitting in such a chair, I should be afraid to lean to the right or the left, for fear of the chair giving way. Give me a Yorkshire rocking-chair, in preference to one of these, where I know of my insecurity, much as I hate such.

Fig. 26.

A chair is a stool with a back-rest, and a stool is a board elevated from the ground or floor by supports, the degree of elevation being determined by the length of the legs of the person for whom the seat is made, or by the degree of obliquity which the body and legs are desired to take when the seat is in use. If the seat is to support the body when in an erect sitting posture, about seventeen to eighteen inches will be found a convenient height for the average of persons; but if the legs of the sitter are to take an oblique forward direction, then the seat may be lower.

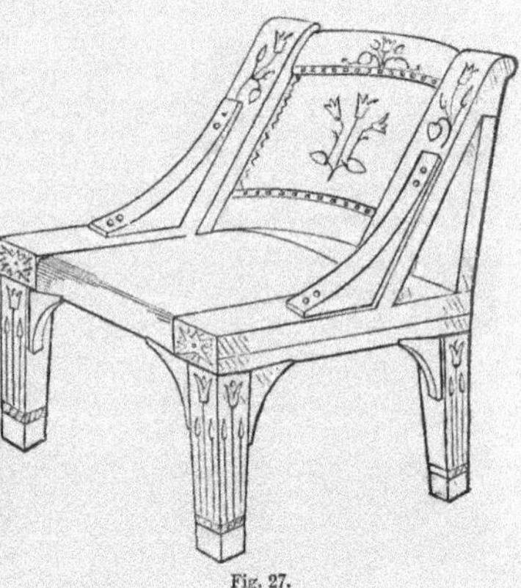

Fig. 27.

A stool may consist of a thick piece of wood and of three legs inserted into holes bored in this thick top. If these legs pass to the upper surface of the seat, and are properly wedged in, a useful yet clumsy seat results. In order that the top of the stool be thin and light, it will be necessary that the legs be connected by frames, and it will be well that they be

FIGURE 9.3 Christopher Dresser, *Principles of Decorative Design* (1873), p. 53. Photograph courtesy of University of California Libraries/Internet Archive.

Having advocated "simplicity of structure and truthfulness of construction" (Dresser 1873: 58), Dresser next considered "the enrichment of parts"; here he recommended that any carving "should be sparingly used" (61). This part of the chapter referred to and illustrated "Mr. Grace's sideboard, by Pugin" (61) and "a painted cabinet by Mr. Burgess [*sic*] (Fig. 42), the well-known Gothic architect, whose architecture must be admired. Both of these works are worthy of study of a very careful kind" (64). Dresser's study of these two pieces found fault in the excessive carving on Pugin's sideboard, while the "much more serious objections" identified and enumerated regarding Burges' painted cabinet[20] related to its roof: "It is very absurd ... to treat the roof of a cabinet, which is to stand in a room, as if it were an entire house, or an object which were to stand in a garden" (65). Interestingly, William Burges had also written on "Furniture" in his published Cantor Lectures *Art Applied to Industry* (1865). Here, Burges defended notable pieces of painted furniture exhibited at the International Exhibition of 1862:

> The works of Marshall, Morris, and Co., in the late Exhibition, were excellent examples of this way of treatment, but then the Firm are all artists, so that we have a right to expect better things than we generally find ... I hope to see a very great deal of this furniture executed, for it speaks and gives us ideas—but then some people dislike nothing so much as ideas, and, upon the whole, would rather not think at all.
>
> (Burges 1865: 76–7)

But, back to Dresser.

Condemning examples of "the false in furniture" discovered while examining French wardrobes and cabinets at the International Exhibition of 1862 ("'Horrible! horrible!' was all I could exclaim"), Dresser also exposed "the series of frauds and shams" he had detected in falsely constructed Gothic furniture designed and manufactured by a large Yorkshire firm of cabinetmakers. Here he equated bad design with bad morals: "How any person could possibly produce such furniture, be he ever so degraded, I cannot think" (Dresser 1873: 66). The chapter continued with comments upon "upholstery as applied to works of furniture, the materials employed as coverings for seats, and the nature of picture-frames and curtain-poles"; he also found space to "notice general errors in furniture, strictly so called" (65).

Much of this discussion referred once more to Eastlake's earlier book. Here, Dresser again copied an illustration, but this time also quoted at length from the text of *Hints*, reproducing two pages of Eastlake's objections to the telescopic dining table "generally made of planks of polished oak or mahogany laid upon an insecure framework of the same material, and supported by four gouty legs, ornamented by the turner with mouldings which look like inverted cups and saucers piled upon an attic baluster" (Eastlake quoted in Dresser 1873: 66). Dresser was in accord; "especially in his remark that, owing to the very nature of its construction, a modern dining-table must be an inartistic object" (67). The chapter continued with four illustrations of mirrors, which Dresser included as "examples of utterly bad furniture" before he turned to the subject of veneering. Unsurprisingly, given his strictures on falsity in furniture, this was condemned as "a practice which should be wholly abandoned" (68). Following this were the promised recommendations for drapery and upholstery, which criticized the "gouty forms" of sofas "now made as though they were feather beds ... so soft that you sink into them, and become uncomfortably warm by merely resting upon them" (70) before he concluded rather abruptly with an illustration of a picture frame taken from the *Building News* of September 7, 1866, which he described as "fanciful but good" (72).

Dresser's *Principles*, the earlier drawing books of Smith, Brown, and Whitaker, and the price books issued by the Society of London Cabinet-Makers are texts that relate to the production of furniture: all were aimed explicitly at a readership of "working men." Yet Dresser's work also incorporated publications usually associated with the distribution and consumption of furniture including exhibition reports, trade catalogs, museum guide books, and advice manuals; texts to which I shall now turn "my careful curiosity."

NINETEENTH-CENTURY TEXTS: THE DISTRIBUTION OF FURNITURE

Walker's diagram suggests several different types of text that relate to the distribution of furniture; the third of the processes of design that moves manufactured goods from producers to consumers. These include publications that were issued for marketing purposes such as advertisements and catalogs, both those produced by the furniture trade for their customers and those produced on a larger scale for exhibitions.

The nineteenth century was famously an "Age of Exhibitions"; the second half of the period witnessed Great Exhibitions, *Expositions universelles*, and world's fairs in London (1851, 1862, and 1871), Paris (1855, 1867, 1878, 1889, and 1900), Vienna (1873), Philadelphia (1876), Melbourne (1880–1), Barcelona (1888), Chicago (1893), and Brussels (1897). These exhibitions, which are discussed elsewhere in this volume, have formed the subject of many studies that have explored themes of imperialism, internationalism versus nationalism, trade, manufacturing, and technological developments in this period.[21] British furniture—the product of all these influences—was exhibited at many international events where it was compared with the furniture manufactured by other nations; especially that exhibited by the French. Indeed, of the five prestigious "Council Medals" awarded at the Great Exhibition in Class 26 none were given to British firms: four went to French manufacturers and one to an Austrian exhibitor.

As was demonstrated at the outset of this chapter, illustrated descriptions can be found in the catalogs and guide books; but detailed information can also be found in the jurors' and artisans' reports and the countless journal and newspaper articles that reviewed the exhibitions. Sometimes these offer very different opinions about the same object. For instance, the virtuoso cabinet made by French firm Fourdinois, which was exhibited at the *Exposition Universelle* in Paris in 1867, was depicted and described in the *Art Journal Illustrated Catalogue of the Universal Exhibition* (Figure 9.4):

> It is impossible, either by pen or pencil, to do justice to the Cabinet of M. Fourdinois, the *chef-d'oeuvre* of the Exhibition, and certainly the best work of its class that has been produced, in modern times, by any manufacturer. But it is not a production of manufacture, not even of Art-manufacture; it is a collection of sculptured works, brought together and made to constitute parts of a cabinet—these "parts" all exquisitely sculptured; "carving" is not a word sufficient to express their delicacy and beauty. We engrave it; yet no engraving, however large, could convey an idea of the perfection of this perfect work.
>
> (1868: 141)

The cabinet was also described in Charles Alfred Hooper's report on "Cabinet Making" published in the *Reports of Artisans selected by a committee appointed by the Society of Arts to visit the Paris Universal Exhibition of 1867* as

> decidedly a perfect gem. The ground is dark wood, and the carving light, but there is this peculiarity in the work, the carving is not planted on, but inlaid, the wood being quite cut through, and, when all glued together, forms one solid mass. This piece of work I consider to be the perfection of cabinet work.
>
> (1867: 6)

And in James Mackie's report on "Woodcarving":

> The ebony cabinet, with carved and many-tinted pear-tree inlay, in the same style of art, is certainly a masterpiece. ... its details are so perfect, that, were it divided into a thousand pieces, each would be a model and a treasure. ... It must be pronounced a work of wonderful beauty.
>
> (1867: 85)

THE PARIS UNIVERSAL EXHIBITION.

It is impossible, either by pen or pencil, to do justice to the CABINET of M. FOURDINOIS, the *chef-d'œuvre* of the Exhibition, and certainly the best work of its class that has been produced, in modern times, by any manufacturer. But it is not a production of manufacture, not even of Art-manufacture; it is a collection of sculptured works, brought together and made to constitute parts of a cabinet—these "parts" all exquisitely sculptured; "carving" is not a word sufficient to express their delicacy and beauty. We engrave it; yet no engraving, however large, could convey an idea of the perfection of this perfect work. The *grand prix* has been allotted to M. Fourdinois, and, we believe, by universal consent of his compeers, for this, his latest and best production, is unrivalled.

derstand that the adaptation they have to accomplish is both direct and indirect; that it extends from principles to designs, and to the manner of working; and that it has to be adjusted to the employment of all modern facilities and appliances, as well as taught to harmonise with the existing state of things. It is enough for us to know that the revival of Art has entered in earnest upon this grand enterprise of adaptation. Time and experience, with repeated efforts, with many failures too, leading to ultimate successes, are required in order to put the second half of the nineteenth century in possession of such a revived Art as may be true both to itself and to the present time. Meanwhile, there is more than a little that is both interesting and valuable, which may be learned by all who love the cause of Art, by observing the progress of the revival as it is now passing under our eyes.

As might naturally have been expected, the first and earliest efforts towards adaptation in the revival of early Art are very generally found to have aimed at such modifications only of early examples, as might be accomplished either by bringing together certain characteristic features of a revived style from different eras

141 N N

FIGURE 9.4 Henri-Auguste Fourdinois (maker) Ebony cabinet, 1867. Image courtesy of University of Southampton Library/Internet Archive.

And *again* in R. Baker's slightly less enthusiastic *Report* on the same trade:

> It is rather over-done in the minuteness and delicacy of detail; the inlaid wood restricts the carver, and the colouring somewhat destroys the effect of the carving. (1867: 103)

Awarded the Grand Prix at the Exposition, Fourdinois' ebony cabinet was acquired by the newly founded South Kensington Museum for £2,750 (an RPI equivalent of £248,900.00 in 2021), but was later described in disparaging terms by Christopher Dresser:

> The South Kensington Museum purchased in the last Paris International Exhibition, at great cost, a cabinet from Fourdonois [*sic*]; but it is a very unsatisfactory specimen, as it is too delicate, too tender, and too fine for a work of utility—it is an example of what should be avoided rather than of what should be followed.
>
> (1873: 63)

Exhibitions generated many fascinating textual representations of furniture, even though "exhibition furniture" such as Fourdinois' ebony cabinet, Morant's Stork Table, and Jennens and Bettridge's "Day-Dreamer" chair give "a completely misleading picture of furniture in common use" (Aslin 1962: 36). Perhaps their extraordinary nature explains why these pieces have so often been examined. However, not all furniture on view and described in the catalogs was "exhibition furniture"; many objects displayed were subsequently successful and widely produced. Famously, Michael Thonet's Vienna bentwood chairs were awarded a bronze medal at the Great Exhibition and, following improvements in manufacturing techniques, a silver medal four years later at the Paris Exposition. Depicted in the *Art Journal Illustrated Catalogue of the International Exhibition* of 1862 (Figure 8.3) they were praised for:

> combining a remarkable degree of lightness with strength and being produced at a singularly small cost. By a peculiar process in manufacture, the wood can be bent to any shape. The designs are generally graceful and good, the great purpose of "use" being always kept in view.
>
> (1862: 291)

Examples of innovative furniture were also shown at events such as the themed exhibitions held annually in London including the International Health Exhibition (1884) and the International Inventions Exhibition (1885). The catalogs published for these events provide interesting descriptions and commentary, even though furniture was not the primary object of interest; indeed, items could only be exhibited if they fulfilled specific requirements:

> Only such exhibits as have a distinct bearing upon health can be admitted. Specimens, therefore, illustrating building construction generally, the decoration of houses, or their furniture, cannot be admitted unless they are shown to have actual reference to the health of the inmates of the houses.
>
> (*International Health Exhibition* 1884: xxxv–xxxvi)

Furniture took center-stage, however, at the exhibitions of the Arts and Crafts Exhibition Society (ACES) at the New Gallery (1888–90) and in the catalogs published for each event. As well as descriptions of the exhibits, the *Catalogue of the Third Exhibition* (1890) included a series of "Introductory Notes," which were later republished in *Arts and Crafts Essays* (1893). These all largely echoed the often-quoted polemic of William Morris, who had earlier argued for

> good citizen's furniture, solid and well made in workmanship, and in design should have nothing about it that is not easily defensible, no monstrosities or extravagances, not even of beauty, lest we weary of it.
>
> (Morris [1882] 1998: 261)

As well as exhibition catalogs written *about* manufacturers, trade catalogs written and published *by* furniture manufacturers and retailers *for* their potential customers are also suggested by Walker's diagram as textual representations associated with the distribution of furniture. Historians of nineteenth-century interior design, decoration, and furniture have also relied heavily on these types of publication, which communicate designs between producers, retailers, and consumers.[22] Similarly, scholars working within the growing field of research into the history of furniture retailing and consumption during the nineteenth century[23] have also relied upon trade catalogs and other printed texts including trade cards[24] and newspaper advertisements;[25] analyzing the role played by these types of printed ephemera in selling furniture.

Representing a commercial development from the furniture pattern book, trade catalogs indicate the divisions of labor within furniture production and distribution, and also show differences in intended readership; advertising actual furniture for potential consumers. William Smee & Sons' *Designs of Furniture* "A Stock of which is Always Kept Ready for Sale at Their Cabinet and Upholstery Manufactory and Warerooms, No. 6, Finsbury Pavement, London" (*c.* 1850), is often cited as one of the earliest examples of a furniture catalog: it comprised 375 pages of numbered illustrations with a brief description for each item. A small sixteen-page trade catalog was issued by Jennens and Bettridge, "specially appointed Papier Mache Manufacturers to their Majesties George IV., William IV., Queen Victoria, and H.R.H. the Prince Albert," immediately after their success at the Great Exhibition, where they received one of the seventy "Prize Medals" awarded for "excellence in production or workmanship" in Class 26. This catalog provided information about the history and production of papier-mâché objects and the innovations patented by Jennens and Bettridge. It also gave a list of prices and featured illustrated descriptions of their papier-mâché products, including the "Day-Dreamer Chair," which had been "Exhibited at the Crystal Palace." Heal's also began issuing their *Illustrated Catalogue of Bedsteads and Priced Bedding* in this decade, however, the majority of the surviving British furniture trade catalogs in the National Art Library in London date from the 1870s onward (Bunston 1971). Published in the era of "Art Furniture," these include catalogs issued by Collinson and Lock's *Sketches of Artistic Furniture* (1871), which featured designs by the architect-designer Thomas Collcutt (1840–1924); James Shoolbred & Company's *Practical Methods of House Furnishing* (1874); and William Watt's *Art Furniture from Designs by E.W. Godwin and Others: With Hints and Suggestions on Domestic Furniture and Decoration* (1877) (Figure 9.5).

Often these catalogs contain remarkably little text, concentrating instead on the all-important illustrations provided by professional designers; several catalogs advertise a direct relationship between designers and manufacturers. Pat Kirkham noted that by the 1860s "designers were regularly employed by West End firms" (1988: 96), while by the 1870s "the professional designer was not only accepted but considered a necessary figure by the leading firms" (105). As well as Collcutt and Godwin, there are other well-known relationships: designs by Bruce Talbert, who had published his second book, *Examples of Ancient and Modern Furniture, Metal Work, Tapestries, Decoration etc.* in 1876, were manufactured by Holland & Son, Gillows, Cox & Son, Jackson and Graham, Marsh, Jones & Cribb, and the Coalbrookdale Iron Company; while Talbert's pupil H.W. Batley (1846–1932), who also published *A Series of Designs for Domestic Furniture* (1883), is known to have designed for Gillows,

FIGURE 9.5 *Art Furniture from Designs by E.W. Godwin FSA*. Photograph courtesy of Smithsonian Libraries/Internet Archive.

James Shoolbred & Company, Collison and Lock, and Smee & Sons (Weber Soros 1999).

Other examples of trade catalog are fortunately more verbose. In particular, Oetzmann and Co.'s lengthy *Hints on House Furnishing and Decoration* (*c.* 1871) was full of useful advice, and in a later version (*c.* 1896) "combined journalism with salesmanship" when it reprinted some illustrated articles first published in *The Lady* that advised a young married couple on furnishing their new home (Edwards 2005: 138). The titles of these trade catalogs, with their *Hints* and *Suggestions*, certainly refer to the genre of domestic advice literature, which became particularly popular from the 1860s following the publication of that quintessential advice manual *Mrs Beeton's Book of Household Management* (1861). Interestingly, several authors of advice literature recommended particular manufacturers and retailers whose trade advertisements were often inserted at the back of the volumes. Robert Edis's published Cantor Lectures on *Decoration and Furniture of Townhouses* (1881), which included "Lecture III: Furniture" recommended specific pieces by several well-known manufacturers:

> I was indebted to Messrs. Jackson and Graham and Messrs. Gillow for the loan of some exceedingly good examples of modern, so-called Chippendale, Adams and Sheraton work, which form the subjects of some of my illustrations.
> (1881: 103)

Similarly, in *Ornamental Interiors: Ancient and Modern* (1887), John Moyr Smith acknowledged his indebtedness "to several publishers, art manufacturers, and importers of artistic objects, whose names are attached to their respective contributions" (1887: iii).

Many studies that have examined Victorian domestic ideology and the gendered construction of "the home" have drawn upon domestic advice books and magazines aimed primarily at female readers.[26] Nineteenth-century women's magazines such as *The Englishwoman's Domestic Journal* (1852–79); *The Queen* (f. 1861); *Myra's Journal* (1875–1912); *Sylvia's Home Journal* (1878–91) and *Woman* (1890–1912) often contained information about the domestic interior and descriptions of its furniture. For example, in an article titled "Influence of Aesthetics on English Society" published in *Sylvia's Home Journal*, the author commented with some irony:

> The aesthetic maxim that all our surroundings are an expression of ourselves, that our furniture betrays us to our friends, is startling enough to good folk who have lived their lives innocently among their chairs and tables without attributing to them any uncanny powers of proclaiming abroad the secrets of their hearts.
> (AC 1879: 420)

Moreover, many articles first published in journals were often later collected and reissued as separate volumes of domestic advice. Elsewhere I have discussed the complicated intertextual relationships between some of the volumes in Macmillan's "Art at Home Series" (1876–83) and Clarence M. Cook's *House Beautiful* (1877), which was based upon his original series of articles "Beds, Tables, Stools and Candlesticks" for *Scribner's Monthly*. My research also demonstrates the problematic nature of visual and textual representations of furniture within this sort of text; notably in Mrs. Orrinsmith's *The Drawing Room* (1878). Commissioned to write new text for British readers around the original images taken from Cook's American articles, Mrs. Orrinsmith resolved any difficulties by simply reorganizing, renaming, and inventing new descriptions for the plates. For example, an illustration that appeared in *The House Beautiful* as "A French Settee" reappeared in *The Drawing Room* as "A 'Sheraton' Sofa," while Cook's description of an "Italian Fire-screen" became "lovely pieces of Japanese embroidery ... worked in glowing silks, representing peacocks' feathers" (Orrinsmith 1878: 78) (Figure 9.6). It is arguable whether this says more about the knowledge of the author, the quality of the image, or the fluidity of its meaning.[27] Nonetheless, this example shows the pitfalls of treating advice literature as straightforward textual (and visual) evidence about how homes were furnished in the nineteenth century.

Recent debates have further problematized the use of advice books as factual documentary sources. Occupying a position somewhere "between fact and fiction" (Lees-Maffei 2003: 1), domestic design advice is a complex source, one often more concerned with the formation of class and gender ideologies than furniture and interior decoration. Indeed, "these non-literary materials did not simply reflect a 'real' historical subject, but helped to produce it through their discursive practices" (Langland 1995: 24). Few scholars, however, have made clear the distinction between advice and evidence or between prescription and practice. Some have commented on this difficulty and others, while acknowledging this dilemma, have nonetheless emphasized the popularity of the genre, suggesting that "it is hard to over-estimate the role of the household book in promoting the ideal pattern of middle-class life" (Attar 1987: 13). A special issue of the *Journal of Design History* (2003) edited by Grace Lees-Maffei, examined domestic design advice and considered the role this type of literature played in the formation of the domestic interior. My own contribution to this special issue offered a comparative analysis of Rhoda and Agnes Garretts's *Suggestions for House Decoration* (1876) and Eastlake's *Hints.* Arguing that domestic advice manuals are not conventional historical evidence, I suggested that they should be understood both as texts that engage with contemporary notions of design and taste, *and* as a genre of Victorian literature; an argument that returns us rather neatly to textual representations of furniture in the nineteenth century.

78 *THE DRAWING-ROOM.* [CHAP.

decorated with a slight relief of the same colour. Lovely pieces of Japanese embroidery are shown below worked in glowing silks, representing peacocks' feathers, most beautiful and useful as a folding screen. Old Venetian leather, richly patterned velvets,

A PEACOCK SCREEN.

or eastern materials, may be considered suitable for screens; but we strongly recommend less expensive materials enriched by personal energy and endeavour —energy, to begin untried work, which afar off seems impossible to untried hands; endeavour, which conduces to the aptitude and dexterity inferred in the oft-used words " artistic taste."

True intention makes sincerity of work. Our greatest living writer says, "All true work is sacred: in all

FIGURE 9.6 An "Italian Screen" reproduced in Clarence Cook's first article for *Scribner's Illustrated* (1876) and later re-titled a "Peacock Screen" by Mrs Orrinsmith in *The Drawing Room* (1878). Photograph courtesy of Robarts – University of Toronto/Internet Archive.

It is tempting to reexamine Charles Eastlake's *Hints*, which was hugely influential both in Great Britain and in America, where it inspired the production of a style of furniture. Eastlake was most indignant and in the Preface to the fourth edition of *Hints* made his feelings on the matter plain:

> I find that American tradesmen continually advertising what they are pleased to call "Eastlake" furniture with the production of which I have nothing whatsoever to do and for the taste of which I should be very sorry to be considered responsible.
>
> (1878: viii)

However, Mr. Eastlake has received quite enough attention already, so instead I shall find another characteristic specimen from this genre to put into my little bucket.

Occasionally classified as a furniture pattern book, the *Encyclopaedia of Cottage, Farm, and Villa Architecture and Furniture*, written by John Claudius Loudon (1783–1843), was first published in 1833 and reissued in eleven editions until 1867. Hugely influential in Great Britain, it was also popular in America and Australia; Loudon commented that the main aim of his book was "to improve the dwellings of the great mass of society, in the temperate regions of both hemispheres" (Loudon 1833: 1). Dealing as it does "with all, literally all, thinkable aspects of the house" (Muthesius 2009: 41), Loudon's *Encyclopedia* has been used by several historians as a source of information about the nineteenth-century home.[28] Figure 9.7 illustrates a page from the *Encyclopedia* which offered advice on suitable furnishings for a cottage. It showed:

> a kind of bench with solid back and arms, for a cottage kitchen, commonly called a settle, and frequently to be met with in public houses. The back forms an excellent screen or protection from the current of air which is continually passing from the door to the chimney. ... Placed in the open floor, where it would seldom require to be moved, there might even be book shelves fixed to this back, and a flap might be hung to it, with a jib bracket, to serve as a reading or writing table, or for other purposes.
>
> (Loudon 1833: 317)

Providing designs and advice for "Furniture for Cottage Dwellings" as well as villas and country houses, Loudon's text offered a broader perspective than other similar sources. As the *Pictorial Dictionary* explained:

> Its title indicates, the *Encyclopedia*, with over 1,100 pages and 2,000 engravings is a mine of information on the homes and furnishings of all classes, in contrast to earlier pattern and similar books which had the upper

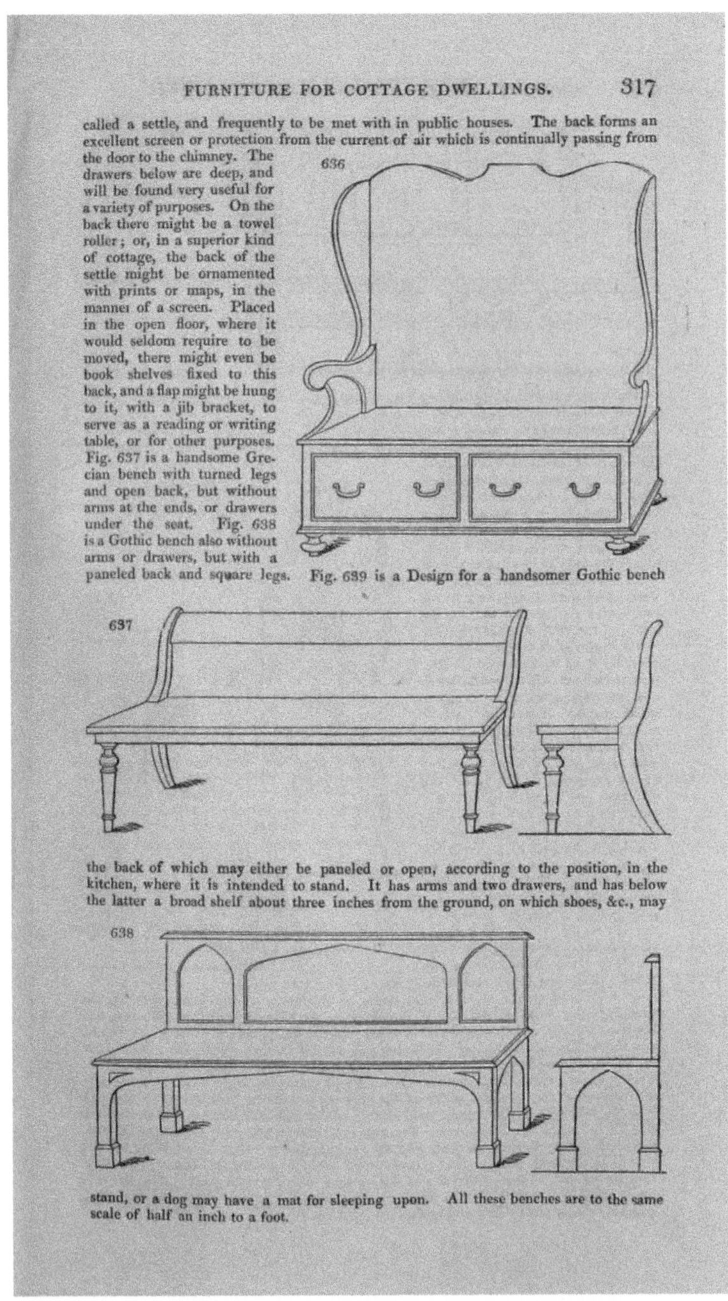

FURNITURE FOR COTTAGE DWELLINGS. 317

called a settle, and frequently to be met with in public houses. The back forms an excellent screen or protection from the current of air which is continually passing from the door to the chimney. The drawers below are deep, and will be found very useful for a variety of purposes. On the back there might be a towel roller; or, in a superior kind of cottage, the back of the settle might be ornamented with prints or maps, in the mannei of a screen. Placed in the open floor, where it would seldom require to be moved, there might even be book shelves fixed to this back, and a flap might be hung to it, with a jib bracket, to serve as a reading or writing table, or for other purposes. Fig. 637 is a handsome Grecian bench with turned legs and open back, but without arms at the ends, or drawers under the seat. Fig. 638 is a Gothic bench also without arms or drawers, but with a paneled back and square legs. Fig. 639 is a Design for a handsomer Gothic bench

636

637

the back of which may either be paneled or open, according to the position, in the kitchen, where it is intended to stand. It has arms and two drawers, and has below the latter a broad shelf about three inches from the ground, on which shoes, &c., may

638

stand, or a dog may have a mat for sleeping upon. All these benches are to the same scale of half an inch to a foot.

FIGURE 9.7 John Claudius Loudon, *An Encyclopaedia of Cottage, Farm, and Villa Architecture and Furniture* (1833), p. 317. Photograph courtesy of the Getty Research Institute/Internet Archive.

> and middle classes mainly in mind. ... It differs from most previous books of the kind in devoting attention to cheap, utilitarian furniture. Nothing else in print of the time gives us such a detailed account of the early Victorian household.
>
> (Joy 1977: xxi)

This assertion is arguable; the *Encyclopedia* is advice, *not* evidence. Its detailed descriptions represent textual ideals rather than factual realities. It does, however, devote a great many of its pages to *ideal* furniture, which could be compared with contemporary sources about the consumption of *actual* furniture; and as my little bucket is almost full, it is toward these texts that I shall now row.

NINETEENTH-CENTURY TEXTS: THE CONSUMPTION OF FURNITURE

If advice is not evidence, then examining the consumption of furniture in the nineteenth century starts to become extremely problematic. How are we to know which items of furniture people actually bought from the wide ranges advertised by retailers in their catalogs, and once acquired, how were these pieces used, customized, and eventually disposed of during the nineteenth century?

One solution has, of course, been to examine the texts written *by* consumers themselves. For instance, Amanda Girling-Budd (2004) combined invoices, account books, and designs from the estimate sketchbooks in the Gillows Archive with diary entries and letters from their clients, the Clarkes of Summerhill in Lancashire. Similarly, Trevor Keeble (2007) made extensive use of the diaries written by the sisters Emily (1819–1901) and Ellen Hall (1822–1902); while Jane Hamlett (2010) consulted diaries, letters, notebooks, inventories, wills and informal bequests, and even lists of wedding presents. These studies draw upon private unpublished sources held in local record offices, but there are several examples of nineteenth-century diaries and collections of correspondence that have been published posthumously and used as historical evidence (see Steinitz 2011). These include the diaries of Mary Ann (Marion) Sambourne (1851–1914), wife of illustrator and *Punch* cartoonist Linley Sambourne (1844–1910), whose house at 18 Stafford Terrace survives as a rare example of an Aesthetic interior.[29]

Another approach is to use surviving images and descriptions of real interiors. Peter Thornton's *Authentic Décor: The Domestic Interior, 1620–1920* (1984) is a visual survey that incorporates illustrations of domestic interiors including paintings of interiors and photographic collections. Along similar lines, Charlotte Gere's *Nineteenth Century Decoration: The Art of the Interior* (1989) is a collection of exclusively nineteenth-century imagery. Unlike Frances Borzello's study *At Home: The Domestic Interior in Art* (2006), neither Thornton nor Gere offered interpretations of the interiors depicted; instead the images (which include some taken from advice manuals) are used as straightforward historical evidence. Indeed, Thornton stated that "these illustrations show rooms as they actually were" (1984: 8). This is, of course, debatable; nonetheless, both studies remain invaluable secondary sources. Many of the images discussed by Thornton and Gere depict the interiors and furnishings of Victorian country houses. There are several studies on this popular Anglo-centric theme that have been published by architectural and social historians, particularly since *The Destruction of the English Country House 1875–1975* exhibition held at the Victoria and Albert Museum in 1974.[30] This "epoch-making" exhibition aroused "public anger at such wanton destruction" and, significantly, also "focussed attention upon the history and the surviving documentation of both destroyed and surviving houses" (Wainwright 1989: 2). The examples of "surviving documentation" included a wide range of textual representations of furniture and interior schemes including unpublished archival sources: inventories; records of sales; insurance policies; diaries; private correspondence; and architectural drawings from the RIBA Archive. Contemporary publications have also been examined including auction catalogs; memoirs and biographies; early nineteenth-century antiquarian studies; topological surveys; articles in architectural journals notably *The Builder, Building News*, and *The British Architect*, as well as periodicals such as *The Gentleman's Magazine* (1731–1922) and *Country Life* (f. 1897). This interest in the Victorian country house—even when it ventures below stairs—illustrates the partial nature of nineteenth-century furniture histories, which of necessity tend to focus upon "opulent" interiors and objects commissioned or collected by the upper classes (Cooper 1979; Wainwright 1989). Indeed, another of the categories of text relating to the consumption of furniture suggested by Walker's diagram is that associated with "museums and private collections." These include the texts written *by* private collectors about their collections such as inventories, catalogs, and guide books and similar publications issued during the nineteenth century by national and regional collections, such as the South Kensington Museum, which represent public consumption.

One of the most significant early nineteenth-century guide books was Thomas Hope's *Household Furniture and Interior Decoration* (1807) (Figure 6.1); a publication usually credited with the introduction of the phrase "interior decoration" into the English language. Thomas Hope (1769–1831) was a designer and collector, whose book described and illustrated his home at Duchess Street and defined Regency style:

> PLATE XI. No. 1 and 2. Front and end of a large library or writing table, flanked with paper presses, or escrutoirs. The tops that terminate these presses present the shape of ancient Greek house roofs. Their extremities

or pediments contain the heads of the patron and patroness of science, of Apollo and of Minerva.

(Hope 1807: 28)

Hope has been the subject of extensive research and exhibitions (Watkin 1968, 2008) as have other notable collectors. For instance, in *The Romantic Interior: The British Collector at Home 1750–1850* (1989), Clive Wainwright examined the development of the modern antiques trade in Britain and offered case studies of significant collections of furnishings amassed in the homes of five well-known collectors.[31] Other textual representations of real furniture can be found in the contemporary magazine features that describe visits to the homes of the rich and famous. An excellent example is Mrs. Mary Eliza Haweis's book *Beautiful Houses* (1882); which like Charles Eastlake's *Hints* was first published in *The Queen* (1880–1). Providing descriptions of "certain well-known artistic houses," Mrs. Haweis described the furniture and interiors found in the homes of artists and architects including Frederick Leighton, Lawrence Alma-Tadema, J.J. Stevenson, Alfred Morrison, and the late William Burges; a theme almost as popular as the Victorian country house. Other similar texts include Moncure Conway's *Travels in South Kensington* (1882) and John Moyr Smith's *Ornamental Interiors* (1887) in which he thanked "the various architects, decorative artists, firms of art decorators, and makers of artistic furniture, who by their courtesy have enabled him to inspect and describe many specimens of artistic work not usually made free to the public" (Moyr Smith 1887: iii–iv).

Some design historians have turned their attention to the furniture found in the provincial and colonial homes of the "middling sort," using family papers, account books, sales catalogs, wills, probate inventories, and house contents lists as textual sources (Nenadic 1994; Keeble 2007; Ponsonby 2007; Hamlett 2010; Hoskins 2013). Further down the social ladder, however, it becomes much harder to establish what type of furniture was found in the homes of the poor. Snippets of factual evidence about the production, retail, and ownership of working-class furniture can be found in important publications that considered the plight of the poor. For instance, Henry Mayhew's articles for the *Morning Chronicle* offer information about the furniture trade while *London Labour and the London Poor* includes a chapter on "Garret-Masters" (1861: 221–31) as does Charles Booth's *Life and Labour of the People in London* (1889). Both texts describe the living conditions of the poor in London. Similarly, Adolphe Smith and John Thomson's photographic articles recording *Street Life in London* (1877) included "Old Furniture," which depicted a secondhand furniture dealer at the corner of Church Lane, Holborn:

whose business was a cross between that of a shop and a street stall. The dealer was never satisfied unless the weather allowed him to disgorge nearly

> the whole of his stock into the middle of the street, a method which alone secured the approval and custom of his neighbours.
>
> (Smith and Thomson 1877: 128)

These texts and official reports, such as the *Royal Commission on the Housing of the Working Classes* (1885), contain references to the furniture owned by the Victorian working classes, which have provided some evidence for historians:

> It could scarcely be called furniture; there was a bed and a big box by the side of the bed, upon which one would lie at night, possibly. The covering of the bed was of a very poor description.
>
> (*Royal Commission* 1885: 258)

There have been interesting studies about the formation of working-class domestic spaces, both rural and urban,[32] but as the authors of *Victorian Interior Style* (1995) have noted, in the nineteenth century:

> Few writers wrote for working-class readers or bothered to describe working-class homes. Few artists or photographers chose to record them. Surviving interiors, even individual items of furniture are rare; in poorer homes most things were used until they were worn out.
>
> (Banham, MacDonald, and Porter 1995: 10)

Descriptions of the homes and furniture owned by all classes of society do, however, appear in the novel, one of the most significant forms of text published in the nineteenth century. Philippa Tristram has commented that "Because the novel is invincibly domestic, it can tell us much about the space we live in; equally, designs for houses and their furnishings can reveal hidden aspects of the novelist's art" (1989: 2). Nineteenth-century fiction is examined in great detail in Tristram's *Living Space in Fact and Fiction* (1989) and in Charlotte Grant's article for *Home Cultures* (2005) and chapter for *Imagined Interiors* (2006) in which she argued "that the novel, as it developed between 1720 and 1920, is a key form of representing and imagining the domestic interior" (2006: 134).

To offer an analysis of the metaphorical meanings of fictional furniture in the nineteenth-century British novel is well beyond the scope of this chapter, but there are several important examples that deserve to be mentioned. Again the problem is the wealth of materials from which to select a "characteristic specimen." Should I examine the furniture in Fanny Price's little east room at *Mansfield Park* (1814), which, significantly, includes a writing desk or the eponymous Emma's rather grander "large modern circular table" that had recently replaced a small-sized Pembroke at Hartfield (Austen [1815] 2008: 325)? Perhaps Mrs. Barton's Pembroke table (Gaskell [1848] 2008: 15) or Mrs Jamieson's "white and gold" chairs at *Cranford* (Gaskell [1851] 1998: 75) should be considered. In *Jane Eyre* (1847), Charlotte Brontë described a whole bedroom suite in the famously womb-like red room that offers a wealth of fictional furniture suitable for Freudian and Feminist analyses:

> A bed supported on massive pillars of mahogany, hung with curtains of deep red damask, stood out like a tabernacle in the centre; the two large windows, with their blinds always drawn down, were half shrouded in festoons and falls of similar drapery; the carpet was red; the table at the foot of the bed was covered with a crimson cloth; the walls were a soft fawn colour with a blush of pink in it; the wardrobe, the toilet-table, the chairs were of darkly polished old mahogany. Out of these deep surrounding shades rose high and glared white, the piled-up mattresses and pillows of the bed, spread with a snowy Marseilles counterpane. Scarcely less prominent was an ample cushioned easy-chair near the head of the bed, also white, with a footstool before it; and looking, as I thought, like a pale throne.
>
> (Brontë [1847] 2006: 8–9)

The novels of Dickens, "a key figure in the nineteenth century's construction of an idealized image of home" are of course filled with furniture and symbolic interiors (Grant 2006: 149–50). A signifier of new money and no taste, the absence of patination on Mr. and Mrs. Veneering's "bran' new" dining table is discussed elsewhere in this volume, but the furniture in Miss Havisham's dressing room described in *Great Expectations* (1865) is just as well known; as is the description of furniture owned by "Our Next Door Neighbour" in *Sketches by Boz* (1839):

> The paper was new, and the paint was new, and the furniture was new; and all three, paper, paint, and furniture, bespoke the limited means of the tenant. There was a little red and black carpet in the drawing-room, with a border of flooring all the way round; a few stained chairs and a pembroke table. A pink shell was displayed on each of the little sideboards, which, with the addition of a tea-tray and caddy, a few more shells on the mantelpiece, and three peacock's feathers tastefully arranged above them, completed the decorative furniture of the apartment.
>
> (Dickens [1839] 1995: 61)

I confess that my personal favorites involve the misadventures of Mr. Pooter's attempts at home improvements recorded faithfully in *The Diary of A Nobody* (1892). Having bought a pot of Pinkford's enamel paint, he determined to try it:

> Went upstairs to the servant's bedroom and painted her washstand, towel-horse, and chest of drawers. To my mind it was an extraordinary improvement, but as an example of the ignorance of the lower classes in matters of taste,

> our servant, Sarah, on seeing them, evinced no sign of pleasure, but merely said "She thought they looked very well as they was before".
>
> (Grossmith [1892] 1995: 42)

While descriptions such as these are of course significant textual representations of furniture that tell us a great deal about the characters depicted, the novel remains an incredibly problematic source for the historian; if indeed it is a source at all. Remember, "Dear Reader," that fictional furniture is not factual evidence.

CONCLUSION

Rowing back with my little bucket now full, I too have attempted "to present some Victorian visions to the [post]modern eye" (Strachey [1918] 2009: 5). The verbal-textual-intertextual representations of nineteenth-century furniture that have been examined with "careful curiosity" in this chapter have been selected to demonstrate the wealth of primary textual materials available for further research. Ranging from price books to advice manuals to novels, and organized using Walker's model of "Production-Consumption," it has also aimed to indicate the wide range of secondary studies of nineteenth-century furniture *and* the different historical disciplines from which they have emanated: furniture history, labor histories, the history of interior design and decoration, architectural history, socioeconomic history, feminist and gender studies, the histories of retail and consumption, and literary history. This is a far cry from the middle of the twentieth century, when Peter Floud drew attention to "the complete absence of any secondary sources" then available for research (Floud in *Victorian and Edwardian Decorative Arts* 1952: 6). Having navigated this "great ocean of material," my selection has focused upon published British sources, but these characteristic specimens have, I hope, succeeded in shooting "a sudden revealing searchlight into obscure recesses, hitherto undivined" (Strachey [1918] 2009: 5).

NOTES

Introduction

1 The influx of immigrants was not entirely positive as there was much backlash to new arrivals, who were often considered lesser than those who had arrived before them and, therefore, not only vilified but also paid less in wages in a lesser job.

2 The economic power of women has been the subject of much conflicting study. See: Sharpe (1995).

Chapter 2

1 Phyfe's furniture, nonetheless, enjoyed a revival in the 1920s when imitations of it were made. F. Scott Fitzgerald even notes in his novel *Tender is the Night* that "She wept ... in a Duncan Phyfe dining-room" (2003: 77).

2 Hagen left behind the 1908 memoir "Personal Experiences of an Old New York Cabinet Maker," as well as the undated "Duncan Phyfe Memorandum," now held at the Winterthur Museum and Library in the Joseph Downs Manuscript Collection. The former contains important details about immigrant furniture makers in New York City in the mid-nineteenth century. The Duncan Phyfe text was reproduced in McClelland (1939: 315–17).

3 This phrase comes from the title of the 2006 exhibition *Hand, Heart and Soul: The Arts and Crafts Movement in Scotland*, the name of which was, in turn, inspired by the architect James A. Morris's lecture in Ayr, Scotland, of October 1904 titled "On the Application of Art to Industry" (Cumming 2006: ix).

4 The example shown here is a nearly identical copy of one by the same maker shown at the 1867 *Exposition Universelle* in Paris.

5 Enrico Colle, "Alla ricerca di uno stile nazionale: arte e industria nell'ebanisteria italiana della seconda metà dell'Ottocento" in De Grassi (2002: 8–31) lists a number of Italian sculptor/carver-cabinetmakers of the second half of the nineteenth century.

6 In Belgium, too, where the Renaissance revival was termed "le style néo-Renaissance flamande" (Flemish neo-Renaissance style), it specifically harked back to an ideal era during which the territory that eventually became Belgium had been a leading cultural and economic center of Europe (Leblanc 2004: 56).

7 Jones says this comes from an unreferenced document in the Barbedienne documentation file at the Musée d'Orsay.
8 A chair made of parrot coal is held by the Kirkaldy Galleries, Fife, Scotland. These pieces can still be valuable today. A table made by Williamson was offered for sale by Phillips Edinburgh in 1999 with an estimate of £15,000–£20,000.
9 Among the other curiosities Pevsner illustrates in his book are a life-saving portmanteau and steamship furniture convertible into a raft (1951b: 42–3).

Chapter 3

1 A model of this chair can be found in the Staatliche Museum, Berlin (Hayward 1965: ill. 27).
2 At that time, the daily salary of an employee in a luxury furniture workshop was approximately 8 francs. Competition organized in 1882 by the Union centrale des arts décoratifs in line with the Exhibition *Le mobilier moderne* (Bibliothèque des arts décoratifs. Archives de l'Union centrale des arts décoratifs, UCAD D1/15).
3 The name "Biedermeier" appeared in the last quarter of the nineteenth century, in reference to a caricature "Papa Biedermeier," a bourgeois figure created by Ludwig Eichrodt (1827–92). The term was at first used to describe paintings before being associated with a type of furniture of restrained geometric appearance, inherited from the Empire style but made with light, native woods.
4 From the French terminology: "confident."
5 Burne-Jones (1904: 59).
6 Jacques-Louis David, *Portrait of Madame Récamier,* 1800, oil on canvas, Musée du Louvre (inv. 3708).
7 An example of this can be found in the Château de Fontainebleau museum (inv. F.553c).
8 For example, a "fauteuil" made of two sofas and two armchairs was exhibited at the Paris 1867 *Exposition Universelle* by Filmer and Son of London, see illustration E59, Meyer (2006: 194).
9 E. Bernard, *Louise Abbema dans l'appartement de Sarah Bernhardt*, photograph, Paris, Musée Carnavalet (inv. Ph 8685).
10 See an example at Charlecote Park in the Library (National Trust, NT 532989).
11 For example, St. Louis Art Museum, (inv. 147:1965). Exhibited at *Inventing the Modern World: Decorative Arts at the World's Fairs, 1851–1939,* Saint Louis Art Museum, April 14, 2012–January 19, 2013.
12 See *Zeitschrift des Vereins zur Ausbildung der Gewerke*, vol. 5 (Munich, 1855), 1–74. The Bavarian State Library.
13 At the London Great Exhibition of the Works of Industry of All Nations in 1851, the juries report: "In the Austrian Collection are some curious chairs and furniture by M. Thonet, of Vienna, in which the wood, inlaid with metal lines, is bent to the required forms without the usual framing." See *Exposition Universelle* (1856: 546).
14 Watercolor by Reinhold Völkel (1873–1938), Historisches Museum, Vienna.
15 Marquetry tables of this type are traditionally attributed to Baldock but there also seems to be a strong connection with the Blake family of inlayers. The Blake firm specialized in this type of marquetry, sometimes combined with mother-of-pearl or ivory. Blake are thought to be the makers of a circular table at Alnwick Castle, acquired by the Duke of Northumberland. Robert Blake was active in the 1820s. By the 1840s the firm were trading as Blake, Geo. & Brothers, inlayers, etc. in

Tottenham Court Road and Mount Street, Mayfair. They were later renamed George Blake & Co. See Geoffrey de Bellaigue, "Edward Holmes Baldock", Part I and II, *The Connoisseur* (1975), 762–3; Martin Levy, "E. H. Baldock and the Blake Family: Further Evidence," *Furniture History Society Newsletter* 158 (2005).

16 Another is now at the Victoria and Albert Museum, previously in the collection of the Earl of Stair (inv. W.36:7–1978), and one at Charlecote Park, acquired in 1837 by George Lucy, still displayed in the Library (National Trust, 532987).

17 Watercolor by Matilda Sharpe, *c.* 1850, Geffrye Museum, London.

18 Salon table designed by Ferdinand List, see Ottillinger et al. (1994: fig. 4).

19 For example, a circular glass top colored blue, raised on a tripod with eagles' heads and feet, made *c.* 1805–7, Pavlosk Palace Museum.

20 Victoria and Albert Museum, London (LOAN: GILBERT.79:1-2008), The Rosalinde and Arthur Gilbert Collection. The scagliola top is signed by Filippo della Valle.

21 Scagliola is made by mixing fine plaster of powdered selenite (gypsum) with alum, glue, water, and pigment to create an effect that imitates marble or *pietra dura*. It was either applied like paint to a wet gesso ground, fixed under heat and polished, or formed into colored pieces and inlaid like a mosaic. The technique was known in ancient Rome and revived in sixteenth-century Italy, later spreading to other places in Europe. Although it is cheaper than marble or other stone surfaces, scagliola is susceptible to damage and has survived in only a few examples (see *Getty Art & Architecture Thesaurus* online at: http://www.getty.edu/research/tools/vocabularies/aat/).

22 The vitrine was made by Pierre Ribaillier aîné (1809–68) and his son-in-law the sculptor Paul Mazaroz (1823–1900), purchased for "28 000 francs" and placed by the emperor in his "cabinet de travail" at the Château de Saint-Cloud (Chevallier et al. 2013).

23 *Furniture Catalogue, Charlesarks & Son, cabinet makers, Arundel, c.* 1880. Geffrye Museum Library.

24 E.H. Baldock bill dated June 17, 1837. See Wainwright (1989).

25 William Allen and Joseph Allen (active 1847–1902) became Philadelphia's greatest furniture making business (Smith 1876).

26 For example, see *Furniture Catalogue, Charlessparks & Son, cabinet makers, Arundel, c.* 1880. Geffrye Museum Library.

27 For example, there are images of Lieutenant L. Walker Munro's Drawing room at Lady Cross Lodge, Brockenhurst, Hampshire; and of Major Joicey's Drawing room at 59 Cadogan Square, London.

28 In grand houses the bedroom gradually became more of a private space in the middle of the eighteenth century. At Petworth House (England) in the mid-1770s, for instance, the 3rd Earl of Egremont (1751–1837) transformed the ground-floor State Bedroom into a library.

29 For example, see National Portrait Gallery, *George Scharf's bedroom, 29 Great George Street, London, c.* 1868–9. Artist and Director of the National Gallery, his own drawings of his home are illustrated in Lasdun (1981: 102).

30 See *Maple & Co Furniture Illustrated catalogue, 1 to 16 Tottenham Place, London,* 1882. Geffrye Museum Library.

31 See *Furniture Catalogue, Charlessparks & Son cabinet makers, Arundel, c.* 1880. Geffrye Museum Library.

32 Louis Held, *Henry van de Velde, Bedroom for Editha von Münchhausen*, 1904. Weimar Art Collection.

Chapter 4

1 It is not simply an appreciation of nice possessions that distinguishes Aunt Chloe and Uncle Tom, but the specialization of spaces and functions within their home. On this development among the American middle class and its relationship to genteel culture, see Bushman (1992) and Grier (1988). When Tom reached Legree's plantation, his "heart sunk when he saw [the quarters]. He had been comforting himself with the thought of a cottage, rude, indeed, but one which he might make neat and quiet, and where he might have a shelf for his Bible, and a place to be alone out of his laboring hours" (Stowe [1852] 1962: 394). On domesticity in *Uncle Tom's Cabin*, see Kelley (1984), Brown (1984), and Tompkins (1986). On the domestic amenities routinely and cruelly denied to slaves, see Northup (1853). Also, see Breeden (1980).

2 The authors are listed in chronological order of their births to convey the longevity of home furnishings as a key component of character development in nineteenth-century literature. See also Logan (2001).

3 John Morley notes, "The idea that Biedermeier furniture is 'bourgeois' is true only in that the bourgeoisie, a class greatly enlarged in the nineteenth century, bought a lot of it" (1999: 264).

4 On this shared culture, consult Ryan (1981) on the United States, Smith (1981) on France, Davidoff and Hall (1987) on England, Reagin (2007) on Germany.

5 Specialized objects and home furnishings "played important roles in a style of life that was highly self-conscious and tightly scripted. They were critical components of an elaborate artifactual system that was central to Victorians' understanding of themselves and their place in the world" (Ames 1992: 8). On the etiquette of mastery and self-regulation in Victorian culture, see Kasson (1990). In the 1870s in Germany, where bourgeois womanhood was linked to impeccable standards of cleanliness, advice literature taught women "how to clean and maintain a plethora of household items, Turkish carpets and mahogany furniture, which were now more widely owned than in previous generations" (Reagin 2007: 26–7). On the earlier simplicity of German furnishings, see Brace (1853).

6 For thoughtful analyses that place etiquette books in the context of nineteenth-century urban life, see Halttunen (1982a) and Kasson (1990). See Leavitt (2002) on the changing nature of prescriptive literature regarding the home. On economy in the English middle-class home, see Boardman (2000). On the significance of frugality and labor in German women's domesticity, see Reagin (2007).

7 Confirming Leslie's opinion regarding the unsuitability of rocking chairs, Webster included rocking chairs under "Invalid Furniture" and "Furniture of the Nursery" (Webster and Parkes 1844: 282, 288). On the meaning of the parlor and its material culture in the United States and England, see Grier (1988) and Logan (2001).

8 Beecher's *A Treatise on Domestic Economy* was first published in 1841 and was reprinted nearly every year from 1841 to 1856.

9 On the relationship between honesty and home design in this period, see Downing (1850).

10 On the significance of domestic settings and values on the American frontier, see Kwolek-Folland (1984) and Radke (2004).

11 For more on the significance of furniture in settlement houses, see Cohen (1980). On the domesticity of English Settlement Houses, see Matthews-Jones (2009).

12 On public parlors, see Grier (1988) and Stevenson ([1991] 2001). "Public domesticity" describes "a hybrid sphere—a social and cultural realm shared by women and men, where deference, privilege, and comfort were determined through commercial rather than personal relationships" (Richter 2005: 12).

13 Zola made a similar point in *Pot Luck* ([1883] 2009: 129). Alphonse Duveyrier's mistress "made him buy her twenty-five thousand francs' worth of furniture," the same red satin-covered drawing room suite as his wife. No longer the marker of a moral home, the furniture is the price of Duveyrier's desire and a symbol of his hypocrisy.

14 The shift in focus was not limited to elite publications. For example, after 1870 *The Rural New Yorker* moved from "an emphasis on frugality to information on fashion trends." By the 1890s "articles still evidence a concern with economy, but now in the form of guidelines on current clothing and furniture styles rather than the virtues of home-made rugs" (Kwolek-Folland 1984: 31).

15 For another account of this decorating trend, see "The Cosey Corner" (1896: 182). The broad reach of these goods is suggested by an advertisement from *The Meriden Daily Republican* from January 13, 1890. A local retailer, Wm. H. Post & Company of Hartford, Connecticut was offering Bagdad curtains, portières and couch covers "at about one-half the usual price" citing "popular demand."

16 Descriptions of immigrant women's furnishings can be found in accounts of middle-class settlement house workers. For example, Esther Barrows recorded an account of the Dipskis, "who displayed a buffet among other new possessions, and on the top of it rested a large cut glass punch bowl. Mrs. Dipski said proudly, 'And so I become American,' as she waved her hand toward the huge piece of furniture, which took 'an inordinately large place in her small room.'" See Barrows (1929: 70). On the preferences of middle-class reformers, see Kittredge (1911). For an analysis of working-class women's furnishings in social and cultural context, see Cohen (1980).

17 This transformation has been characterized as a shift "from the parlor to the living room" (Halttunen 1982b). See also Grier (1992). On the transition from furniture as a badge of morality to the expression of personal identity at the end of the nineteenth century in England, see Cohen (2006), especially chapter 5, "Home as Stage: Personality and Possessions."

18 On the Arts and Crafts movement and a new language of the moral home, see Boris (1986). On utopian and feminist challenges to the nineteenth-century domestic ideal, there is no better source than Hayden (1981). See also Wright (1980) on reform and domestic architecture at the end of the nineteenth century.

Chapter 5

1 This room, in the records, corresponds in each palace to the *grand cabinet*. It is also frequently referred to as the Salon de l'Empereur.

2 1844–5, Versailles, Musée national du château.

3 The Order of the Reunion, established in 1811, by Napoleon as an order of merit awarded to Frenchmen and foreigners, rewarding their services in the civil service, magistracy, and army. It was directed particularly to those who were from areas newly annexed to France, such as the Kingdom of Holland. It was abolished in 1815.

4 1810, Versailles, Musée national du château.

5 Many examples of this painting are still conserved today, notably at the Musées nationaux des châteaux de Versailles et de Compiegne (MV 3890 and C 67D1), and at the Musée d'art Roger-Quillot, Clermont-Ferrand.
6 *Le Recueil des Ceremonies du marriage de l'Empereur* by Percier and Fontaine indicate there may be an exception to this rule. Plate X, *L'Empereur et l'Imperatrice recevant sur leur trône dans le palais des Tuileries, les hommages et les félicitations de tous les corps de l'État, le lendemain de leur mariage (3 avril 1810)*, shows Napoleon and Marie Louise sitting side by side under the thone's canopy. The pair of armchairs used on this occasion to replace the unique throne of the emperor are unknown.
7 It was used at the coronation at Notre Dame on December 2, 1804, before being divided into parts, notably to be used in the bedroom of Louis XVIII. Pieces of the balustrade are found today at the Louvre, Fontainebleau, and the Mobilier national.
8 Collection of the German Embassy in France. I would like to thank Dr Jörg Ebeling for providing me with information on the photograph.
9 See Young (1995: 97, fig. 59).
10 This information was communicated to me by the registrar of the Canadian Senate. I would like to thank the Honorable Serge Joyal, Senator of Canada.
11 See Young (1995: 99, fig. 61).
12 This system is still in place today, but as in the case of Westminster, a second throne has since been added for the consort of the sovereign title.

Chapter 6

1 John Bowes (1811–85) was an avid collector and the founder of the Bowes Museum, in Barnard Castle, Teesdale, Durham, England, established in 1869 and opened to the public in 1892.
2 Although India and Sri Lanka (Ceylon) had been important suppliers of furniture in the eighteenth century, in the nineteenth century, they seem to have supplied far fewer items of furniture.
3 Charpentier was a founding member of the decorative arts group Les Cinqs, which had been established in 1895, with members: architect Tony Selmersheim (1871–1971), designer Felix Aubert (1866–1940), sculptor Jean Dampt (1854–1945), and painter Étienne Moreau-Nélaton (1859–1927). In 1896, Plumet joined the group, and they became Les Six, and later Art dans Tout.
4 This was in opposition of such groups as the Working Men's party and trade unions (Price 2000: 276–7).
5 For a very thorough review of all the exhibitions from 1851 to 1887, not only those that displayed industrial products, see Simmonds (1887).
6 For more discussion on the rivalries at the exhibitions, see Ames (1974: 1–27).

Chapter 8

1 This precedent owes much to influential eighteenth-century pattern books, especially those by Thomas Chippendale, Robert Adam, and George Hepplewhite.
2 Notably Duncan Phyfe came to America in the 1780s from near Inverness in Scotland (Cornelius 1922); and Charles-Honoré Lannuier first trained in France as an *ébéniste* before moving to New York in 1803 (Waxman 1960).
3 Caqueteuse chairs tended to have wide, flaring seats with narrow backs and curving arms.
4 From 1790 the French distanced themselves from the period directly preceding the French Revolution and referred to it as the *ancien régime*.

5 In accordance with tradition, Guilmard has adapted the same approach by separating the *sièges* from the *meubles*.

Chapter 9

1 Key early studies include: Pevsner (1951a, b), Musgrave (1961), Aslin (1962), Jourdain and Fastnedge (1965), Symonds and Whineray (1965), and Jervis (1968).
2 Edward Joy has noted that this official total is slightly misleading as "Several numbers are missing and exhibitors are known to have entered twice" (Joy 1977: 307, n. 1).
3 Victoria and Albert Museum Collections (V&A: 25:1 to 3–1852), see Victoria and Albert Museum (1998b).
4 For the story of the revival of interest in Victorian architecture, design and the decorative arts, see Lubbock (1978), Watkin (1980), Wainwright (1986), and Burton (2004).
5 The table by George J. Morant & Sons exhibited at the Great Exhibition in 1851 is very similar to the one displayed in the British Galleries of the Victoria & Albert Museum, which was purchased by the museum from Lady Ashton (Madge Garland, former fashion editor of British *Vogue* and first Professor of Fashion at the Royal College of Art). Her husband Sir Leigh Ashton was director of the Victoria and Albert Museum from 1945 until 1955. Michelangelo Barberi and George Morant & Son, *Table*, Carved, painted and gilt wood, with metal parts, the top marble inlaid with micro-mosaic, *c.* 1851, Victoria and Albert Museum Collections (W.34:1, 2–1980), see Victoria and Albert Museum (1998c).
6 The Archive of Art and Design hold the following collections: Crace Family (1692–1992) (ARC1089), Holland & Son (1821–1968) (ARC51241), Heal & Son Holdings plc (1810–2009) (ARC51256), and E.W. Godwin (ARC51012). Besides the London-based archives, others such as the Joseph Downs Collection of Manuscripts and Printed Ephemera at the Winterthur Library (2020–1), which includes the papers of such American firms as Herter Brothers in New York, provide a wealth of unpublished textual representations of furniture for this period.
7 On the Craces, see Aldrich (1990). The studies of Liberty's include Adburgham (1975), Calloway (1992), Ashmore (2008), and Bennett (2012). On Gillows, see Goodison and Hardy (1970), Stuart (1996), a special edition of *Regional Furniture* (1998); Girling-Budd (2004), Mircoulis (2005), and Stuart (2008). On Holland & Son, see Jervis (1970), Anderson (2005c, 2012), and Girling-Budd (2004). On Heal's, see Goodden (1984) and Heal (2014). For E.W. Godwin, see Aslin (1986), Kinchin (2005), and Weber Soros (1999).
8 For the architect-designers, respectively, see Wainwright (1976, 1994), Wedgwood (1990), Crook (1981), Halén (1990), Durant (1993), Whiteway (2004), Lyons (2004), MacDonald (1987), Jervis (1989), Durant (1992), Hitchmough (1997), O'Donnell (2011), Crawford (1985), Billcliffe (1979b), Crawford (1995), and McKean and Baxter (2012).
9 Glenn (1979), Wainwright (1988), Barty-King (1992), Hall (1996), Edwards (1998, 2012), and Mircoulis (1998, 2001).
10 See the example in the V&A Collection (V&A, CIRC.250&A/1to B/1-1961), see Victoria and Albert Museum (1998a).
11 Kirkham (1982), Carruthers (1989), Collard (1996a), and Ellwood (1996).
12 Boynton (1967), Millar (1996), Jones (1997), and Banham (2001).
13 Evans (1997) and *Century Guild of Artists* (2008).

14 Carruthers (1978), Comino [Greensted] (1980), Carruthers and Greensted (1999), Andrews (2015), and Roscoe (2014).
15 Mayes (1960), Oliver (1966), Joy (1977: 217–61), Blankenhorn (1985), Reid (1986), Kirkham, Mace, and Porter (1987), and Kirkham (1988: i, iii–iv, vi–xii, 1–195, and 197–221).
16 Revisions to the London Price Books were published in 1803, 1811, 1824, 1836, and 1866; Supplements were published in 1815, 1825, 1831, 1836, 1846, 1863, and 1866.
17 Weil (1979), Gilbert (1982), Cotton (1988), and Jones (1989).
18 The history of the Government Schools of Design has been recounted in Bell (1963), MacDonald ([1970] 2004), Forty (1986: 58–61), Frayling (1987), Raizman (2003: 57–77), and Romans (2005, 2007).
19 Redgrave's own writings and contribution to art education in this period, are discussed in MacDonald ([1970] 2004: 234–41), who directs his readers to *The Manual of Design* compiled from Redgrave's various reports and addresses and published as one of the South Kensington Art Handbooks in 1876: this included a chapter "On Domestic and Other Furniture."
20 This piece of furniture is the Yatman Cabinet (1858) now in the V&A. See Victoria and Albert Museum (2001).
21 Greenhalgh (1988), Auerbach (1999), Edwards (2008), and Jackson (2008).
22 Cornforth (1978), Thornton (1984), Gere (1989), Long (2002), and Muthesius (2009).
23 Some historians have examined these publications for information about the physical spaces of furniture retail including well-known areas of London associated with the trade, see Kirkham, Mace, and Porter (1987), Kirkham (1988), and Edwards (2011). Manufacturers' showrooms; furniture displays in department stores; specialist furniture and furnishing shops; and shop window displays have also been studied. Several furniture historians have explored the development of the modern trade in antiques and the secondhand market, for example, Muthesius (1988), Wainwright (1989), Nenadic (1994), Collard (1996b), Lomax (1997), Edwards and Ponsonby (2008), and Westgarth (2009). In addition, the services offered by furniture manufacturers and retailers both before and after the sale such as the provision of installment credit, interior decoration, and the maintenance of furniture have also been discussed. See Muthesius (1992), Girling Budd (2004), Edwards (2005, 2006, 2013), and Shimbo (2015).
24 There are collections of furniture-makers' trade cards at the British Museum, the Bodleian Library and Waddesdon Manor; see the articles by Scott (2004), Berg and Clifford (2007), and Stobart (2008).
25 Crom (1989), Stabler (1991), and Smith (1992).
26 Branca (1975), Calder (1977), Davidoff and Hall (1987), Langland (1995), Kinchin (1996), Grier (1997), Ferry (2003, 2007, 2014), Flanders (2003), Ponsonby (2003), Keeble (2007), and Hamlett (2010).
27 Unfortunately Thad Logan used this example from Mrs. Orrinsmith's *The Drawing Room* to demonstrate the popularity of Japanese style screens made fashionable by the Aesthetic movement, see Logan (2001: 120).
28 Aslin (1962), Joy (1977), Davidoff and Hall (1987), Tristram (1989), Long (2002), and Young (2003).
29 Preserved by their descendants, it was opened to the public in 1980 by the Victorian Society, an organization that was founded at 18 Stafford Terrace in 1958 by the

Sambournes' granddaughter, Anne, 6th Countess of Rosse. See Nicholson (1998). The Diaries are being transcribed, see the Royal Borough of Kensington and Chelsea (n.d.).

30 Strong et al. (1974), Wilson (1977), Girouard (1979), Franklin (1981), and Wainwright (1989).

31 These are Sir Horace Walpole's Strawberry Hill; William Beckford's Fonthill Abbey; Sir Walter Scott's Abbotsford; Charlecote Park, home to the Lucy family; and, Sir Samuel Rush Meyrick's Goodrich Court.

32 Porter (1992), Tinniswood (1995), Payne (1998), Hewitt (1999), and Livesey (2007).

BIBLIOGRAPHY

PERIOD PUBLICATIONS

American Architect and Building News (1876–1909), New York: The American Architect.
L'Art Décoratif (1898–1922), Paris.
The Art Journal (1839–1912), London and New York: George Virtue.
The Art Workers' Quarterly (1902–6), London: Chapman & Hall.
The Bazaar, The Exchange and Mart (1868–2009), London.
The Builder. An Illustrated Weekly Magazine for the Architect, Engineer, Archaeologist, Constructor, & Art-Lover (1843–1966), London.
The Cabinet Maker and Art Furnisher (1880–1902), London: J. Williams Benn and Bros.
The Decorator and Furnisher (1882–98), New York: E.W. Bullinger.
Furniture Gazette (1872–96), London.
Harper's New Monthly Magazine (1850–1900), New York: Harper & Brothers.
The Illustrated London News (1842–2003), London: William Little.
The Magazine of Art (1878–1904), London and New York: Cassell, Petter and Gallpin.
The Mechanics' Magazine: Museum, Register, Journal, and Gazette (1823–53), London: M. Salmon.
The Portfolio (1870–93), London: Seeley, Jackson, and Halliday.
Repository of the Arts (1764–1834), London: Rudolph Ackermann.
The Studio (1893–1964), London.

SECONDARY SOURCES

Aaseng, Nathan (2002), *Business Builders in Real Estate*, Minneapolis, MN: The Oliver Press.
Abbott, Mary (1898), "Individuality of Homes," *House Beautiful*, February.
Abelson, Elaine (1989), *When Ladies Go A-thieving*, New York: Oxford University Press.

AC (1879), "Influence of Aesthetics on English Society," *Sylvia's Home Journal*, December: 420–1.
Ackermann's Repository (1813), London: Repository of Arts, Literature, Commerce, Manufactures, Fashions and Politics.
Adburgham, Alison (1975), *Liberty's: A Biography of a Shop*, London: Allen & Unwin.
Addams, Jane (1910), *Twenty Years at Hull House*, New York: MacMillan Company.
Agius, Pauline (1978), *British Furniture 1880–1915*, Woodbridge, UK: Antique Collectors Club.
Agius, Pauline (1984), *Ackermann's Regency Furniture & Interiors*, Marlborough, UK: Crowood Press.
Alcouffe, Daniel (1978), *The Second Empire, 1852–1870: Art in France under Napoleon III*, Philadelphia: Philadelphia Museum of Art.
Alcouffe, Daniel, Anne Dion-Tenenbaum, Marc Bascou, and Philippe Thiébaut (1988), *Le arti decorative alle grandi esposizioni universali: 1851–1900*, Milan: Idealibri.
Aldrich, Megan, ed. (1990), *The Craces: Royal Decorators, 1768–1899*, London: John Murray; Brighton: The Royal Pavilion, Art Gallery and Museums.
Aldrich, Megan (1997), *Gothic Revival*, London: Phaidon Press.
Altick, Richard ([1957] 1998), *The Common Reader: A Social History of the Mass Reading Public 1800–1900*, rev. edn., Columbus: Ohio State University Press.
Ames, Kenneth (1974), "The Battle of the Sideboards," *Winterthur Portfolio*, 9: 1–27.
Ames, Kenneth (1992), *Death in the Dining Room and Other Tales of Victorian Culture*, Philadelphia: Temple University Press.
Ames, Winslow (1970), "The Transformation of Château-sur-Mer," *Journal of the Society of Architectural Historians*, 29 (4): 291–306.
Anderson, Christina M. (2005a), "A Great Exhibition Sideboard by Matthew Bland of Halifax," Newsletter of *The Furniture History Society*, 158: 5–6.
Anderson, Christina M. (2005b), "Swiss Carving at the International Exhibitions," in Jay Arenski, Simon Daniels, and Michael Daniels (eds.), *Swiss Carvings: The Art of the "Black Forest" 1820–1940*, Woodbridge, UK: Antique Collectors' Club.
Anderson, Christina M. (2005c), "W. Bryson and the Firm of Holland and Sons," *Furniture History*, 41: 217–30.
Anderson, Christina M. (2012), "Further Evidence of the Comprehensive Nature of the Firm of Holland and Son," *Furniture History*, 48: 211–16.
Andrews, John (2015), *Arts and Crafts Furniture*, rev. edn., Woodbridge, UK: Antique Collectors Club.
Antin, Mary (1912), *The Promised Land*, Boston: Houghton Mifflin Company.
Apicella, Mary Ann (2008), *Scottish Cabinetmakers in Federal New York*, Published by author.
Appadurai, Arjun (1986), *The Social Lives of Things: Commodities in Cultural Perspective*, Cambridge: Cambridge University Press.
"Arms and the Chair" (1876), *New York Times*, June 14: 4.
"The Artistic Home" (1895), *The Album*, 2 (23) (July 8): 43.
Art Journal Illustrated Catalogue of the Industry of All Nations 1851 (1851), London: George Virtue.
Art Journal Illustrated Catalogue of the International Exhibition (1862), London: J.S. Virtue.
Ashmore, Sonia (2008), "Liberty and Lifestyle: Shopping for Art and Luxury in Nineteenth Century London," in David Hussey and Margaret Ponsonby (eds.),

Buying for the Home: Shopping for the Domestic from the Seventeenth Century to the Present, 73–90, Farnham, UK: Ashgate.

Aslin, Elizabeth (1962), *Nineteenth Century English Furniture*, London: Faber and Faber.

Aslin, Elizabeth (1986), *E.W. Godwin: Furniture and Interior Decoration*, London: John Murray.

The Atheneum, or the Spirit of English Literature and Fashion (1831–2), XX—fourth series, October 1831–April 1832, Boston: Kane & Co.

Attar, Dena (1987), *A Bibliography of Household Books Published in Britain 1800–1914*, London: Prospect Books.

Atterbury, Paul and Clive Wainwright (1995), *A.W.N. Pugin: Master of Gothic Revival*, New Haven, CT: Published for the Bard Graduate Center for Studies in the Decorative Arts, New York by Yale University Press.

Auerbach, Jeffrey (1999), *The Great Exhibition of 1851: A Nation on Display*, New Haven, CT: Yale University Press.

Auerbach, Jeffrey A. and Peter H. Hoffenberg, eds. (2008), *Britain, the Empire, and the World at the Great Exhibition of 1851*, Aldershot, UK: Ashgate Publishing.

Auslander, Leora (1988), "The Creation of Value and the Production of Good Taste: The Social Life of Furniture in Paris, 1860–1914," Ph.D. thesis, Brown University, published by University of Michigan.

Auslander, Leora (1996), *Taste and Power: Furnishing Modern France*, Berkeley: University of California Press.

Austen, Jane ([1813] 1988), *Pride and Prejudice*, Oxford: Oxford University Press.

Austen, Jane ([1815] 2008), *Emma*, London: Penguin Classics.

Baker, Malcolm (2007), "The Cult of the Catalogue: Representing the Fonthill, Stowe, and Hamilton Palace Collections," in Roberta Panzanelli and Monica Preti-Hamard (eds.), *La Circulation des Oeuvres d'Art: The Circulation of Works of Art in the Revolutionary Era*, 201–10, Rennes: Presses Universitaires de Rennes.

Baker, R. (1867), "Wood-Carving," in *Reports of Artisans selected by a committee appointed by the Society of Arts to visit the Paris Universal Exhibition of 1867*, 102–6, London: Published for the Society for the Encouragement of Arts, Manufactures and Commerce by Bell and Daldy.

Banham, Joanna, ed. ([1997] 2015), *Encyclopaedia of Interior Design*, London: Routledge.

Banham, Joanna and Jennifer Harris (1984), *William Morris and the Middle Ages: A Collection of Essays, Together with a Catalogue of Works Exhibited at the Whitworth Art Gallery*, Manchester, UK: Manchester University Press.

Banham, Joanna, Sally MacDonald, and Julia Porter (1991), *Victorian Interior Style*, New York: Crescent Books.

Banham, Joanna, Sally MacDonald, and Julia Porter (1995), *Victorian Interior Style*, London: Studio Editions.

Banham, Julie (2001), "Johnson & Appleyards Ltd of Sheffield: A Victorian Family Business," *Regional Furniture*, 15: 43–63.

Bard, Christine and Nicole Pellegrin (1999), "Femmes travesties, un mauvais genre," *Clio*, 10.

Barrows, Esther (1929), *Neighbors All: A Settlement Notebook*, Boston: Houghton Mifflin.

Barry, Charles and H.T. Ryde (1849), *Illustrations of the New Palace of Westminster: A History of the Palace of Westminster*, London: Warrington and Sons.

Barty-King, Hugh (1992), *Maples Fine Furnishers: A Household Name for 150 Years*, London: Quiller Press.
Beard, Geoffrey and Christopher Gilbert, eds. (1986), *The Dictionary of English Furniture Makers 1660–1840*, Leeds: W.S. Maney and Son.
Beckerdite, Luke (1998), *American Furniture*, Milwaukee, WI: Chipstone Foundation.
Beecher, Catharine (1845), *A Treatise on Domestic Economy*, New York: Harper & Brothers.
Bell, Quentin (1963), *The Schools of Design*, London: Routledge and Kegan Paul.
Bennett, Daryl (2012), *Liberty's Furniture 1875–1915: The Birth of Modern Interior Design*, Woodbridge, UK: Antique Collectors Club.
Berg, Maxine and Helen Clifford (2007), "Selling Consumption in the Eighteenth Century: Advertising and the Trade Card in Britain and France," *Cultural and Social History*, 4 (2): 145–70.
Bergdoll, Barry and Peter Christensen, eds. (2008), *Home Delivery: Fabricating the Modern Dwelling*, Part 1, New York: The Museum of Modern Art.
Billcliffe, Roger (1979a), *Charles Rennie Mackintosh: The Complete Furniture, Furniture Drawings and Interior Designs*, New York: Taplinger Pub. Co.
Billcliffe, Roger (1979b), *Complete Furniture: Furniture Drawings and Interior Designs, Mackintosh, Charles*, London: Lutterworth Press.
Black, Robert Monro (1983), *The History of Electric Wires and Cables*, London: Peter Peregrinus.
Blanc, Charles (1882), *Grammaire des arts décoratifs, décoration intérieure de la maison*, Paris: Renouard, H. Loones, Succ.
Blankenhorn, David (1985), "'Our Class of Workmen': The Cabinet-Makers Revisited," in Royden Harrison and Jonathan Zeitlin (eds.), *Divisions of Labour: Skilled Workers and Technological Change in Nineteenth Century Britain*, 19–46, Brighton, UK: Harvester Press.
Boardman, Kay (2000), "The Ideology of Domesticity: The Regulation of the Household Economy in Victorian Women's Magazines," *Victorian Periodicals Review*, 33 (2): 150–64.
Boris, Eileen (1986), *Art and Labor*, Philadelphia: Temple University Press.
Borzello, Frances (2006), *At Home: The Domestic Interior in Art*, London: Thames and Hudson.
Bouzin, Claude (2000), *Dictionnaire du meuble*, Paris: Charles Massin.
Boynton, Lindsay (1967), "High Victorian Furniture: The Example of Marsh and Jones of Leeds," *Furniture History*, 3: 54–91.
Boynton, Lindsay, ed. (1996), *Gillow Furniture Designs 1760–1800*, Woodbridge, UK: Antique Collectors Club.
Brace, C.L. (1853), *Home-Life in Germany*, New York: Charles Scribner.
Branca, Patricia (1975), *Silent Sisterhood: Middle Class Women in the Victorian Home*, London: Croom Helm.
Brawer, Nicholas (2001), *British Campaign Furniture: Elegance under Canvas, 1740–1914*, New York: Harry N. Abrams.
The British Museum: Historical and Descriptive (1850), Edinburgh: William and Robert Chambers.
Breeden, James (1980), *Advice Among Masters*, Westport, CT: Greenwood Press.
Brincourt (1889), "Paris," *The American Architect and Building News*, 26 (709) (July 27): 39.

Britton, John (1827), *The Union of Architecture, Sculpture and Painting*, London: John Britton.

Brontë, Charlotte ([1847] 2006), *Jane Eyre*, London: Penguin Books.

Broun, Dauvit, R.J. Finlay, and Michael Lynch, eds. (1998), *Image and Identity: The Making and Re-making of Scotland Through the Ages*, Edinburgh: John Donald Publishers.

Brown, Gillian (1984), "Getting in the Kitchen with Dinah: Domestic Politics in Uncle Tom's Cabin," *American Quarterly*, 36 (4): 503.

Brown, Richard (1822), *The Rudiments of Drawing Cabinet and Upholstered Furniture*, London: Printed for the author.

Brown, Richard (1835), *The Rudiments of Drawing Cabinet and Upholstery Furniture*, London: Taylor.

Bryant, Julius, ed. (2012), *Art and Design for all: The V&A Museum*, London: V&A Publishing.

Bryant, Julius and Susan Weber, eds. (2017), *John Lockwood Kipling. Arts & Crafts in the Punjab and London*, New York: Bard Graduate Center Gallery; New Haven, CT: Yale University Press.

Bunston, John (1971), *English Furniture Designs 1800–1914: A Bibliography of 120 Pattern Books and Trade Catalogues in the Library of the Victoria and Albert Museum*, London: National Art Library/Victoria and Albert Museum.

Burges, William (1862), "The International Exhibition," *Gentleman's Magazine and Historical Reviews*, July, vol. 213: 3–12.

Burges, William (1865), *Art Applied to Industry*, Oxford: John Henry and James Parker.

Burton, Anthony (2002), "The Uses of the South Kensington Art Collections," *Journal of the History of Collections*, 14 (1): 79–95.

Burton, Anthony (2004), "The Revival of Interest in Victorian Decorative Art and the Victoria and Albert Museum," in Miles Taylor and Michael Wolff (eds.), *The Victorians since 1901: Histories, Representations and Revisions*, 121–37, Manchester, UK: Manchester University Press.

Busch, Jason T., Catherine L. Futter, Regina Lee Blaszczyk, Martin P. Levy, Jane Shadel Spillman, Annamarie V. Sandecki, Ethan Robey, Stephen Harrison, Kevin W. Tucker, Karin A. Jones, and Dawn Reid (2012), *Inventing the Modern World: Decorative Arts at the World's Fairs, 1851–1939*, New York: Skira Rizzoli International Publications.

Bushman, Richard (1992), *The Refinement of America*, New York: Knopf.

Butler, E.M., ed. (1957), *A Regency Visitor: The English Tour of Prince Puckler-Muskau Described in his Letters 1826–1828*, London: Collins.

Butler, Josephine (1869), *Woman's Work and Woman's Culture*, London: Macmillan.

Byers, C.A. (1925), *Modern Priscilla Home Furnishing Book*, Boston: Priscilla Publishing Company.

The Cabinet-Maker's Assistant (1853), Bishopbriggs, UK: Blackie & Son.

Calder, Jenni (1977), *The Victorian Home*, London: Batsford.

Calloway, Stephen, ed. (1992), *The House of Liberty: Masters of Style and Decoration*, London: Thames and Hudson.

Carruthers, Annette (1978), *Ernest Gimson and the Cotswold Group of Craftsmen*, Leicester, UK: Leicestershire Museums, Art Galleries and Record Service.

Carruthers, Annette (1989), "'Like Incubi and Succubi': A Table by Webb or Morris," *Craft History*, 2: 55–61.

Carruthers, Annette (2003), *The Arts and Crafts Movement in Scotland*, New Haven, CT: Yale University Press.

Carruthers, Annette (2013), *The Arts and Crafts Movement in Scotland*, London: Paul Mellon Centre for Studies in British Art.

Carruthers, Annette and Mary Greensted (1999), *Good Citizens Furniture: The Arts and Crafts Collections at Cheltenham*, London: Lund Humphries.

Catalogue d'un Riche Mobilier, voitures, vins precieux, curiosites, vases grecs, tableaux, piano, etc. (1833), Paris: Imprimerie Selligue.

Century Guild of Artists (2008), Oxford: Oxford University.

Chabert, H. (1865), "De L'Ameublement des appartements modernes," in *Le Moniteur de l'Ameublement*, (February): 17.

Charpy, Manuel (2015), "La rareté partagée. Commerces et consommations des antiquités et des curiosités au XIXe siècle (Paris, Londres et New York)," in Natacha Coquery and Alain Bonnet (eds.), *Le commerce du luxe, Production, exposition et circulation des objets précieux du Moyen Âge à nos jours*, 289–99, Paris: Mare et Martin.

Chen, Constance J.S. (2010), "Merchants of Asianess: Japanese Art Dealers in the United States in the Early Twentieth Century," *Journal of American Studies*, 44 (1): 19–46.

Chevallier Bernard, Denis d'Arnaud, Aurélia Rostaing, Jean-Denis Serena, Marc Walter, and Sabine Arqué (2013), *Saint-Cloud, le palais retrouvé*, Saint-Cloud: Swan Editeur-éditions du Patrimoine.

The Cincinnati Directory for the year 1829: to which are appended, lists of State, County, & City Officers... (1829), Cincinnati, OH: Robinson and Fairbank.

Clark, John. A. (1840), *Rome, and its Wonders, and Its Worship*, London: Bagster & Co.

Clark, Kenneth (1950), *The Gothic Revival: An Essay in the History of Taste*, London: Constable.

"Class XXVI. Report on Decorative Furniture and Upholstery, including Paper-Hangings, Papier Mache, and Japanned Goods" (1852), in Royal Commission, *Reports by the Juries on the Subjects in the Thirty Classes into which the Exhibition Was Divided*, 544–52, London: W. Clowes and Sons.

Coffin, Sarah (2008), *Rococo: The Continuing Curve, 1730–2008*, New York: Cooper-Hewitt, National Design Museum.

Cohen, Deborah (2006), *Household Gods: The British and Their Possessions*, New Haven, CT: Yale University Press.

Cohen, Lizabeth (1980), "Embellishing a Life of Labor: An Interpretation of the Material Culture of American Working-Class Homes, 1885–1915," *Journal of American Culture*, 3 (4): 752–75.

Collard, Frances (1985), *Regency Furniture*, Woodbridge, UK: Antique Collectors' Club.

Collard, Frances (1996a), "Furniture" in Linda Parry (ed.), *William Morris*, 155–79, London: Philip Wilson/V&A Publications.

Collard, Frances (1996b), "Town and Emanuel," *Furniture History*, 32: 81–9.

Collard, Frances (2003), "Historical Revivals, Commercial Enterprise and Public Confusion: Negotiating Taste, 1860–1890," *Journal of Design History*, 16 (1): 35–48.

Colvin, Howard (1978), *A Biographical Dictionary of British Architects, 1600–1840*, London: John Murray.

Comino [Greensted], Mary (1980), *Gimson and the Barnsleys: Wonderful Furniture of a Commonplace Kind*, London: Evans Brothers.

Comino Greensted, Mary (1982), *Gimson and the Barnsleys: Wonderful Furniture of a Commonplace Kind*, London: Evans Brothers.

Cooper, Jeremy (1972), "Victorian Furniture: An Introduction to the Sources," *Apollo*, 19: 115–23.

Cooper, Nicholas (1979), *The Opulent Eye: Late Victorian and Edwardian Taste in Interior Design*, London: Architectural Press.

Coquery, Natacha and Alain Bonnet, eds. (2015), *Le commerce du luxe, Production, exposition et circulation des objets précieux du Moyen Âge à nos jours*, Paris: Mare et Martin.

Cordier, Sylvain (2008), "Deux projects pour le fauteuil du trône de Louis XVIII par Dugourc et Saint-Ange", *Revue de l'Art*, 160: 69–71.

Cordier, Sylvain (2012a), "The Bellangé Album and New Discoveries in French Nineteenth Century Decorative Arts," *Metropolitan Museum Journal*, 47: 119–47.

Cordier, Sylvain (2012b), *Bellangé, ébénistes: Une histoire du goût au XIXe siècle*, Paris: Mare et Martin.

Cordier, Sylvain, ed. (2018), *Napoleon: The Imperial Household*, New Haven, CT: Yale University Press.

Cornelius, Charles (1922), "Furniture from the Workshop of Duncan Phyfe," *American Magazine of Art*, 13 (12): 521–8.

Cornforth, John (1978), *English Interiors 1790–1848, The Quest for Comfort*, London: Barrie & Jenkins.

"Correspondence: The Paris Industrial Exhibition" (1879), *The American Architect and Building News*, 6 (200) (October 25): 134.

"The Cosey Corner" (1896), *Decorator and Furnisher*, 27 (March): 182.

Cotton, Gerry (1988), "'Common' Chairs from the Norwich Chair Makers' Price Book of 1801," *Regional Furniture*, 2: 68–92.

Courtin, Nicolas (2014), "Les chambres de Louis XIV," in Alexandre Maral, Nicolas Milovanovic, and Mathiew Da Vinha (eds.), *Louis XIV, l'image et le mythe*, 125–42, Paris: Presses universitaires de Rennes/Centre de recherches du château de Versailles.

"Cozy Corners for Parlors" (1890), *Ladies Home Journal*, July: ii.

Crane, Stephen (1896), *Maggie a Girl of the Streets*, New York: D. Appleton and Company.

Crane, Stephen ([1898] 1993), *The Open Boat and Other Stories*, New York: Dover Publications.

Crane, Walter (1905), "Of the Arts and Crafts Movement," in *Ideals in Art, Papers Theoretical Practical Critical*, 1–34, London: George Bell & Sons.

Crawford, Alan (1985), *C.R. Ashbee: Architect, Designer, and Romantic Socialist*, New Haven, CT: Yale University Press.

Crawford, Alan (1995), *Charles Rennie Mackintosh*, London: Thames & Hudson.

Crawford, Alan (2005), *C.R. Ashbee: Architect, Designer and Romantic Socialist*, New Haven, CT: Yale University Press.

Crom, Theodore R. (1989), *Trade Catalogues 1542 to 1842*, Melrose: Theodore Crom.

Crook, J. Mordaunt (1981), *William Burges and the High Victorian Dream*, Chicago: University of Chicago Press.

Crook, J. Mordaunt (1982), *The Strange Genius of William Burges, "art-architect", 1827–1881*, Cardiff: National Museum of Wales.

Cumming, Elizabeth (2006), *Hand, Heart and Soul: The Arts and Crafts Movement in Scotland*, Edinburgh: Birlinn.

Cunningham, Colin and Prudence Waterhouse (1992), *Alfred Waterhouse, 1830–1905: Biography of a Practice*, Oxford: Oxford University Press.

de Bellaigue, Geoffrey (1991), *Carlton House: The Past Glories of George IV's Palace*, London: The Queen's Gallery.

Davidoff, Leonore and Catherine Hall (1987a), *Family Fortunes*, Chicago: University of Chicago Press.

Davidoff, Leonore and Catherine Hall (1987b), *Family Fortunes: Men and Women of the English Middle Class, 1780–1850*, London: Hutchinson.

Davis, Diana (2020), *The Tastemakers: British Dealers and the Anglo–Gallic Interior, 1785–1865*, Los Angeles: Getty Publications.

"Decorative Fine-Art Work at Philadelphia: Furniture in the British Section" (1876), *The American Architect and Building News*, 1 (November 18): 372–3.

Deflassieux, Françoise (2005), *Guide des meubles et des styles*, Paris: SOLAR.

De Grassi, Massimo, ed. (2002), *Valentino Panciera Besarel 1829–1902*, Belluno: Provincia di Belluno Editore.

de Honnecourt, Villard ([13th century] 2009), *The Portfolio of Villard de Honnecourt*, repr., London: Routledge.

Denon, Baron Dominique-Vivant (1802), *Voyage dans la basse et la haute d'Egypte*, London: James Ridgway.

"Designs for Furniture and Decoration at the Academy" (1881), *The Furniture Gazette*, 15 (June 4): 362.

Department of Practical Art (1852), *A Catalogue of the Articles of Ornamental Art, selected from the exhibition of the works of industry of all nations in 1851, &c.* with an introduction by Owen Jones, London: Stationery Office.

Dickens, Charles (1839), *Oliver Twist, or, the Parish Boy's Progress*, London: Richard Bentley.

Dickens, Charles ([1839] 1995), *Sketches by Boz*, London: Penguin Classics.

Dickens, Charles ([1865] 1997), *Our Mutual Friend*, repr., London: Penguin.

Dion-Tenenbaum, Anne (2005), "Les marchands de curiosités à travers les achats du Garde-Meuble sous la monarchie de Juille," in Monica Preti-Hamard and Philippe Sénéchal (eds.), *Collections et marché de l'art en France 1789–1848*, 229–41, Rennes: Presses Universitaires de Rennes, INHA.

"The Domestic Use of Design" (1873), *Furniture Gazette*, April 12: 4.

Donnelly, Max (2001), "British Furniture at the Philadelphia Centennial Exhibition, 1876," *Furniture History Society*, 37: 91–120.

Doordan, Dennis P. (1995), *Design History: An Anthology*, Boston: The MIT Press.

D'Osmond, Louise-Eléonore-Charlotte-Adélaide (1907), *Récits d'une Tante: Mémoires de la Comtesse de Boigne, née d'Osmond*, Paris: Mercure de France.

Doty, Mrs. D. (1893), *The Town of Pullman*, Pullman, Illinois: T.P. Struhsacker.

Downing, Andrew Jackson (1850), *The Architecture of Country Houses*, New York: D. Appleton.

Dresser, Christopher (1870), "Art Furniture," in *The Technical Educator*, 311–13; 376–8; 403–6, London: Cassell & Co.

Dresser, Christopher (1873), *Principles of Decorative Design*, London: Cassell, Petter and Galpin.

Dresser, Christopher (1876), *Studies in Design*, London: Cassell, Petter and Galpin.

Du Bois, W.E.B. (1901), "The Problem of Housing the Negro: The Home of the Slave," *Southern Workman*, (30): 492.

Durant, Stuart (1992), *CFA Voysey*, London: John Wiley.
Durant, Stuart (1993), *Christopher Dresser*, London: John Wiley.
Eastlake, Charles L. (1868), *Hints on Household Taste in Furniture, Upholstery, and Other Details*, London: Longmans, Green.
Eastlake, Charles (1874), *Hints on Household Taste in Furniture, Upholstery, and Other Details*, Boston: James R. Osgood and Company.
Edis, Robert W. (1881), *Decoration & Furniture of Town Houses: A Series of Cantor Lectures Delivered before the Society of Arts 1880*, London: C.K. Paul & Co.
Edwards, Anthony David (2008), *The Role of International Exhibitions in Britain, 1850–1910: Perceptions of Economic Decline and the Technical Education Issue*, Amherst, NY: Cambria Press.
Edwards, Clive D. (1995), "British Imports of American Furniture in the Later Nineteenth Century," *Furniture History*, 31: 210–16.
Edwards, Clive D. (1998), "The Firm of Jackson and Graham," *Furniture History*, 34: 238–65.
Edwards, Clive D. (2005), *Turning Houses into Homes: A History of the Retailing and Consumption of Domestic Furnishings*, Aldershot, UK: Ashgate.
Edwards, Clive D. (2006), "Buy Now—Pay Later. Credit: The Mainstay of the Retail Furniture Business," in John Benson and Laura Ugolini (eds.), *Cultures of Selling: Perspectives on Consumption and Society Since 1700*, 127–52, Aldershot: Ashgate.
Edwards, Clive D. (2011), "Tottenham Court Road: The Changing Fortunes of London's Furniture Street 1850–1950," *London Journal*, 36 (2): 140–60.
Edwards, Clive D. (2012), "'Art Furniture in the Old English Style': The Firm of Collinson and Lock, London, 1870–1900," *West 86th: A Journal of Decorative Arts, Design History, and Material Culture*, 19 (2): 255–81.
Edwards, Clive D. (2013), "Complete House Furnishers: The Retailer as Interior Designer in Nineteenth-Century London," *Journal of Interior Design*, 38 (1): 1–17.
Edwards, Clive D. and Margaret Ponsonby (2008), "Desirable Commodity or Practical Necessity? The Sale and Consumption of Second Hand Furniture 1750–1900," in David Hussey and Margaret Ponsonby (eds.), *Buying for the Home: Shopping for the Domestic from the Seventeenth Century to the Present*, 117–38, Aldershot, UK: Ashgate.
Ellwood, Giles (1996), "Three Tables by Philip Webb," *Furniture History*, 32: 127–40.
Elmes, James (1831), *London and Its Environs in the Nineteenth Century*, London: Jones and Co.
"English Furniture" (1876), *The American Architect and Building News*, 1 (December 2): 389–97.
"English Furniture at the Exhibition" (1878), *The American Architect and Building News*, 4 (155) (December 14): 198–9.
Etiquette du Palais Imperial (1806), Paris: Imprimerie impériale.
Evans, Stuart (1997), "Century Guild Inventions: The Century Guild of Artists at the International Inventions Exhibition, London, 1885," *Journal of the Decorative Arts Society 1850–The Present*, 21: 46–53.
"Exhibition of Decorative Art" (1881), *The Furniture Gazette*, 15 (June 4): 361.
"Exhibition of the Produce of French Industry at the Louvre" (1819), *The Literary Gazette*, (144) (October 23): 681.
"The Exhibition of Rooms at the Crystal Palace, London" (1892), *Decorator and Furnisher*, (20): 97.

Exhibition of the Works of Industry of all Nations 1851, Reports by the Jurors on the Subjects in the Thirty Classes into which the Exhibition was Divided, By the Authority of the Royal Commission (1852), London: Spicer Brothers.

"Exhibition of Works in Wood" (1884), *The Furniture Gazette*, 15 (May 31): 449.

Exposition artistique et rétrospective de la Société Archéologique de Tarn-et-Garonne (1897), Montauban: Forestié.

Exposition des produits de l'industrie Belge en 1835 (1835), Brussels: H. Remy.

Exposition Universelle de 1855, rapports du jury mixte international (1856), Paris: Imprimerie impériale.

Exposition Universelle d'Anvers. Catalogue official general (1894), Brussels: Mertens.

Falke, Jakob von (1873), *Die Kunst im Hause: Geschichtliche und kritisch-ästhetische Studien über die Decoration und Ausstattung der Wohnung*, Vienna: Gerold.

Farnam, Anne (1979), "H. H. Richardson and A. H. Davenport: Architecture and Furniture as Big Business in America's Gilded Age," in Paul Kebabian and William Lipke (eds.), *Tools and Technologies: America's Wooden Age*, 80–92, Burlington: Robert Hull Fleming Museum, University of Vermont.

Faure, Gressin-Demoulin et Valérius (1836), *La Belgique industrielle de l'exposition des produits de l'industrie en 1835*, Brussels: Louis Hauman et Comp.

Favardin, Patrick (1979), "La villa ou l'avènement d'un nouveau mode d'habitation," in "L'architecture et le décor sous le Second Empire," *Monuments Historiques*, 102: 57–61.

Fennimore, Donald (1981), "American Neoclassical Furniture and Its European Antecedents," *American Art Journal*, 13 (4): 49–65.

Ferrey, Benjamin (1978), *Recollections of A.W.N. Pugin and His Father Augustus Pugin*, London: The Scolar Press.

Ferry, Emma (2003), "'Decorators may be compared to doctors': An Analysis of Rhoda and Agnes Garrett's Suggestions for House Decoration 1876," *Journal of Design History*, 16 (1): 15–33.

Ferry, Emma (2007), "'Information for the ignorant and aid for the advancing ...' Macmillan's Art at Home Series. 1876–83," in Jeremy Aynsley and Kate Forde (eds.), *Design and the Modern Magazine*, 134–55, Manchester, UK: Manchester University Press.

Ferry, Emma (2014), "'Any lady can do this without much trouble ...' Class and Gender in The Dining Room (1878)," *Interiors: Design Architecture Culture*, 5 (2): 141–59.

Fetridge, William Pembroke (1873), *The American Traveller's Guide: Harper's Handbook for Travellers in Europe and the East ... Twelfth Year*, New York: Harper & Brothers.

Fitzgerald, Francis Scott ([1933] 2003), *Tender is the Night*, repr., New York: Scribner.

Flanders, Judith (2003), *The Victorian House: Domestic Life from Childbirth to Deathbed*, London: Harper Collins.

Flestrin, Quinbus (Edward Fay) (1892), "Interview with William Morris," *The Clarion*, November 12: 8.

"Forthcoming Furniture Exhibition" (1881), *The Furniture Gazette*, May 7: 295.

Forty, Adrian (1992), *Objects of Desire: Design and Society since 1750*, London: Thames and Hudson.

Fourdinois, Henri (1885), *De l'état actuel de l'industrie du mobilier*, Paris: E. Rouveyre.

Franklin, Jill (1981), *Gentleman's Country House and Its Plan, 1835–1914*, London: Routledge & Kegan Paul.

Frayling, Christopher (1987), *The Royal College of Art, One Hundred and Fifty Years of Art and Design*, London: Hutchinson.

"French Woodwork at South Kensington" (1895), *The Studio*, 6: 25–9.

"Furnishing Items at the Building Exhibition, 1882" (1882), *The Cabinet Maker and Art Furnisher*, 2 (22) (April 1): 197.

"Furniture Shown at the Melbourne Exhibition" (1881), *The Furniture Gazette*, February 19: 124.

Gabet, Olivier (2011), "Trône livré pour l'ambassade de Prusse à Paris," in Jacques Charles Gaffiot (ed.), *Trônes en majesté*, 294–5, Paris: éditions du Cerf.

Galignani and Company (1838), *Galignani's New Paris Guide: containing an accurate statistical and historical description of all the institutions, public edifices ... an abstract of the laws affecting foreigners ...*, Paris: A. and W. Galignani and Company.

Garets, Comtesse des (née Marie de Larminat) (1928), *Souvenires d'une demoiselle d'honneur de l'impératrice Eugénie*, Paris: Calmann lévy.

Garric, Jean-Philippe, ed. (2016), *Charles Percier: Architecture and Design in an Age of Revolutions*, New Haven, CT: Published for the Bard Graduate Center for Studies in the Decorative Arts, New York by Yale University Press.

Gaskell, Elizabeth ([1848] 2008), *Mary Barton*, Oxford: Oxford World Classics.

Gaskell, Elizabeth ([1851] 2011), *Cranford*, Oxford: Oxford World Classics.

Gastinel-Coural, Chantal (1991), "Salle du trône du château des Tuileries: bois du meuble d'été (deux fauteuils de représentation, deux tabourets de pied, paravent à six feuilles, écran, quatre candélabres)," in *Un âge d'or des arts décoratifs, 1814–1848*, Paris: Réunion des musées nationaux [exhibition catalog].

Gere, Charlotte (1989), *Nineteenth Century Decoration: Art of the Interior*, London: Weidenfeld & Nicolson.

Gere, Charlotte and Michael Whiteway (1993), *Nineteenth-Century Design: From Pugin to Mackintosh*, London: Weidenfeld and Nicolson.

Gilbert, Christopher (1982), "The Cabinet-Makers Book of Prices 1793: Part II—London and Provincial Books of Prices: Comment and Bibliography," *Furniture History*, 18: 11–21.

Girling-Budd, Amanda (2004), "Comfort and Gentility: Furnishings by Gillows, Lancaster 1840–55," in Susie McKellar and Penny Sparke (eds.), *Interior Design and Identity*, 27–47, Manchester, UK: Manchester University Press.

Girouard, Mark (1979), *The Victorian Country House*, New Haven, CT: Yale University Press.

"The Glasgow International Exhibition 1888" (1888), *The Art Journal*, 50: 14.

Glenn, Virginia (1979), "George Bullock, Richard Bridgens and James Watt's Regency Furnishing Schemes," *Furniture History*, 15: 54–67.

Goodden, Susanna (1984), *A History of Heal's*, London: Lund Humphries.

Goodison, Nicholas and John Hardy (1970), "Gillows at Tatton Park," *Furniture History*, 6: 1–39.

Goodman, Dena (2009), *Becoming a Woman in the Age of Letters*, Ithaca, NY: Cornell University Press.

Grant, Charlotte (2006), "'One's self, and one's house, one's furniture': From Object to Interior in British Fiction, 1720–1900," in Jeremy Aynsley and Charlotte Grant (eds.), *Imagined Interiors: Representing the Domestic Interior since the Renaissance*, 134–53, London: V&A Publications.

Graves, J.T. (1883), *The Winter Resorts of Florida*, Passenger Department, Savannah, FL, and Western Railway Co.

Greenhalgh, Paul (1988), *Ephemeral Vistas: The Expositions Universelles, Great Exhibitions and World's Fairs, 1851–1939*, Manchester, UK: Manchester University Press.

Greenhalgh, Paul (1993), *Quotations and Sources on Design and the Decorative Arts*, Manchester, UK: Manchester University Press.

Greensted, Mary (1991), *Gimson and the Barnsleys: Wonderful Furniture of a Commonplace Kind*, Stroud, UK: Sutton Publishing.

Grier, Katherine (1988), *Culture & Comfort*, Rochester, NY: Strong Museum.

Grier, Katherine (1992), "The Decline of the Memory Palace: The Parlor after 1890," in Jessica H. Foy and Thomas J. Schlereth (eds.), *American Home Life, 1880–1930*, 49–74, Knoxville: University of Tennessee Press.

Grier, Katherine (1997), *Culture and Comfort: Parlor Making and Middle Class Identity, 1850–1930*, Washington DC: Smithsonian Books.

Grossmith, George and Weedon Grossmith ([1892] 1995), *The Diary of a Nobody*, London: Penguin Classics.

Guida della città di Firenze: e suoi contorni … (1828), Florence: Presso Antonia Campani.

Gurney, Peter J. (2006), "'The Sublime of the Bazaar': A Moment in the Making of a Consumer Culture in Mid-Nineteenth Century England," *Journal of Social History*, 40 (2): 385–405.

Habermas, Jürgen (1991), *The Structural Transformation of the Public Sphere*, Cambridge, MA: The MIT Press.

Halén, Widar (1990), *Christopher Dresser*, London: Phaidon Christies.

Hall, Michael (1996), "'Furniture of Artistic Character': Watts and Company as House Furnishers, 1874–1907," *Furniture History*, 32: 179–204.

Halttunen, Karen (1982a), *Confidence Men and Painted Women*, New Haven, CT: Yale University Press.

Halttunen, Karen (1982b), "From Parlor to Living Room: Domestic Space, Interior Decoration, and the Culture of Personality," in S. Bronner (ed.), *Consuming Visions*, 157–90, Winterthur: Henry Francis du Pont Winterthur Museum.

Hamlett, Jane (2010), *Material Relations: Domestic Interiors and Middle-Class Families in England, 1850–1910*, Manchester, UK: Manchester University Press.

Harper's New Monthly Magazine (1876), no. 315, August (London).

Harris, John (2007), *Moving Rooms: The Trade in Architectural Salvages*, New Haven, CT: Yale University Press.

Havard, Henry (1883–), *L'art dans la maison, grammaire de l'ameublement*, Paris: Rouveyre et G. Blond.

Haweis, Mrs. H.R. (1881), *The Art of Decoration*, London: Chatto and Windus.

Hayden, Dolores (1981), *The Grand Domestic Revolution*, Cambridge, MA: MIT Press.

Hayward, Helena, ed. (1981), *World Furniture: An Illustrated History*, 1st edn. 1965; 2nd edn. 1977, New York: Crescent.

Hazard's Register of Pennsylvania (1831), 8 (20) (November 12): 305–8.

Heal, Oliver (2014), *Sir Ambrose Heal and the Heal Cabinet Factory 1897–1939*, London: Oblong Creative.

Heal and Sons (1854), *Officers Portable Furniture Catalogue*, May, London: Heal and Sons.

Heckscher, Morrison H., with the assistance of Lori Zabar (2005), *John Townsend: Cabinetmaker*, New York: The Metropolitan Museum of Art.

Hellman, Mimi (2011), "Enchanted Night: Decoration, Sociability, and Visuality after Dark," in Charissa Bremer-David (ed.), *Paris: Life & Luxury in the Eighteenth Century*, 91–113, Los Angeles: J. Paul Getty Museum.

Hepplewhite, George (1788), *The Cabinet-Maker and Upholsterer's Guide*, London: I. & J. Taylor.

Herda-Mousseaux, Rose-Marie, Patrick Rambourg, and Guillaume Séret (2015), *Thé, café ou chocolat? L'essor des boissons exotiques à Paris au XVIIIe siècle*, Paris: Paris Musées, Musée Cognacq-Jay.

Herrmann, Wolfgang (1992), "Introduction," in Heinrich Hübsch, Rudolf Wiegmann, Carl Albert Rosenthal, Johann Heinrich Wolff, and Carl Gottlieb Wilhelm Bötticher, *In What Style Should We Build? The German Debate on Architectural Style*, Los Angeles: The Getty Center for The History of Art.

Hertford, Marquess of (1981), *The Hertford-Mawson Letters*, May 12, 1851, London: The Wallace Collection.

Hewitt, Martin (1999), "District Visiting and the Constitution of Domestic Space in the Mid-19th Century," in Inga Bryden and Janet Floyd (eds.), *Domestic Space: Reading the Nineteenth-Century Interior*, 121–41, Manchester, UK: Manchester University Press.

Hicklin, John and A. Wallis (1869), *Bemrose's Guide to Derbyshire: A Complete Hand-Book for the County*, London: Bemrose and Sons.

Hiesinger, Kathryn B. and Joseph Rishel, eds. (1978), *The Second Empire: Art in France under Napoleon III*, Philadelphia: Philadelphia Museum of Art.

Hill, Rosemary (2007), *God's Architect: Pugin & the Building of Romantic Britain*, London: Allen Lane.

Himmelheber, Georg (1983), *Die Kunst des deutschen Möbels*, Frankfurt: C.H. Beck Publishers.

History and Commerce of New York 1891 (1891), 2nd edn., New York: American Publishing and Engraving Co.

"History of the Great Exhibition" (1851), *The Art Journal Illustrated Catalogue*, London: George Virtue.

"The History of the Kensington Loan Collection—I" (1881), *The Furniture Gazette*, 15 (April 23): 268–9.

Hitchmough, Wendy (1997), *CFA Voysey*, London: Phaidon.

Hoganson, Kristin (2007), *Consumers' Imperium*, Chapel Hill: University of North Carolina Press.

Hooper, Charles Alfred (1867), "Cabinet Making," in *Reports of Artisans selected by a committee appointed by the Society of Arts to visit the Paris Universal Exhibition of 1867*, 1–25, London: Published for the Society for the Encouragement of Arts, Manufactures and Commerce by Bell and Daldy.

Hope, Thomas (1807), *Household Furniture and Interior Decoration*, London: Longman, Hurst, Rees and Orme.

Hoskins, Lesley (2013), "Social, Economic, and Geographical Differences in Mid-Nineteenth-Century Homes: The Evidence from Inventories," *Regional Furniture*, 27: 93–119.

Howard, Vicki (2008), "'The Biggest Small-Town Store in America': Independent Retailers and the Rise of Consumer Culture," *Enterprise & Society*, 9 (3): 457–86.

Howe, Katherine S., Alice Cooney Frelinghuysen, and Catherine Hoover Voorsanger (1994), *Herter Brothers: Furniture and Interiors for a Gilded Age*, New York: Harry N. Abrams.

The Illustrated Catalogue of the Universal Exhibition (1868), published with the *Art Journal*, London: George Virtue.

"An Indian Room" (1889), *Decorator and Furnisher*, (14): 38.

"An Interior in the Turkish Style" (1894), *Decorator and Furnisher*, (25): 16.

"Interiors in the Oriental Style" (1896), *Decorator and Furnisher*, (27): 103.

International Health Exhibition, Official Catalogue (1884), London: William Clowes and Sons.

"An Italian Renaissance Dining-Room" (1896), *Decorator and Furnisher*, (29): 69.

Jackson, Anna (2008), *Expo: International Expositions 1851–2010*, London: V&A Publications.

Jefferys, James (1950), *The Distribution of Consumer Goods: A Factual Study of Methods and Costs in the United Kingdom in 1938*, Cambridge: Cambridge University Press.

Jervis, Simon (1968), *Victorian Furniture*, London: Wardlock.

Jervis, Simon (1970), "Holland and Sons and the Furnishing of the Athenaeum," *Furniture History*, 6: 43–61.

Jervis, Simon (1984), *Dictionary of Design and Designers*, London: Puffin.

Jervis, Simon (1989), "Charles, Bevan and Talbert," in Susan M. Wright (ed.), *The Decorative Arts of the Victorian Period*, 15–29, London: The Society of Antiquaries.

Jervis, Simon (2005), "Charles Davis, the 15th Duke of Norfolk, and the Formation of the Collection of Furniture at Arundel Castle," *Furniture History*, 41: 231–48.

Jervis, William Pervis (1896), *Rough Notes on Pottery*, Newark, NJ: W.P. Jervis.

Jones, Claire (2014), *Sculptors and Design Reform in France, 1848 to 1895: Sculpture and the Decorative Arts*, Farnham, UK: Ashgate.

Jones, David (1987a), "Coal Furniture in Scotland," *Furniture History*, 23: 35–8.

Jones, David (1987b), *Looking at Scottish Furniture: A Documented Anthology, 1570–1900*, Glasgow, UK: Crawford Centre for the Arts.

Jones, David (1989), "Scottish Cabinet Maker's Price Books, 1805–1825," *Regional Furniture*, 3: 27–39.

Jones, Owen (1842), *Plans, Elevations, Sections, and Details of the Alhambra, from Drawings Taken on the Spot in 1834 by Jules Goury, and in 1834 and 1837*, vol. 1, London: O. Jones.

Jones, Owen (1856), *The Grammar of Ornament*, London: Day and Son.

Jones, Robin (1997), "Arthur Foley: A Nineteenth-Century Furniture Manufacturer in Salisbury," *Regional Furniture*, 11: 42–9.

Jourdain, Margaret and Ralph Fastnedge (1965), *Regency Furniture*, London: Country Life.

Joy, Edward (1977), *Pictorial Dictionary of 19th Century Furniture Design*, Woodbridge, UK: Antique Collectors Club.

J.W. Mason & Company (1874), *Illustrated Catalogue of Chairs and Furniture*, New York: Mason & Co.

Kaplan, Amy (1992), *The Social Construction of American Realism*, Chicago: University of Chicago Press.

Kasson, John (1990), *Rudeness & Civility*, New York: Hill and Wang.

Kavanagh, Thomas M. (1993), *Enlightenment and the Shadows of Chance: The Novel and the Culture of Gambling in Eighteenth-Century France*, Baltimore: Johns Hopkins University Press.

Keeble, Trevor (2007), "'Everything Whispers of Wealth and Luxury': Observation, Emulation and Display in the Well-to-Do Late-Victorian Home," in Elizabeth Darling and Lesley Whitworth (eds.), *Women and the Making of Built Space in England 1870–1950*, 69–86, Aldershot, UK: Ashgate.

Kelley, Mary (1984), *Private Woman, Public Stage*, New York: Oxford University Press.

Kenny, Peter M., Frances F. Bretter, and Ulrich Leben (1998), *Honoré Lannuier, Cabinetmaker from Paris: The Life and Work of French Ébéniste in Federal New York*, New York: Metropolitan Museum of Art and Harry N. Abrams.

Kenny, Peter, Michael K. Brown, Frances F. Bretter, and Matthew A. Thurlow (2011), *Duncan Phyfe: Master Cabinet Maker in New York*, New York: Metropolitan Museum of Art.

Kerber, Peter Björn (2011), "Perfectibility and Its Foreign Causes: Reading for Self-Improvement in Eighteenth-Century Paris," in Charissa Bremer-David (ed.), *Paris: Life & Luxury in the Eighteenth Century*, 75–90, Los Angeles: J. Paul Getty Museum.

Ketchum, William C., Jr. with the Museum of American Folk Art (1995), *American Cabinetmakers: Marked American Furniture, 1640–1940*, New York: Crown Publishers.

Kiene, Michael (2015), "Antique Polychromy Applied to Modern Art and Hittorff's Saint Vincent de Paul in Paris, the Architectural Showpiece of the Renouveau Catholique," *Vincentian Heritage Journal*, 32 (2): article 5. Available online: http://via.library.depaul.edu/vhj/vol32/iss2/5 (accessed May 23, 2021).

Kinchin, Juliet (1996), "The Gendered Interior: Nineteenth Century Essays on the 'Masculine' and the 'Feminine' Room," in Pat Kirkham (ed.), *The Gendered Object*, 12–29, Manchester, UK: Manchester University Press.

Kinchin, Juliet (2005), "Designer as Critic: E. W. Godwin and the Aesthetic Home," *Journal of Design History*, 18 (1): 21–34.

Kirkham, Pat (1982), "William Morris's Early Furniture," *Journal of William Morris Studies*, 4 (3): 25–8.

Kirkham, Pat (1988), "The London Furniture Trade, 1700–1870," *Furniture History*, 24: i, iii–iv, vi–xii, 1–195, and 197–221.

Kirkham, Pat, Rodney Mace, and Julia Porter (1987), *Furnishing the World. The East London Furniture Trade 1830–1980*, London: Journeyman Press.

Kirkham, Pat and Susan Weber, eds. (2013), *History of Design: Decorative Arts and Material Culture, 1400–2000*, New York: Bard Graduate Center.

Kisluk-Grosheide, Daniëlle, O. Wolfram Koeppe, and William Rieder (2006), *European Furniture in The Metropolitan Museum of Art*, New York: Metropolitan Museum of Art.

Kittredge, Mabel (1911), *Housekeeping Notes*, Boston: Whitcomb & Barrows.

The Knight of Glin and James Peill (2007), *Irish Furniture: Woodwork and Carving in Ireland from the Earliest Times to the Act of Union*, London: Paul Mellon Centre for Studies in British Art.

Kornwolf, James D. (1972), *M. H. Baillie Scott and the Arts and Crafts Movement: Pioneers of Modern Design*, Baltimore: Johns Hopkins University Press.

Kwolek-Folland, Angel (1984), "The Elegant Dugout: Domesticity and Moveable Culture in the United States, 1870–1900," *American Studies*, 25 (2): 21–37.

Langdon, William B. (1843), *A Descriptive Catalogue of the Chinese Collection now exhibiting at the St. George's Place, Hyde Park Corner*, London: Printed for the proprietor.

Langeois, David (2004), "Paire de tabourets provenant du Premier salon des officiers ou Salon bleu du Grand appartement du roi au palais de Tuileries, par Pierre-Gaston Brion," *Galerie Perrin, catalogue 2004*, Paris: Self-published.
Langland, Elizabeth (1995), *Nobody's Angels: Middle-Class Women and Domestic Ideology in Victorian Culture*, Ithaca, NY: Cornell University Press.
Lasc, Anka I. (2013), "Interior Decorating in the Age of Historicism: Popular Advice Manuals and the Pattern Books of Édouard Bajot," *Journal of Design History*, 26: 1–24.
Lasdun, Susan (1981), *Victorians at Home*, London: Weidenfeld and Nicolson.
Leach, William (1984), "Transformations in a Culture of Consumption: Women and Department Stores, 1890–1925," *Journal of American History*, 71 (2): 319–42.
Leavitt, Sarah (2002), *From Catharine Beecher to Martha Stewart*, Chapel Hill: University of North Carolina Press.
Leblanc, Claire, ed. (2004), *Art et Industrie: Les arts décoratfs en Belgique au XIXe siècle*, Brussels: Musées royaux d'Art et d'Histoire.
Ledoux-Lebard, Denise (1965), *Les Ébénistes Parisiens du XIXe siècle (1795–1870): leurs oeuvres et leurs marques*, Paris: F. De Nobele.
Lees-Maffei, Grace (2003), "Introduction—Studying Advice: Historiography, Methodology, Commentary, Bibliography," *Journal of Design History*, 16 (1): 1–14.
Leon, Derrick (1949), *Ruskin: The Great Victorian*, London: Routledge & K. Paul.
Les arts du bois, des tissus et du papier (1883), Paris: A. Quantin, Imprimeur-Editeur.
Leslie, Eliza (1864), *Miss Leslie's Behaviour Book*, Philadelphia: T.B. Peterson and Bros.
Lessard, Michel (1999), *Meubles anciens du quebec; au carrefour de trois cultures*, Montreal: Editions de l'Homme.
Levy, Martin (1998), *Napoleon in Exile: The Houses and Furniture Supplied by the British Government for the Emperor and His Entourage on St. Helena*, Leeds, UK: Furniture History Society.
Levy, Martin (2009–10), "Review: Gillows of Lancaster and London, 1730–1840: Cabinetmakers and International Merchants: A Furniture and Business History by Susan E. Stuart," *Studies in the Decorative Arts*, 17 (1): 208–13.
Lewis, Arnold, James Turner, and Steven McQuillin (1987), *The Opulent Interiors of the Gilded Age: All 203 Photographs from "Artistic Houses,"* New York: Dover Publications.
L.H.S. (1893), "Furniture—Different Styles, Where to Purchase and How to Use," *The Bazaar, The Exchange and Mart*, 68 (June 26): 1143–4.
Livesey, Ruth (2007), "Women rent collectors and the rewriting of space, class and gender in East London, 1870–1900," in Elizabeth Darling and Lesley Whitworth (eds.), *Women and the Making of Built Space in England 1870–1950*, 87–107, Aldershot, UK: Ashgate.
Loetscher, Michel (2005), *Spindler, un siècle d'art en Alsace*, Strasbourg: Nuée Bleue.
Logan, Thad (2001), *The Victorian Parlour: A Cultural Study*, Cambridge: Cambridge University Press.
Lomax, James (1997), "Buying Antiques in Early Victorian Leeds: The 1843 Exhibition," *Furniture History*, 33: 275–85.
"London" (1888), *The American Architect and Building News*, 24 (673) (November 17): 231.
London Cabinet-Makers' Union Book of Prices (1811), London: Printed by Ballantine & Byworth, for the committee.
Long, Helen (2002), *Victorian Houses and Their Details: The Role of Publications in Their Building and Decoration*, London: Architectural Press.

Lorimer, Robert (1897), *Notes on the Work and Influence of William Morris*, unpublished lecture.

Loudon, John Claudius ([1836] 1883), *Encyclopedia of Cottage, Farm and Villa Architecture and Furniture*, 1st edn., London: Published for the author.

Lubbock, Jules (1978), "Victorian Revival," *Architectural Review*, 163: 161–7.

Lucie-Smith, Edward (1988), *Furniture A Concise History*, London: Thames and Hudson.

Lyons, Harry (2004), *Christopher Dresser*, Woodbridge, UK: Antique Collectors Club.

MacDonald, Sally (1987), "Gothic Forms Applied to Furniture: The Early Work of Bruce James Talbert," *Furniture History*, 23: 39–66.

MacDonald, Stuart ([1970] 2004), *The History and Philosophy of Art Education*, repr., Cambridge: Lutterworth Press.

Mackie, James (1867), "Wood-carving," in *Reports of Artisans selected by a committee appointed by the Society of Arts to visit the Paris Universal Exhibition of 1867*, 84–101, London: Published for the Society for the Encouragement of Arts, Manufactures and Commerce by Bell and Daldy.

Madigan, Mary Jean Smith (1975), "The Influence on Charles Eastlake on American Furniture Manufacture, 1870–90," *Winterthur Portfolio*, 10: 1–22.

Mansel, Philip (1988), *The Court of France, 1780–1830*, Cambridge: Cambridge University Press.

Mansel, Philip (2015), *The Eagle in Splendour: Inside the Court of Napoleon*, new edn., London: I.B. Taurus.

Maple & Co Furniture Illutrated Catalogue (1882, 1889), London.

Margolin, Victor (2014), *World History of Design*, London: Bloomsbury.

Marin, William A. (1931), "Sod Houses and Prairie Schooners," *Minnesota History Magazine*, (12): 138.

Marx, Karl (1864), "Address and the Provisional Rules of the International Working Men's Association," London.

Marx, Karl (1864), *Pamphlet in Inaugural Address and Provisional Rules of the International Working Men's Association, along with the "General Rules"*, London. Online Version: Marx & Engels Internet Archive (marxists.org) 2000.

Matthews-Jones, Lucinda (2009), "Centres of Brightness: The Spiritual Imagination of Toynbee Hall and Oxford House, 1880–1914," Ph.D. diss., University of Manchester.

Mayes, J.L. (1960), *The History of Chair Making in High Wycombe*, London: Routledge & Kegan Paul.

Mayer, Roberta A. (1996), "The Aesthetics of Lockwood de Forest: India, Craft, and Preservation," *Winterthur Portfolio*, 31 (1): 1–22.

Mayhew, Henry (1861), *London Labour and the London Poor: a cyclopaedia of the condition and earnings of those that will work, those that cannot work, and those that will not work*, vol. 2, London: Griffin, Bohn and Company.

McClelland, Nancy V. (1939), *Duncan Phyfe and the English Regency*, New York: William R. Scott.

McKean, John and Colin Baxter (2012), *Charles Rennie Mackintosh: Architect, Artist, Icon*, Broxburn, Scotland: Lomond Books.

The Mechanics' Magazine: Museum, Register, Journal, and Gazette (1831), XV, London, M. Salmon.

Mencken, August (1957), *The Railroad Passenger Car*, Baltimore: Johns Hopkins University Press.

Merklen, Colette (1974), *L'oeuvre de Rupert Carabin 1862–1932*, Paris: Galerie du Luxembourg.

Merrill, Linda (1998), *The Peacock Room: A Cultural Biography*, New Haven, CT: Yale University Press.

Meyer, Franz Sales (1888), *Handbook of Ornament*, Karlsruhe.

Meyer, Jonathan (2006), *Great Exhibitions: London–New York–Paris–Philadelphia, 1851–1900*, Woodbridge, UK: Antique Collectors' Club.

Millar, Luke (1996), "The Notebook of John Davies, Cabinet Maker, Carmarthen, 1844–55," *Regional Furniture*, 10: 66–99.

Mirault, Claude-François (1834), *Rapport concernant la peinture en émail sur lave de volvic émaillée, fait à la Société libre des beaux-arts*, Paris: J. Gratiot.

Mircoulis, Laura (1998), "Charles Hindley & Sons, London House Furnishers of the Nineteenth Century: A Paradigm of the Middle-Range Market," *West 86th: A Journal of Decorative Arts, Design History, and Material Culture*, 5 (2): 69–96.

Mircoulis, Laura (2001), "The Furniture Drawings of Charles Hindley & Sons, 134 Oxford Street, London," *Furniture History*, 37: 67–90.

Mircoulis, Laura (2005), "Gillow and Company's Furniture for a Liverpool Maecenas: John Grant Morris of Allerton Priory," *Furniture History*, 41: 189–216.

Morley, John (1993), *Regency Design 1790–1840: Gardens, Buildings, Interiors, Furniture*, New York: Harry N. Abrams.

Morley, John (1999), *The History of Furniture*, Boston: Bullfinch Press.

Morris, William ([1882] 1998), "'The Lesser Arts of Life': A Lecture delivered in support of the Society for the Protection of Ancient Buildings," in *Lectures on Art and Industry* from *The Collected Works of William Morris*, vol. 22, 235–69, London: Longmans Green and Company.

Morris, William (2012), *The Collected Works of William Morris: With Introductions by His Daughter May Morris*, Cambridge: Cambridge University Press.

Morteleque, M. (1830), "On Enamel Paintings executed upon Stone," *Gill's Technological & Microscopic Repository; or Discoveries and Improvements in the Useful Arts*, 6: 184–6.

Mourey, Gabriel (1896), "Studio–Talk," *The Studio*, 9 (45) (December): 211–12.

Mourey, Gabriel (1897a), "Decorative Art in the Salon du Champ de Mars," *The Studio*, 11 (51) (June): 36–47.

Mourey, Gabriel (1897b), "Studio–Talk," *The Studio*, 10 (47) (February): 55–6.

Mourey, Gabriel (1898), "Decorative Art in Paris: The Exhibition of 'The Six'," *The Studio*, 13 (60) (March): 81–91.

Moyr Smith, John (1887), *Ornamental Interiors: Ancient and Modern*, London: Crosby Lockwood and Co.

"Mr Pugin on Christian Art" (1845), *The Builder*, 3: 367.

Musée national du Château de Chambord (2011), "Trônes d'Henri V," in Jacques Charles-Gaffiot (ed.), *Trônes en majesté: l'autorité et son symbole*, Paris: Éditions Château de Versailles.

Musgrave, Clifford (1961), *Regency Furniture 1800–30*, London: Faber & Faber.

Mussey, Robert D., Jr. (2002), *The Furniture Masterworks of John & Thomas Seymour*, Salem, MA: Peabody Essex Museum.

Muthesius, Stefan (1988), "Why Do We Buy Old Furniture? Aspects of the Authentic Antique in Britain 1870–1910," *Art History*, 11 (2): 231–54.

Muthesius, Stefan (1992), "We Do Not Understand What is Meant by a 'Company' Designing": Design versus Commerce in Late Nineteenth-Century English Furnishing," *Journal of Design History*, 5 (2): 113–19.

Muthesius, Stefan (2009), *The Poetic Home, Designing the 19th-Century Domestic Interior*, London: Thames and Hudson.

Nenadic, Stana (1994), "Middle-Rank Consumers and Domestic Culture in Edinburgh and Glasgow 1720–1840," *Past and Present*, 145 (1): 122–56.

Nesbit, Molly and Françoise Reynaud (1992), *Eugène Atget, intérieurs parisiens: un album du musée Carnavalet*, Paris: Musée de Carnavalet.

Newton, Charles (2005), "Dresser and Owen Jones," *Journal of the Decorative Arts Society 1850–the Present*, 25: 30–41.

Nicholson, Shirley (1998), *A Victorian Household: Based on the Diaries of Marion Sambourne*, Stroud, UK: Sutton Publishing.

Northup, Solomon (1853), *Twelve Years a* Slave, London: Sampson Low, Son & Company.

Nouvel-Kammerer, Odile (2007), *L'Aigle et papillon, symbols des pouvoirs sous Napoléon 1800–1815* [Symbols of Power: Napoleon and the Art of the Empire Style 1800–1815], Paris: Les Arts décoratifs; New York: American Federation of Arts/Abrams New York.

Oates, Phyllis Bennett (1998), *The Story of Western Furniture*, Chicago: New Amsterdam Books.

O'Donnell, Anne (2011), *C.F.A. Voysey: Architect Designer Individualist*, Warwick: Pomegranate Europe.

Official Descriptive and Illustrated Catalogue of the Great Exhibition of the Works of Industry of All Nations, 1851 (1851), vol. 2, London: Spicer Brothers.

Oliver, Andrew (2014), *American Travelers on the Nile Early U.S. Visitors to Egypt, 1774–1839*, Cairo: American University in Cairo Press.

Oliver, Andrew (2015), *American Travelers on the Nile: Early U.S. Visitors to Egypt, 1774–1839*, Oxford: Oxford University Press.

Oliver, J.L. (1966), *Development and Structure of the Furniture Industry*, Oxford: Pergamon Press.

Orrinsmith, Mrs. Lucy (1878), *The Drawing Room*, London: Macmillan.

Ostergard, Derek, ed. (1987), *Bentwood and Metal Furniture, 1850–1946*, Seattle: University of Washington Press.

Ottillinger, Eva B. (1989), "August Kitschelt's Metal Furniture Factory and Viennese Metal Furniture in the Nineteenth Century," *Furniture History*, 25: 235–49.

Ottillinger, Eva B., Johanna Sophia, and Renata Stein (1994), "Imperial Patronage and Self-Promotion in Mid-Nineteenth-Century Vienna: A Table by Anton Müller in the Hofmobiliendepot," *Studies in the Decorative Arts*, 1/2: 87–97.

Paine, Albert Bigelow (1912), *Mark Twain: A Biography; the Personal and Literary Life of Samuel Langhorne Clemens*, New York: Harper.

Pardailhé-Galabrun, Annik (1988), *La naissance de l'intime*, Paris: Presses universitaires de France.

"Paris" (1889), *The American Architect and Building News*, 26 (721) (October 19): 181–2.

Parker, Rozsika (1984), *The Subversive Stitch: Embroidery and the Making of the Feminine*, London: Women's Press.

Parry, Linda, ed. (1996), *William Morris*, London: Victoria and Albert Museum.

Pavoni, Rosanna (1997), *Reviving the Renaissance: The Use and Abuse of the Past in Nineteenth-Century Italian Art and Decoration*, Cambridge: Cambridge University Press.

Payne, Christiana (1998), "Rural Virtues for Urban Consumption: Cottage Scenes in Early Victorian Painting," *Journal of Victorian Culture*, 31: 45–68.

Payne, Christopher (1981), *Nineteenth Century European Furniture*, Woodbridge, UK: Antique Collectors' Club.

Payne, Christopher (2003), *François Linke 1855–1946 The Belle Epoque of French Furniture*, Woodbridge, UK: Antique Collectors' Club.

Payne, Christopher (2013), *European Furniture of the Nineteenth Century*, Woodbridge, UK: Antique Collectors' Club.

Percier, Charles and Pierre Leonard Fontaine (1798), *Palais, Maisons, et autres édifices modernes dessinés à Rome*, Paris: Baudouin.

Percier, Charles and Pierre Leonard Fontaine (1801, 1812), *Recueil de Decorations Intérieures*, Paris: Pierre Didot l'ainé.

Pergam, Elizabeth (2014), "Selling Pictures: The Illustrated Auction Catalogue," *Journal of Art Historiography*, 11: 1–25.

Pevsner, Nikolaus (1951a), "Art Furniture of the Eighteen Seventies," *Architectural Review*, 111 (661): 43–50.

Pevsner, Nikolaus (1951b), *High Victorian Design: A Study of the Exhibits of 1851*, London: Architectural Press.

Phillips Edinburgh (1998), *Fine Furniture Sale*, March 27, lot 232.

Phillips Edinburgh (1999), *Fine Furniture Sale*, March 26, lots 158–62.

Piggott, Jan (2004), *Palace of the People: The Crystal Palace at Sydenham 1854–1936*, London: C. Hurst and Co.; Madison: University of Wisconsin Press.

Pincemaille, Christophe (2002), *L'imperatrice Eugénie*, Paris: Payot.

Pollen, John Hungerford (1874), *Ancient & Modern Furniture and Woodwork in the South Kensington Museum*, London: Chapman and Hall.

Ponsonby, Margaret (2003), "Ideals, Reality and Meaning: Homemaking in England in the First Half of the Nineteenth Century," *Journal of Design History*, 16 (3): 210–14.

Ponsonby, Margaret (2007), *Stories from Home: English Domestic Interiors, 1750–1850*, Farnham, UK: Ashgate.

"Popular Miscellany" (1884), *Popular Science Monthly*, 25 (October): 855–63.

Porter, Val (1992), *Life behind the Cottage Door*, Stanstead, UK: Whittet Books.

Praz, Mario (1982), *An Illustrated History of Interior Decoration: From Pompeii to Art Nouveau*, London: Thames & Hudson.

Price, Stephen P. (2000), "Mechanics' Institutes of the City of New-York and the conception of Class Authority in Early Modern America, 1830–1860," *New York History*, 81 (3): 269–99.

Pugin, Augustus Charles (1821), *Specimens of Gothic architecture, accompanied by historical and descriptive accounts*, London: M. A. Nattali; Plates published by J. Taylor.

Pugin, Augustus Welby Northmore (1835), *Gothic Furniture in the Style of the Fifteenth Century*, London: Ackerman & Co.

Pugin, Augustus Welby Northmore (1836), *Contrasts: or, A Parallel between the Noble Edifices of the Fourteenth and Fifteenth Centuries, and Corresponding Buildings of the Present Day; shewing the Present Decay of Taste*, London: Printed for the author and published by him.

Pugin, Augustus Welby Northmore (1841), *The True Principles of Pointed or Christian Architecture*, London, J. Weale.

Pugin, Augustus Welby Northmore (2001), *The Collected Letters of A.W.N. Pugin*, edited by Margaret Belcher, Oxford: Oxford University Press.

Pullman Company (1893), *The Story of Pullman*.

Radke, Andrea G. (2004), "Refining Rural Spaces Women and Vernacular Gentility in the Great Plains, 1880–1920," *Great Plains Quarterly*, 24 (4): 227–48.

Raizman, David (2003), *History of Modern Design*, London: Laurence King.

Raizman, David (2013), "Giuseppe Ferrari's Carved Cabinet for the 1876 Centennial Exhibition: Presentation Furniture in the Cultural Context of World's Fairs," *West 86th*, 20 (1): 62–91.

Ramond, Pierre (2000), *Masterpieces of Marquetry: From the Régence to the Present Day*, Los Angeles: J. Paul Getty Museum.

Rapport sur les produits de l'industrie française (1824), Paris: Imprimerie royale.

Raynor, Samuel (1853), *The Parlor*, New York: Samuel Raynor.

Reagin, Nancy (2007), *Sweeping the German Nation: Domesticity and National Identity in Germany, 1870–1945*, Cambridge: Cambridge University Press.

Redgrave, Richard (1852), "Supplementary Report on Design," in *Reports by the juries on the subjects in the thirty classes into which the exhibition was divided: Exhibition of the Works of Industry of All Nations, 1851*, 708–49, London: Clowes.

Regional Furniture (1998), vol. 12.

Reid, Huw (1986), *The Furniture Makers: A History of Trade Unionism in the Furniture Trade 1868–1972*, Oxford: Malthouse Press.

Reports by the Juries on the Subjects in the Thirty Classes into Which the Exhibition was Divided (1852), London: Spicer Brothers.

Repton, Humphry (1816), *Fragments on the Theory and Practice of Landscape Gardening, including some remarks on Grecian and Gothic Architecture*, London: Printed by T. Bensley for J. Taylor.

Richards, Thomas (1990), *The Commodity Culture of Victorian England: Advertising and Spectacle, 1851–1914*, Stanford, CA: Stanford University Press.

Richardson, Margaret (1983), *Architects of the Arts and Crafts Movement*, London: Trefoil Publications.

Richter, Amy (2005), *Home on the Rails: Women, the Railroad, and the Rise of Public Domesticity*, Chapel Hill: University of North Carolina Press.

Richter, Amy (2015), *At Home in Nineteenth-Century America*, New York: New York University Press.

Riddell, Richard (2004), "Tatham, Charles Heathcote (1772–1842)," *Oxford Dictionary of National Biography*, 55, Oxford: Oxford University Press.

Roberts, Hugh (1989), "Royal Thrones 1760–1840," *Furniture History*, 25: 61–85.

Roberts, Hugh (2001), *For the King's Pleasure: The Furnishing and Decoration of George IV's Apartments at Windsor Castle*, London: The Royal Collection.

Robinson, John Charles, ed. (1881), *Catalogue of the Special Loan Exhibition of Spanish and Portuguese Ornamental Art, South Kensington Museum, 1881*, London: Chapman & Hall.

Robinson, John Martin (1979), *The Wyatts: An Architectural Dynasty*, Oxford: Oxford University Press.

Roche, Daniel (1997), *Histoire des choses banales: Naissance de la consommation dans les sociétés traditionnelles, XVII–XIXe siecle*, Paris: Fayard.

"A Roman Studio" (1884), *Decorator and Furnisher*, (5): 87.

Romans, Mervyn (2005), *Histories of Art and Design Education: Collected Essays*, Chicago: University of Chicago Press.

Romans, Mervyn (2007), "An Analysis of the Political Complexion of the 1835/6 Select Committee on Arts and Manufactures," *International Journal of Art and Design Education*, 26 (2): 215–24.

Ronfort, Jean Nérée, ed. (2009), *André Charles Boulle (1642–1732), Un nouveau style pour l'Europe*, Somogy: Museum für Angewandte Kunst Francfort.
Roqueplain Nestor (1869), "Le bric à brac," in *La vie parisienne. Regain*, ch. 20, Paris: Michel Lévy.
Roscoe, Barley (2014), "Stoneywell and the Gimsons: Furniture and Family History," *Furniture History*, 50: 351–65.
Roubo, André-Jacob (1772), *L'art du menuisier en meubles*, Paris: Académie Royale des Sciences.
Royal Commission on the Housing of the Working Classes (1885), London: Eyre and Spottiswoode.
Ruskin, John (1900), *Ruskin's Works: The Seven Lamps of Architecture; Lectures on Architecture and Painting; The Study of Architecture*, edited by Dana Estes, Boston: Dana Estes & Co.
Ruskin, John (1964), *The Genius of John Ruskin: Selections from His Writings*, edited by John D. Rosenberg, Charlottesville: University of Virginia Press.
Ruskin, John and John Atkinson Hobson (1899), *Ruskin's Works*, Boston: D Estes.
Ryan, Mary (1981), *Cradle of the Middle Class*, Cambridge: Cambridge University Press.
Rydell, Robert W., John E. Findling, and Kimberly D. Pelle (2000), *Fair America: World's Fairs in the United States*, Washington, DC: Smithsonian Institution Press.
Said, Edward (1993), *Culture and Imperialism*, London: Chatto & Windus.
Samoyault, Jean-Pierre (1987), "L'ameublement des salles du trône dans les palais impériaux sous Napoléon Ier," *Bulletin de la Société d'histoire de l'art français*: 185–206.
Samoyault, Jean-Pierre (2009), *Mobilier français, Consulat et Empire*, Paris: Editions Gourcuff Gradenigo.
Samoyault, Jean-Pierre (2012), *Mobilier français, Consulat et Empire*, Montreuil: Gourcuff Gradenigo.
Samoyault-Verlet, Colombe (1978), "Furnishings," in *The Second Empire: Art in France under Napoleon III*, 74–6, Philadelphia: Philadelphia Museum of Art.
Samoyault-Verlet, Colombe (1991), "L'ameublement des châteaux Royaux à l'époque de la Restauration" and "Louis Philippe de 1830 à 1840," in *Un âge d'or des arts décoratifs: 1814–1848*, 42–9, Paris: Réunion des musées nationaux.
Sancho, J. (2011), "Trône du roi Charles III d'Espagne," in Jacques Charles-Gaffiot (ed.), *Trônes en Majesté: L'Autorité et son symbole*, 282–3, Paris: éditions du Cerf.
Sander, Jochen (2004), "Der 'Leere Thron' im höfischen Zeremoniell des 18. Jahrhunderts," in Margit Kern, Thomas Kirchner, and Hubertus Kohle (eds.), *Geschichte und Ästhetik, Festschrift für Werner Busch zum 60. Geburstag*, 121–38, Munich: Deutscher Kunstverlag.
Sargentson, Carolyn (1997), *Merchants and Luxury Markets: The Marchands Merciers of 18th Century Paris*, London: V&A Publications.
Savage, Peter (1980), *Lorimer and the Edinburgh Craft Designers*, Edinburgh: Harris.
Schoemaker, Theo and Kiers Judikje (1995), *The Age of Ugliness: Showpieces of Dutch Interior Design 1835–1895*, Zwolle: Waanders.
Schoeser, Mary and Christine Boydell, eds. (2002), *Disentangling Textiles: Techniques for the Study of Designed Objects*, London: Middlesex University Press.
Scobey, David (2002), *Empire City: The Making and Meaning of the New York City Landscape*, Philadelphia: Temple University Press.
Scott, Katie (2004), "The Waddesdon Manor Trade Cards: More Than One History," *Journal of Design History*, 17 (1): 91–104.

Scott, Katie (2005), "Image-Object-Space," *Art History*, 28 (2): 137–50.

Seconde exposition publique des produits de l'industrie Française (1801), Paris: l'impremerie de la République.

Sedgwick, Catharine (1837), *The Poor Rich Man, and The Rich Poor Man*, New York: Harper & Brothers.

Semper, Gottfried (1852), *Wissenschaft, Industrie und Kunst: Vorschlage zur Anregung nationalen Kunstgefuhles, bei dem Schlusse der Londoner Industrie-Ausstellung*, Braunschweig: F. Vieweg und Sohn.

Sharpe, Pamela (1995), "Continuity and Change: Women's History and Economic History in Britain," *Economic History Review*, n.s., 48 (2) (May): 353–69.

Shen, Lindsay Macbeth (1992), *A Comment on Tradition: Robert S. Lorimer's Furniture Design*, Red Peroba Publishing.

Sheraton, Thomas (1793–4), *The Cabinet-Maker and Upholsterer's Drawing-Book, in Three Parts*, London: Thomas Bensley.

Sheraton, Thomas (1802), *The Cabinet-Maker and Upholsterers' Drawing Book in Four Parts*, 3rd rev. edn, London: T. Bensley.

Sheraton, Thomas (1803), *The Cabinet Dictionary, Containing an Explanation of all the Terms Used in the Cabinet, Chair and Upholstery Branches*, London: W. Smith.

Shimbo, Akiko (2015), *Furniture-Makers and Consumers in England, 1754–1851: Design as Interaction*, Farnham, UK: Ashgate.

Sidgwick, Mrs. A. (1912), *Home Life in Germany*, Chautauqua, NY: Chautauqua Press.

Simmonds, P.L. (1887), "National & International Exhibitions," *The Jubilee Chronicle* (London): 62–7.

Simond, Louis (1815), *Journal of a Tour and Residence in Great Britain 1810–11*, Published for the author.

"Sketches of Furniture from the Furniture Exhibition" (1883), *Scientific American Supplement*, (391) (June 30): 6236.

Skull, Edwin (1860), *Edwin Skull of High Wycombe Broadsheet*, High Wycombe: Published for the author.

Sloboda, Stacey (2010), "Fashioning Bluestocking Conversation: Elizabeth Montagu's Chinese Room," in Denise Amy Baxter and Meredith Martin (eds.), *Architectural Space in Eighteenth-Century Europe: Constructing Identities and Interiors*, 129–48, Burlington, VT: Ashgate.

Smart Martin, Ann (2011), *Buying into the World of Goods: Early Consumers in Backcountry Virginia*, Baltimore: Johns Hopkins University Press.

Smeins, Linda (1999), *Building an American Identity: Pattern Book Homes and Communities, 1870–1900*, Walnut Creek, CA: Altamira Press.

Smith, Adolphe and John Thomson (1877), *Street Life in London*, London: Sampson Low, Marston, Searle and Rivington.

Smith, Bonnie (1981), *Ladies of the Leisure Class*, Princeton, NJ: Princeton University Press.

Smith, Gaye (1992), *Trade Catalogues: A Hundred Years 1850–1949*, Manchester, UK: Manchester Metropolitan University Library.

Smith, George (1826), *The Cabinet-Maker and Upholsterer's Guide: Being a Complete Drawing Book; in which will be comprised Treatises on Geometry and Perspective, as applicable to the above branches of mechanics*, London: Jones and Company.

Smith, Walter (1876), *The Masterpieces of the Centennial International Exhibition, Industrial Art*, vol. 2, *Industrial Art*, Philadelphia: Gebbie & Barrie.

Snodin, Michael (1984), *Rococo: Art and Design in Hogarth's England*, London: Trefoil Books.

Sotheby's London (2001), June 13, *Important English Furniture*.
Sparke, Penny (2013), *An Introduction to Design and Culture: 1900 to the Present*, London: Routledge.
Stabler, John (1991), "British Newspaper Advertisements as a Source of Furniture History," *Regional Furniture*, 5: 93–102.
Stamp, Gavin (2002), *An Architect of Promise: George Gilbert Scott Junior (1839–1897) and the Late Gothic Revival*, Spalding, UK: Shaun Tyas.
Steffens, Martin (2003), *Schinkel*, Berlin: Taschen.
Steinbach, Susan (2012), *Understanding the Victorians: Politics, Culture and Society in Nineteenth-Century Britain*, London: Routledge.
Steinitz, Rebecca (2011), *Time Space and Gender in the Nineteenth Century British Diary*, Basingstoke, UK: Palgrave Macmillan.
Stevenson, Louise ([1991] 2001), *The Victorian Homefront: American Thought and Culture, 1860–1880*, Ithaca, NY: Cornell University Press.
Stobart, Jon (2008), "Selling (Through) Politeness," *Cultural and Social History*, 5 (3): 309–28.
Stowe, Harriet Beecher ([1852] 1962), *Uncle Tom's Cabin*, Cambridge, MA: Belknap Press.
Strachey, Lytton ([1918] 2009), *Eminent Victorians*, Oxford: Oxford World Classics.
Strong, Roy, John Harris and Marcus Binney (1974), *The Destruction of the English Country House 1875–1975*, London: Thames & Hudson.
Stroud, Dorothy (1966), *Henry Holland: His Life and Architecture*, London: Country Life.
Stuart, Susan E. (1996), "Three Generations of Gothic Chairs by Gillows," *Furniture History*, 32: 33–45.
Stuart, Susan E. (2008), *Gillows of Lancaster and London 1730–1840: Cabinet-Makers and International Merchants. A Furniture and Business History*, Woodbridge, UK: Antique Collectors, Club.
"Studio–Talk" (1898), *The Studio*, 13 (60) (March): 118–20.
"Studio–Talk" (1899a), *The Studio*, 15 (70) (January): 286–7.
"Studio–Talk" (1899b), *The Studio*, 16 (72) (March): 136–9.
Symonds, R.W. and B.B. Whineray (1965), *Victorian Furniture*, London: Country Life.
Tatham, Charles Heathcote (1803, 1810, and 1836), *Etchings, Representing the Best Examples of Ancient Ornamental Architecture; Drawn from the Originals in Rome and Other Parts of Italy*, London: John Gardiner.
Tatham, Charles Heathcote (1811), *The Gallery at Brocklesby in Lincolnshire: the seat of the Right Honourable Lord Yarborough and The Gallery at Castle Howard in Yorkshire: the seat of the Earl of Carlisle*, London, T. Gardiner; Longman, Hurst, Rees, Orme, and Brown.
Teukolsky, Rachel (2009), *The Literate Eye: Victorian Art Writing and Modernist Aesthetics*, Oxford: Oxford University Press.
Thackeray, William Makepeace (1862), *The Adventures of Philip on his Way Through the World; Showing Who Robbed Him, Who Helped Him, and Who Passed Him By*, New York: Harper & Brothers.
The Royal Borough of Kensington and Chelsea (n.d.), "18 Stafford Terrace: Marion Sambourne's Diaries." Available online: https://www.rbkc.gov.uk/subsites/museums/18staffordterrace/archives/thesambournefamilydiaries-1/marionsambournediaries.aspx (accessed May 15, 2021).
Thicknesse, Philip (1777), *A Year's Journey Through France and Part of Spain*, London: R. Cruttwell.

Thomas, George E. (2002), "'The Happy Employment of Means to Ends': Frank Furness's Library of the University of Pennsylvania and the Industrial Culture of Philadelphia," *Pennsylvania Magazine of History and Biography*, 126 (2): 249–72.

Thornton, Peter (1984), *Authentic Décor: The Domestic Interior 1620–1920*, London: Weidenfeld & Nicolson.

Tiersten, Lisa (2001), *Marianne in the Market: Envisioning Consumer Society in Fin-de-Siècle France*, Berkeley: University of California Press.

Tinniswood, Adrian (1995), *Life in the English Country Cottage*, London: Weidenfeld Nicolson Illustrated.

Tompkins, Jane (1986), *Sensational Designs*, New York: Oxford University Press.

Tracy Charles (2001), *Continental Church Furniture in England: A Traffic in Piety*, Woodbridge, UK: Antique Collectors' Club.

Tristram, Philippa (1989), *Living Space in Fact and Fiction*, London: Routledge.

Tully, John (2009), "A Victorian Ecological Disaster: Imperialism, the Telegraph and Gutta-Percha," *Journal of World History*, 20 (4): 559–79.

Verlet, Pierre (1966), *La maison du XVIIIe siècle en France. Société, décoration, mobilier*, Paris: Editions Baschet et Cie. Plaisir de France.

Verlet, Pierre (1972), *Styles, meubles, décors, du Moyen Age à nos jours*, Paris: Larousse.

Verlet, Pierre (1982), *Les meubles français du XVIIIe siècle*, 2nd edn., Paris: Presses universitaires de France.

Victoria and Albert Museum (1998a), "Adjustable-Back Chair," September 29. Available online: http://collections.vam.ac.uk/item/O9236/morris-adjustable-back-chair-bird-adjustable-back-chair-webb-philip/ (accessed May 15, 2021).

Victoria and Albert Museum (1998b), "Armoire," July 2. Available online: http://collections.vam.ac.uk/item/O8162/armoire-pugin-augustus-welby/ (accessed May 15, 2021).

Victoria and Albert Museum (1998c), "Table," July 6. Available online: http://collections.vam.ac.uk/item/O8202/table-barberi-michelangelo-chevalier/ (accessed May 15, 2021).

Victoria and Albert Museum (2001), "The Yatman Cabinet," July 19. Available online: http://collections.vam.ac.uk/item/O61225/the-yatman-cabinet-cabinet-burges-william/ (accessed May 15, 2021).

Victorian and Edwardian Decorative Arts (1952), London: Victoria and Albert Museum [exhibition catalog].

Vincent, Clare (1967), "John Henry Belter's Patent Parlour Furniture," *Furniture History*, 3: 92–9.

Viollet-le-Duc, Eugène-Emmanuel (1863), *Entretiens sur l'architecture*, Paris: Q. Morel et cie.

Viollet-le-Duc, Eugène-Emmanuel (1877), *Lectures on Architecture*, London: Sampson Low, Marston, Searle and Rivington.

Wainwright, Clive (1976), "AWN Pugin's Early Furniture," *Connoisseur*, 191 (767): 3–11.

Wainwright, Clive (1986), "Tell Me What You Like and I'll Tell You What You Are," in Adrian J. Tilbrook (ed.), *Truth, Beauty and Design: Victorian, Edwardian and Later Decorative Art*, 7–14, London: Tilbrook and Fischer Fine Art.

Wainwright, Clive (1988), *George Bullock: Cabinet-Maker*, London: John Murray.

Wainwright, Clive (1989), *The Romantic Interior: The British Collector at Home, 1750–1850*, New Haven, CT: Studies in British Art, Yale University Press.

Wainwright, Clive (1994), "Furniture," in Paul Atterbury and Clive Wainwright (eds.), *Pugin: A Gothic Passion*, 127–42, London: V&A Publications.

Wainwright, Clive and Charlotte Gere (2002a), "The Making of the South Kensington Museum I: The Government Schools of Design and Founding Collection, 1837–51," *Journal of the History of Collections*, 4 (1): 3–23.
Wainwright, Clive and Charlotte Gere (2002b), "The Making of the South Kensington Museum II: Collecting Modern Manufactures: 1851 and the Great Exhibition," *Journal of the History of Collections*, 4 (1): 25–43.
Wainwright, Clive and Charlotte Gere (2002c), "The Making of the South Kensington Museum III: Collecting Abroad," *Journal of the History of Collections*, 4 (1): 45–61.
Walker, John A. (1989), *Design History and the History of Design*, London: Pluto Press.
Walker, Mack (1964), *Germany and the Emigration, 1816–1885*, Cambridge, MA: Harvard University Press.
Ward-Jackson, Peter (1984), *English Furniture Designs of the Eighteenth Century*, London: Victoria and Albert Museum.
Waring, John Burley (1863), *Masterpieces of Industrial Art and Sculpture at the International Exhibition, 1862, in Three Volumes*, London: Day and Son.
Watkin, David (1968), *Thomas Hope 1769–1831 and the Neo-classical Ideal*, London: John Murray.
Watkin, David (1980), *The Rise of Architectural History*, London: Architectural Press.
Watkin, David (2000), *Sir John Soane: The Royal Academy Lectures*, Cambridge: Cambridge University Press.
Watkin, David (2008), *Thomas Hope: Regency Designer*, New Haven, CT: Yale University Press.
Watkin, David and Philip Hewat-Jaboor, eds. (2008), *Thomas Hope: Regency Designer*, New Haven, CT: Published for the Bard Graduate Center for Studies in the Decorative Arts, New York by Yale University Press.
Waxman, Lorraine (1960), "Arrival of Charles-Honore Lannuier in America," *Winterthur* Newsletter, June 27: 7.
Weber Soros, Susan (1999a), "Rediscovering H.W. Batley (1846–1932), British Aesthetic Movement Artist and Designer," *Studies in the Decorative Arts*, 6 (2): 2–41.
Weber Soros, Susan (1999b), *The Secular Furniture of E.W. Godwin*, New Haven, CT: Yale University Press.
Weber Soros, Susan, ed. (1999c), *E.W. Godwin: Aesthetic Movement Architect and Designer*, New Haven, CT: Published for the Bard Graduate Center for Studies in the Decorative Arts, New York by Yale University Press.
Weber Soros, Susan and Catherine Arbuthnott (2003), *Thomas Jeckyll: Architect and Designer, 1827–1881*, New Haven, CT: Published for the Bard Graduate Center for Studies in the Decorative Arts, Design, and Culture, New York, by Yale University Press.
Webster, T. and Mrs. W. Parkes (1844), *An Encyclopaedia of Domestic Economy*, London: Longman, Brown, Green, and Longmans.
Wedgwood, Alexandra (1990), "JG Crace and AWN Pugin," in Megan Aldrich (ed.), *The Craces: Royal Decorators 1768–1899*, 137–45, London: John Murray.
Weil, Martin Eli (1979), "A Cabinetmaker's Price Book," *Winterthur Portfolio* 13: 175–92.
Westgarth, Mark (2005), "The Emergence of the Antique Curiosity Dealer, 1815–*c*.1850, the Commodification of the Historical Object," Ph.D. thesis, University of Southampton, UK.

Westgarth, Mark (2009), *A Biographical Dictionary of Nineteenth Century Antique and Curiosity Dealers*, Glasgow, UK: Regional Furniture Society.
Wharton, Edith and Ogden Codman (1897), *The Decoration of Houses*, New York: Charles Scriber's Sons.
Wheatley, Henry B. (1884), "Decorative Art in London," *Decorator and Furnisher*, 3 (4) (January): 139.
Whitaker, Henry (1847), *The Practical Cabinet-Maker and Upholsterer's Treasury of Designs*, London: Peter Jackson, Late Fisher, Son, & Co.
Whiteway, Michael (2004), *Shock of the Old: Christopher Dresser's Design Revolution*, London: V&A Publications.
Wilson, Michael (1977), *The English Country House and Its Furnishings*, London: Batsford.
Winterthur Library (2020–1), "Library." Available online: http://winterthur.org/library (accessed May 15, 2021).
"The Winter Exhibition of the Berlin Industrial Museum" (1890), *The Architect and Building News*, 27: 174.
Wolowski, M. (1855), "Meubles," *Exposition Universelle de 1851, Travaux de la Commission française de l'industrie des Nations, publiée par ordre de l'Empereur*, 7 (26): 40.
"Women's Complaint about Car Seats" (1885), *Railway Age*: 722.
Wornum, Ralph Nicholson (1851), "The Exhibition of 1851 as a Lesson in Taste," in *The Art Journal Illustrated Catalogue: The Industry of All Nations 1851*, I***–XXII***, London: George Virtue.
Wornum, Ralph Nicholson (1860), *Analysis of Ornament. The Characteristics of Styles: An Introduction to the Study of the History of Ornamental Art*, London: Chapman and Hall.
Wright, Gwendolyn (1980), *Moralism and the Model Home*, Chicago: University of Chicago Press.
Yamamori, Yumiko (2008), "Japanese Arts in America, 1895–1920, and the A.A. Vantine and Yamanaka Companies," *Studies in the Decorative Arts*, 15 (2): 96–126.
Young, Carolyn A. (1995), *The Glory of Ottawa, Canada's First Parliament Buildings*, Montreal and Kingston: McGill/Queen's Press.
Young, Linda (2003), *Middle-Class Culture in the Nineteenth Century: America, Australia and Britain*, Basingstoke, UK: Palgrave Macmillan.
Zeigler, Robert H. (2002), *American Workers, American Unions*, Baltimore: Johns Hopkins University Press.
Zeisler, Wilfried (2014), *L'objet d'art et de luxe français en Russie (1881–1917): Fournisseurs, clients, collections et influences*, Paris: Mare et Martin.
Zeisler, Wilfried (2015), "De New York à Saint-Pétersbourg, le commerce international du luxe à la belle-époque," in Natacha Coquery and Alain Bonnet (eds.), *Le commerce du luxe, Production, exposition et circulation des objets précieux du Moyen Âge à nos jours*, 81–8, Paris: Mare et Martin.
Zola, Émile ([1877] 2009), *L'Assommoir*, Oxford: Oxford University Press.
Zola, Émile ([1883] 2008), *The Ladies' Paradise*, translated by Brian Nelson, Oxford: Oxford University Press.
Zola, Émile ([1883] 2009), *Pot Luck*, Oxford: Oxford World's Classics.

INDEX